Reading Ladders for Human Relations

5th Edition

Reading Ladders for Human Relations

5th Edition

VIRGINIA M. REID
Editor

and the Committee on
Reading Ladders for
Human Relations of the
National Council of
Teachers of English

**American Council
on Education**

Washington, D.C.

© 1972 by American Council on Education
One Dupont Circle, Washington, D.C. 20036
Library of Congress Catalog Card Number 72-87462
ISBN Paper 0-8268-1373-9
ISBN Cloth 0-8268-1375-5

016.370196
Am 36n
1972

Foreword

Since 1947, *Reading Ladders for Human Relations* has been used by teachers and parents, in thousands of classrooms and homes, to select books to enrich the young, the intermediate, as well as the mature reader. This fifth edition, published in cooperation with the National Council of Teachers of English, follows the format of earlier ones but has been revised and updated in content through the help of teachers, librarians, and specialists in children's books and human relations. The latest contributions add important, new dimensions to this literature guide that will prove valuable, I am sure, to all those who work with young people.

ROGER W. HEYNS, *President*

v

CT A

Preface

This fifth edition of *Reading Ladders for Human Relations* is a greatly expanded version of the first edition which appeared in 1947; but it shares with all the previous editions the same major aim—to help teachers, librarians, and other adults working with children and young people in the delicate task of extending sensitivity toward people, their values, and their ways of living.

It is hoped that this edition, like the former ones, will serve to advance the cause of better human relations. "Besides direct experience with people of diverse background," Hilda Taba said in 1947, "books, especially drama and fiction, can serve this purpose." At that time Dr. Taba was director of Intergroup Education in Cooperating Schools. In 1955 Margaret Heaton, Dr. Taba's able partner in this pioneer project, added that "books make vivid the problems of human relations and give access to them in new dimensions."

The influence of Hilda Taba and Margaret Heaton lives on long after their untimely deaths. Their idea of using literature to extend sensitivity and their method of organizing books around themes important in human relations continue to be popular.

Each revision of *Reading Ladders* has created changes. This volume is no exception. While retaining many desirable features of earlier editions, this fifth edition includes the following changes:

1. Reduction from six to four themes to avoid some duplication.
2. Division of each ladder into subcategories for easier identification of books dealing with a particular aspect of human relations.
3. Cross-listing of books both by theme and age group.
4. Inclusion of many books published since 1962 and books published earlier but new to *Reading Ladders for Human Relations*.

5. Rewriting of annotations for some books included in previous editions to show their relationship to the ladder in which they have been placed.
6. Expansion of annotations to help the reader decide how he might use the books.
7. Addition of quoted passages from books for children and young adults in the introductions to each ladder.
8. Expansion of the instructional strategies to include drama, book talks, book illustrations, and other ways to further the responses of children and young people to literature.

Each committee member served with another member as a team to prepare one ladder. One had responsibility for primary and intermediate readers, the other for secondary students and mature readers. Some also shared in the preparation of the introductory essays.

Two special contributions were made by Patricia Cianciolo, associate professor of elementary education, Michigan State University, and Elizabeth A. Morse, coordinator, Young Adult Service, Contra Costa County Library, California.

The chairman and the committee appreciate the leadership of the cochairman, Jesse Perry, in the sections dealing with junior, senior, and mature readers, and his contributions to the introductory material of the book.

We appreciate also the guidance given by J. Oscar Lee, director of education, National Conference of Christians and Jews, Inc.; Charlotte Huck, Ohio State University; Maxine Delmare, Texas A & I University; and Joanne Dale, consultant in English language arts, Los Angeles County School District, California. Each attended one meeting of the committee to give guidance and support.

For their wise counsel, we wish to thank Jean Wilson, supervisor of secondary English, Oakland Public Schools, California; Dorothy Petitt, English Department, San Francisco State College; and Effie Robinson, director of Human Relations Department, San Francisco, California, Housing Authority.

We give grateful acknowledgment to Matilda Ebert, library catalog clerk, Teachers' Professional Library, Oakland Public Schools, California, who supplied reviews for each book under consideration, and to the secretaries of the committee, Ella Tuvell and Debbie Dettmer.

I am personally grateful to various members of the Association of Children's Librarians of Northern California for reactions to annotations and titles. In particular, I wish to thank Jesse Boyd, retired director of libraries, Oakland Public Schools; Mae Durham, School of Librarianship, University of California, Berkeley; Rosemary Glenn, children's librarian, Los Gatos Union School District; Connie Kidder, children's librarian, Berkeley Public Library; Oraville Tuttle and Annie Robertson, librarians, Oakland Public Library.

Without the cooperation of the publishers, this book could not be possible. They not only supplied books requested, they also brought to the attention of the committee books which they felt merited inclusion. Conferences with juvenile editors and public relations persons were also helpful.

This book has required much teamwork, but even more will be required of librarians, teachers, and all adults who work with young people if the experiences and understandings stored in these books are to serve the intended purpose.

It is hoped that this edition, like the previous ones, will enhance learning and living together.

VIRGINIA M. REID, *Chairman*

Acknowledgments

Committee on Reading Ladders for Human Relations, Fifth Edition

VIRGINIA M. REID, Oakland Public Schools, California; *Chairman*

JESSE PERRY, Alameda County School Department, California; *Associate Chairman*

DONALD J. BISSETT, Wayne State University

MAUDE EDMONSON, Merced City Schools, California

JAMES E. KERBER, Ohio State University

DOROTHY MACDOUGALL, SCN, Nazareth College of Kentucky

ROBERT B. MARSHALL, Knoxville College

EFFIE LEE MORRIS, San Francisco Public Library, California

E. JANE PORTER, University of Delaware

IRIS M. TIEDT, University of Santa Clara

ROBERT DYKSTRA, University of Minnesota; *ex officio*

JOANNE DALE, Los Angeles, California; *Consultant*

Contributors

DOROTHY L. AUSTIN, Chenoweth Elementary School, Merced, California

MARY E. BARRETT, Ohio State University

SANDRA BASSETT, Middle Elementary Teaching Team Project, Ohio State University

x

BERNICE ANN BAUR, Graduate Student, Ohio State University

SHIRLEY A. BEACHUM, Student Teacher, Ohio State University

BARBARA BEACHY, Teacher-Librarian, Horace Mann School, Oakland, California

FRANCES LOPEZ BECKERS, Regional Migrant Center, Merced, California

SHEILA BENDER, Reston, Virginia

JANE BOTHAM, San Francisco Public Library, California

ELLIOT ALAN BOXERBAUM, Student, Ohio State University

MARCIA BRILL, Middle Elementary Teaching Team Project, Ohio State University

RUDOLPH J. BUFANO, University of Pennsylvania

ADRIENNA COX, Wayne State University

CONSTANCE L. CREGO, Student, Ohio State University

HARRIET B. CRUMP, Shelby County Board of Education, Tennessee

LAURICE CUCULICH, Tenaya School, Merced, California

BERNICE E. CULLINAN, New York University

HELEN C. DAVIS, Burbank Elementary School, Merced, California

GRETCHEN K. DELACRUZ, Shaffer School, Atwater, California

SHIRLEY EATON, Braddock Elementary School, Annandale, Virginia

W. GEIGER ELLIS, JR., University of Georgia

MILDRED ESHNAUR, Merced County Schools, California

MARTHA FAULKENBERRY, Ada Givens School, Merced, California

ALISON JEAN FURLONG, Student, Ohio State University

JOAN I. GLAZER, Ohio State University

WILLIAM HAMLIN, Wayne State University

FRANCES HASLAM, Franklin School, Oakland, California

ANGELA HAYES, SCN, St. John School, Bellaire, Ohio

JANET HICKMAN, Ohio State University

RUTH W. HILL, Peter Burnett Junior High School, San Jose, California

EMILIE HOENISCH, Merced County Schools, California

SUSAN HOLZHAUSER, Student, Ohio State University

PHYLLIS HUFF, Middle Elementary Teaching Team Project, Ohio State University

DIANA JORDAN, Cleveland State University, Ohio

B. JO KINNICK, Oakland Public Schools, California

ELIZABETH R. LANE, Shelby County Board of Education, Tennessee

JEAN MARIE LEE, Sather Gate Book Shop, Berkeley, California

DOROTHY M. LINDSAY, Student Teacher, Hamilton Elementary School, Columbus, Ohio

ELIZABETH H. LOCKHART, Contra Costa County Library, California

EVELYN McCAUGHEY, Margaret Sheehy School, Merced, California

NANCY McCLELLAN, University of Oregon

BARBARA MILLER, Louisville Free Public Library, Kentucky

PAUL W. MILLER, Loudoun County School Board, Virginia

RUTH MOLINE, Ohio State University

BEVERLY MOORE, Dos Palos Joint Union School, California

ELIZABETH MORSE, Contra Costa County Library, California

VERA MUTHLEB, Wayne State University

JANET L. PARSONS MYERS, Honolulu School District, Hawaii

ROSEMARY W. PEARSON, Middle Elementary Teaching Team Project, Ohio State University

MARGARET E. POARCH, State Library of Ohio, Columbus

MARGIE POWELL, Student Teacher, Ohio State University

SHIRLEY REED, Curriculum Center, Merced City Schools, California

CAROL SCHWARTZ, Librarian, Oak Park Public Schools, Michigan

VIRGINIA SHATTUCK, Riviera School, Merced, California

RUDINE SIMS, Wayne State University

LILLIAN SMITH, Roosevelt Junior High School, Oakland, California

L. JANE STEWART, Ohio State University

JOAN E. STRIBLING, Librarian, Chenoweth Elementary School, Merced, California

LINDA R. STRONG, Student Teacher, Ohio State University

MARJORIE A. TSUJI, Sunnyvale School District, California

LORETTA J. WEBB, University of Santa Clara

JOEL B. WEST, Limestone College, Gaffney, South Carolina

CHRISTINE WHITMER, Middle Elementary Teaching Team Project, Ohio State University

CAROLYN WILLIAMS, Student, Ohio State University

ELIZABETH WRIGHT, San Francisco Public Library, California

National Council of Teachers of English Committee on Publications

ROBERT F. HOGAN, Executive Secretary, National Council of Teachers of English; *Chairman*

BLYDEN JACKSON, University of North Carolina at Chapel Hill

ROBERT E. PALAZZI, Burlingame High School, California

BETTE J. PELTOLA, University of Wisconsin—Milwaukee

PAUL O'DEA, Director of Publications, National Council of Teachers of English; *ex officio*

NANCY BEACH, Editorial Services, NCTE Headquarters

NORMA PHILLIPS MEYERS, Design, NCTE Headquarters

NOTES

P   Paperback edition
P/several   Paperback edition, more than one available
O.P.   Out of print
ed.   Editor
il.   Illustrator
comp.   Compiler
*   An asterisk in the left margin indicates that the main annotation appears elsewhere in the book.

Abbreviations of the publishers' names are explained in the Directory of Publishers, page 313.

Prices were verified in recent issues of *Books in Print* and *Paperbound Books in Print,* but it is important to note that publishers' prices are subject to change without notice.

Contents

Statement of Purpose

Literature is a mirror by which man is reflected; it is through books that one might gain knowledge about people who live in another country, in another community or whose ethnic or cultural background may be different from one's own.

It is, therefore, the purpose of *Reading Ladders for Human Relations* to list books that may increase the social sensitivity of young people and to extend their experience, appreciation, and understanding of their own life styles and the life styles of others. Information alone, however, is not enough to effect attitude change. There still needs to be a "gut level" experience, even if merely vicarious, for there to be significant change in one's attitude toward a different socioeconomic, cultural, religious or ethnic group.

Books can play a unique role in fostering better human relationships among all people, especially if those books selected genuinely and realistically reflect the multi-cultural and multi-ethnic composition of that society. The insights gained from this exposure may be related to those immediate problems and socioeconomic conditions, such as family and peer relationships, racial isolation, poverty and religious prejudice young readers may face. A book such as Frank Bonham's *Durango Street* gives a realistic picture of young people coping with family and peer problems.

On the other hand, books such as Jeanette Eyerly's *The Girl Inside* or Lee Kingman's *The Year of the Raccoon* may help instill a strong concept of self in those young people who have, because of outside forces, developed a poor image of themselves.

A human relations program centered upon literary experiences has the potential for clarifying moral imperatives and expanding social consciousness as readers explore the problems of racism, pov-

1

erty, and cultural isolation. It is the intent of *Reading Ladders for Human Relations* to foster an understanding of the social, psychological, economic, and cultural factors that are inherent in a pluralistic society and to create an awareness that these differences must be recognized and accepted if there is to be a "real" extension of the democratic process. It is the committee's hope that through books readers may interact in order to insure more positive personal, school, and community relationships.

Librarians and teachers may jointly contribute to a school human relations program through books. The teacher's enthusiasm for books may carry over to the students. Often there is an increased willingness to share reading experiences when the teacher has instilled in the student the will to read, especially if the books have relevancy for those experiences brought by the student to a particular reading activity.

The librarian, by calling the attention of the teacher to the wide variety of vicarious experiences in books, can enlarge the teacher's perception. For example, a class may have discussed how physical handicaps affect the adjustment of individuals to groups, to friends, to self-concepts. Asked to develop a reading program around such a theme, a thoughtful librarian suggests not only books about physical handicaps, but also books about social handicaps, such as racial identity or lack of educational opportunity. Librarians can name, from their wide knowledge, books that offer experiences relevant to particular problems of growth. Teachers can provide for the discussion of books in order to develop group appreciations and attitude change. Community mores and attitudes should be considered carefully before recommending certain of these books to students.*

The library is really an extension of the school. Its responsibility is to serve the community, be it the school community or citizens outside of a particular school site.

In planning for the use of books, teachers must consider particular goals. They must project a sequence of steps in the learning process and must select the material appropriate to each step. Two goals are all important: appreciation of common human needs and values, and sensitivity to the differences and similarities among people, their opportunities, cultural values, and expectations. Teachers may have to concentrate on areas where differences currently hinder cooperation between groups and on areas where extension of experience is needed.

Furthermore, maturity in understanding incidents which involve sex or profanity is only one kind of maturity. Many other kinds are

---

* Teachers' and students' selections of books are discussed in *The Students' Right to Read* (NCTE, 1962).

derived from depth and breadth of living and from an understanding of the complexity of influences that play upon individuals and groups. The books on this list have been thoughtfully discussed and selected to test and develop capacity for broad understanding, tolerance of contradictory values, broad interests and concerns, and depth of emotional experience.

Because racism and religious bigotry are two of the most important social issues young readers will have to face in the 70s, it is imperative that students have the opportunity to openly and freely discuss, with expert guidance, all of the ramifications of these pertinent social problems. Those books that have been selected afford an opportunity for a variety of viewpoints. However, the books themselves are merely a vehicle to foster dialogue; what the students do with those ideas and perceptions gained from discussing books is really the most important aspect of a reading program whose goal is developing positive human relationships.

JESSE PERRY

Design of the Reading Ladders

The books annotated in the fifth edition of *Reading Ladders for Human Relations* develop four themes. The themes explore the individual's concept of himself; his relationship to his family, peers, and others, or his alienation from those groups; his appreciation or lack of appreciation of persons from other socioeconomic, cultural or ethnic groups; and his need to cope with change, including all of the traumatic experiences change can produce.

The themes in *Reading Ladders* represent points of view on which people may take issue. Because one lives in a multi-cultural, multi-ethnic society, it is only through diversity of opinion and honest appraisal of those opinions that wholesome relationships can evolve.

Teachers and librarians should use the theme groupings merely as suggestions and develop their own groupings for particular individual student needs.

Arrangement of the Ladders

Within each theme books are arranged by maturity level and then listed alphabetically by author. The assignment or cross-reference of a given title to a given ladder or a given sequence is only suggestive; any complex work will have more facets than can be reflected here. Teachers and librarians using these lists should judge for themselves whether books suggested for one theme can also be used for another, or which of them represents increasingly complex emotional experiences for their students. Capacity to comprehend and to respond to reading depends at least as much on the maturing effect of previous learning experiences in school and at home as it does on age, reading ability, and intelligence. Many books usually recommended for young children may be read by more mature students for a different, more complex analysis.

Maturity-level designations were made on the basis of the following criteria:

For Primary Readers: These are picture books and easily read books of interest to young children. Some are meant to be read aloud, others can be read by children in the first three grades; still others may be useful in introducing a topic which will be further developed at a later date.

For Intermediate Readers: These are books of interest to preteenage children. With some exceptions, these stories are about boys and girls from eight to twelve. Several titles are of equal interest to intermediates—grades four to six—and juniors—grades seven to nine. Teachers and librarians should consult both the Intermediate and Junior Reader lists.

For Junior Readers: These particular selections focus upon concerns of boys and girls in early adolescence such as family and peer group relationships and growing in maturity.

For Senior Readers: Selections represented in this ladder deal with those concerns and desires expressed by young people in what has become a more complex society since the fourth edition of *Reading Ladders*. Problems of war and peace, male-female relationships, racism, and poverty are explored in these books as they represent a wide range of human relations concerns.

For Mature Readers: The books in this section represent different kinds and ranges of maturity, yet there are no simple criteria for identifying maturity. Books listed here may pose questions related to sex or contain what to some may be profane or offensive language. Such incidents may prevent the readers from analyzing a book in relationship to its accurate presentation of an aspect of the "human condition."

Readers bring very different ethical and religious values to bear on their evaluations of certain books; therefore, the committee strongly suggests careful examination and discussion by teachers, parents, students, and both school and public librarians of those books that might provoke questions of morality. It is important, however, that students not be restricted access to worthwhile books. Several organizations, including the National Council of Teachers of English and the American Library Association, can give guidance to persons who are concerned about safeguarding the students' right to read.

Use of This Book

To ensure maximum use of *Reading Ladders for Human Relations*, teachers and librarians should publicize its existence to faculty members, parents, and all adults interested in children and youth. Talks before groups of parents, social workers, and leaders in scouting and character-building agencies may cite specific books to show how ladders have been developed and may be used.

Reading Ladders has proved effective when used as the focus in preservice and inservice workshop sessions with teachers, in teacher training programs, as a model for projects and publications by curriculum development teams, and during a book fair entitled "Books for Brotherhood."

When adults who are interested in children's reading ask for printed guides, *Reading Ladders for Human Relations* may properly be included in materials recommended to them. When radio and television programs, newspapers, and educational publications present booklists for children's reading, *Reading Ladders* should appear among them. Teachers and librarians should be alert to see that it is included in bibliographies of children's literature as well as on special lists for use by social workers, psychologists, psychiatrists, and other specialists who work with young people.

Librarians and teachers need to be aware of the considerable range among the books in *Reading Ladders*. They include philosophical interpretations of the problems of childhood and adolescence; problems involving complex political and social backgrounds; incidents which may shock some readers because of language or frank presentation of sex or drug problems; deep or unique emotional experiences not within the adolescent's normal range; and portrayal of individuals so complex and many-faceted that only the most sophisticated and mature readers will understand them.

Many of these books can be read by students in their senior high school years; some are already on high school reading lists. In recent years, teachers and librarians have made available more and more of the best adult books in libraries and on reading lists. Those who guide the reading of young people recognize that modern living and mass media have exposed more young people to complex and bewildering problems than ever before.

Symbols Used in the Ladders

In order to provide space for a number of new books, the full annotation for a specific volume appears only once, under that theme for which it is considered particularly pertinent. However, the better the book, the more complexity it has. If a book is considered useful in a theme other than the one under which the annotation appears, only the author and the title of the book are listed. An asterisk (*) in the left margin indicates that the annotation appears elsewhere in this book and its location is shown in the author and title indexes.

The bibliographical material includes an abbreviation of the publisher's name (consult the Directory of Publishers beginning on page 313, for full names and addresses), the publication date for that edition, and publishers of paperback editions when known. Paperback editions are indicated by "P"; if more than one paperback edition is available, the word *several* replaces the publisher's name. Some volumes are issued in paperback and do not appear in hardbound. It should be kept in mind, however, that paperbacks go out of print quickly and new paperback editions are being issued constantly. Also, conceivably, there may be instances where the only hardbound edition listed is illustrated, but the corresponding paperback edition is an abridgment of the original. These same differences may, of course, occur among various editions of hardbound books, especially frequently reprinted classics.

Out-of-print books are indicated by "O.P." following the bibliographical data. Prices have been verified in recent issues of *Books in Print* and *Paperbound Books in Print* (published by R. R. Bowker Company), but it is important to note that prices change frequently. For current bibliographical information, teachers should consult the most recent editions of *Books in Print* and *Paperbound Books in Print*.

Choice of Materials

The books in the four ladders are listed with the following purposes in mind: to develop a positive self-image; to create a sensitivity to the experiences, needs, and feelings of others; to develop an appreciation of differences as well as similarities among people;

to extend insights into different life styles; and to help children and young people adjust to change in a dynamic, demanding world. Because of the committee's primary interest in fostering human relations, the members chose books that had the most relevant content. By this criterion some books that are not of superior literary merit may be listed. These should be considered as place holders until a better book on the subject becomes available. Members of the committee are aware of and concerned about the number of such entries. They are even more concerned about books of excellence which may have been overlooked. On the other hand, many older or classic titles which do provide insights into human relationships are included, even though in time or setting they may often seem somewhat remote from the 70s. Furthermore, some titles, previously listed, have been dropped because they give the reader a false picture of today. Unfortunately, few books exist which accurately reflect certain identifiable cultures; however, forces currently at work in society are bringing about changes in attitude which may influence the future publication of such books.

Other Criteria Used in Selection

1. Books which contain the essentials of all good literature: plot, content, theme, characterization, and format.
2. Books which, through text or illustration, belittle no people either through condescension, deprecatory statements, or ridicule.*
3. Books which are natural and convincing instead of those which are contrived and which suggest superficial treatment in solving difficult problems humans face.
4. Books whose illustrations supplement the text in adding content or contributing to the mood.
5. Books which recognize minority groups' participation in and contribution to history and culture of our country.
6. Books which prevent the carrying forward of old prejudices and stereotypes into the new generation.
7. Books which can help each reader realize his identity, appreciate his individuality, and respect his heritage.
8. Books containing subject matter appropriate to the age—nonfiction which is accurate and meaningful and fiction which is true to life and has a valid theme.
9. Books no longer in print are included because they may still be

---

* Consult "Criteria for Teaching Materials in Reading and Literature" of the NCTE Task Force on Racism and Bias in the Teaching of English for a more complete discussion of this concept.

found in libraries, and increased demand for and use of these books might possibly bring them back into print.

Because it is the intent of *Reading Ladders* to be selective rather than comprehensive, several cautions are provided for teachers and librarians selecting additional books:

Select books of reasonable quality.

Choose books which contain an honest and authentic portrayal of the human condition.

Be on the alert for evidences of lack of sensitivity to racial, ethnic, and religious feelings.

Evaluate books for human relations by evidences of descriptive behavior, motivating forces, presentation of a variety of hypotheses for each behavior pattern, discussion of methods of dealing with problems in human relations, integrative forces in reaching solutions to problems, and sensitivity to a variety of alternatives in choice making.

Be aware of the excellent books which were overlooked by the committee or were publishd too late to make the deadline for supplying books to the committee.

JESSE PERRY

*I was looking in books for a bigger world
in which I lived. In some blind and instinctive
way I knew what was happening in those
books was also happening all around me. And
I was trying to make a connection between the
books and the life I saw and the life I lived.*

*You think your pain and your heartbreak
are unprecedented in the history of the world,
but then you read. It was books that taught
me that the things that tormented me the most
were the very things that connected me with
all the people who were alive, or who had ever
been alive.*

JAMES BALDWIN

Understanding Oneself and Others through Literature

The previous edition of *Reading Ladders* identified the need
for literature to promote social sensitivity and to fill the individual
needs of children. Implicit in social sensitivity is an awareness of
common values and an appreciation of differences among peoples.
Those who compiled this edition of *Reading Ladders* worked from
the assumptions that literature is an effective means of preserving,
transmitting, and improving the cultures that make up our pluralistic
society; that liking and trusting others can increase as we share
their feelings through literature; and that transfer of learning is
possible from books to real life.

*Literature is an effective means of preserving, transmitting, and
improving the cultures that make up our pluralistic society.* Change
is a normal and inescapable result of those sociocultural and physical worlds on whose stages we act out our life's roles. Often, however, change is difficult to understand and accept. Books can serve
for readers as a bridge between generations, between the past and
the present, between what is and what ought to be. Children's
horizons can be broadened through vicarious encounters during
their quest for self-understanding and acceptance of others.

Through literature a child can be introduced to those aspects
of life that make up the human condition. In addition to his basic

needs as an individual, the child must satisfy needs that are shaped and directed by the social system and the culture in which he functions.

Moral values is a label under which we can discuss with students the necessity for people to get along with each other, either on an individual basis or in groups. Literature motivates children to see, hear, and read more and better stories; helps them explore new interests; enables them to tackle new problems; provides them with meaningful reading experiences; and exposes them to the great literary heritage of the past and present.

Liking and trusting others can increase as we share their feelings through literature. The job of today's author is not to solve children's problems, but to help children become aware that there are considerable feelings of tension whenever human beings make decisions and that anyone who has had to make decisions recognizes these feelings. Good literature can assist teachers in seeing that a child is left with at least a question in his mind, such as, Why are they like this? Is this the way people are? This may enable or force a child to look a little more closely, a little more acutely, at the people around him. It is through literature that a child gets the chance to be a participant, to be really *in* the lives of others as well as his own.

Transfer of learning is possible from books to real life. Certain basic needs are common to all people and to all times in history. A child's needs are at first intensely and narrowly personal but quickly broaden and become more widely socialized. In the struggle to satisfy both personal and societal needs, the child is constantly seeking to maintain a balance between personal happiness and social approval. Books can help directly and indirectly.

Books which focus on the individual while dealing with social values have the greatest chance of reaching children. The reader will see in a situation, good or bad, how probable it might be that he would do the same thing or react with the same emotion. The reader or listener has something to think about and perhaps the urge to ask himself, Is there a solution?

G. Robert Carlsen says, "The book that is psychologically oriented in its dominant plot line outlives the one that simply tells what happened." Therefore, wise authors and teachers do not limit themselves or children to one locale or topic but write and search for books of the human spirit because these books have the best chance of "living" for and with children.

"The books that are successful with the young reader are generally told from the personal viewpoint of one character rather than in the objective third person. They detail what it feels like to be ashamed of one's parents, to be afraid in a crowd, to be lonely and on the sidelines, to be pushed to the limits of one's physical endurance in a sport event and fail, and to enter a contest and be only second best," states Carlsen.* Emily Neville said it another way: "Young people need to get the idea that their problems have been confronted before; that they are not alone."

Today there are varieties and types of literature for children that have never existed before. Much of today's fiction is vitally concerned with current social problems. Parents, teachers, and librarians need to be aware of the increased dimensions of each child's growth as they guide the child's selection of books and other experiences in media and the arts. Young people must be viewed as individuals with their own rights, needs, interests, responsibilities, and capabilities. This recognition suggests a need for literature that captures the continuing wonders, humors, and disappointments of childhood.

Characters in literature must move toward full development in their struggles for survival, maturity, and self-understanding. These persons then become believable human beings. Values that are written about will probably never lead to heroics, but they may lead to fuller humanity for every child. The mission of teachers, librarians, and families is to give young people a lifelong source of strength and enjoyment by exposing them to good books of many kinds.

Necessary to developing a love of literature in young people are good books, a well-defined literature program, and knowledgeable teachers. The teacher is the key to the process as the builder of programs, provider of time to read, initiator of activities, and spark plug who shows children his own enthusiasm for literature as a joyous and rewarding form of recreation.

There is disagreement over the value of bibliotherapy. Emily Neville notes that the parents and adults of this world are not perfect and that it is an author's and teacher's job to reassure children that other adults know this. Perhaps the child can then write or talk about a parent who is imperfect. However, there can be danger in giving a child a story which deals with his particular problem. In the process of growing older, a child may be confronted with pressures and problems too difficult for him to sustain or solve. To give such a child, already harassed, a story about a hero who conquers a similar fault may simply make the child more self-conscious or resentful of the virtuous example in the book. The child needs to

---

* *Books and the Teen-Age Reader,* p. 44. Copyright 1971 by G. Robert Carlsen. Published by Bantam Books. Used by permission of Harper & Row, Publishers.

discover books that encourage belief that life is worthwhile. Some form of indirect guidance through books can be valuable; adults who deal with the young in a way that is intimate and unique, professional and yet instinctive, have it in their power to provide the best hope for the student's future.

JAMES E. KERBER

Ways of Working With Young People and Books

Much social insensitivity is apparent today in our culture. Books can—and do—have their influence in helping young people to be more aware of the social problems and conflicts all about them. When authors sensitively portray the human person with his strengths and weaknesses, the message comes through. The teacher's task is to help the one who has read the book to crystallize his own ideas and when appropriate to share his insights with others. Just as the selection of the book should be the student's, so should the option of sharing with others. Some of the discoveries may be too intimate or painful to reveal in group situations. However, most children and young adults do enjoy and profit from various group and individual activities through which they convey their thinking and feeling about a book to their peers.

Books May Be Shared in Many Ways

When children can interest others in the books they find most enjoyable, the experience often becomes much more memorable for both the reader and the audience, particularly if the onus of book reporting is removed, and the student is encouraged to vary his participation. The young child who has read *Evan's Corner* by Elizabeth Hill, for example, might share the story by means of a flannel board presentation. Just as Evan finally gives some of his time to his younger brother, so the need within each person to share is shown, and the power of the story is multiplied when children explain this to each other.

Drawing a picture is simpler than working with flannel cutouts.

Some children may want to draw Charley's house or the school he attends as they are described in Rebecca Caudill's *Did You Carry the Flag Today, Charley?* The young readers will be fixing in their minds the things they learned about the Appalachian culture as it is portrayed in this delightful book which shows that material achievements are not everything.

Older children who have read the same book may want to share their reactions by means of a panel discussion. They may, for example, want to discuss the feelings of each member of the family about Teddy in the book *Don't Take Teddy* by Babbis Friis-Baastad. Were Mikkel's feelings those of a normal boy his age? How does society in general stand on the issue of mental retardation? Do people really stop and stare?

Or a group may want to discuss *The Young Unicorns* by Madeleine L'Engle. The suspense and soaring theme cannot help but awaken readers to the importance of free will. A complex cast of characters is woven into an intricate and exciting story.

Perhaps individuals would like to present oral reports on books that deal with various social phenomena. Someone might compare the reaction of the young American girl to the death of her brother in *Home From Far* by Jean Little with the Japanese boy's reaction to the death of his parents in Pearl Buck's *The Big Wave*. The cultural differences between these two situations are marked, and yet the human suffering is so much the same that universal principles concerning life and death will begin to be learned.

An ideal story for a puppet show would be Russell Hoban's *Baby Sister for Frances*. Children could show in their rendition of the story their understanding of the social implications of Frances's behavior. Family relationships are beautifully delineated in this picture book.

Tape recorded presentations could well focus on books which use diaries, journals, or letters to help develop the plot. *Across Five Aprils* by Irene Hunt shows feelings toward war and could be appropriately studied in the light of our present crisis. The notebook of *Harriet the Spy* by Louise Fitzhugh could be examined for its underlying references to modern society. What can be said about the set of values Harriet is developing?

If the equipment is available, a videotape presentation can be a vehicle for encouraging social awareness through a critical reaction to books. (A strip of pictures drawn through a frame can also be used effectively as a make-believe TV.) Such a presentation of *Let's Be Enemies* or *The Quarreling Book* by Charlotte Zolotow could be both enjoyable and thought-provoking.

If there is a class newspaper, a regular column may feature the comparison of books with similar themes. The realistic *Shadow of a*

Bull by Maia Wojciechowska and a book of fantasy, *The Gammage Cup* by Carol Kendall, could be compared, because they treat in quite different ways the idea of nonconformity. Which book makes the point more strongly? The newspaper could also contain a column which features the most exciting part of a story as a current news event.

For an individual activity which can bring balance to the generally group-centered activities of the school day, young people may turn to creative writing in order to respond to a book. To be most successful, the topic for a piece of writing should be the student's own idea rather than one assigned by the teacher. The problem in a story can be looked at through the eyes of a character who seems unpleasant, unkind or even dishonest. The action in Martha Ward's book *Ollie, Ollie Oxen Free* might be described by Ollie's father. The reader would then perhaps be less harsh in his judgments of this man who failed so frequently in his duties as a father. Older students might write of the two sides of man's nature represented by the boys in Ray Bradbury's *Something Wicked This Way Comes* or find Oliver difficult to fathom as they respond to Nina Bawden's *Tortoise by Candlelight*. For young people to gain sensitivity toward characters who seem insensitive to others is a big step upward on the ladder of human relations.

Book reports, both oral and written, should be encouraged as creative expressions, never as a way of proving that a book has been read. A report based on the point of view of a minor character in the story reveals much of the reader's knowledge of the human relationships involved. A letter written from one character to another in a story will reveal these same insights. A more mature student could read the book from the point of view of one character while several others each read from the viewpoint of other characters in the same story. This could lead to an interesting panel discussion of "the story as I saw it." The sharing of books in these ways will involve young people much beyond the discussion of plot, which too frequently characterizes reports on their reading.

Creating Interest in Books

Examining the ways books may be shared presupposes that young people do *read*. Far too many children grow to adulthood without ever experiencing the thrill of becoming truly lost in a book that is impossible for them to put down. In some homes and classrooms we must begin with a variety of efforts to create even an initial interest in books. The adult who knows and loves good books can do much to foster this interest.

People of all ages love to hear a good story. When it is told well, a kind of spell holds the audience and for that time nothing much matters beyond the story's charm. An endless supply of stories for such telling may be found in literature in the oral tradition, most of which has come down to us through many generations of story-tellers. Fortunately, most public librarians and many school librarians keep the art alive in their storytelling sessions.

There are also books that cry out to be read aloud! The number of adults who practice this art is much greater than the number of storytellers. The two-year-old on a parent's lap enjoys the cadence of the voice and the enthusiasm of the tale's recounting. Words and pictures start to come together and form a whole new world. Less novel, but just as exciting, is the situation for the six-, eight-, or ten-year-old. Teachers and librarians who read aloud to their students in the upper elementary grades and in high school or have encouraged students to read to younger children are creating bonds with books that might otherwise never develop.

But the world of verbal symbols is a complicated one, and the mind and imagination need concrete stimuli to keep them operating enthusiastically. Nothing could be a bigger boon to the reading interests of young people than seeing films made from books that have become their favorites. A book can come alive in a dramatized or animated version or be enhanced by a series of pictures and a musical background along with the narration.

Another way to create interest in reading is inviting authors or illustrators to come to class or showing a film in which a writer tells about his books or his reasons for writing them. The three author-illustrators in the film *The Lively Art of Picture Books* communicate not only their enthusiasm and reasons for writing but also something of the complex task of creating a book. Records, audio tapes, and video tapes are other ways of bringing young people and authors and illustrators together.

An attractive bulletin board will frequently catch the eye—and interest—of young people if it arouses their curiosity about an adventure, a character, or a particular time and place in history. A picture submitted by a reader depicting a story's most exciting scene, questions that can be answered in an enjoyable search through the pages of a book, or games and puzzles created by children might prove to be more absorbing than the most elaborate teacher-made display. Book displays in the classroom or book fairs on a school-wide basis create interest if children are deeply involved in their planning and presentation.

Much can be done to help young readers appreciate the best of what has been written for them, but at the same time adults must learn about the young people's interests. A basic honesty is called for; and the teacher, librarian, or parent must proceed cautiously when making an effort to broaden reading interests. In a world where facts are in demand, many young people seem to be ignoring fantasy. Young readers need to be led to see that fantasy shows the truth by exploring the why of things. Who can read *The Forgotten Door* by Alexander Key and not be affected by the message it conveys? For this nation, the *how* is much more readily answered than the *why*. Works which engage the imagination of the reader may be the books which give hope for the future.

If it is true that books can influence children only if they give them delight, then a further role of teachers, librarians, and others concerned with such influence would be to make sure that children have the opportunity to be delighted. Time for reading for enjoyment should be set aside daily.

Teachers can broaden literary understanding by helping children to recognize consistent patterns and differences in books. Through discussion of the components of characterization, theme, plot, and setting, children may gain competency not only in judging a book's quality but also in appreciating the author's skill in creating a believable story. When children examine them more closely and critically, books begin to have a deeper influence; and the young readers can show their increased awareness of human relationships through debating social issues raised in books, seeing human problems in historical context, or discussing problems related to technological change, poverty, minority groups, war and peace.

A Team Effort Is Required

Children are not born knowing the many opportunities that are theirs for the taking, and this includes opportunities with books. It is possible for a child to get to school without ever having encountered a book, but there are enough concerned adults around to make sure that a child does not move through our schools without a meaningful introduction to some of the best books available to him. Having parents, librarians, teachers, and other significant adults in the child's world working as a team to get young readers and books together would be an ideal approach.

Sensitive teachers not only know the interests of their students but also understand the deeper concerns underlying these interests. They realize, for example, that the popularity of books like *Hot Rod* represents a fascination not just with cars, per se, but with power and powerlessness. An increasing number of teachers are looking critically at literature for children and young people in order to become better qualified to act as guides in book selection. The school librarian is the person most capable of assisting these teachers.

It is true that there are not enough school librarians, but the dedication of those who are available gives evidence of the potential of this part of the "lure-to-books" team.

The public librarian also stands ready and eager to assist students, teachers, and parents. Parents who are themselves avid readers teach their children the way to the public library quite early, in both a metaphorical and a literal sense. Children find the librarian a helpful friend who knows a wide range of materials and who promotes good reading through attractive book displays, lists of the especially fine books available, book talks and read-aloud presentations in the library itself.

Other members of this "let's read" team may include school guidance counselors, reading resource people, book store personnel, and leaders of youth organizations. These special people know ways of whetting the appetite for good reading of all types. If the members of this team will make an increasing effort to know the best of books for young people, those best books will have a good chance of being shared. Adults may be amazed at the ingenuity of young people in conveying a message once they are convinced that it is a point worth getting across.

E. JANE PORTER AND DOROTHY MACDOUGALL, SCN

Book Talks: A Way of Recommending Books

The book talk, long a technique used by librarians, is one of the most effective ways of introducing books to children and young adults. Basically a book talk is an oral presentation of books to an individual or to a group. A book review calls attention to a single title; a book talk presents a number of books related to a particular theme or topic. Designed to encourage the reading habit, a book talk can provide an enriching cultural experience, it can motivate to action, or it can deepen human understanding. But above all it should stimulate a desire to read.

A natural outgrowth of daily association with books is a desire to share them with others, a compelling need to share with individuals and with groups the ideas expressed, the new avenues opened, the reassurances given, the questions asked, the questions answered. Because librarians and teachers are excited about books, they want to make books and reading so exciting and essential to children and young adults that reading continues as a lifelong habit. It is through book talks that this excitement can be generated and transmitted.

The titles selected for a book talk should be based upon a consideration of the audience—the age, sex, interests, and intellectual attainments of the group. Other elements that influence selection of titles include the size and general purpose of the group and the place of presentation, whether classroom, club, or assembly. Titles chosen should be of interest to the group and should be books that are worth the time devoted to them. They should be books that the librarian or teacher has enjoyed reading and can therefore present with enthusiasm. Selections should include books that the group might otherwise miss and may include books which reflect seasonal interests or timely subjects. Both fiction and nonfiction should be included whenever possible. Three to twelve books can be introduced in one book talk, the number being determined by the amount of time allowed for the talk (usually from 20 to 45 minutes), the number of titles suitable for development of the theme, and the manner of presenting individual titles.

Ways of Organizing the Talk

There are as many approaches and treatments of the book talk as there are teachers and librarians and these will vary with the individual and with the group. Every presentation of a book, whether in the library or in the classroom, is in essence a book talk, an informal "quickie" book talk, perhaps, but a book talk nonetheless. The more formal book talk is generally developed in one of three ways: by theme, by similar components, or from a single title.

Theme

Books can be grouped around a special theme, such as living or traveling in another country. Adjustment to the rigorous life of the Canadian frontiers and its hardships is the background for *Mrs. Mike* by Benedict and Nancy Freedman, a story that shows the maturing effects of marriage on a young girl. Teenager Robert Westbrook records his impressions of Russia in *Journey behind the Iron Curtain,* and Sansan in *Eighth Moon* relates what it was like to grow up in Communist China. These three books convey realistic pictures of different cultures and different ways of living, providing the young person with an appreciation of cultural differences while at the same time underlining human similarities.

The school or public librarian may be invited to speak to an English class when it is exploring creative literature which provides an understanding and appreciation of minority groups in American society. Or he may be asked to present a selection of titles to a history class pursuing topics related to the current civil rights movement within an historical perspective. Or the librarian may also be asked by a home economics teacher to discuss books on grooming, personality, and teenage problems.

Similar Components

Linking books together by association of related characters, incidents, or settings is another approach that can be used for the book talk. *A Girl Like Me* by Jeanette Eyerly, *Mr. and Mrs. Bo Jo Jones* by Ann Head, *Too Bad About the Haines Girl* by Zoa Sherburne, and *House of Tomorrow* by Jean Thompson all reveal the inner and outer struggle of teenagers confronted by an unwanted pregnancy. Each reacts to this knowledge differently but each ultimately confronts it directly and emerges a stronger individual as a result.

Single Title

Another technique is to comment at length on one particular title, using it as an introduction to a brief treatment of several others related by author, subject or setting. The experiences and insights of white journalist John Griffin who darkened his skin to live as a black man could be explored at length in a discussion of *Black Like Me,* relating these experiences to those of Susan Gregory in *Hey, White Girl,* the only white girl in one of Chicago's black high schools, or to the experiences of a teenage black girl living with a white family in New England as portrayed in *One Summer in Between* by Melissa Mather. *I Am the Darker Brother* by Arnold Adoff, an anthology of poems by black Americans, and *Who Look at Me* by June Jordan, a narrative poem with paintings by well-known artists, provide the black young person with self-identity and give the white teenager an appreciation and understanding of the black experience. *You Can't Make It by Bus* by James Summers reflects the conflicts of a Mexican-American teenager who is torn between the philosophies held by his father and those promoted by the leaders of the Chicano movement. It could be used with *La Raza* and *The New Indians* by Stan Steiner to present the feelings of other minority groups as they struggle for identity.

Once the approach has been determined, preparation should begin well in advance of the presentation. Books should be read and reread noting significant incidents and character portrayal. Although the talk should be prepared in writing either fully or in outline, the book presentation should never be read. Fully written talks should become so familiar that the prepared text can be discarded and notes composed to speak from. Intimacy, spontaneity, and friendliness should characterize delivery. An overly prepared speech can put a real barrier between the speaker and the audience and take away all flexibility. The unexpected should be expected, indeed invited, and the children and young adults should be encouraged to comment. The success of the book talk can be judged both by their response to the talk and their eagerness to check out the books presented.

ELIZABETH A. MORSE

Discussion: A Process of Involvement

Discussion in the classroom is aimed chiefly at promoting growth in students' ability to listen, to think, and to speak; effective discussion cannot exist without a combination of these skills. As James Moffett writes in *A Student-Centered Language Arts Curriculum,* "Discussion is a process of amending, appending, diverging, converging, elaborating, summarizing, and many other things." * Through the use of discussion the student learns to interact with others, usually his peers, and he gains understanding of topics under discussion.

Discussion is an appropriate activity in all classrooms, especially in the subject areas of English and social studies. It is particularly helpful in the study of human relations. To develop the necessary skills, discussion must be a functional part of the curriculum, not an unplanned extra. Discussion must occur in frequent, regular, and purposeful activities through which students learn specific techniques and assume responsibility for their success. Students can, for example, recognize reasons for discussion (to persuade, to solve a problem, to exchange opinions, to share ideas, to release strong feelings); and they can understand that discussion participants have certain responsibilities (to contribute to the discussion; to listen to others; to weigh the relevance of contributions; to recognize problems of fact, definition, and value; to keep discussion impersonal; to be willing to make concessions).

---

* Houghton Mifflin, 1968, p. 46.

Grouping for Discussion

Two methods of grouping for discussion are successful in the classroom: whole class discussion and small group discussion. Both techniques are recommended because each serves a different purpose.

The interaction possible in a larger group of perhaps thirty students is especially effective when students exchange opinions about a topic of general interest. For maximum participation in a large group, seat the students in a circle so that all faces can be seen, as suggested by William Glasser in *Schools without Failure*. Discussion should be focused on a topic about which everyone has information so that all can contribute; for example, a short story read aloud in class, ideas in a novel the class is reading together, or a topic discussed after reading several works which focus on a common theme.

For maximum participation and involvement of the individual student in discussion, the small group of three to six students proves ideal, providing repeated opportunities for each individual to speak. Individuals can share ideas actively as they question, answer, elaborate, and revise informally. Some of the following activities are recommended for small-group approaches to the study of human relations.

If each student has read one book in a given *Reading Ladders* category, for example, each student can present his book to the group in an informal oral book review, encouraging other group members' responses. Such interaction would not be possible in a larger group. Time is also more available for discussion by the other participants.

What things do we believe in? How do we get our values? These questions might be discussed after students have read Charlotte Mayerson's *Two Blocks Apart* which compares the backgrounds of Juan and Peter and their different ways of viewing life. In the small group each student can become involved and has an opportunity to share his personal experiences. Hopefully, students will get to know each other better, too.

Questioning Can Develop Discussion

The posing of provocative questions is one way to encourage the desire to know, to dig deeper, to visualize situations in a new way and to relate these feelings to others. Skillful questioning can be one of the teacher's greatest allies for encouraging discussion, developing thinking, and guiding learning. Inquiry, judgment, and interpretation of literature may be strengthened when questions are skillfully used as springboards for student interaction and involvement. Learning is more than accumulating and remembering knowledge. It is reacting, thinking, and solving problems.

The dialogue that may develop as a result of skilled questioning offers opportunities for students to express many points of view; to free, rather than control ideas; and to extend, rather than limit thought. A teacher can use this strategy to encourage students to move beyond the parroting of obvious facts to question, compare, and evaluate situations which may ultimately lead to the remodeling of their own ideas and beliefs.

The creative use of questioning has, furthermore, excellent possibilities for helping students to visualize characters, action, or settings, to discern relationships, and to develop critical and creative responses. This technique may promote students' discovering that what they say and think is important. The teacher can help raise the students' level of thinking to a point where understanding and appreciation may begin.

Sequencing, moving from the concrete to the abstract, offers opportunity for students to build on previous experiences and to add new insights. The teacher uses questions at different levels of abstraction moving along the continuum from factual observation and recall to the interpretation and critical analysis of concepts and then to the application of learning to new situations.

Relating Facts

The questions at this simple level ask the student for literal understanding as he recognizes information and enumerates facts. Although this type of questioning is the most commonly used, it does little to stimulate critical or creative thinking. Examples of questions in this category include:

Who were the characters in *The Learning Tree* (by Gordon Parks)?
What happened at the end of this book?
What do we call a stingy person?
What words did the author use to describe Sarah Winger?
Who are Newt's Friends?

Interpreting Meanings

The questions at this developmental level ask the student to synthesize ideas. Thought-provoking questions may lead students to make inferences, recognize central thoughts, see relationships, draw conclusions, make critical judgments, develop an understanding of the author's ideas, and relate the content of the story to his own experience. Examples that might be used include:

Why do you suppose Lou became upset in *The Soul Brothers and Sister Lou* (Kristin Hunter)?
Why is it important that the boys have a club house?
How is this book like *The Outsiders* (S. E. Hinton)?
Why are these boys collecting weapons?
How do you know the boys don't trust white people?
Can you tell how Louretta felt when she received the first check?
Why is the city providing money for the group?
What do you think will happen next?
How is Louretta different from her sister?

Thinking Creatively

At the most advanced level of abstraction students are asked to imagine, hypothesize, rearrange, and create concepts and understandings in new situations. Questions that might fall in this range on the continuum include:

In Ann Nolan Clark's *Secret of the Andes* did you feel as if you traveled with the boy Cusi?
In what ways were Cusi's feelings different from feelings you have had? In what ways were they the same?
Did you feel that the author had done a lot of background reading or that she had visited the country? Why?
Did you find the factual or the imaginative parts of the book more interesting? Why?
What did you imagine about the gold ear plugs?
If you could visit any setting pictured in the book, where would you choose? Why?
Why do you think the book earned the Newbery Award?

In implementing discussion skills, it is clear that we must give careful attention to the progressive development of questioning that encourages dialogue and discussion. Arthur Combs, writing in the 1970 ASCD Yearbook, states:

If we would prepare youth properly for the human world they must live in and for the human problems they must solve, the curriculum . . . must provide students opportunities to explore human questions. Vital questions of values, beliefs, feelings, emotions, and human interrelationships in all forms must be integral parts of the curriculum.*

IRIS M. TIEDT AND MAUDE EDMONSON

---

* "An Educational Imperative; The Humane Dimension," *To Nurture Humaneness: Commitment for the '70's*, p. 181. Copyright 1970 by Association for Supervision and Curriculum Development. Used by permission.

What Can the Illustrations Offer?

There is substantial evidence to support the idea that illustrations in books provide an important and effective means of learning facts, attitudes, and values. The child need not even know how to read, yet by merely looking at the pictures he may be greatly influenced by the contents of the book. Careful observation of pictures shows him details about himself and others which he may already know or which he had neither noticed nor understood previously. An illustration can show the young reader new ways of seeing, it can sharpen his view, it can give him a deeper understanding of the relation between nature and man. In a powerful nonverbal way an artistic book illustration can express man's innermost thoughts and feelings; and if the reader is thoughtful or perceptive, an illustration may have a profound effect on him.

It is a goal of this publication to facilitate understanding of oneself and others through literature. Since the impact of illustrations (and text, of course) is known to be intense and subjective, it is imperative that when one selects and uses books for a goal such as this, he is obliged to examine the illustrated books. In each case their appropriateness may be determined if they evidence the characteristics discussed below.

Styles of Illustrating Vary

Children should be encouraged to read and examine picture books and illustrated books for the pleasure they may bring to them.

Little or nothing will be gained from the message that the text and illustrations offer unless the reader can enjoy reading the book and can respond favorably to the artist's interpretation of the story. Individuals vary in their appreciation of illustrations that accompany stories or factual books. One reader may be delighted with *The Jazz Man* written by Mary Weik and profusely illustrated by Ann Grifalconi with exquisite woodcut prints. Another reader may be affected more deeply by the expressionistic paintings such as those by Charles Keeping in *Joseph's Yard*. A third reader may prefer the fairly representational full color paintings by John Steptoe for his picture book *Stevie* or the sensitive, poignant portrayal of blacks by Tom Feelings for picture books such as *Lamani Goes to Market* written by his wife, Muriel Feelings, or for books for more mature readers such as *To Be a Slave* by Julius Lester.

Illustrations may be done in realistic styles, photographs, or in the less inhibited modern art styles. They may be drawings, paintings, woodcut prints or other graphic art forms that children can interpret and enjoy. If the goals of this publication are to be realized to a significant degree, the books that depict human relationships should be sensitively illustrated and should exemplify the same high quality as the text.

Illustrations Facilitate Identification

The illustrations in children's books should be childlike, yet not coy or naive or condescending. The pictures must radiate sincere human emotions, warmth, and hope. They should evidence storytelling qualities so that such literary components as action, mood, theme, setting, and plot are revealed in a manner that encourages the reader to exercise his own imagination and go beyond the text. Within the limits of the strength and openness of her imagination, the eleven- or twelve-year-old girl who examined the simple sketches by Bea Holmes that appear in *Sue Ellen* by Edith Hunter would be easily led to enlarge on the story elements. She would be led to confront each problem as Sue Ellen did and to identify with this thoroughly believable, impoverished child. She would gradually experience with Sue Ellen the feeling of accomplishment as she advanced in learning, confidence, and self-respect. *The Boy Who Wouldn't Talk*, a charming and sympathetic story by Lois K. Bouchard with Ann Grifalconi's line and wash drawings might help the male reader to realize fully the difficulties a Puerto Rican boy in New York City experiences when he fails to adjust to a new environment where everyone speaks a language different from his own.

Illustrations Help Self-Concept

The visual message transmitted by a book's illustrations may determine in large measure the concept of self that the viewer constructs. Illustrated books may be used to help the reader view himself in an adequate and positive manner; they may help him to consciously accept himself as he views himself in the social setting in which he must function and grow up. Examine Nancy Grossman's illustrations for *Evan's Corner* by Elizabeth S. Hill and June Jordan's twenty-seven paintings of black American life for her book *Who Look at Me.* In neither of these books does one find a stereotyped conception of the attributes or social values of a class of persons. The readers are exposed to several life styles, thus giving the black child models upon which he could build a valid and positive self-image. Books abound which depict a diversity of Caucasian characteristics. It is hoped that such diversity might be available for young people of all ethnic groups. When young people understand, respect, and admire diversity, they need not fear differences in color, ability or life situation.

Illustrated books can be used to help children of all ages realize that their wishes, feelings, and actions are a normal part of the process of growing up. This edition of *Reading Ladders for Human Relations* includes many books which emphasize basic human emotions and human frailties. The black and white photographs of Miyuke, her teacher-father, and young brother in *Why, Mother, Why?* by Miyuke Furuya sustain the tone of this genuinely moving but unsentimental book about death. Although the brief, unrhymed evocative poems are by a ten-year-old Japanese girl, the book is recommended also for young adult collections. The free pencil sketches that John Wilson made to illustrate *Striped Ice Cream,* written by Joan Lexau, emphasize the genuine human traits in family situations that are portrayed in this realistic story. The line and wash illustrations by Symeon Shimin that appear in *Santiago* by Pura Belpre may also serve to present readers, especially Puerto Rican children, a view of themselves as acceptable and productive members of our society. We become as we imagine ourselves to be. Illustrated books such as these might help the readers become beautiful, functioning human beings.

Illustrations Extend the Child's World

Illustrations should serve to extend the reader's perception to worlds beyond his own. A picture is a window and it is through this window that the reader may learn about individuals who live in an environment which differs from his own. Illustrations constitute a powerful and pervasive means of communicating a respect for the concept that minorities should not be permitted to lose their identities in anonymity. One should appreciate the challenge of being different and luxuriate in the unity, achievement, and exhilaration offered by pluralistic societies. Having read the story and examined John Gundeflinger's pencil sketches in Gil Rabin's *False Start,* the thoughtful, sensitive reader should experience and empathize with the effects that the living conditions, the tenseness, and sometimes humorous situations existing in a Jewish ghetto may have on adults and children. Leonard Weisgard's red, brown, and black drawings, done in a style suggestive of primitive art for Mary Perrine's story *Salt Boy,* a simple low-keyed account of a Navajo Indian boy, would help the reader acquire a wealth of information and healthy attitude about the uniqueness and similarities of this particular cultural group. Most young children would appreciate the realities of city life which are so artistically depicted by Ezra Jack Keats in *Goggles,* a picture book account of a dog that outsmarts several bullies, big boys from the neighborhood. Likewise, older readers would find that the simple but effective woodcut prints by Gil Miret for *Wigwam in the City* depict so well the experiences and emotions of Susan Bearskin and her family when they leave their reservation home in Wisconsin and move to Chicago.

Each illustration should emphasize the richness and diversity of the human experience, for it is especially in the affective domain of the educative process that art leads the reader to a better understanding of himself and others.

PATRICIA JEAN CIANCIOLO

From Literature to Drama to Life

Drama means many things, from the unstructured play of a preschool child to a highly formal theater production. There are strong educational uses for both formal and informal activities. The values of each are quite different. Creative dramatics is one of the informal dramatic activities in which children create dramatic scenes, usually of a semi-improvisational nature. Acting out a scene from a story is probably the most common form of using creative dramatics in relation to literature. It is certainly a useful activity in helping children develop the ability of active response to people and situations in stories. Story dramatizations are done most effectively with children in grades three through seven.

In order to act out a scene well, a child must think and talk and act like a character in a story. He must make the story situation real to himself. When children act out scenes from books, the scenes can no longer lie flat on the page; they must come to life. The processes which children go through planning and playing scenes are exercises in trying to feel and be someone else. When these scenes become a classroom activity, the class must discuss the scene in order to play it. When scenes revolve around problems in human relations, the class must discuss those problems.

The potential for acting out scenes then becomes potential for a more active response to literature, potential for trying on different roles, potential for discussing human problems.

Choosing Appropriate Scenes

Stories that act out well have at least one vivid character around whom the action revolves. The remaining characters are usually uncomplicated and clear-cut. Particularly when children are first dramatizing stories, they need interesting characters to stimulate their imaginations, characters that are understandable to them. Children inexperienced in drama can, for example, soon learn to act out well the role of a child with a problem such as the loss of a father and brother in a car accident. But acting out an adult's reaction to the same problem will be more difficult for them.

Stories to act out must have action. That action must be transferable to the playing area, and the players must be able to show the action. The action should be easy to imagine and easy to transfer into dialogue and movement in a scene. Characters should be able to show how they feel, not just talk about their feelings. A story can tell what happened; a dramatization must be able to show it happening. Some action is impractical for children to act out. At home, a 10-year-old girl may kiss her father without hesitation. Kissing a 10-year-old boy portraying her father in a dramatization is a completely different situation, one that usually brings revolt or silliness that ruins a dramatization. Boys like to act out fight scenes or war scenes, but again, these scenes may get out of hand with children inexperienced in dramatization. In order for a story to act out well, children need scenes where the action can be shown and scenes where the plot can be acted without an invitation to embarrassment or chaos.

Many kinds of stories act out well. Light, humorous stories are fun to dramatize. The story that dramatizes a basic human problem or predicament is the story that presents opportunities for children to grow in understanding of other people and themselves. Children tend to approach these stories more seriously, too, and will work hard on an honest interpretation of the scene. A story that attempts to come to grips with a problem understandable to children will stimulate their best efforts and can become a unique experience in human relations learning.

Steps Essential to Acting Out a Scene

When children are used to acting out stories, a good story told or read is all the motivation needed to provide the interest and stimulation to act it out. When children are first beginning to learn how to act out scenes, the teacher may have to convince children that they can act the story out and that acting it out will be pleasant. Sometimes a game, a pantomime, practice characterizations, or even having children read the dialogue from a story provides this motivation. When children have never acted out a scene before, it is wise to begin with a simple scene and to have them volunteer to act out the characters. Soon other children will want to join in.

Planning

In many respects the planning step is the one crucial to the success of acting out a scene. For many children, improvising dialogue and action is not easy at first. They may feel put on the spot and forget what comes next. When that happens, children get silly or stop the action of a scene and the dramatization collapses. In order to free children to feel their way into characterizations and to create honest action and dialogue, the teacher should help them make general plans for the scene but not plan every detail. The planning step prevents those pitfalls that might make children unable to express themselves creatively.

A review of the incidents reminds the potential players of the sequence of events and helps avoid the embarrassment of forgetting something essential to the scene. Discussion of characters provides clues for dialogue and action to help portray the characters. Sometimes several children actually make up one or two lines of dialogue to show alternative ways of portraying a character. They might react to questions such as, How would Jennie walk? talk? What would her reaction to Charlie be? Is she carrying anything in this part of the story?

Whenever possible, properties are pantomimed to relieve the players of the job of handling them in the scene. Often children want to use properties, not predicting the difficulties of using them well or the hilarity when a broom falls out of a hand or a hat slips down over the eyes. Setting the stage is another important part of planning. Where will the table be? Where would be the best place for the door? To feel secure, children need to know where in the playing area they will be moving. Otherwise in the middle of the scene one child is likely to be whispering "Stand over here" to another.

Planning a specific beginning will help children get off to a good start and planning a specific ending will help them to know when to quit. Beginnings and endings are important. When they do not go well, giggles may prevail and make it difficult for players to concentrate.

Most creative drama leaders choose characters at the very end of the planning process, thereby ensuring that all children participate in the planning. When Suzi Ann knows she is going to be the mother in the story from the beginning of the planning, she has a tendency to listen only to the planning about the mother.

In first dramatizations, it is sometimes wise to use volunteers for the first few scenes. As soon as possible give all children a chance to participate by asking each in turn *who* (not if) he would like to be in the scene. This procedure guarantees the prodding of the nonparticipant.

With children inexperienced in acting out a story, the planning step seems to consume a disproportionate amount of time. With beginning groups it may take seven minutes to plan a two minute scene. It must be remembered, however, that planning itself is creative and, if effective, it releases further creativity. It is also the time for examining closely the characters involved and the problems the characters face. As groups get used to dramatization, they become more adept at planning and the planning step takes less and less time and becomes more vital. Children take over the leadership and sense instinctively what needs to be planned and what can be improvised.

Playing

When planning has gone well, children are able to progress through the acting out of the scene with concentration and honest expression. Those chosen to act out the scene do so, other children and the leader serving as an audience—not to be entertained, but to evaluate whether or not the story is being acted out effectively. It is absolutely necessary that the actors are left to their own creativity. Coaching from the sidelines ruins their concentration and creativity. Observers play an active role looking and listening to discover how and when the story is being acted out well. Those acting will not know what worked well until they are told by those watching.

Under rare circumstances the leader intervenes during the performance, but will stop it completely only if it is disintegrating. Sometimes by playing a scene badly through to the end, children learn that planning and concentration are necessary for good scenes. Sometimes the embarrassment of a poor scene is so discouraging to children that a leader is justified in stopping a scene not going well.

Well-planned scenes play well, an experience which teaches children and their adult leaders how much of what to plan. The playing period is the test of planning. Were the characters understood? Was the action clear? Did we make provision for what was necessary to tell in the scene by acting it out? The playing will tell.

Evaluation

The acting out experience is incomplete and much of the educational value is lost unless the playing step is followed by an evaluation by those acting out the story and those observing. During the process of evaluation, critical thinking is encouraged, the values of the scene are further explored, and players are rewarded by comments of their peers and their leader. This healthy interaction of personalities can be an exciting experience of individuality within the group process. To take fullest advantage of the evaluation step, the leader usually observes several conventions.

Positive comments are elicited first; the leader invites comments about which things in the scene went well. Specific contributions by players are noted. The leader looks for at least one good thing each player has done during the scene. If students bring these points out, the leader need not. Genuine appreciation for good individual and group effort results in honest praise that does wonders for the players. The leader can encourage positive comments by such questions as, What parts of the story were told best? Why? If you were seeing this scene and hadn't heard the story, which parts would you understand best? When was the playing most real?

Those parts of the scene that could be improved are discussed next. Leaders usually don't talk about bad actors or scenes, rather pointing out which parts of the story could be told better with more planning and effort: How could we improve this scene?

Replanning and replaying

Evaluation leads naturally into replanning and replaying a scene. The evaluation will mean little unless children have time to adjust to their evaluations and replay the scene with a new set of characters. Sometimes a second playing of the scene will satisfy children, sometimes they will replay a scene five or six times before their interest is diminished. It is often more exciting to play one scene over and over again making it better each time than to move on to a new scene from a story.

The Role of the Adult Leader

When working with stories with human relations themes, leaders should keep focusing children's attentions on the honesty of character portrayals to keep children from seeing characters as stereotypes. As children focus on characters and their problems, they can be helped to think of story characters as real people by remembering similar feelings and frustrations. Children soon develop their abilities to identify with a wider range of people and problems. Discussion may be a bit formal or even strained until children get used to discussing feelings, but soon they will be free to make such comments as, She wouldn't be that sweet. She was mad. She couldn't help but be mad. How would you feel if someone came up to you and . . . ?

When real feelings like these come out into the open, the leader is well rewarded for patient leadership during the planning and acting out process.

Acting out a story is a group process and strong leadership is needed if groups are to become productive. Human interaction is potentially explosive as well as therapeutic. The leader in creative dramatics needs to be effective in group processes. He leads rather than directs.

Acting out a story can become a creative experience for children only when the adult can become a leader who focuses children's thoughts and feelings, who facilitates the group process and the acting out process, who encourages the timid and holds the aggressive in check, who builds an atmosphere where individuals can be creative in the middle of the group process. Children are amazingly responsive to such leadership. If they are not accustomed to similar leadership, it may take a while longer for them to adjust, but catch on they will, and they will thrive on it. Stories will come alive and humanity will jump from the page and be examined more closely by groups of children who have the advantage of acting out stories.

DONALD J. BISSETT

Useful Books for Teachers

ALLSTROM, ELIZABETH. *Let's Play a Story*. il. by Janet Smalley. Friend Pr, 1957, O.P.

ALA. *Let's Read Together: Books for Family Enjoyment*. 3rd ed. ALA, 1969, $1.50.

ARBUTHNOT, MAY HILL. *Children and Books*. 3rd ed. Lothrop, 1964, $15.00.

———. *Children's Reading in the Home*. Lothrop, 1969, $7.50.

ASCD. *Learning about Role-Playing for Children and Teachers*. ASCD, 1960, O.P.

BAKER, AUGUSTA. *The Black Experience in Children's Books*. N.Y. Public Library Office of Children's Services, 1970, $.50.

BARNES, DOUGLAS, ED. *Drama in the English Classroom*. NCTE, 1968, $1.50.

BECHTEL, LOUISE S. *Books in Search of Children: Essays and Speeches*. ed. by Virginia Haviland. Macmillan, 1969, $6.95.

BROWN, INA CORINNE. *Understanding Other Cultures*. P/P-H, 1963, $2.45.

BURTON, DWIGHT. *Literature Study in the High Schools*. 3rd ed. HR & W, 1969, $7.50.

BUTLER, FRANCELIA, ED. *The Great Excluded: Critical Essays on Children's Literature*. U Conn English Dept., 1971, $3.65.

CAHN, EDGAR S., ED. *Our Brother's Keeper: The Indian in White America*. World Pub, 1969, $3.95.

CARLSON, RUTH KEARNEY. *Emerging Humanity: Multi-Ethnic Literature for Children and Adolescents.* Wm C Brown, 1972, $3.95.

CARLTON, LESLIE. *Reading, Self-Directive Dramatization and Self-Concept.* Merrill, 1968, $2.95.

CHAMBERS, DEWEY W. *Literature for Children: Storytelling and Creative Drama.* P/Wm C Brown, 1970, $1.95.

CIANCIOLO, PATRICIA. *Literature for Children: Illustrations in Children's Books.* P/Wm C Brown, 1970, $1.95.

COGER, LESLIE I., AND MELVIN R. WHITE. *Reader's Theatre Handbook.* Scott F, 1967, $4.25.

CROSBY, MURIEL. *An Adventure in Human Relations.* Follett, 1965. O.P.

FADER, DANIEL N., AND ELTON B. McNEILL. *Hooked on Books: Program and Proof.* P/Berkley Pub, 1968, $.75.

FENWICK, SARA INNIS. *A Critical Approach to Children's Literature.* U Chi Pr, 1967, $4.50.

FITZGERALD, BURDETTE. *Let's Act the Story.* Fearon, 1957, $1.75.

GIBSON, JOHN S. *The Intergroup Relations Curriculum: A Program for Elementary School Education.* Vol. 1. Lincoln Filene/Tufts, 1969, $2.50.

GLANCY, BARBARA J. *Children's Interracial Fiction.* AFT, 1969, $1.00.

GLASSER, WILLIAM. *Schools without Failure.* Har-Row, 1969, $4.95.

GOELL, YOHAI. *Bibliography of Modern Hebrew Literature in English Translation.* Katv, 1968, $10.00.

GRAMBS, JEAN D. *Intergroup Education: Methods and Materials.* P/P-H, 1968, $3.50.

HAVILAND, VIRGINIA. *Children's Literature: A Guide to Reference Sources.* Library of Congress, 1966, $2.50.

HOETKER, JAMES. *Dramatics and the Teaching of Literature.* NCTE, 1969, $1.50.

HUCK, CHARLOTTE S., AND DORIS Y. KUHN. *Children's Literature in Elementry School.* 2nd ed. HR & W, 1968, $11.50.

HUUS, HELEN. *Children's Books to Enrich the Social Studies: For the Elementary Grades.* NCSS, 1966, $2.50.

JACKSON, MILES M., ED. *A Bibliography of Negro History and Culture for Young Readers.* P/U Pitt Pr, 1968, $2.50.

JOYCE, WILLIAM W., AND JAMES A. BANKS, EDS. *Teaching the Language Arts to Culturally Different Children.* P/A-W, 1971, $3.95.

KARL, JEAN. *From Childhood to Childhood.* John Day, 1970, $6.50.

KEATING, CHARLOTTE MATTHEWS. *Building Bridges of Understanding.* Palo Verde, 1967, $5.95.

LARRICK, NANCY. *A Parent's Guide to Children's Reading.* rev. enl. ed. P/PB, 1969, $.95.

————. *A Teacher's Guide to Children's Books.* Merrill, 1960. O.P.

LENSKI, LOIS. *Adventures in Understanding.* Friends of the Florida State Library, 1968, O.P.

LOBAN, WALTER. *Literature and Social Sensitivity.* NCTE, 1954, O.P.

MEIGS, CORNELIA, ET AL. *A Critical History of Children's Literature.* rev. ed. Macmillan, 1969, $12.95.

MOFFETT, JAMES. *Drama: What Is Happening.* NCTE, 1967, $1.25.

————. *Student-Centered Language Arts Curriculum, Grades K-13: A Handbook for Teachers.* HM, 1968, $8.95.

PILGRIM, GENEVA HANNA, AND MARIANA K. MCALLISTER. *Books, Young People, and Reading Guidance.* 2nd ed. Har-Row, 1960, $11.50.

PURVES, ALAN. *Elements of Writing about a Literary Work: A Study of Response to Literature.* P/NCTE, 1968, $1.50.

ROBINSON, EVELYN. *Readings about Children's Literature.* P/McKay, 1966, $3.95.

ROLLINS, CHARLEMAE, ED. *We Build Together.* NCTE, 1967, $1.50.

ROSENBLATT, LOUISE M. *Literature as Exploration.* rev. ed. P/Noble, 1968, $2.00.

RUSSELL, DAVID H. *Children Learn to Read.* 2nd ed. Xerox, 1961, $10.50.

————. *Dynamics of Reading.* Xerox, 1970, $6.25.

SANDERS, SANDRA. *Creative Plays with Children.* P/Schol Bk Serv, 1970, $1.25.

SHAFTEL, FANNIE AND GEORGE. *Building Intelligent Concern for Others through Role-Playing.* NCCJ, 1967 (pamphlet).

————. *Role Playing the Problem Story: An Approach to Human Relations in the Classroom.* NCCJ, 1952, O.P.

SIKS, GERALDINE. *Creative Dramatics, An Art for Children.* Har-Row, 1958, $9.00.

SILBERMAN, CHARLES E. *Crisis in Black and White.* P/Random, 1964, $1.95.

SMITH, DORA V. *Fifty Years of Children's Books.* NCTE, 1963, $4.75 (P/NCTE, $2.95).

SQUIRE, JAMES R., ED. *Response to Literature.* P/NCTE, 1968, $1.50.

———. *The Responses of Adolescents while Reading Four Short Stories.* P/NCTE, 1964, $1.50.

STEINER, STAN. *The New Indians.* Har-Row, 1969, $7.95.

TABA, HILDA, ET AL. *Literature for Human Understanding.* ACE, 1948, O.P.

TIEDT, IRIS M. AND SIDNEY W. *Unrequired Reading: An Annotated Bibliography for Teachers and School Administrators.* P/Oreg St U Pr, 1967, $1.50.

TOOZE, RUTH, AND BEATRICE P. KRONE. *Literature and Music as Resources for Social Studies.* P-H, 1955, $11.95.

WARD, WINIFRED. *Drama with and for Children.* U.S. Dept. of H.E.W., 1960.

———. *Playmaking with Children from Kindergarten through Junior High School.* 2nd ed. Appleton, 1957, $5.75.

WILSON, JAMES. *Responses of College Freshmen to Three Novels.* P/NCTE, 1966, $1.00.

WITTY, PAUL A. *Development in and through Reading.* National Society for the Study of Education, 60th Yearbook, Part I. P/U Chi Pr, 1961, $4.25.

Book Review Sources

The Booklist and Subscription Books Bulletin. ALA. Semimonthly.

Branch Library Book News. N.Y. Public Library. Monthly.

Bulletin of the Center for Children's Books. U Chi Pr. Monthly except August; reviews books for preschool through grade 10.

Elementary English. NCTE. Monthly, October through May, for elementary teachers.

English Journal. NCTE. Monthly, September through May, for high school English teachers.

The Horn Book Magazine. Horn Book. Bimonthly; contains articles, reviews of children's books, and information about authors and illustrators.

Interracial Books for Children. CIBC. Quarterly.

Library Journal. Bowker. Semimonthly, except monthly, July and August.

New York Times Book Review. New York Times. Sundays; weekly reviews and special issues on children's books.

Publishers' Weekly. Bowker. Weekly.

Saturday Review. Saturday Review Corp. Weekly; reviews books for children and youth.

Scholastic Teacher. Scholastic Magazines. Monthly, September through May; both elementary and secondary teacher supplements.

School Library Journal. Bowker. Monthly, September through May.

Top of the News. ALA. Quarterly by the Children's and Young Adult Services Divisions.

Wilson Library Bulletin. Wilson. Monthly except July and August.

LADDER 1

*I writing this to let you know how I feel about
everything around me, one first I hate flowers
and the smell of them. I hate to go to funeral
homes and look at dead people.
I like to be surrounded by guys and gals of
my own and be hip and know whats going on
around this messed-up world. Everybody hates
school, but I am different. I like school, I like
to be where people are. I mean the teachers
and hear them talk gibberish talk. I like to see
and hear the kids own things and opinion on
the crummy world.**

LADDER 1

Creating a Positive Self-Image

Never before have so many of our children and young people
been so well informed, socially conscious, and humanely oriented.
At the same time they face more problems and confusion than
young people have ever before encountered. The current problem
of alienation in the United States is wider, deeper and more diverse
than at any time in our history. Young people are angry at what
they consider to be the sham they see everywhere they look and
hear every time they listen. The scientific achievements and technological innovations which have contributed to our well-being
have limited the range of exuberant experience for which young
people have an instinctive need. Creative and responsible young
people are searching for a moral philosophy to deal with a world
twitching in peril. Their new system of values is built primarily
on a kind of personalism, on a search for self-knowledge, and especially on respect for the individual. Some have fought to overcome their individual isolation through the solidarity of political
activism; some have tried to escape through sexual experimentation
and drugs. Others have been unable to cope with the real world
at all.

Today's young people are confronted with the necessity of making choices of a very personal nature, often with long-range effects.
They are rebelling against the hypocrisy they see in the adult

* From *The Me Nobody Knows: Children's Voices from the Ghetto*, edited
by Stephen M. Joseph. Copyright © 1969 by Stephen M. Joseph. Reprinted
by permission of Avon Books, New York.

world. Their younger brothers and sisters are exposed to these same concerns. They need reassurance to give them a feeling of dignity and self-worth. The child in his search for identity must feel sufficiently secure if the world is not to be such a threatening place for him. He must like and accept himself before he can relate to others. Children and young people also demand that others find out who they are.

In their efforts to develop a healthy self-image, young people can be helped in their search by introduction to books presenting a wide variety of human experiences.

The books in this ladder have been chosen to help find a positive self-image through (1) recognizing one's strengths and weaknesses, (2) growing into maturity and accepting oneself, (3) identifying with the heritage of one's family, and (4) developing personal values.

The concepts in the books chosen in this first ladder are involved in all the ladders that follow. Many books mentioned below apply equally in several ladders and some are annotated in another ladder. The books selected are written from a personal point of view in order that the reader may immediately identify with the character around whom the action revolves. But who can say what will have the most meaning to the reader? The background and experience of the reader will affect his appreciation and understanding, because books can be read on many levels.

For example, *Manchild in the Promised Land* by Claude Brown offers a black child potential identification in his personal search for a positive self-image. Young people of other ethnic backgrounds may learn to appreciate our pluralistic society and understand the black experience with which the black child is identifying. Given a new awareness, any reader can recognize the quality of "soul" in the basic human emotions arising in the harsh ghetto life.

Beginning with the first step on the ladder, in the recognition of the strengths and weaknesses in all persons, young people can be challenged, tested, and taught to rely on their own strengths. *Camilla* of the Madeleine L'Engle story gradually recognizes the child-like person her mother is and discovers that she, Camilla, is strong enough to overcome the situation caused by her parents' divorce. It is the firmness of Timothy, the wise old illiterate West Indian sailor in Theodore Taylor's *The Cay,* which provides the support for the newly-blinded boy when their ship is torpedoed during World War II. After Timothy's death, the boy finds that he has the courage and skill to survive until rescued.

As the incidence of mental illness increases, young people who are associated with these conditions in their own lives need to know how their peers have reacted. Books like *I Never Promised You a*

Rose Garden by Hannah Green and *Lisa, Bright and Dark* by John Neufeld offer a rare glimpse of the world of those who suffer emotional disabilities.

Growing into maturity and understanding can be a slow and painful process. In Paul Zindel's *The Pigman,* John and Lorraine thoughtlessly play a part in the death of an old man who has befriended them. It is then that they realize and accept responsibility for their actions. In contrast fifteen-year-old Nicholas assumes the task of returning a group of Greek children to their homeland after World War II in *Ring the Judas Bell* by James Forman. He completes his mission despite the testing of his convictions and emerges as a mature and outstanding personality. *The Rock and the Willow* by Mildred Lee can be a satisfying reading experience for girls whose own lives seem drained by physical labor. In a small Alabama town, Ernie's dreams seem remote from the reality of the hard life she lives but her dreams keep her growing and the work makes her ready when the opportunity comes to leave.

Related to the choice of facing or escaping reality are decisions about drugs and sex. In both *The Peter Pan Bag* by Lee Kingman and *Escape from Nowhere* by Jeannette Eyerly, teenage girls are caught between the emptiness of the straight world and the disintegration of the drug scene. Preoccupation with their growing bodies and inability to control their emotions is another problem girls face. In *Too Bad about the Haines Girl* by Zoa Sherburne, Melinda becomes pregnant, decides against abortion, and realizes she must tell her parents. The solution they reach together is not revealed. One solution is presented in the forced marriage of Ann Head's teenaged *Mr. and Mrs. Bo Jo Jones.* They also face the complications of different social backgrounds. Rarely mentioned is another sexual problem that disturbs young boys. The brief and innocent homosexual episode in John Donovan's *I'll Get There: It Better be Worth the Trip* provides a compassionate glimpse into the feelings of the boys involved.

In some recent books tough-minded and determined black youth look with dignity at their blackness. Hetty, the grandmother in Margaret Walker's *Jubilee,* is a forceful and proud former slave who fights with the determination of a mother to provide a better life for her family. She will not be defeated. The black voices in *Black Out Loud,* compiled by Arnold Adoff, speak their love, hate, protest, and pride in their heritage. Knowing that others know who you are, where you have come from, and why you are as you are goes beyond pride in one's heritage to strengthen the positive feelings of self. For all ethnic minorities, the need is great. Stan Steiner's *La Raza* traces the Chicano movement and his *The New Indians* defines the concept of "red power" as these groups struggle to force the majority to recognize their need for self-determination.

Closely related to identification is the development of personal values. In Hermann Hesse's *Siddhartha,* the mystical search of a young East Indian for the meaning of existence leads him to experience all the modes of life in his culture. In a different milieu, Malcolm X in his autobiography explores on a gut level the meaning of life. Siddhartha sets out to withdraw from the world, Malcolm X finds out about life by existing.

Books which mirror life and develop respect for humanity can reinforce basic convictions and help young people to commit themselves to exploring their individual potential to the fullest. The literature now available holds out more hope than other current artistic media.

EFFIE LEE MORRIS

Recognizing One's Strengths and Weaknesses

Primary

ANNO, MITSUMASA. *Topsy-Turvies.* il. by author. Weatherhill, 1968, $3.50. *Topsy-Turvies,* called *Pictures to Stretch the Imagination,* is just what it says it is. Funny little men are viewed in impossible situations, walking on ceilings, hanging pictures on the floor, and sliding up bannisters. Everyone who looks at the pictures in this wordless book sees something different, and the same person looking at it several times never sees quite the same thing twice.

ARUEGO, JOSE. *Look What I Can Do.* Scribner, 1971, $4.95. A simple nonsensical joke about the follow-the-leader romp of two caribou is told in a few words with lighthearted humorous drawings of scenes from the Philippines.

BONSALL, CROSBY. *The Case of the Hungry Stranger.* il. by author. Har-Row, 1963, $2.50. A group of neighborhood boys form a club to solve mysteries. Their first case involves the disappearance of Mrs. Meech's blueberry pie. Each boy learns to use his special talents to interpret the clues and solve the mystery.

CLIFTON, LUCILLE. *Some of the Days of Everett Anderson.* il. by Evaline Ness. HR & W, 1970, $3.95 (P/HR & W, $1.25). "Daddy's back is broad and black and Everett Anderson loves to ride it." Who is Everett Anderson? He is any child who has ever missed his daddy, played in the rain, been afraid of the dark, or wondered about the stars.

DAVIS, CHRISTOPHER. *Sad Adam—Glad Adam.* il. by Stan Tusan. Macmillan, 1966, $3.50. Adam's wish is to be able to read. He tries to read the books that his parents read to him, but he cannot. By the time he starts first grade, he decides that since no one can teach him to read, it does not pay to try. One day Adam's friend tells him that he learned to whistle by practicing. After that Adam tries very hard to learn to read and finally succeeds.

GODDEN, RUMER. *The Fairy Doll.* il. by Adrienne Adams. Viking Pr, 1956, $3.00. Everyone thinks Elizabeth just can't do anything right, that is, until Great Grandmother gives Elizabeth a Fairy Doll to help her. This doll is something very special, and magical things happen to Elizabeth, with the Fairy Doll to help her. When her precious doll disappears, Elizabeth makes a startling discovery about herself. A delicate story which should appeal primarily to girls.

GOFFSTEIN, M.B. *Goldie the Dollmaker.* il. by author. FS&G, 1969, $3.50. Goldie lives by herself in a little house in the forest. It is there that she makes her dolls, which are in great demand because of their beauty and fine craftsmanship. Goldie uses much care and the best materials available for the dolls as if each were for a very special person. The dolls seem to glow with love. This book shows that a special talent should be used to the utmost, for the result will reflect the extra effort.

HORVATH, BETTY. *Hooray for Jasper.* il. by Fermin Rocker. Watts, 1966, $2.95. Jasper is too little to do anything. His brothers and sisters do not let him join their games. Jasper tries everything to make himself physically larger, but fails. It is when he discovers that he can grow mentally that Jasper is truly happy.

JOHNSTON, JOHANNA. *That's Right Edie.* il. by Paul Galdone. Putnam, 1966, $3.69. Like almost every other small child, Edie loves to "write." Her difficulty is that what she thinks of as writing is only scribbling to everyone else. Edie's teacher, parents, and friends try to help her understand the need for other people to be able to read her writing. An occasion that demands a legible signature proves to Edie that she can print clearly if she really wants to.

JUHL, JERY. *The Big Orange Thing.* il. by Charles E. Martin. Bradbury, 1969, $3.95. Disappointed because his teacher is unable to recognize the best duck he has ever drawn, Charlie sets out to relax. Relaxing means constructing something, and his creation is entirely constructed of orange materials. When he takes this to school, Charlie earns the admiration of everyone.

* KAY, HELEN. *An Egg Is for Wishing.*

KRAUS, ROBERT. *Leo the Late Bloomer.* il. by Jose Aruego. Windmill, 1971, $4.95. Leo the Tiger cannot do anything right, but his mother has faith that he will bloom late. His growing pains and his belated debut should prove of interest and support to other slow starters.

LEXAU, JOAN M. *The Homework Caper.* il. by Syd Hoff. Har-Row, 1966, $2.50. Bill's little sister, Susan, feels neglected. When the wrong homework turns up in Bill's book, his best friend, Ken, helps solve the mystery. The culprit is Susan.

————. *The Rooftop Mystery.* il. by Syd Hoff. Har-Row, 1968, $2.50. It's moving day in the city for Sam. He must carry his sister's doll four blocks to their new apartment. A boy's job? The doll disappears. Sam and his friend Albert must solve the rooftop mystery of the lost doll.

* LIPKIND, WILLIAM, AND NICOLAS MORDVINOFF. *Chaga.*

MCDONNELL, LOIS EDDY. *Stevie's Other Eyes.* il. by Brinton Turkle.

Friend Pr, 1962, $2.95. Six-year-old Stevie shows his courage in over-coming his blindness. Shunned by other boys his age, Steve attends a school for the blind where he makes many friends and learns to use his "other eyes." Stevie soon gains the admiration and friendship of the boys who earlier avoided him, for by using his other senses, Steve opens the door to many things he can do by himself. This is an excellent story of a young boy's ability to overcome a handicap.

McGovern, Ann. *Black Is Beautiful.* il. with photographs by Hope Wurmfield. Four Winds, 1969, $3.50 (P/several). A child can now see that there are many beautiful things that are black—including people. This book is appropriate for the primary grades because pictures tell the story. There is not an overemphasis on race, but rather a presentation of many beautiful things that are black.

————. *Little Wolf.* il. by Nolan Langner. Abelard, 1965, $3.50. While the others his age show their worth by hunting animals, Little Wolf prefers discovering the many wonders of the woods and caring for its helpless and lame creatures. When the chief's only son is taken ill after eating poison berries, Little Wolf's knowledge of the forest saves him. The attractive green- and brown-tone illustrations complement the text with its forest setting.

Molarsky, Osmond. *Song of the Empty Bottles.* il. by Tom Feelings. Walck, 1968, $4.25. Thaddeus, a young Negro boy, spends his Thursday afternoons at the Neighborhood House where children gather to sing. Thaddeus does not sing, but listens to the director play the guitar. After a talk with the director, Thaddeus learns that he can have a guitar of his own if he can save $15. Determined to own the instrument, Thaddeus collects empty bottles and newspapers to save money. Thinking he will never save enough, Thaddeus is ready to give up until the director tells him that if Thaddeus will compose a song, he will pay him $10. To a boy who loves music, the idea is wonderful, but, Thaddeus finds that making up a song is not so easy.

Olds, Helen D. *Jim Can Swim.* il. by Ezra Jack Keats. Knopf, 1963, $2.95. Eight-year-old Jim, while spending three weeks with his cousins at their island resort home, overcomes his fear of water.

Ormsby, Virginia H. *What's Wrong with Julio?* il. by author. Lippincott, 1965, $2.95. Five Spanish-speaking children in an English-speaking classroom are the center of this story. The children help themselves by teaching each other the English and Spanish words for many objects, but Julio refuses to participate. It is discovered that Julio's parents are far away and he is homesick for them. The class joins together and saves enough money for Julio to call home.

Ryan, Cheli. *Hildilid's Night.* il. by Arnold Lobel. Macmillan, 1971, $4.50. Some of Lobel's best illustrations convey the folk quality and humor of this simply told story of an old woman who hates the night and tries mightily to get rid of it. Finally, she turns her back on it—

and it's morning. A story that might allay the night fears of young listeners or readers.

SCOTT, ANN HERBERT. *Sam.* il. by Symeon Shimin. McGraw, 1967, $3.95. Everything Sam would like to do or attempts to do seems to get him in trouble with his mother, father, brother, or sister. When the family realizes how upset he is, they begin to discover jobs that are just right for Sam. At the same time Sam begins to understand his own limitations and abilities.

SHULEVITZ, URI. *One Monday Morning.* il. by author. Scribner, 1967, $3.95. The small boy of this unusual picture book faces the dreariness of a rainy day through his tenement window. He calls upon his imagination to create playing-card characters who pay him gratifying homage. The illustrations contrast the colorful expressions of the child's fantasy with his dingy neighborhood.

SINDALL, MARJORIE. *Three Cheers for Charlie.* il. by Margaret Gill. Criterion, 1968, $2.95. Charlie has never traveled far from his crowded street in London, until he is given the opportunity to vacation at a real farm. Unfamiliar experiences frighten him and Sally is always teasing him about being scared. When he saves the young chicks from being burned, he proves to himself and his new friend that he is really a brave boy.

STANLEY, JOHN. *It's Nice to Be Little.* il. by Jean Tamburine. Rand, 1965, $2.95. Most very young boys and girls have never thought about how nice it is to be small! This text allows children to recognize the advantages and strengths of being closer to so many things: ants, flowers, grass, and pets.

UNWIN, NORA S. *Sinbad, the Cygnet.* il. by author. John Day, 1970, $4.50. Sinbad the swan is much weaker than his brother Simon. On their first long trip up-river Sinbad finds it hard to follow his family. Through his determination he manages to overcome each obstacle and gain the strength to make the following tasks easier. Sinbad finally gets over the waterfall, the greatest obstacle, and joins the family of swans heading proudly up-river.

WISE, WILLIAM. *The Cowboy Surprise.* il. by Paul Galdone. Putnam, 1961, $2.68. Mike and Sally are unhappy because they have to wear glasses. Sometimes the other children make fun of them. Everything changes, however, when Wild Bill, a famous cowboy, and his horse come to town to perform. The other children become envious because Mike and Sally wear glasses just like Wild Bill's.

ZOLOTOW, CHARLOTTE. *Mr. Rabbit and the Lovely Present.* il. by Maurice Sendak. Har-Row, 1962, $2.95 (P/Schol Bk Serv, $.75). The little girl wants to give her mother a nice birthday present but says she has nothing to give her. Mr. Rabbit helps her to see that even though her mother would like emeralds or a blue lake, she will be most happy with the basket of fruit in colors of the rainbow because it is something the little girl can give!

Intermediate

* Adoff, Arnold. *Malcolm X.*

* Anckarsvard, Karin. *Doctor's Boy.*

Bawden, Nina. *The Witch's Daughter.* Lippincott, 1966, $3.50. An exciting suspense story involving much more than the capture of jewel thieves. Perdita, a lonely orphan, is rejected by the other children because of her unusual power to see into the future. Through the arrival of a blind girl, Janey, and Janey's brother Tim, Perdita comes to realize that her powers are not a sign of witchcraft, but a special talent.

Bosworth, J. A. *A Bird for Peter.* il. by Howard Simon. Criterion, 1963, $3.00. Twelve-year-old Peter Corbie is spending the winter and spring with his grandparents on their farm in Arizona so that his health will improve. Peter finds a baby roadrunner and persuades his grandparents to let him raise it. During the following months changes in Peter, the bird, and desert life are vividly and accurately presented. Peter grows in his understanding of his pet's need to live its own free life in the desert.

Brink, Carol Ryrie. *Caddie Woodlawn.* Macmillan, 1935, $3.95 (P/ several). Caddie's adventures on the Wisconsin frontier are very realistic and exciting (and glimpses of history appear also) as the Woodlawns rejoice at hearing that the Civil War has ended and later mourn the assassination of President Lincoln. Caddie is an adventurous tomboy who seems to resist accepting her sex role. However, her personal values are good throughout, and as she continues to understand the female role, one is certain that she will grow up to be a lovely young lady as her father has predicted.

————. *Two Are Better than One.* il. by Fermin Rocker. Macmillan, 1968, $4.50. The story tells in a realistic manner of problems that girls face as they are growing up. The book has a theme that young girls of today can identify with and understand.

Carruth, Ella Kaiser. *She Wanted to Read: The Story of Mary Macleod Bethune.* il. by Herbert McClure. Abingdon, 1966, $2.25 (P/ WSP, $.60). Mary Macleod Bethune grew up on a cotton plantation in South Carolina. The first person in her family to learn to read and write, Mary dedicated her life to helping black children get an education. Fighting the Ku Klux Klan and overcoming other hardships, she started many schools, becoming a college president and a civic leader.

* CATHERALL, ARTHUR. *Camel Caravan.*

CHRISTENSEN, GARDELL DANO. *Buffalo Kill.* il. by author. Nelson, 1959, $3.10 (P/WSP, $.50). A twelve-year-old Indian boy is chosen to wear a buffalo hide and to lure the buffalo herd from the prairie to a cliff where they will be driven to their deaths. The year's supply of meat and hides, as well as his own status of manhood, depends on Winter Weasel's success.

COATSWORTH, ELIZABETH. *Jock's Island.* il. by Lillian Obligado. Viking Pr, 1963, $3.19 (P/Viking Pr, $.65). A border collie's unending loyalty is the theme of this story. Jock lives on an island in a volcanic area, with his master Old Tom. Jock's job is to care for his master's sheep, a job which he does with deep devotion even though his relationship with his master is purely one of respect, excluding the usual love bond between dog and master.

CRETAN, GLADYS YESSAYAN. *All except Sammy.* il. by Symeon Shimin. Little, 1966, $3.00. Coming from a very musical family is great—if you are also musical. This is Sammy's problem: he can't seem to play an instrument of any kind. A solution begins to evolve while Sammy is touring an art gallery on a homework assignment. Intrigued with the skill of painters, he decides he wants to learn the skill himself. The next family picture shows Sammy in the center of his family, displaying the poster he made for the family concerts. At last a part of the musical family, Sammy realizes that playing an instrument isn't the only thing a boy can do.

* DE TREVINO, ELIZABETH B. *I, Juan De Pareja.*

DOUTY, ESTHER MORRIS. *Charlotte Forten: Free Black Teacher.* Garrard, 1971, $2.59. A simply-written narrative biography of Charlotte Forten, granddaughter of the Negro businessman and abolitionist James Forten. Many quotations from a journal kept by Charlotte Forten are incorporated into the account. It focuses on her childhood in Philadelphia, her education in Salem, Massachusetts, and on her experiences, in her twenties, as a teacher among the freed slaves on the Carolina Sea Islands during the Civil War. The remainder of her life is capsuled in an afterword.

FELTON, HAROLD W. *Jim Beckwourth, Negro Mountain Man.* Dodd, 1966, $3.50 (P/Apollo Eds., $1.75). Jim Beckwourth leaves his blacksmith apprenticeship in St. Louis to go into the wilderness. There he becomes one of the best hunters, trappers, and guides among the mountain men. He also learns the dangers and hardships of life among Indians and wild animals. Finally Jim is named chief of the Crows, whom he guides wisely for many years.

————. *Nat Love, Negro Cowboy.* il. by David Hodges. Dodd, 1969, $3.50. After his father's death, fifteen-year-old Nat decides to go to the West to seek his fortune. There his skill and courage finally win him both fame and respect.

————. *Edward Rose—Negro Trail Blazer.* Dodd, 1967, $3.50. The Indians ignore color and accept Ed Rose for what he is—a fine hunter and trapper and an honest and courageous man!

FLORY, JANE. *One Hundred and Eight Bells.* il. by author. HM, 1963, $3.50. Daydreaming and forgetfulness cause twelve-year-old Setsuko Sagawas many heartaches. Aspiring to be an artist like her father, she finds her daydreaming gets in the way of her ambitions. Realizing her shortcomings, Setsuko tries again and again to reform, but never seems able to stick to her goal. Growing up helps, and the girl slowly becomes less forgetful. On New Year's Day she resolves to try harder, and finds that her family loves her as she is. A good family story of present day Japan.

FRIEDMAN, FRIEDA. *Ellen and the Gang.* il. by Jacqueline Tomes. Morrow, 1963, $3.95. Twelve-year-old Ellen feels uncertain of her parents' love because her talented younger sister and studious older brother seem to get all the attention and admiration. She strikes back by secretly becoming involved with a gang. Later, Ellen rejects the gang members, who have been using her. Assured of her parents' love, she devotes the remaining part of her summer to helping supervise the playground.

FRIIS-BAASTAD, BABBIS. *Kristy's Courage.* il. by Charles Geer. HBJ, 1965, $3.50. Kristy is a small girl who has been hit by a car and must learn to live with a scar and nearly unintelligible speech. Teased or ignored by the children in her school, Kristy learns to accept herself and deal with her classmates' reactions.

GRAHAM, LORENZ. *Every Man Heart Lay Down.* il. by Colleen Browning. TY Crowell, 1970, $3.75. The foreword of *How God Fix Jonah* has been made into a striking picture book. The story of the birth of Jesus is told in a rhythmic, poetic idiom of "Africans' newly come to English" speech. It will appeal to readers younger and older.

* ————. *A Road Down in the Sea.*

GRAY, ELIZABETH JANET. *I Will Adventure.* il. by Corydon Bell. Viking Pr, 1962, $4.00. Andrew Talbot finds life difficult when he has to follow in the path of five older brothers. To make matters worse, he finds his physical size embarrassing. At last a rich uncle visits Andrew's house and invites the boy to become a page at his home.

HAMILTON, VIRGINIA. *The Time-Ago Tales of Jahdu.* il. by Nonny Hogrogian. Macmillan, 1969, $4.50. Lee Edward, a young Negro child, stays with Mama Luka during the day while his mother works.

Mama Luka tells tales about Jahdu, a boy with magical power. As Lee Edward grows older, so does Jahdu. Lee Edward realizes that like Jahdu, he also has magical power—pride!

HARNDEN, RUTH. *Summer's Turning.* il. by John Gretzer. HM, 1966, $3.25. Instead of going to the seashore with his parents Mark has to spend the summer with his aunt, practicing and improving his reading. The summer seems dull until Mark meets a girl named Tony. Tony is not an ordinary girl for she can do just about everything a boy can do—only better. Both Tony and Mark go through the process of becoming aware of the other person and of not being so self-centered.

HARRISON, DELORIS. *The Bannekers of Bannaky Springs.* il. by David Hodges. Hawthorn, 1970, $4.25. This is more a story of Benjamin Banneker's parents and his grandparents than it is of the great self-taught scientist, astronomer, and mathematician himself. His white grandmother, having completed her seven-year indenture, bought Bannaky, a proud African prince whom she later married. The relationship between Benny and the tiny brave grandmother he called "Big Ma-Ma" is one to be remembered.

HICKOK, LORENA A. *The Story of Helen Keller.* il. by Jo Polseno. G&D, 1958, $2.95 (P/G&D, $.60). The tender, moving story of the life of Helen Keller. A child left deaf, dumb, and blind after an illness at two years of age overcomes her plight and becomes one of the most remarkable women of all time. Miss Keller's acceptance of self and the way she matured despite her handicaps should be an inspiration to anyone reading this book.

HOLMAN, FELICE. *Professor Diggins' Dragons.* il. by Ib Ohlsson. Macmillan, 1966, $4.25. This story centers around a summer at the sea with the professor and five children engaged in an unusual form of dragon hunting. The five highly individualistic children grow in maturity and self-knowledge as they collect water specimens with the wise and good-humored professor.

JOHNSON, JAMES WELDON AND ROSAMUND. *Lift Every Voice and Sing.* Hawthorn, 1970, $3.95. Often called the Negro national anthem, this verse, written at the turn of the century, still forms a bond between black Americans today and their past. Excellent charcoal illustrations trace with drama and dignity the history of the Afro-American.

JONES, ADRIENNE. *Sail, Calypso.* il. by Adolph Le Moult. Little, 1968, $4.95. A lonely summer, an abandoned boat, and two boys make a wonderful story of friendship. Clay, a Negro whose family are migrant workers, is the first to find the boat and makes plans to return and spend his time fixing it up. The white boy, Paul, finds the boat a day later, but also claims his right to fix it up. Refusing to work at the same time, they agree upon the plan of taking turns alone with the boat on an every other day basis. After considerable antagonism they realize that the boat can be fixed much faster if they work together.

As the boys become united in their efforts, they find that friendship is even more valuable than the boat they worked all summer to restore.

* KOHN, BERNICE. *Talking Leaves: The Story of Sequoyah.*

LAWSON, ROBERT. *They Were Strong and Good.* il. by author. Viking Pr, 1940, $3.50. *They Were Strong and Good* presents the author's childhood impressions of his father and mother and their fathers and mothers. None of them made a name in history; they were just strong and good individuals. Through a book like this, the teacher can help children identify with their heritage and with their ancestors. To know and understand one's ancestors can help a child be proud of his origin, build faith in himself, and develop a more positive self-image.

LE GUIN, URSULA K. *Wizard of Earthsea.* il. by Ruth Robbins. Parnassus, 1968, $4.50 (P/Ace Bks, $.75). The boy, Sparrowhawk, later to become Ged, learns the rules and the means of wizardry as well as his own heart as he faces his destiny in this powerful fantasy-allegory. Though set as prose, the rhythms of the language are truly and consistently poetical.

MANN, PEGGY. *The Street of the Flower Boxes.* il. by Peter Burchard. Coward, 1966, $3.29 (P/WSP, $.60). The local gang has fun at the expense of a new family on the street: the boys rip up the flowers that the newcomers have planted. Young Carlos returns to the house later, on his grandmother's orders, to apologize for the damage he has done. This results in the boy agreeing to be a "watcher" of the flowers that will be planted. Struck with how pretty the flowers look on the slum street, Carlos opens up a business of selling window flower boxes which he and his friends have carefully made.

* MEYERS, SUSAN. *The Cabin on the Fjord.*

O'DELL, SCOTT. *The Black Pearl.* il. by Milton Johnson. HM, 1967, $3.75. Ramon Salazar, son of a pearl fisherman in Baja California, finds a black pearl weighing 62.3 carats in the cove of Manta Diablo, a giant manta ray feared by the inhabitants of Baja. His father gives it to the church and is assured that the act will protect his family from harm. Ramon discovers that it is not the pearl but his father's weakness in believing in it, which causes the loss of the fishing fleet in a storm.

PARKINSON, ETHELYN. *Today I Am a Ham.* il. by Ralph McDonald. Abingdon, 1968, $3.95. Young Eric Crane finds life difficult when he is kicked off the junior high football team. Being a coach's son makes matters worse, for Eric knows his father's dream is for his son to be an athlete, which Eric isn't. Turning his interests to ham radios, Eric proves that sports aren't everything. The boy becomes hero of the town by using his radio to help during an emergency. He also surprises everyone by finally becoming the athlete he dreamed of being.

PETRY, ANN. *Harriet Tubman: Conductor on the Underground Railroad.* TY Crowell, 1955, $3.95 (P/WSP, $.75). Harriet, born a slave, dreamed of the day when she would become free. Hearing about the many escapes from the plantation through the underground railroad, she escaped this way, north to freedom. She then started making trips to free other slaves, once running, hiding, coaxing, and praying until 300 slaves got through to safety. Harriet became known as "Moses" and was feared by every plantation owner.

POTTER, BRONSON. *Antonio.* il. by Ann Grifalconi. Atheneum, 1968, $3.50. Antonio, the son of a Portuguese fisherman, is unable to go to sea and fulfill his dream of becoming a fisherman because of a stiff hand. His unhappiness and his yearnings persist until a severe storm gives him the opportunity to save the village boats, to show his ability to think in time of stress, to display his strength, and to overcome his feelings of inadequacy.

* RHOADS, DOROTHY. *The Corn Grows Ripe.*

ROBERTSON, KEITH. *Henry Reed's Babysitting Service.* il. by Robert McCloskey. Viking Pr, 1966, $3.50 (P/G&D, $.60). Fourteen-year-old Henry Reed, with the help of his friend Midge Glass, sets up a baby-sitting service and encounters all kinds of adventures.

* ROBINSON, JACKIE, AND ALFRED DUCKETT. *Breakthrough to the Big League.*

ROBINSON, LOUIE, JR. *Arthur Ashe: Tennis Champion.* il. with photographs. Doubleday, 1967, $3.50 (P/several). This is the story of a young Negro boy, Arthur Ashe, who fights against the white world of tennis for a chance to play. An excellent book that touches race, acceptance of self, and the need to strive towards a goal that may sometimes seem unattainable.

ROBINSON, VERONICA. *David in Silence.* il. by Victor Ambus. Lippincott, 1965, $3.50. Deaf and dumb, David suffers fear and the derision of the young people of his new neighborhood. With Michael as a friend, David is finally able to win their respect by proving his worth as a person. Realistically and tenderly written, this book shows true sympathy and understanding for the deaf.

SMITH, VIAN. *Tall and Proud.* il. by Don Stivers. Doubleday, 1966, $3.25 (P/WSP, $.60). A thrilling story of how a young girl overcomes her handicap of polio to walk again. An only child of parents who have little money to spare, Gail spends much of her time, before becoming ill, writing about and drawing horses. Satisfied to be home after many months in the hospital, Gail does not work to regain the use of her left leg. Her father searches for a means to get Gail back on her feet, and buys a horse for her. Overcoming the pain of exercise with determination, Gail begins to recover. When noises warn Gail that her horse may be in danger, she puts her pain aside to walk and warn him.

* SNYDER, ZILPHA KEATLEY. *The Egypt Game.*

* SOUTHALL, IVAN. *Hills End.*

SPERRY, ARMSTRONG. *Call It Courage.* il. by author. Macmillan, 1940, $3.50 (P/Macmillan, $.95). Mafatu, son of Tavana Nui, had one mission in life: to conquer his fear of the sea, a fear which had bothered him since he was a baby when his mother was taken by the sea. He faces and overcomes many dangers and finally returns to his own people.

* STERLING, PHILIP, AND RAYFORD LOGAN. *Four Took Freedom: The Lives of Harriet Tubman, Frederick Douglass, Robert Small, and Blanche K. Bruce.*

TALBOT, CHARLENE JOY. *Tomás Takes Charge.* il. by Reisie Lonette. Lothrop, 1966, $3.50. Papa leaves one day and never returns. A brother and sister, Tomás and Fernanda, find themselves all alone in New York. The children manage to set up housekeeping in a vacant apartment. In the market Tomás finds food that people have left behind. Both children learn to work together with courage in order to survive in the city.

* TAYLOR, THEODORE. *The Cay.*

* TERZIAN, JAMES P. *Mighty Hard Road: The Story of Cesar Chavez.*

THORVALL, KERSTIN. *Gunnar Scores a Goal.* il. by Serge Hollerbach. HBJ, 1968, $2.75. Nine-year-old Gunnar finds himself having to compete with two older brothers who are constantly teasing him. He also must face the fact that there are many things older boys can do that he cannot. With the discovery that he can play a decent game of soccer, Gunnar comes into his own and soon earns the respect of his older brothers.

TREFFINGER, CAROLYN. *Li Lun, Lad of Courage.* il. by Kurt Wiese. Abingdon, 1947, $3.00. Li Lun refuses to go on his first fishing voyage, a manmaking event in his village. Li Lun's father punishes him by commanding him to grow rice on the desolate mountaintop. With courage and dedication, he accomplishes his task and becomes a hero to all of the village. Li Lun's courage and persistence gives the reader a sense that he also has these qualities.

UNITAS, JOHNNY, AND ED FITZGERALD. *Pro Quarterback: My Own Story.* S & S, 1965, $4.50. Johnny Unitas developed a positive self-image as well as professional success through learning to recognize and use his own strengths and weaknesses, and through developing his own personal values. Boys will particularly like the emphasis on actual Baltimore Colts games.

* UNRAU, RUTH. *Who Needs an Oil Well?*

VIERECK, PHILLIP. *The Summer I Was Lost.* il. by Ellen Viereck. John Day, 1965, $3.95. Paul is a boy who is never good in school work or in athletics. His parents send him to camp to teach him to be more self-reliant. On a wilderness hike a storm comes up and Paul finds himself separated from the rest of the group. The rest of the story tells of Paul's brave efforts to survive and the maturity and self-reliance he gains through them.

* WATSON, SALLY. *Other Sandals.*

* WRIGHTSON, PATRICIA. *A Racecourse for Andy.*

Junior

ADOFF, ARNOLD. *Brothers and Sisters: Modern Stories by Black Americans.* Macmillan, 1971, $5.95. A wide spectrum of styles, points of view, and writing skill is offered in this collection of short stories by black Americans, all but two of which have been previously published. The tone is mostly somber, often introspective, with each story revealing a psychological reaction on the part of the protagonist, usually a child or young person, to the experiences of his life. Although not written for young people, mature adolescents will find among the wide variety offered many stories that will move them and perhaps lead them to read the more complete works by such authors as Baldwin, Hughes, and Wright as well as the works of younger writers.

* ———. *Malcolm X.*

* ALCOCK, GUDRUN. *Turn the Next Corner.*

* ALEXANDER, RAE PACE (comp.) *Young and Black in America.*

BEYER, AUDREY WHITE. *Dark Venture.* il. by Leo and Diane Dillon. Knopf, 1968, $4.50. Demba, a twelve-year-old African boy, is captured by an enemy tribe and sold into slavery. Transported to Barbados, he and Adam White, the ship's surgeon, become friends. Although Demba is treated as less than human at times, he remains honest, loyal, and proud, as his father had taught him to be. The story displays the feelings of both whites and blacks who were caught in the web of slavery and shows how its various facets affect their characters.

BONTEMPS, ARNA. *Lonesome Boy.* il. by Felix Toposki. HM, 1955, $3.25. Back in print is the haunting story of Bubber and his beloved trumpet which he blows "too strong, too long." This book should find a larger and more appreciative audience now.

BRO, MARGUERITTE. *Sarah.* Doubleday, 1949, $3.95 (P/G & D, $.95). Sarah must choose between following her father's wish that she become an artist and developing her greater ability as a musician.

* BULL, ANGELA. *Wayland's Keep.*

BUTLER, BEVERLY. *Light a Single Candle.* Dodd, 1962, $3.50 (P/WSP, $.60). At the age of fourteen Cathy Wheeler has an unsuccessful eye operation. Her keen desire to be an artist does not make it any easier for her to accept the fact that she is blind. For the eighteen months following the operation she struggles to become a well-adjusted person, overcoming unhappy experiences at the state school for the blind, training with a guide dog, and at the local high school. The author, blind herself, writes sympathetically and realistically of Cathy and her handicap.

CURRY, JANE LOUISE. *The Change-Child.* il. by Gareth Floyd. HBJ, 1969, $4.25. Glowing with the color and magic of Celtic mythology, this engrossing tale, set in the reign of Elizabeth I, affords the reader an opportunity to better understand the concerns of man.

DE TREVINO, ELIZABETH B. *I, Juan De Pareja.* FS & G, 1965, $3.25. The story in this Newbery Award winner is told through the eyes of Juan, a slave, who tells of his relationship with the 17th century Spanish artist, Velasquez. Rebellious in his attitude and actions, he taught himself to paint, but was never recognized as an artist despite his unique talent.

* DOUTY, ESTHER MORRIS. *Charlotte Forten: Free Black Teacher.*

* EMERY, ANNE. *Mountain Laurel.*

EQUIANO, OLAUDAH. *The Slave Who Bought His Freedom: Equiano's Story.* Dutton, 1971, $4.50. Olaudah Equiano, an Ibo slave, had many adventures on the sea, in America, and in England, and educated himself in reading, mathematics, and navigation.

EYERLY, JEANNETTE. *The Girl Inside.* Lippincott, 1968, $3.95 (P/Berkley Pub, $.60). A sympathetic, understanding, and honest treatment of a teenage girl's attempts to reconcile the girl outside with the girl inside.

* FELTON, HAROLD W. *Nat Love, Negro Cowboy.*

GARFIELD, LEON. *Smith.* il. by Antony Maitland. Pantheon, 1967, $3.95. Twelve-year-old Smith is one of the best pickpockets in all of eighteenth-century London. One day he steals a document from an old gentleman minutes before the man is murdered. Determined to discover why the document is valuable, he sets out to learn to read. Befriending a blind judge whose daughter tutors him, Smith finds himself accused of killing the man whose document he stole.

GLYN, CAROLINA. *The Unicorn Girl.* Coward, 1966, $4.00. Fullie feels inadequate when faced with the demands of growing up and escapes the anguishes of adolescence by retreating into a world of fantasy. For Fullie, the unicorn symbolized her alienation, her "disgustedness" with herself. The humor and pathos of this highly original and imaginative novel will delight the reader.

HENRY, MARGUERITE. *Mustang: Wild Spirit of the West.* Rand, 1966, $3.95. Wild horses used to roam our western plains by the millions: now there are only a few scattered herds. Annie Johnston is determined to save them, and she carries her battle for protective legislation all the way to the White House. Thanks to "Wild Horse Annie," the magnificent wild mustang has been saved from extinction.

HICKOK, LORENA A. *The Touch of Magic.* Dodd, 1961, $3.95. An orphan, Anne Sullivan was mistreated by those responsible for her care. Unwanted, neglected, threatened, her life was filled with tragedy and loss. However, she found a way to become educated and was later able to return her famous pupil, Helen Keller, to the world of the living.

* KLABEN, HELEN. *Hey, I'm Alive!*

* LE GUIN, URSULA K. *Wizard of Earthsea.*

L'ENGLE, MADELEINE. *Camilla.* TY Crowell, 1965, $4.50. Camilla's first loves, her struggles with school life and friends, and her relationship to a disabled veteran give her the maturity to see her parents as individuals and to accept their divorce.

McGRAW, ELOISE JARVIS. *Moccasin Trail.* Coward, 1952, $4.50. Left for dead after a savage attack by a grizzly bear, Jim Keath was found and restored to health by a band of Crow Indians. For nine years Jim lived with the tribe, and he became a full-fledged warrior. On an extended trapping expedition, he met his younger brothers and sister, who needed him to help them establish a new home in Oregon. Born white and raised Indian, Jim was caught between two worlds and belonged to neither. Eventually the special skills he acquired among the Indians enabled him to find his own niche.

* NEUFELD, JOHN. *Lisa, Bright and Dark.*

* NEWLON, CLARKE. *Famous Mexican Americans.*

* O'DELL, SCOTT. *The Black Pearl.*

OGBURN, CHARLTON, JR. *Big Caesar.* HM, 1958, $3.25. Ronnie Gaines wants a diesel truck more than anything. All he has is "Big Caesar" which his father drove before he died. Ron rebuilds Big Caesar from the motor out and during the town's worst blizzard Big Caesar helps Ronnie rescue a number of cars, increasing the old truck's value in Ronnie's eyes.

PLATT, KIN. *The Boy Who Could Make Himself Disappear*. Chilton, 1968, $4.95 (P/Dell, $.75). Twelve-year-old Roger, unloved, unwanted, and handicapped by a severe speech impediment, withdraws into a world of schizophrenia.

* QUIMBY, MYRTLE. *The Cougar*.

* ROBINSON, VERONICA. *David in Silence*.

* SHERBURNE, ZOA. *Stranger in the House*.

* SOMMERFELT, AIMÉE. *No Easy Way*.

SULLIVAN, MARY W. *Jokers Wild*. il. with photographs by Michael H. Roberts. Field, 1970, $2.70. *Jokers Wild* is the story of a teenager trying to organize his life in the midst of family chaos. Through his abilities and friendships in a musical group and his hard work on a newspaper route he is able to turn misfortune into a financial asset. With the help of kind adults he is able to plan for his future.

SUTCLIFF, ROSEMARY. *Warrior Scarlet*. Walck, 1958, $5.50. Drem has a crippled arm: how can he ever become a warrior and earn the right to wear the scarlet cloth that is reserved for the men of his tribe? In spite of many setbacks, Drem's courage and grim determination enable him to win the respect of his people and the right to wear the scarlet robe. The book provides an accurate view of life and customs in Bronze Age Britain.

* SWARTHOUT, GLENDON AND KATHRYN. *Whichaway*.

* WELLS, HELEN. *Doctor Betty*.

* WOJCIECHOWSKA, MAIA. *The Hollywood Kid*.

———. *A Single Light*. Har-Row, 1968, $3.95 (P/Bantam, $.75). Her mother dies when she is born, and no one bothers to name her. Filled with shame for having a deaf daughter, her father ignores her. When the parish priest takes her in to help clean the church, she finds an old and extremely valuable statue. This event affects the lives of everyone in her village. Set in a tiny hamlet in southern Spain, *A Single Light* is concerned with the basic human need to love.

Senior

* ADOFF, ARNOLD. *Brothers and Sisters: Modern Stories by Black Americans*.

* ALEXANDER, RAE PACE (comp.) *Young and Black in America*.

* BRADDON, RUSSELL. *When the Enemy Is Tired*.

CHEVIGNY, HECTOR. *My Eyes Have a Cold Nose.* Yale, 1946, $3.50. A young professional writer finds the sudden onset of blindness a handicap but not a tragedy. He describes how his seeing eye dog helps him, how he continues with his writing, and how he overcomes his handicap.

FREEDMAN, BENEDICT AND NANCY. *Mrs. Mike.* Coward, 1947, $4.50 (P/ Berkley Pub, $.75). Sixteen-year-old Katherine O'Fallon moves from Boston to Alberta, falls in love with Sergeant Mike of the Canadian Mounted Police, and settles in a new home close to the Arctic Circle. Adjustment to rigorous life on this frontier and its hardships is the background for a story that shows the enriching and maturing effect of marriage on Kathie.

GIBSON, BOB, AND PHIL PEPE. *From Ghetto to Glory: The Story of Bob Gibson.* P-H, 1968, $5.95 (P/Popular Lib, $.75). Bob Gibson narrates the story of his long, uphill battle for success. Born in a ghetto, the youngest of a family of seven fatherless children, he comes to learn the meaning of hardship and prejudice. His story of his relationship with his eldest brother is an example of family unity and of the influence one person can have on another's success. Through refusing to play a role imposed upon him by society, Bob goes on to become a hero of that society.

* GODDEN, RUMER. *The River.*

GREEN, HANNAH. *I Never Promised You a Rose Garden.* HR & W, 1964, $4.95 (P/NAL, $.95). Deborah's everyday surroundings become a gray shadow world as she slips deeper into her secret Kingdom of Yr. Once a pleasant retreat from reality, Yr is now a frightening place which claims increasingly larger segments of her days. Deborah is ill, and treatment in a mental hospital is necessary. With the help of her doctor, Deborah finds the strength to fight her way back to health. Told with deep understanding and compassion, Deborah's story provides a rare glimpse into the world of those who suffer from mental illness.

GREGORY, SUSAN. *Hey, White Girl!* Norton, 1970, $4.95 (P/Lancer, $.95). This book relates the experiences of the only white girl at a ghetto school in Chicago. Provides insight into problems of ghetto inhabitants and schools and an understanding of the changing racial situation.

GRIFFIN, JOHN HOWARD. *Black Like Me.* HM, 1961, $4.95 (P/NAL, $.75). A white journalist undergoes medical treatment to change the color of his skin and travels as a Negro in the deep South.

HEMON, LOUIS. *Maria Chapdelaine: A Tale of the Lake St. John Country.* Translated by W. H. Blake. Macmillan, 1934, $4.95 (P/Doubleday, $.85). On a small farm deep in the Canadian north woods, Maria Chapdelaine lives with her family. Told with extraordinary beauty,

Maria's story is simple: she falls in love, and she must decide how she will spend the rest of her life. Primitive conditions and harsh climate do not make for easy living, but life itself is good. Love, duty, and courage are the elements of this tale of French Canada.

HERZOG, MAURICE. *Annapurna: The First Conquest of an Eight Thousand Meter Peak.* Dutton, 1953, $6.50 (P/Popular Lib, $.75). The scaling of Annapurna, the highest mountain ever climbed by man, is related by the leader of the French Himalayan Expedition. More than a record of adventure and scientific investigations, it is the story of nine men who appreciate one another's qualities and who together face joy, pain, and even death. The conquest of the mountain becomes a symbol of the men's courage and understanding.

JOSEPH, STEPHEN M., (ed.). *The Me Nobody Knows: Children's Voices from the Ghetto.* World Pub., 1969, $4.95 (P/Avon, $.95). Sensitive teachers with a positive attitude toward learning and children inspired these perceptive writings. The ghetto children tell it like it is—about themselves, their neighborhood, their world.

* KILLILEA, MARIE L. *Karen.*

MARSHALL, CATHERINE. *A Man Called Peter.* McGraw, 1951, $5.95 (P/ several). Coming to the United States in 1927 as a poor Scottish immigrant, Peter Marshall rose in nineteen years to the office of Chaplain of the U.S. Senate. Wherever he preached, he left behind him churches with larger and more energetic congregations than he met when he came. Through his inspirational leadership he touched the lives of thousands, dedicating his whole life to God and his fellow men.

* MEHTA, RAMA. *The Life of Kesbau.*

MEHTA, VED. *Face to Face.* Little, 1957, $5.95 (P/Penguin, $1.95). Ved, a young Hindu who became blind at the age of three, tells of his childhood and early teens in India and the test of his courage and determination as he attempted to make a full life for himself. He gave up an easier, happier life in America in order to return to India to help in the rehabilitation of his country's blind.

* MERRIAM, EVE. *Growing up Female in America: Ten Lives.*

NEVILLE, EMILY. *Fogarty.* Har-Row, 1969, $3.50. A twenty-three-year-old law school dropout and unsuccessful off-Broadway playwright returns to his hometown to be a teacher.

* NEWLON, CLARKE. *Famous Mexican Americans.*

* OGBURN, CHARLTON, JR. *Big Caesar.*

* PARKS, GORDON. *A Choice of Weapons.*

* SEVERN, BILL. *Toward One World: The Life of Wendell Wilkie.*

* WOODY, REGINA J. *The Young Medics.*

Mature

HESSE, HERMANN. *Narcissus and Goldmund.* trans. by Ursule Molinaro. FS & G, 1968, $5.95 (P/FS & G, $2.25). Medieval Europe is the background for the lifelong friendship between the austere monk Narcissus and his cheerful student Goldmund. When the Mariabronn cloister can no longer contain Goldmund, he leaves his friend in order to search for some goal in life. For years he wanders across Germany, running the gamut of human experience at all levels of society. Discovering that he was born to be an artist, he concentrates his search on a master who can teach him his craft. Goldmund's adventures are more than a series of entertaining episodes, for they provide a perceptive view of the development of an artist.

WILLIAMS, TENNESSEE. *The Glass Menagerie.* P/New Directions, 1945, $1.60. This lyrical and tenuous play centers on a mother and daughter who live in their illusions. Laura, the daughter, uses her crippled leg as a shield against reality; Amanda, the mother, lives in a world populated by gracious Southern ladies and gentlemen of a bygone era. Tom, the son, is torn between the mundane reality of his job at the shoe factory and the poetic feeling in his soul.

Growing into Maturity and Accepting Oneself

Primary

ANDERSON, NEIL. *Meet Sandy Smith.* il. by Mary Stevens. Hale, 1954, $2.70. (P/WSP, $.60). Sandy, a boy from a Western ranch, moves to New York City. He enjoys exploring in his tall apartment building, but he finds it difficult to make friends.

BELL, GINA. *Who Wants Willy Wells?* il. by Jean Tamburine. Abingdon, 1957, $2.00. There's a new baby at home. Willy feels unwanted so he runs away. He soon returns, however, and begins to realize how nice his parents, and even his little brother, really are.

BROTHERS, AILEEN, AND CORA HOLSCLAW. *Just One Me.* il. by Jan Balet. Follett, 1967, $1.95. Jimmy imagines himself as being such things as a road, a merry-go-round, and a plane; but he decides that if there is "just one me, that's what I really want to be."

DE JONG, MEINDERT. *Puppy Summer.* il. by Anita Lobel. Har-Row, 1965, $3.79. One day Jon and Vestri go to a neighboring farm to choose a puppy. They end up taking three puppies. The children must now learn to accept the responsibility of caring for and feeding Smith, Brown, and Jones.

* DE REGNIERS, BEATRICE, AND IRENE HAAS. *A Little House of Your Own.*

DUNCAN, LOIS. *Giving Away Suzanne.* il. by Leonard Weisgard. Dodd, 1963, $2.99. Mary Kay trades her troublesome little sister for a gold-fish. She soon realizes, however, that although Suzanne was trouble-some at times, she was much more enjoyable and entertaining than a fish.

EICKE, EDNA. *The Children Who Got Married.* il. by author. S & S, 1969, $3.50. This is a unique book written in a child's scrawl. Two children play a game of house. They take a honeymoon, really a ride around the block, use three toys as their children, and play out the role of father seeking a job.

FIFE, DALE. *Who's in Charge of Lincoln?* il. by Paul Galdone. Coward, 1965, $2.97. An imaginative eight-year-old boy tells the most fantastic tales ever; therefore, the morning his mother goes to the hospital, no one believes that a horse has fallen on Mrs. Readywell's leg. Lincoln is left alone in their New York apartment with no one in charge of him.

GRIFALCONI, ANN. *City Rhythms.* il. by author. Bobbs, 1965, $4.95. Jimmy Peters tries to solve his father's riddle about the city having a rhythm of its own. Jimmy begins to listen, look, and move very alertly. He notices and remembers everything going on around him, and finally he begins to sense what his father meant.

* HOBAN, RUSSELL. *Bedtime for Frances.*

* ———. *A Birthday for Frances.*

———. *Ugly Bird.* il. by Lillian Hoban. Macmillan, 1969, $3.95. *Ugly Bird* is a very ugly bird; he is so ugly in fact that only his mother loves him and all the other birds make fun of him. Looking for an escape from his ugliness, the little bird changes himself into a hand-some stone, a shiny fish, a little pebble, and a buzzing bee. Through these roles he finds out that it is not so bad to be an ugly bird after all.

HOCKER, KARLA. *The Three Times Lost Dog.* il. by Helge Kuckei. Atheneum, 1967, $3.50. Christian, against his parents' wishes and knowledge, keeps a dachshund puppy named Pixie. After losing his puppy, forgetting to feed and water him, and causing trouble with the guests at his father's inn, Christian finally develops the maturity needed to care responsibly for the small dog.

IWASAKI, CHIHIRO. *Staying Home Alone on a Rainy Day.* il. by author. McGraw, 1969, $3.95. Allison feels proud and grown-up when her mother goes to the store and leaves her home alone for the first time. When a storm comes and her mother is delayed the house suddenly seems empty and frightening. With delicate watercolor illustrations the author-artist shows how the child overcomes her fears and learns to enjoy the beauty of the rain.

KEMPNER, CAROL. *Nicholas.* il. by author. S & S, 1968, $4.50. Every day Nicholas walks with his mother to the subway as she goes off to work, but he is never permitted to ride on these exciting trains. Accidentally shoved aboard by a crowd of people, Nicholas gains some maturity and independence.

KUSKIN, KARLA. *The Bear Who Saw the Spring.* il. by author. Har-Row, 1961, $3.79. This book deals with the change of the seasons, running parallel with the changes living things go through as they grow to maturity. The child learns that it is natural for animals to be born, to live, and then to die.

LENZEN, HANS GEORG. *The Blue Marble.* il. by Marie-Luise Pricken. Abelard, 1969, $3.95. The blue marble represents a child's dream world where things he has read, or seen, or heard about come to life. But they are not ordinary things—they are what life itself is all about: love, religion, happiness, and sorrow. The blue marble holds in it the thoughts of its owner and one day the boy sees a little girl who he knows needs the marble. He gives it to her and sends her off into the world of hopes and dreams and security that the blue marble holds.

LEXAU, JOAN M. *I Should Have Stayed in Bed.* il. by Syd Hoff. Har-Row, 1965, $3.50. After "getting up on the wrong side of the bed," and having a terrible morning, Sam goes back to bed to start the day again. Even though he and his good friend Albert are late for school, it promises to be a good day after all.

LITTLE, JEAN. *Spring Begins in March.* il. by Lewis Parker. Little, 1966, $3.95. Meg Copeland, youngest of four children, feels she is a total failure at home and school. Promised a room of her own, Meg faces disappointment when her grandmother moves in with the family and Meg must continue to share a room with her sister. Failing at school doesn't seem to bother Meg until she realizes that the teacher does not plan to promote her. Facing her shortcomings, Meg finally asks for help from her sister. With tutoring, Meg manages to prove that she is a good student.

* LOVELACE, MAUD HART. *The Valentine Box.*

MANNHEIM, GRETE. *The Two Friends.* Knopf, 1968, $3.95. Jenny is beginning school, and all of her family try to make this exciting and scary time a little easier. There are many new experiences and many new people to meet, but Jenny's special friend is Nancy. The real photographs of very natural scenes should make this multiracial book most helpful for primary children and their parents.

MASON, MIRIAM E. *The Middle Sister.* il. by Grace Paull. Macmillan, 1947, $3.50. Sarah Samantha knows the only thing that will make her brave is Uncle Romeo's shiny lion's tooth. In return for the tooth she agrees to make him an apple dumpling from her apple tree, Miss Appleseed. When the family decides to move to a homestead, Sara Samantha chooses Miss Appleseed as her one treasure to take along. Through many adventures with animals and Indians in a strange new land, Sarah is already brave by the time she receives the tooth.

RASKIN, ELLEN. *Spectacles.* il. by author. Atheneum, 1968, $3.50. Iris Fogel does not see things just as others do. The chestnut mare, for example, is really the babysitter. And to Iris's dismay, she must begin to wear glasses. Then she can see objects in not just one, but two ways!

REESINK, MARYKE. *The Fisherman's Family.* il. by Georgette Apol. HBJ, 1968, $3.95. Jan attempts to help his family through a crisis when he learns his father is lost at sea.

* SARGENT, SHIRLEY. *Yosemite Tomboy.*

SIMON, NORMA. *What Do I Do?* il. by Joe Lasker. A Whitman, 1969, $3.50. A Puerto Rican girl, like all children, needs to develop the "I can do" feeling. In her inner-city environment, she strives to feel competent and capable. The constant question, "What do I do?" permits the reader, as well as the Puerto Rican child, to reflect upon himself and to formulate personal answers to the problems of growing up.

* TOLSTOY, LEO. *Twenty-Two Russian Tales for Young Children.*

WRIGHT, BETTY REN. *This Room Is Mine.* il. by Judy Stang. Western Pub, 1966, $2.39. Chris and Mary are sisters who share the same bedroom. Each is fearful that the other will use her things, so they divide the room in half, each vowing not to use the other's half of their room. After a very short experiment the girls discover that part of growing up is sharing.

Intermediate

* ALCOCK, GUDRUN. *Run, Westy, Run.*

* BARNES, NANCY. *The Wonderful Year.*

* BAWDEN, NINA. *The Runaway Summer.*

BOLTON, IVY. *Wayfaring Lad.* il. by Lorence F. Bjorklund. P/WSP, 1967, $.60. Young Richard Nolan loses his mother at an early age, and is just getting over the death of his father, when he is sent off to a neighboring settlement by a cousin who has no use for him. Proving himself to be a hard worker, honest and brave, Richard saves the settlement.

BOND, GLADYS BAKER. *A Head on Her Shoulders.* il. by Richard Kennedy. Abelard, 1963, $3.00 (P/WSP, $.60). The Wards' plan to move to the West is changed at the last minute when Papa breaks his leg and Brita, the oldest of four children, must take the responsibility of moving the other children, the livestock, and the family belongings to Spokane Falls, where the parents will meet the children later.

* BUCK, PEARL. *The Big Wave.*

* BURLESON, ELIZABETH. *Middl'un.*

* BYARS, BETSY. *The Midnight Fox.*

* CHESSMAN, RUTH. *Bound for Freedom.*

* COATSWORTH, ELIZABETH. *Jon the Unlucky.*

COCKETT, MARY. *Ash Dry, Ash Green.* il. by Diana Stanley. Criterion, 1968, $2.95. *Ash Dry, Ash Green* is a realistic, informative story of a young boy's fascination with a little seed growing into a tall tree. John finally saves the tree from later harm by having it transplanted into his own yard.

* CORCORAN, BARBARA. *A Row of Tigers.*

GAGE, WILSON. *Miss Osborne-the-Mop.* il. by Paul Galdone. World Pub, 1969, $3.95 (P/WSP, $.60). Jody and Dill resent the idea of having to spend their entire summer vacation together until something strange happens. Jody changes Dill into a squirrel! What fun they have together performing magic tricks. But magic cannot always be controlled, for example, when Jody brings to life a mop that refuses to go back into the closet. The two are faced with the problem of what to do with the mop.

* GARST, SHANNON. *Cowboy Boots.*

HAUGAARD, ERIK CHRISTIAN. *Hakon of Rogen's Saga.* il. by Leo and Diane Dillon. HM, 1963, $3.00. Hakon, living at the end of the Viking period, is the rightful heir to the island of Rogen. Because of Hakon's youth, his uncle tries to take possession of Rogen. As he deals with treachery, vengeance, and dishonesty, Hakon develops from a boy into a man.

HEPPE, MARGARET, AND LULU HATHAWAY. *Especially Rosita.* il. by Heff Heisler. P/Friend Pr, 1968, $1.75. Mr. Rankin, a traveling business-man, is seldom home. Mrs. Rankin has her social obligations. Jean is involved in her own affairs, and Arthur, often left to himself, is on the road to becoming a juvenile delinquent. Rosita, an exchange student from Ecuador living with the family, and Pastor Cliff help to bring this family together.

HUSTON, ANNE, AND JANE YOLEN. *Trust a City Kid.* il. by J. C. Kocsis. Lothrop, 1966, $3.75. Twelve-year-old Reg, a Negro boy from Man-hattan, spends a summer with a Quaker family on a farm in Pennsyl-vania. Unable to accept genuine kindness and love, Reg finds the going hard. He exhibits a negative attitude toward his host family and is suspicious of everyone's motives. Finding a stray horse and keeping him a secret involves Reg in a series of petty thefts, but his attitude changes when the horse is assured a home with the Quaker family.

* JACKSON, JACQUELINE. *The Taste of Spruce Gum.*

* KONIGSBURG, E. L. *About the B'nai Bagels.*

———. *From the Mixed-Up Files of Mrs. Basil E. Frankweiler.* Athen-eum, 1968, $3.95. A delightful account of two runaways, Claudia and Jamie Kincaid. Claudia masterminds the trip which takes them to the Metropolitan Museum of Art. A new statue called "Angel" mesmerizes Claudia with its beauty and she becomes engrossed in discovering the maker. This leads them to Mrs. Frankweiler's house and files. This grand old dame gives her the key to unlock the secret, thus making it possible for Claudia to return home.

* ———. *Jennifer, Hecate, Macbeth, William McKinley and Me, Elizabeth.*

* KRUMGOLD, JOSEPH. *And Now, Miguel.*

LANSING, ELISABETH HUBBARD. *Liza of the Hundredfold.* il. by Dorothy Bayley Morse. P/WSP, 1968, $.50. An only daughter, Liza has not yet learned that at twelve her father expects her to take her mother's place in the house. Still in the tomboy stage, Liza resents being left out of her older brother's activities. After a serious argument between surrounding neighbors and her father, Liza assumes the role of sym-pathizer and helps get the neighbors back together. Unknowingly, she lets some of her tomboyishness slip aside while she tends to her "family."

LINDE, GUNNEL. *The White Stone.* il. by Imero Gobbato. HBJ, 1966, $3.50. Fia and Hampus challenge each other to do different daring feats to win the possession of a beautiful white stone which is precious to both of them. The stone possesses great powers, causing the children to create ever more exciting games for themselves and to do things which neither would have dared before.

* MILLER, LUREE, AND MARILYN SILVERSTONE. *Gurkhas and Ghosts.*

* NORRIS, GUNILLA B. *The Top Step.*

OTTLEY, REGINALD. *Boy Alone.* il. by Clyde Pearson. HBJ, 1966, $3.75.
Working as a "wood and water Joey," a boy learns to admire the
special talents the other workers have and attempts to do his very
best in all he does. Running away with Rags, the pup he has raised,
the boy becomes lost and is found by the man who owns Rags. The
man gives the boy the dog, love, and security.

PHIPSON, JOAN. *The Boundary Riders.* il. by Margaret Horder. HBJ, 1963,
$3.50. Three children, Jane and Bobby Thompson and their cousin
Vincent, are sent out on a week's mission to check the boundary
fences on their ranch in Australia. Finishing their task early, the
children decide not to return home but rather to explore the countryside. Unfortunately, they become lost in the foothills with no food
and only twelve matches. Survival becomes a very important factor
as the children must battle the weather, hunger, and fear.

* RYDBERG, ERNIE. *The Dark of the Cave.*

SARGENT, SHIRLEY. *Yosemite Tomboy.* il. by Victoria de Larrea. Abelard,
1967, $3.50. Young Jan Kern is suddenly shifted from living with
her family to boarding with friends of her parents. She and her older
brother attend school while waiting for their parents to move. Jan
discovers that the other girls do not care for her tomboyish ways.

* SERRAILLIER, IAN. *The Silver Sword.*

* SMITH, GEORGE HARMON. *Wanderers of the Field.*

* STEELE, WILLIAM O. *The Year of the Bloody Sevens.*

TOLSTOY, LEO. *Twenty-Two Russian Tales for Young Children.* trans. by
Miriam Morton. il. by Eros Keith. S & S, 1969, $4.50. A beautiful
book with stories that will appeal to primary and intermediate children. These stories were written and then translated in a style that
will allow them to be enjoyed orally or silently.

* WARREN, MARY PHRANER. *A Snake Named Sam.*

WOODY, REGINA. *Almena's Dogs.* il. by Elton C. Fax. G & D, 1968, $2.50.
Young Almena's first love is dogs. Her greatest ambition is to become
a "dog doctor." One of her friends wins a dog through a write-in contest and gives it to Almena, but her parents tell her that their apartment will not allow dogs. Unhappily, Almena gives up her present
but later finds fulfillment when she begins to work with handicapped
children.

Junior

AAHPER (ed.). *Drug Abuse: Escape to Nowhere.* P/Smith, Kline and French Laboratories, 1967, $2.00. Essentially a guide for educators, *Drug Abuse* contains information of value to students from junior high on, their parents, teachers and concerned members of the community. Dealing with such topics as the commonly used drugs, how they are used, their effects, how to identify the user, and methods of therapy, the book makes no attempt to preach or make moral judgments. Those working with young people will find the bibliography most helpful; it lists books, films, pamphlets, government publications, and articles in medical and scientific journals.

AMES, FRANCIS. *That Callahan Spunk.* Doubleday, 1965, $4.95. Weary of New England's cramped, confining atmosphere, John Conway stakes a homestead claim in Montana in the early 1900s. His wife Trix and their son Tom join him. Tom takes a job as a cowboy with a rancher neighbor. Although he is totally unprepared for the job, "that Callahan spunk," his grandmother's legacy, spurs him on.

* ARNOLD, ELLIOTT. *A Kind of Secret Weapon.*

ARTHUR, RUTH M. *Portrait of Margarita.* il. by Margery Gill. Atheneum, 1968, $4.25. An airplane crash leaves Margarita a lonely orphan in an English boarding school until her cousin Francis becomes her guardian. When she joins Francis in Italy, Margarita finds herself attracted to a young man, Pietro, who very much resembles Cousin Francis. As she matures she begins to realize that her relationship with her cousin is a father-daughter relationship and that her relationship with Pietro is a true romance.

BURCH, ROBERT. *Queenie Peavy.* il. by Jerry Lazare. Viking Pr, 1966, $3.50. "I don't care" is tomboy Queenie's outward reaction as she contends with the taunts of her rural Georgia classmates about her father, who is in the penitentiary. Faced with a sheriff's investigation and the possibility of the reformatory when wrongly accused of breaking some windows, Queenie decides truth and reality are more important than toughness and pretense.

* BUTLER, MARJORIE. *The Man Who Killed a Bear with a Stick.*

* CARSON, JOHN F. *The Twenty-Third Street Crusaders.*

* CAVANNA, BETTY. *Going on Sixteen.*

CHESSMAN, RUTH. *Bound for Freedom.* il. by Anne Linton. Abelard, 1965, $3.25. James and Davy, two bonded servants aboard a ship bound for Boston, form a deep friendship in their common need for companionship as they anticipate new lives under their unknown masters. James is bought by a fair and gentle farmer in whose home the twelve-year-old is nurtured as a member of the family. Davy is abused by a harsh master intent upon working him to exhaustion. The action is halted frequently for looks at the 18th century surroundings.

DALY, MAUREEN. *Seventeenth Summer.* Dodd, 1942, $3.50 (P/WSP, $.60). During Angie Morrow's seventeenth summer, she goes out with Jack Duluth for the first time. Their dating pattern is normal: cokes at the drugstore, rides in Jack's jalopy and on Swede's boat. As the summer passes, their friendship grows naturally until near the end Jack feels compelled to tell Angie he loves her, because she is going away to college and he is moving back to Oklahoma. The story is healthy in its approach to life and the pains of adjusting to physical and emotional development with the opposite sex as well as relationships with members of the family.

* DE ANGELI, ARTHUR CRAIG. *The Door in the Wall.*

DONOVAN, JOHN. *I'll Get There: It Better Be Worth the Trip.* Har-Row, $3.95 (P/Dell, $.75). Death, divorce, and a tentative, bewildering relationship with another boy are part of a thirteen-year-old boy's trip to adulthood.

* EVARTS, HAL G. *Smuggler's Road.*

EYERLY, JEANNETTE. *A Girl Like Me.* Lippincott, 1966, $3.75 (P/Berkley Pub, $.60). This novel tells of the high school days of a teenager who is faced with the problem of dating, of a friend's pregnancy, and of learning that she had been adopted.

———. *Escape from Nowhere.* Lippincott, 1969, $3.95. A teenage girl's conflict over the emptiness of the straight world and the disintegration of the drug world.

* FARJEON, ANNABEL. *Maria Lupin.*

FORMAN, JAMES. *Ring the Judas Bell.* FS & G, 1965, $3.25. Nicholas, a fifteen-year-old shepherd, assumes the responsibility of shepherding a group of Greek children back to their homeland from Albania, where they had been taken when they were kidnapped. Based on the experiences of thirty thousand Greek children after World War II, the author has written a powerful novel wherein Nicholas' strength of his convictions are tested to the limit.

FRANK, ANNE. *Anne Frank: The Diary of a Young Girl.* trans. by B. M. Mooyart. Doubleday, 1967, $4.95 (P/several). Few are unfamiliar with Anne Frank, thirteen years of age, documentor of a secret life and Nazi terror. Forced into hiding by the Nazi occupation of Amsterdam, eight Jews lived in fear of discovery and death for two years. They faced almost unbearable conditions of material and spiritual deprivation, yet their lives, and especially that of Anne, are an ever-lasting monument to courage, faith, and hope for mankind.

FRITZ, JEAN. *Brady.* il. by Lynd Ward. Coward, 1960, $4.25. Living in a divided community before the Civil War, Brady is embarrassed by his father's militant attitude against slavery. As he comes to agree with his father, the boy shows the initiative and courage of a man.

* GEORGE, JEAN CRAIGHEAD. *Gull Number Seven Thirty-Seven.*

HAUGAARD, ERIK CHRISTIAN. *The Little Fishes.* il. by Milton Johnson. HM, 1967, $3.75. Guido, an orphan beggar boy in Naples during World War II, searches for food as well as meaning in life. With Anna and her small brother Mario he begins a journey to find a home. When Anna asks him why he doesn't hate the people who are warring, he replies, "It is understanding that makes the difference between us and animals. And when you understand you can feel a kind of happiness even in the worst misery."

* HAUTZIG, ESTHER. *The Endless Steppe: Growing up in Siberia.*

HENTOFF, NAT. *A Doctor among the Addicts.* Rand, 1968, $4.95. Dr. Marie Nyswander is a psychiatrist who specializes in the problems of drug addiction. Her success with the methadone treatment for heroin addicts in New York has led to the establishment of methadone programs in many other cities.

HOLM, ANNE S. *North to Freedom.* HBJ, 1965, $3.95. David, a prisoner of war, is given a chance to escape and is told only to make his way to Denmark. Distrusting human beings, he makes his way silently from Eastern Europe and on the journey regains his faith in mankind.

HUNT, IRENE. *Across Five Aprils.* il. by Albert John Pucci. Follett, 1964, $4.95 (P/several). The "five Aprils" of the title are those of the Civil War—1861-1865. A family living in southern Illinois is one of many split by sympathy for either the North or the South. Young Jethro Creighton becomes the man of the family when his brothers enlist in the Union and the Confederate armies and his father falls ill. Jethro learns to understand himself and his role within the family as he accepts the responsibility of the farm work, as well as coping with the reactions of the neighbors to a family with sons fighting on both sides.

———. *Up a Road Slowly.* Follett, 1966, $4.95. Julie grows up in the home of her aunt, a schoolteacher, who takes her in after her mother dies. Her resentment of the adults around her changes to love and understanding as she learns to accept people for themselves. Her uncle nurtures her interest in writing and supports her through a romance with the wrong boy.

HYDE, MARGARET O. *Mind Drugs.* P/PB, 1969, $.95. A series of articles by authorities on what is known about mind-altering drugs and their effects. A factual objective summary of great value to teachers, parents, and children.

KINGMAN, LEE. *The Peter Pan Bag.* HM, 1970, $3.75 (P/Dell, $.75). A teenage girl leaves home to find freedom, only to become involved in the drug scene.

LEE, MILDRED. *The Rock and the Willow.* Lothrop, 1963, $4.25 (P/WSP, $.75). There is little chance that Enie's dreams of travel will ever come true, for life is hard on a small Alabama farm in the 1930s. Birth and death, hard work, and her first love all help Enie to mature. She is ready when the opportunity to go down that big new highway comes.

————. *Honor Sands.* Lothrop, 1966, $4.50. Fourteen-year-old Honor feels hemmed in at times by her mother's constant attention and her family's love. Like most girls her age she is over-sensitive and tends to exaggerate situations. Honor's crush on a teacher makes her feel set apart from her friends. She begins to suspect something more than friendship in her father and Aunt Catherine's relationship but this is wholly imagined. To add to her problems, Honor's best friend begins to date. A realistic novel of an only child growing into maturity.

* MACPHERSON, MARGARET. *The Rough Road.*

MADDOCK, REGINALD. *The Pit.* Little, 1968, $4.75. A forceful story of Butch, a rough boy whose father beats him every night. Because of the role he plays as a ruffian, he is falsely accused of theft. How he proves his innocence and becomes a hero on the boggy moors is excitingly told.

* MOSKIN, MARIETTA D. *A Paper Dragon.*

* NEVILLE, EMILY. *It's Like This, Cat.*

* NEWELL, HOPE. *A Cap for Mary Ellis.*

* OTTLEY, REGINALD. *Boy Alone.*

* PEDERSEN, ELSA. *House upon a Rock.*

RAWLINGS, MARJORIE KINNAN. *The Yearling.* Scribner, 1938, $6.95 (P/Scribner, $2.45). Young Jody Baxter lives a lonely life in the scrub forest of Florida until his parents unwillingly consent to his adopting an orphan fawn. When the fawn destroys the meager crops, Jody realizes that the situation offers no compromise. In the sacrifice of what he loves, he leaves his own yearling days behind.

RICHARDSON, GRACE. *Douglas.* Har-Row, 1966, $3.50. Douglas, a scholarship student expelled from a private school, barely scrapes through college and fails miserably when he tries to go it alone in London.

RINKOFF, BARBARA. *Name: Johnny Pierce.* Seabury, 1969, $3.95. Johnny Pierce, fifteen years old, feels that at times he is not really his father's son. A younger sister who has "spells" and must be treated with caution and a younger brother who seems to get all his parents' attention cause Johnny to feel left out and neglected. Falling in with a gang, Johnny soon finds himself in real trouble. When his father does not punish him, he reflects upon his family life and sees himself as an important member of the family.

SHERBURNE, ZOA. *Too Bad about the Haines Girl.* Morrow, 1967, $3.95. Melinda, almost eighteen and engaged to be married, is faced with the fact that she is pregnant. Unable to carry out the planned abortion she accepts the bitter fact that she must tell her parents.

STEELE, WILLIAM O. *The Year of the Bloody Sevens.* il. by Charles Beck. HBJ, 1963, $3.95. The year 1777 is one of Indian massacres, and Kelsey Bond travels westward to rejoin his father. Having to go it alone when two companions are killed, Kelsey learns a lot about hiding and scouting and finally rejoins his father at Logan's Fort, where he has an opportunity to become a hero.

STOLZ, MARY. *A Love, or a Season.* Har-Row, 1964, $4.43. A summer of love and passion in the lives of two teenagers who try desperately to understand and to control the new, strange, and delightful emotions which threaten to overwhelm them.

TUNIS, JOHN R. *His Enemy, His Friend.* Morrow, 1967, $3.50 (P/Avon, $.75). Hans Von Kleinschrodt, one of the soldiers occupying Nogent-Plage on the Normandy coast during World War II, is nevertheless a friend of the villagers, until a German officer is murdered. Hans is ordered to have six hostages, all friends, killed. Although he did not give the order, he is remembered as "The Butcher" when he returns to the area during peacetime to participate in a soccer game, and a crazed Frenchman decides to take matters into his own hands. One's loyalty to country and self are carefully examined as is the entire moral question of war.

* WILKINSON, SYLVIA. *A Killing Frost.*

YOUNG, BOB AND JAN. *Where Tomorrow?* Abelard, 1971, $4.00 (P/WSP, $.60). When her junior year ends, Bunny Taylor quits school to go to work. A job in a department store is fun until she is laid off. Bunny finds that she can get only part-time work or collect unemployment checks. Meeting the River Rats, a gang of high school dropouts, she drifts with them for months, overlooking their thefts. One night she finds herself running from the police and decides to seek her high school counselor's help.

ZINDEL, PAUL. *My Darling, My Hamburger.* Har-Row, 1969, $3.95 (P/Dell, $.75). Teenage Liz faces an abortion while her admiring girlfriend tentatively explores the world of boys and dates.

————. *The Pigman*. Har-Row, 1968, $3.95 (P/Dell, $.60). Two teen-agers take turns chapter by chapter relating the story of their friend-ship with a lonely old man. Although they are very fond of Mr. Pignati and aware at times of their need for his company, one thoughtless act on their part has a great deal to do with his death. It is only after-wards that John and Lorraine realize the enormity of their irresponsi-bility and attempt to explain it by writing the book. The lesson is painful, all the more so when told from John and Lorraine's point of view.

Senior

* AAHPER (ed.). *Drug Abuse: Escape to Nowhere.*

* BORLAND, HAL. *When the Legends Die.*

CAPOTE, TRUMAN. *A Christmas Memory*. Random, 1966, $5.00. Each year Buddy and Miss Sook bake pecan-rich fruitcakes which they give to their friends. Through the Christmas rituals of cake baking, tree cutting and trimming, gift making and giving, emerges the wonderful relationship which exists between a lonely boy and his elderly cousin.

CATHER, WILLA. *My Antonia*. HM, 1947, $6.95 (P/HM, $2.25). The privations, hard work, and grim tragedy of existence in a pioneer settlement in Nebraska bring out the sturdy self-reliance of this Bohemian girl.

* CRANE, CAROLINE. *Wedding Song.*

FERBER, EDNA. *A Peculiar Treasure*. Doubleday, 1938, $5.95 (P/Lancer, $.95). An ambitious American Jewish girl tells of the struggle and hard work that began with her reporting job at the age of seventeen and brought her recognition as a writer of short stories and novels.

* FREEDMAN, BENEDICT AND NANCY. *Mrs. Mike.*

HART, MOSS. *Act One*. Random, 1959, $7.95 (P/Ballantine, $1.25). This autobiography of the famous playwright is filled with zest whether the writer is telling about his poverty-stricken childhood in the Bronx or the agony of rewriting endlessly in an effort to produce a successful play. This is more than a book about show business; it is the story of a wise man who tells about the things which influenced him as he changed from a stage-struck boy to an adult.

* HEAD, ANN. *Mr. and Mrs. Bo Jo Jones.*

* HUNTER, KRISTIN. *The Soul Brothers and Sister Lou.*

LOTT, MILTON. *Backtrack*. HM, 1965, $4.95. This novel provides a penetrating view into the lives of two human beings. Ringo, who has blocked memories of his violent youth, is disturbed by Luis, an adolescent who is as vulnerable and defenseless as Ringo once had been. Through their relationship, both Ringo and Luis arrive at self-understanding.

McCULLERS, CARSON. *Member of the Wedding.* HM, 1946, $4.95 (P/several). Frankie Adams, a tall thirteen-year-old girl, is a loner in a small southern town. The only balm to her loneliness is six-year-old John Henry. When her brother comes home from the army, Frankie at last has someone to belong to, but when he marries and doesn't take her on the honeymoon, she is forced to grow up. After floundering, she manages to accept the situation and herself.

MATHER, MELISSA. *One Summer in Between.* Har-Row, 1967, $4.95. A summer of courage and love for a nineteen-year-old black girl from South Carolina living with a white family in Vermont.

* MAUERMANN, MARY ANNE. *Strangers into Friends.*

* NAYLOR, PHYLLIS REYNOLDS. *Dark Side of the Moon.*

* NORTH, STERLING. *So Dear to My Heart.*

PARKS, GORDON. *The Learning Tree.* Har-Row, 1963, $6.95 (P/Fawcett World, $.95). A black boy grows up in a Kansas town amid crime, violence and prejudice. Absorbing and learning through each experience, he manages to finish high school.

* PEDERSEN, ELSA. *Fisherman's Choice.*

RUSSELL, TERRY AND RENNY. *On the Loose.* il. by authors, Sierra, 1967, $7.95 (P/Ballantine, $3.95). The authors of this book are in their teens; through their intimate association with nature, they come to understand themselves, and thus all men, better. The photographs give the book a beauty that reinforces the text.

* SANSAN. *Eighth Moon.*

STEINBECK, JOHN. *The Red Pony.* Viking Pr, 1945, $3.37 (P/Bantam, $.60). Though Jody is the dominant character in this book, it is not about him. It is a story of the pain of becoming an adult; it is the story of a child's wisdom and a man's foolishness; it is the age-old story of birth and death, love and hate, pleasure and pain. The boy Jody encounters all these things in the painful process of becoming a man.

SUTCLIFF, ROSEMARY. *The Mark of the Horse Lord.* Walck, 1965, $5.50. Phaedrus, the gladiator, wins his freedom by slaying his opponent in the arena. Accepting a strange offer of a kingdom, he is groomed to masquerade as the rightful heir to the Dalriadain. The author breathes life into a distant past amid the violence and romance of Britain before

Christ. The struggle of the tribe he represents becomes that of Phaedrus and his triumph is well-earned. Through the identity of another, he learns his own.

* THOMAS, PIRI. *Down These Mean Streets.*

* WOJCIECHOWSKA, MAIA. *Tuned Out.*

Mature

BUCK, PEARL. *To My Daughter, with Love.* John Day, 1967, $4.95. From this shared talk with her seven daughters, Pearl Buck has distilled the articles and speeches which are collected in this volume. Personal values, love and marriage, woman's role, the sexual revolution are among the subjects which Miss Buck treats with candor, gentle understanding, and great wisdom.

* FRY, ROSALIE K. *September Island.*

SANDBURG, CARL. *Always the Young Strangers.* HBJ, 1952, $6.95. A poet tells of his boyhood and youth in a small town in Illinois, playing pranks with the gang, listening to folk tales, and growing up with the community.

YABLONSKY, LEWIS. *Synanon: Tunnel Back.* P/Penguin, $1.95. Synanon came into existence in 1958 when Chuck Dederich, an ex-alcoholic, and a group of hard-core drug addicts banded together in an effort to cure their addiction. From the first clubhouse, a dilapidated storefront building in Ocean Park, California, Synanon has grown into a large institution, with branches on the East Coast as well as a number of centers in California. In Synanon, ex-drug addicts live and work together in a community where they participate in meaningful group sessions.

Identifying with One's Heritage

Primary

BOLLINGER, MAX. *The Fireflies.* il. by Jiri Trnka. Atheneum, 1970, $4.95. For Prosper, the young firefly, growing up does not come all at once. He must learn to fly in a wind, to find his way when he is lost, to know what to fear and what not to fear. Finally he must learn to answer for his own children the questions he asked when he was young.

BOURNE, MIRIAM ANNE. *Emilio's Summer Day.* il. by Ben Shecter. Har-Row, 1966, $3.27. On a hot, breezeless day in the city Emilio tries to entertain himself without moving too quickly. The welcome interruption of the street washer is the highlight of the day.

BUCK, PEARL S. *The Chinese Story Teller.* il. by Regina Shekerjean. John Day, 1971, $4.95. One day Grandmother who had been born in China tells Susan and Redy an old Chinese tale of how cats and dogs came to dislike one another. The illustrations are patterned after one of the oldest and most beautiful folk arts in China. These paper cut outs are pasted on paper windowpanes at New Year's and are known as "Window Flowers."

* DESBARATS, PETER. *Gabrielle and Selena.*

HAWKINSON, LUCY. *Dance, Dance, Amy-Chan!* il. by author. Whitman, 1964, $2.95. During Amy's and her younger sister Susie's visit to their Japanese grandparents in the city, they learn Japanese customs and make preparations to participate in a Japanese street dance. Amy misses the first dance while looking for lost, scared Susie. The children discover that basic similarities in family relationships and interdependence exist among all peoples.

* JUSTUS, MAY. *A New Home for Billy.*

KOTZWINKLE, WILLIAM. *Elephant Boy.* il. by Joe Servello. FS & G, 1970, $3.95. In the days of the caveman, a father introduces his son to the wildlife of that time. The boy's struggle is toward gaining a name of his own. The young boy received his name Elephant Boy from the hair of the elephant's tail and the teeth of the elephant that were strung into a necklace by his father and Shining Stone, another caveman. He now must try to gain a name of his own.

* MILES, MISKA. *Annie and the Old One.*

RADLAUER, RUTH AND ED. *Father is Big.* il. by Harvey Mandin. Bowmar, 1967, $3.24. By looking at his father's clothes, at the size of his hands and body, and at the tools he uses, the boy learns to identify with his father.

STEIN, R. CONRAD. *Steel Driving Man: The Legend of John Henry.* il. by Darrell Wiskur. Childrens, 1969, $3.00. The story of John Henry is dramatically told.

Intermediate

* ARMSTRONG, WILLIAM H. *Sounder.*

BAILEY, BERNADINE. *Jose.* HM, 1969, $2.40 (teacher's guide, $.45). Jose, a Puerto Rican boy living in Chicago, struggles with his job, the English language, curiosity that gets him involved in a riot, and limited ability in swimming.

* BARRETT, ANNE. *Midway.*

COOK, OLIVE R. *Serilda's Star.* il. by Helen Torrey. McKay, 1959, $2.95 (P/WSP, $.50). Serilda trades her precious gold locket and chain for a sick, sorrel mare. The horse recovers and gradually regains her strength, finally becoming the envy of all who see her. One day she disappears, and all fear that she has been stolen, setting the stage for an exciting ending.

* DE GEREZ, TONI. *2 Rabbit 7 Wind: Poems from Ancient Mexico.*

GLASGOW, ALINE. *Pair of Shoes.* il. by Symeon Shimin. Dial, 1971, $4.95. Using the flavor and idiom of the folk tale, Aline Glasgow tells the short story of a 12-year-old boy's growth in understanding of the nature of pride. In the 19th century Polish family, one pair of shoes is shared by three children. Jacob demands shoes of his own for his bar mitzvah, for how can he be a man without them. When his sister breaks her ankle and something must be sold to pay the doctor, Jacob sacrifices the shoes and gains understanding. His invalid father profits too by the lesson and decides to sell three of his beautifully bound books to buy shoes for the children.

HAMILTON, VIRGINIA. *Zeely.* il. by Symeon Shemin. Macmillan, 1967, $4.95 (P/Macmillan, $.95). Imaginative eleven-year-old Geeder is stirred when she sees Zeely Tayber, who is dignified, stately, and six-and-a-half feet tall. Geeder thinks Zeely looks like the magazine picture of the Watusi queen. Through meeting Zeely personally and getting to know her, Geeder finally returns to reality.

* HAUGAARD, KAY. *Mykeko's Gift.*

HOUSTON, JAMES. *Eagle Mask: A West Coast Indian Tale.* il. by author. HBJ, 1966, $3.30. This is the story of a young northwest coast Indian boy who proves his skill, courage, and bravery during the three days he spends in the forest.

* JONES, HETTIE (comp.) *The Trees Stand Shining.*

LEWITON, MINA. *Candita's Choice.* il. by Howard Simon. Har-Row, 1959, $3.95. An eleven-year-old girl leaves her Puerto Rican home to start a new life in New York City. There she must learn a new language and new customs, as well as overcome her shyness. With help from a teacher, a neighbor boy, and a nurse's aid, Candita develops her self-image and finds happiness and security in her decision to remain in the United States.

MILES, MISKA. *Annie and the Old One.* il. by Peter Parnall. Little, 1971, $3.95. Annie wonders at many things about life, growing up, and the passage of time, things her mother and grandmother seem to understand. She fears for the day when her beloved grandmother will no longer be alive. For Annie, as long as the rug her mother is weaving stays on the loom, her grandmother will be with them, so she undoes each days' weaving. She soon realizes that this will not stop time and that she herself must now learn to work the loom.

NESS, EVALINE. *Exactly Alike.* il. by author. Scribner, 1964, $4.95. A confused little girl named Elizabeth is confronted with four brothers (Bertie, Benny, Buzzie, Biff) who are constantly annoying her. The problem is that all four brothers are frecklefaced and look exactly alike. As time goes on, Elizabeth finds a clue to the mystery of who is who.

OAKES, VANYA. *Willy Wong: American.* il. by Weda Yap. Messner, 1951, $3.50 (P/WSP, $.50). Willy Wong, who is a Chinese-American and lives in Chinatown, leads an interesting life. While Willy wants to be considered all-American by his American friends, he also begins to find out a lot of fascinating things about China, his Chinese ancestors, and how his great-grandfather helped to build the first American railroad. This information helps to increase Willy's pride in his heritage and so inspires the theme of the model he enters in a United Nations contest.

* PATTON, WILLOUGHBY. *Manuel's Discovery.*

POULAKIS, PETER (ed.). *American Folklore.* il. by Marian Ebert. P/ Scribner, 1969, $2.00. A collection of folk tales gathered from the United States and its many subcultures. These excellent selections emphasize pride in one's family heritage and the development of personal values.

SCHAEFER, JACK. *Old Ramon.* il. by Harold West. HM, 1960, $3.25. "You will go with Ramon for this season. You have had too much of the printed books. You will watch Ramon and learn. If he will talk to you, you will learn more." With these words, the boy's father sends him to summer pasture with old Ramon and the flock. They are accompanied by two dogs, old Pedro and young Sancho; the latter takes the boy as master. The boy ponders on his relationship to nature, to animals, and to his own past.

* SORENSEN, VIRGINIA. *Plain Girl.*

* SPEEVACK, YETTA. *The Spider Plant.*

Junior

ADOFF, ARNOLD. *Black on Black: Commentaries by Negro Americans.* Macmillan, 1968, $5.95 (P/Macmillan, $1.25). The author presents some of the best literature by Negro Americans written during the last century, showing the continual rediscovery of the barrier which keeps black Americans from achieving equality in white America. Among the distinguished writers included are Frederick Douglass, W. E. B. DuBois, Walter White, Langston Hughes, Richard Wright, Gordon Parks, Ralph Ellison, James Baldwin, Dick Gregory, Bill Russell, Malcolm X, Ossie Davis, Martin Luther King, Jr., LeRoi Jones, Stokeley Carmichael, and Charles V. Hamilton. Brief biographical notes have been included.

* ————. *Black Out Loud: An Anthology of Modern Poems by Black Americans.*

* CAVANNA, BETTY. *Jenny Kimura.*

* CRANE, CAROLINE. *Don't Look at Me That Way.*

* DE GEREZ, TONI. *2 Rabbit 7 Wind: Poems from Ancient Mexico.*

DOUGLASS, FREDERICK. *The Mind and Heart of Frederick Douglass, Excerpts from Speeches of the Great Negro Orator.* TY Crowell, 1968, $4.50. Grouped under ten headings are excerpts from over sixty speeches which Frederick Douglass, the brilliant and prophetic nineteenth-century Afro-American orator and reformer, delivered during his crusade against slavery and the nation's continual denial of equal rights to Negroes even after the Civil War. The book is a companion volume to Douglass' autobiography, *Life and Times of Frederick Douglass.*

* FRANCHERE, RUTH. *Stampede North.*

HAMILTON, VIRGINIA. *The House of Dies Drear.* il. by Eros Keith. Macmillan, 1968, $4.95 (P/Macmillan, $.95). The abolitionist Dies Drear supposedly had treasures hidden in his house that served him in helping slaves escape. The modern day family that lives in this house finds the true treasure as they uncover their family heritage.

HINTON, S. E. *The Outsiders.* Viking Pr, 1967, $3.95 (P/Dell, $.60). The orphaned Curtis brothers, Pony, Soda, and Darry, can stay together only so long as they stay out of trouble, not an easy task for members of a poor eastside gang in constant warfare with the Socs, westside rich kids.

* JOHNSTONE, PAUL K. *Escape from Attila.*

* JONES, HETTIE (comp.) *The Trees Stand Shining.*

* LAMPEL, RUSIA. *That Summer with Ora.*

LESTER, JULIUS. *To Be a Slave.* il. by Tom Feelings. Dial, 1968, $3.95 (P/Dell, $.75). Through the words of the slave, interwoven with strongly sympathetic commentary, the reader learns what it is to be another man's property; how the slave feels about himself; and how he feels about others. Every aspect of slavery, regardless of how grim, has been painfully and unrelentingly described.

* RICHTER, CONRAD. *A Country of Strangers.*

WENTWORTH, ELAINE. *Mission to Metlakatla.* HM, 1968, $3.50. When William Duncan leaves a comfortable life in England to serve as a missionary to the Tsinshian Indians, he is surprised to find a highly cultured people. Contact with the white settlers streaming into the Pacific Northwest threatens to destroy their society. Duncan engineers a move to an island in United States territory which enables the tribe to preserve its unity.

WIBBERLEY, LEONARD. *Island of the Angels.* Morrow, 1965, $4.50. In this fast-moving novel a fisherman, a recluse who lives near Ensenada, fights nature's elements to save a teenager from death from diphtheria. Each discovers that he needs to be wanted and cared for.

* YATES, ELIZABETH. *Amos Fortune, Free Man.*

Senior

ASTROV, MARGOT. *American Indian Prose and Poetry.* P/Putnam, 1962, $2.45. The contents of this volume are selected from ten culture areas of Indians of North and South America. The groups represented are the northern woodlands, the basin area, the great plains, the deserts of the Southeast, California, Northeast, Far North, Mexico, Central America, and Peru. The poetry is selected from the ritualistic observances of Indian life. The prose selections represent speeches, childhood recollections, and similar narratives.

* FRANK, ANNE. *Anne Frank: The Diary of a Young Girl.*

FULLER, IOLA. *The Loon Feather.* HBJ, 1940, $5.95 (P/HBJ, $.95). Educated in a convent, Oneta, daughter of an Indian chieftain, returns to the tribal ways she loves.

* HANSBERRY, LORRAINE. *Raisin in the Sun.*

* HILL, GRACE L. *A Patch of Blue.*

MEANS, FLORENCE C. *Our Cup Is Broken.* HM, 1969, $3.95. Sara, a Hopi Indian, goes to live with a white family for nine years after the death of her parents. After an unhappy love affair with a white boy, she returns to the reservation in the hope that she can leave behind the white man's ways and adopt the life of her ancestors. However, she is unable to accept the Indians' ancient religion and way of life, and the Hopi cannot accept what in her seem to be eccentricities. A Hopi boy rapes her and she bears a daughter who is blind. Ultimately she marries, but her life, while not without hope, is fraught with the tragedy of being caught between two cultures.

MOMADAY, N. SCOTT. *House Made of Dawn.* Har-Row, 1968, $4.95 (P/

NAL, $.95). The Pulitzer award winner in 1969, this novel is a post-World War II account of a Kiowa Indian who cannot come to grips with reservation life following his service as a G.I. He commits a senseless murder and is given a light sentence on the condition that he resettle in Los Angeles under an Indian rehabilitation service. He continues to drink heavily to cover up for a life that has no meaning. He returns to the reservation with hopes of finding himself.

MORIN, RAUL. *Among the Valiant*. Borden, 1966, $5.00. This is the first full-length factual account of the Mexican-American soldier of World War II and the Korean conflict to be written by a native-born American of Mexican descent. Much of the material in the book is based on the author's own experiences in the United States and in the front lines during World War II.

* PECK, RICHARD (ed.). *Sounds and Silences.*

SAROYAN, WILLIAM. *The Human Comedy*. HBJ, 1943, $5.75 (P/Dell, $.60). Homer Macauley, the fastest messenger boy for the telegraph office in the San Joaquin Valley, comes from an Armenian family. The story stresses loyalty to a small group and shows how its influence may be felt in the community.

SOMMERFELT, AIMÉE. *My Name Is Pablo*. Criterion, 1965, $3.95. Living in humble surroundings outside Mexico City, Pablo is a good student who aspires to further education so that in his adult years he will not be trapped in perpetual poverty. A Norwegian family becomes aware of the young teenager and adopts him. However, Pablo's family still needs his financial support as a shoeshine boy. His work leads him through a set of hair-raising experiences, to the inhuman conditions of a Mexican jail and the life of a dope pusher. The book conveys vividly the harshness of peasant life in Mexico and will give youth some good insights into what the Mexican-American faces in our own society.

STEINER, STAN. *La Raza: The Mexican Americans*. Har-Row, 1970, $8.50. Interviews with inhabitants of the Southwest explore the abuses, exploitations and prejudices toward Mexicans, Spanish-Americans, and Chicanos.

THOMPSON, ERA BELL. *American Daughter*. U Chi Pr, 1946, O.P. Era Bell Thompson, a young Negro woman, relates the ups and downs of her family as they moved from an Iowa city to a North Dakota farm where they shared the community life of Scandinavian settlers. Era Bell worked her way through college and then went to Chicago, where she struggled to get a suitable job and to adjust herself to living conditions on the city's south side.

* WALKER, MARGARET. *Jubilee.*

* WATERS, ETHEL, AND CHARLES SAMUELS. *His Eye Is on the Sparrow.*

* WEST, JESSAMYN. *Friendly Persuasion.*

* WOJCIECHOWSKA, MAIA. *Shadow of a Bull.*

Mature

* BOOTH, ESMA RIDEOUT. *The Village, the City and the World.*

* BROWN, CLAUDE. *Manchild in the Promised Land.*

* JARRELL, RANDALL. *The Animal Family.*

JOYCE, JAMES. *A Portrait of the Artist as a Young Man.* Viking Pr, 1916,
$3.95 (P/Viking Pr, $1.65). A giant literary figure of our time recounts the story of his own development, an imaginative record of
his hopes, fears, and frustrations.

* LAWRENCE, D. H. *Sons and Lovers.*

* MALCOLM X AND ALEX HALEY. *The Autobiography of Malcolm X.*

SALINGER, J. D. *Catcher in the Rye.* Little, 1951, $4.95 (P/Bantam,
$1.25). A boy faces the adult world and does not want to enter it.
Adults are "phonies." Holden Caulfield, a boy who holds high values
and who will not let hypocrisy have a part in his life, cannot accept
man as he really is.

STEELE, WILLIAM O. *Wayah of the Real People.* il. by Isa Barnett.
HR & W, 1964, $3.50. A young Cherokee Indian boy comes to learn
the white man's ways at Barberton Hall in Williamsburg in spite of
his grandfather's warning that soon he will not be good for either
of the two worlds, the white man's or the Indian's. When he returns
at the end of the year to his people, he finds that he is able to help
his people with his knowledge of the white man's ways.

STEINER, STAN. *The New Indians.* Har-Row, $7.95 (P/Dell, $2.45). The
"red power" drive is presented by American Indians from many different tribes as interviewed by the author.

Developing Personal Values

Primary

ARDIZZONE, EDWARD. *Peter the Wanderer.* il. by author. Walck, 1964,
$4.50. A young boy, Peter, meets an old sailor who has spent his

entire life searching for a lost treasure. The old sailor shows the boy a golden key which will open the iron treasure chest. After the sailor leaves, Peter finds the key, which the sailor has apparently lost. Realizing how important the key is to the old man, Peter sets out to find him. On the way Peter is confronted with hardship and greedy, evil people intent on taking the treasure. In the end Peter is rewarded for his patience, unselfishness, and loyalty.

BOYD, MARY E. *Joy.* il. by Joan Dresher. Gibson, 1969, $1.95. A book written in charming and simple verse. Joy can come from experiencing such things as visiting a sick friend, catching a butterfly, running barefoot through the grass, taking your first pony ride, etc.

BROWN, MARCIA. *Once a Mouse.* il. by author. Scribner, 1961, $4.95. In this fable from India, a hermit saves the life of a mouse, changing him in turn into a cat, a dog, and a tiger, who then turns upon him. ". . . And the hermit sat thinking about big—and little."

COMBS, PATRICIA. *Lisa and the Grompet.* il. by author. Lothrop, 1970, $3.78. Lisa is always being told what to do. She decides to run away into the woods and there meets a grompet who never had anyone tell him what to do. They can help each other, for Lisa needs to tell someone what to do and the grompet wants someone to tell him what to do. Lisa changes her attitudes and sees the value of doing what she has been told.

DUVOISIN, ROGER. *Petunia.* il. by author. Knopf, 1950, $3.50. Petunia the goose finds a book and, proud of her new wisdom, is free with her advice. Not until all the barnyard is in a turmoil does Petunia learn that wisdom must be in the mind and in the heart.

FISHER, AILEEN L. *My Mother and I.* il. by Kazue Mizumura. TY Crowell, 1967, $3.95. A little girl comes home from school to find that her mother has been called to care for "Gran" for two weeks. During this period she thinks about creatures such as frogs and butterflies who have no mothers to love them. When her mother returns, she expresses her feelings with a hug and a comment that she is glad she is not a frog or a bug.

* HILL, ELIZABETH. *Evan's Corner.*

HIPPOPOTAMUS, EUGENE H. *Hello Hippopotamus.* Windmill Bks, 1969, $3.95. This is the first in a series of stories about Eugene Hippopotamus, by Eugene Hippopotamus, for boys and girls who really like hippopotomuses. Eugene believes he's the ugliest of the ugly, but he quickly discovers that love can make anyone handsome.

HOGAN, BERNICE. *A Small Green Tree and a Square Brick Church.* il. by Meg Wohlberg. Abingdon, 1967, $2.50. A little boy explores the wonders of nature and the city. He discovers that it is not the building or the ornaments which make the church; it is the people.

* KEATS, EZRA JACK. *A Letter to Amy.*

KOREN, EDWARD. *Don't Talk to Strange Bears.* il. by author. S & S, 1969, $4.95. An appealing story for younger children that follows little Nat as he attempts to obey literally his mother's instructions not to talk to strangers. The unusual cartoon illustrations depicting a multitude of animals make this book exciting and fun.

MACDONALD, GOLDEN. *The Little Island.* il. by Leonard Weisgard. Doubleday, 1946, $3.95. Children often think of themselves as little islands, self-contained and with no responsibilities toward others. This book explains that the little island really is a part of the big world, too.

McNULTY, FAITH. *When a Boy Wakes up in the Morning.* il. by Leonard Weisgard. Knopf, 1962, $2.95. Jamie likes to get busy as soon as he wakes up. But it's not much fun if no one else is around to appreciate your playing. Mother and Father are still sleeping and have warned Jamie about hammering on his toys. However, they haven't said anything about all the other ways that there are to make noise in the morning.

OLSEN, AILEEN. *Bernadine and the Water Bucket.* il. by Nola Langner. Abelard, 1966, $3.50. Every day Bernadine and her mother go into the village to get drinking water. Bernadine can hardly wait to go by herself—how grown-up she will be. One day her mother is busy so she sends Bernadine alone to get the water. After getting the water, Bernadine heads home, but by the time she arrives she has her bucket filled with many things besides water.

OTSUKA, YUZO. *Rota's Great Canoe.* il. by Hisakatsu Hijikata. Weatherhill, 1970, $3.95. This Polynesian folk tale tells the story of a boy named Rota who learned a lesson about the forest and its guardian spirits. These spirits are very angry when Rota cuts down their favorite tree to build a canoe, and they use their magic to prevent him from completing his project. When Rota explains that he needs the canoe to visit his father who is chief on another island, the forest spirits use their magic to help build the canoe.

RASKIN, ELLEN. *Nothing Ever Happens on My Block.* il. by author. Atheneum, 1968, $2.95. Chester is convinced that he lives in the dullest, quietest, most uneventful neighborhood of all in the entire world. If he'd only notice what the reader can see going on around him, he'd change his mind.

* SENDAK, MAURICE. *Where the Wild Things Are.*

SIMON, NORMA. *Benjy's Bird.* A Whitman, 1965, $2.95. Benjy's mother, his dog friends, and a baby robin fallen from its nest help Benjy to understand and to appreciate the joy of life and nature. When the cool autumn appears, Cheery, Benjy's pet robin, follows instincts and seeks a warmer climate. Other children can identify with Benjy to help them discover that sad and happy feelings are a normal part of life.

THAYER, JANE. *Quiet on Account of Dinosaur*. il. by Seymour Fleishman. Morrow, 1964, $3.50. In this fanciful tale, Mary Ann's interests in prehistoric animals lead her to discover a real live dinosaur. Dandy the dinosaur is as friendly as a puppy and everyone loves him, but Mary Ann discovers that the hustle, bustle, and noise of our world and time are just too much for him. With the cooperation of all the people in the world, the story ends with a happy dinosaur and a new, very famous scientist—Mary Ann.

TURKLE, BRINTON. *Thy Friend, Obadiah*. il. by author. Viking Pr, 1969, $3.95. Who wants a sea gull following him around like a pet? A boy named Obadiah who lives in old Nantucket has just such a problem. The silly bird annoys Obadiah every day, and at night the gull roosts outside his bedroom window. One very cold day when Obadiah needs a friend, the bird is gone and the boy misses it. The gull shows up later with a fish hook caught in its beak. After Obadiah has removed the hook, he discovers it is pleasant to make a real friend, and both the boy and the gull are happy. The story can help children to realize that we all need friends.

UCHIDA, YOSHIKO. *Sumi and the Goat and the Tokyo Express*. il. by Kazue Mizumura. Scribner, 1969, $2.50. A story showing that even with all our technical and industrial advances there are times when we must stop and realize that we are all human beings.

———. *Sumi's Prize*. il. by Kazue Mizumura. Scribner, 1964, $4.05. Since Sumi always wanted to win a prize, she enters the village kite contest on New Year's Day. She is sure she has won until the mayor's top hat is caught by the wind and her butterfly kite crashes as she tries to rescue the hat. Sumi's special prize helps make up for the disaster.

WILSON, JULIA. *Becky*. il. by John Wilson. TY Crowell, 1966, $3.75. Becky is given money for her birthday to buy herself a doll. After looking all day for her "special" doll the one she finds costs more money than she has. Presented with the opportunity to steal the doll, she turns away from the temptation. Because of her honesty, Becky's mother gives her the extra money.

Intermediate

* BAKER, BETTY. *Walk the World's Rim.*

* BELL, THELMA HARRINGTON. *The Two Worlds of Davy Blount.*

BERNARD, JACQUELINE. *Journey toward Freedom*. G & D, 1967, $5.95 (P/Dell, $.60). Sojourner Truth leaves her job as a domestic servant to teach against slavery and preach about her God. Born a slave, she works in the North helping freedmen from the South to find work, land, and freedom.

* BRODSKY, MIMI. *The House at 12 Rose Street.*

BUCKLEY, PETER. *Okolo of Nigeria.* il. by author. Hale, 1962, $2.94. Okolo wants to become a teacher. He learns the value of patience and hard work as he earns the money to go to school.

* BURCH, ROBERT. *Renfroe's Christmas.*

* CALHOUN, MARY. *Honestly, Katie John.*

CARLSON, NATALIE SAVAGE. *The Empty Schoolhouse.* il. by John Kaufman. Har-Row, 1965, $4.50. (P/Dell, $.75). When the Louisiana parochial schools are desegregated, Lullah is happy that she can attend school with her white friend, Oralee. But the situation is soon marred by the jeers and brutality of those opposed to integration. Even Oralee rejects Lullah and finds companionship with white children. When Lullah is shot in the ankle by an agitator, the community realizes its cruelty and peace returns to the district.

* CLEAVER, VERA AND BILL. *Lady Ellen Grae.*

COLES, ROBERT. *Dead End School.* il. by Norman Rockwell. Little, 1968, $3.95 (P/Dell, $.75). Jim, his mother, and his sister have just moved into the inner city. His mother is disturbed with the new school and its administration and gets the whole community aroused over miserable school conditions. Finally, the school board agrees to bus some of the children to a newer school. Jimmy must adjust to his ghetto neighborhood, his new school, and the comments of some of his friends.

COLMAN, HILA. *Classmates by Request.* Morrow, 1964, $3.95 (P/Morrow, $1.50). Carla, a white girl, is one of ten teenagers who decide to request a transfer to an all Negro school and thus help to integrate a city school. To Ellen, the Negro heroine, this is only a "token step." Many human problems and understandings of a complex nature arise for impatient Carla and angry Ellen as they struggle to learn to live with others and finally realize that all goals cannot be reached directly.

* CRANDELL, MYRA CLARK. *Molly and the Regicides.*

GATES, DORIS. *Little Vic.* il. by Kate Seredy. Viking Pr, 1951, $3.95 (P/WSP, $.60). This is a story about a Negro boy who follows a race horse named Little Vic from one owner to another, keeping faith in the horse's ability to win, contrary to other people's opinions. It is the boy who later rides Little Vic to the winner's circle of a very important race.

HAYWOOD, CAROLYN. *Eddie the Dog Holder.* il. by author. Morrow, 1966, $4.75. This story shows how a young boy can turn his leisure time into something profitable with the help of a friend.

HOFF, CAROL. *Chris.* il. by Robert Patterson. Follett, 1960, $3.48. Chris has been forced to transfer schools many times because of his father's work. He has no friends, cares nothing about school, and believes that the only way to be noticed is to be either a bully or a pest. His father and teacher insist on improved behavior, and Chris becomes a friend of the leader of the class. He comes to realize that a friend is one who can be depended upon without needing constant reassurance of that friendship.

HOLLAND, ISABELLE. *Amanda's Choice.* Lippincott, 1970, $3.95. Amanda's mother has died and her father, who seems to resent her, has left her with a series of governesses and housekeepers. Amanda begins to feel that the only way to have people notice her is to be a constant trouble-maker.

HOUSTON, JAMES. *The White Archer: An Eskimo Legend.* il. by author. HBJ, 1967, $3.50. After twelve-year-old Kungo's parents are killed and his sister is captured by Indians, a seal hunter finds him in the frozen Arctic wilderness and brings him into his home for two years. Kungo learns to hunt and becomes a great archer. Still haunted by a desire to avenge his family, Kungo leaves to fulfill this desire. Just as he reaches his goal he sees another far better one.

* IK, KIN YONG. *Blue in the Seed.*

JEWETT, SARAH ORNE. *A White Heron.* il. by Barbara Cooney. TY Crowell, 1963, $3.50. Sylvy loves to roam in the out-of-doors. Her only friends are animals. She makes friends with a hunter who is searching for a rare white heron. Sylvy must then decide between the wildlife friend and a new friend with a gun. She decides to remain loyal to the white heron and her own world.

LARRICK, NANCY. *On City Streets.* il. by David Sagarin. M. Evans, 1968, $4.95 (P/Bantam, $.75). Children from rural and suburban areas can catch a vivid glimpse of life in the city from the clear photographs and the well written poems. Children from the big city can see themselves in the poetry and photographs.

L'ENGLE, MADELEINE. *Dance in the Desert.* il. by Symeon Shimin. FS & G, 1969, $4.95. A fanciful tale that shows that a child's trust and love are the most powerful of all strengths.

————. *A Wrinkle in Time.* FS & G, 1962, $3.95. This Newbery Award winner describes the adventures of Meg, brother Charles, and friend Calvin as they experience a tesseract, or wrinkle in time, in their search for Meg's father.

McDONNELL, LOIS EDDY. *Susan Comes through the Fire.* il. by Jim Walker. P/Friend Pr, 1969, $1.75. Young Susan is on an outing with her parents and a girl friend when she accidentally pours gasoline on their campfire, instead of water. The resulting burns put Susan in the hospital for many months. Resentment builds as Susan is confined to bed. After a few trips to a playroom where other injured children play, Susan realizes that many others have been hurt more than she has. This is the beginning of Susan's road to recovery. She overcomes her grief and begins to help other children at the hospital. After she leaves, Susan returns to help with the other children in the ward.

MADIAN, JON. *Beautiful Junk: A Story of the Watts Towers.* il. by Barbara and Lou Jacobs, Jr. Little, 1968, $3.95. Charlie is dissatisfied with all of the junk near his home. While smashing bottles one day, he is confronted by an old man with a wheelbarrow full of "junk." Curiosity overcomes the boy and he follows the old man, who invites him to see the creations he has made with all his junk. The sensitive photography of the real towers is extremely impressive.

MASON, MIRIAM E. *Caroline and the Seven Little Words.* il. by Paul Frame. Macmillan, 1967, $4.95. When Caroline announces in school one day that she is going to be a doctor, everybody laughs. No pioneer girl can do a man's job. The proper place for a woman is doing a woman's job—sewing, cooking, and the like. Caroline, along with her five uncles, finds that perhaps her dream will come true, if she tries hard enough. Sequel to *Caroline and Her Kettle Maud.*

NORRIS, FAITH, AND PETER LUMN. *Kim of Korea.* il. by Kurt Wiese. P/ WSP, 1967, $.60. Kim, ten-year-old war orphan, meets Len, a wounded American soldier who wants to take him to America and adopt him. Kim learns that the Americans are leaving Korea from Inchon and he must find Len. On his journey from Seoul, Kim has many adventures which give insights into the culture of Korea and the people of the wartorn country as they are rebuilding their lives. When Kim reaches Inchon he must decide if he really wants to leave his country.

* ORMONDROYD, EDWARD. *Time at the Top.*

PHIPSON, JOAN. *Good Luck to the Rider.* il. by Margaret Horder. HBJ, 1968, $3.50. Barbara, a frail twelve-year-old Australian girl, feels that she must be as good a horseback rider as her older sister. Barbara finds a colt in the woods whose mother has been killed and decides to raise the colt herself. Through her love for this colt, Barbara overcomes her own weakness.

POTTER, BRONSON. *Isfendiar and the Bears of Mazandaran.* Atheneum, 1969, $3.75. il. by David O. White. Isfendiar, a charcoal burner's son in a small Iranian village, sets off on a journey to find adventure and the answer to the question, "What do you say to a vain child, one who has been so blinded by his luck that he cannot find happiness?"

Haidar the hunter offers to take him on a hunting trip with some rich men of Tabiz. They are followed by a fabled bear and Isfendiar is able to kill it with his Bedouin knife. He returns to his native village able to answer his question.

* SHOTWELL, LOUISA R. *Roosevelt Grady.*

SMITH, ERIC B., AND ROBERT MEREDITH. *Pilgrim Courage.* il. by Leonard Everett Fisher. Little, 1962, $4.25. The personal account of the travels of a religious group from England to Holland and finally to America. The story is based on the personal papers of William Bradford and Edward Winslow who were in this group of pilgrims. The personal values and contributions of special talents of each member of this courageous undertaking as well as the exactness of the illustrations add a great deal to the worth of this book.

STERLING, DOROTHY. *Captain of the Planter: The Story of Robert Smalls.* il. by Ernest Crichlow. Doubleday, 1958, $3.95 (P/WSP, $.50). This is the story of Robert Smalls, a Negro whose parents were slaves and who was a slave himself. His early years were filled with memories of a mother who wished for her son to be a free man and attempted to gain this for her boy by making him learn manners and the ways of the white men. As he grew, Robert learned that no matter how much of a man he was, he would always remain a "boy" in the eyes of some. Following the Civil War, Smalls went into an active political life and fought desperately for his people and his own manhood.

UCHIDA, YOSHIKO. *The Promised Year.* il. by William M. Hutchinson. HBJ, 1959, $3.50. Keiko has never been to the United States. It is hard to leave Japan and her family but she knows that Aunt Emi and Uncle Henry are anxiously awaiting her in California, where her home will be for one year. As Keiko disembarks from the ship, she instantly recognizes her aunt and uncle. She takes a liking to Aunt Emi, but Uncle Henry looks disapprovingly at both Keiko and her big, black cat Tama. A problem arises which Tama and Keiko help solve, and Uncle Henry is won over.

* ———. *The Sea of Gold and Other Tales from Japan.*

* VAN DER VEER, JUDY. *Higher than the Arrow.*

* WIBBERLEY, LEONARD. *Journey to Untor.*

Junior

* ALMEDINGEN, E. M. *A Candle at Dusk.*

* BONHAM, FRANK. *The Nitty Gritty.*

* BRADBURY, BIANCA. *Lots of Love, Lucinda.*

* COLMAN, HILA. *Classmates by Request.*

CRANDELL, MYRA CLARK. *Molly and the Regicides.* il. by Paul Frame. S & S, 1968, $3.95. What could be more adventuresome than to discover two regicides seeking refuge in New Haven Town? These regicides, previously judges in England, are ordered arrested by Charles II, King of England (1661), for condemning his father to death. Not wishing to be caught, General Whalley and Captain Goffe make their way to America, where they are pursued by the king's men. When young Molly and her twin brother Mark find that the judges are at the inn next door to them, they try to help them.

* DUNN, MARY LOIS. *The Man in the Box: A Story from Vietnam.*

FORMAN, JAMES. *The Traitors.* FS & G, 1968, $3.95. Paul Eichhorn, a quiet and thoughtful person, becomes frightened for the safety of his pastor father when he begins to speak out against the Nazi regime. He sees his brother Kurt become an ardent Nazi soldier and his best friend, a young Jewish boy, disappear mysteriously. With a courage born of desperation, Paul and his father gather a small group together and prevent the German army from capturing the town.

FRITZ, JEAN. *I, Adam.* il. by Peter Burchard. Coward, 1963, $4.95. Adam Crane leaves the sea where his father is captain of a whaling vessel and accepts his role as farmer on his family's new land. His friend, however, has more positive feelings about his own future as a sailor. In six months, Adam finally realizes his true love is learning.

GALT, TOM. *Peter Zenger: Fighter for Freedom.* TY Crowell, 1951, $4.50. This biography tells about Zenger's printing apprenticeship, his association with the chief printer of New York, and his scandalous but truthful attacks on Governor William Cosby. The book climaxes in the arrest and imprisonment of Zenger for libel and in Philadelphia lawyer Andrew Hamilton's eloquent appeal for his acquittal. A "not guilty" verdict is decided at the trial in 1735.

GRAHAM, LORENZ. *North Town.* TY Crowell, 1965, $4.50. *North Town* is an excellent story about a Negro boy named David whose family moves from South Town to North Town where they believe conditions will be better. As first it does not appear so, but then things begin to fit together so that David can once more strive for his future goals.

* ———. *South Town.*

* GRANGER, PEG. *Canyon of Decision.*

* HARRIS, CHRISTIE. *Forbidden Frontier.*

HUNTSBERRY, WILLIAM E. *The Big Wheels.* Lothrop, 1967, $3.95 (P/ Avon, $.60). Beaver persuades five of his close friends to join to-

gether to swing the school elections so that each will have a major
office in the various organizations. All the boys are talented and are
convinced by Beaver that they can lead the students better than
anyone else. They are extremely successful and it isn't until Beaver
begins to talk about continuing the same operation in college that
Doc, the narrator, begins to realize why he has objected.

JOHNSON, ANNABEL AND EDGAR. *Pickpocket Run*. Har-Row, 1961, $3.79.
The hero, just graduated from high school, knows that he must get
away from the small town where he lives. Good jobs are scarce. The
town, known by truckers as a "tourist trap" and "pickpocket run,"
boasts only that it has a movie house, two dance halls, and nine
saloons. If the hero stays, he will be forced to work in his father's
service station, and he cannot stomach the way his father cheats the
tourists upon whom he depends for a living. Before he is able to make
definite plans, the boy gets into difficulty with a gang. The theme is
unusual for this age group—a young man's struggle between his
pride in working on cars and his coping with his father's dishonest
business practices.

LATHAM, JEAN LEE. *Trail Blazer of the Seas*. il. by Victor Mays. HM,
1956, $3.95. Matthew Fontaine Maury, a Tennessee farm boy,
achieves a naval career in spite of strong parental disapproval.

LIPSYTE, ROBERT. *The Contender*. Har-Row, 1967, $3.50 (P/Bantam,
$.75). Dropout Alfred Brooks wants to be somebody special and be-
gins training as a boxer. He soon learns that in being a contender it
is the climbing that makes the man, and that "getting to the top is
an extra reward." He succeeds in learning to climb and pledges to
help his friend James, who has become a heroin addict, to take his
first hopeful steps.

* MASON, MIRIAM E. *Caroline and the Seven Little Words*.

* NEUFELD, JOHN. *Edgar Allen*.

O'DELL, SCOTT. *The King's Fifth*. il. by Samuel Bryant. HM, 1966,
$3.95. Esteban de Sandoval, a map maker, joins a conquistador party
in a search for the legendary Seven Cities of Cibola. The journey
teaches him the power of man's greed. Although their goals are
questionable, the conquistadors are pictured with courage and style.

PEYTON, K. M. *Flambards*. il. by Victor G. Ambrus. World Pub, 1968,
$4.95. Christina, an orphaned heiress, is sent to live with her Uncle
Russell on a rural English estate called Flambards. Uncle Russell is
a frustrated rude person whose one love is horses and who rules his
household with an iron hand. His older son Mark shares his passion
for horses, but William, the second son, deliberately lets his broken
leg heal improperly to avoid riding and also to be able to pursue his
interest in airplanes. Christina slowly realizes that Flambards will

never change. With World War I imminent and the automobile beginning to prove its usefulness, she decides to be a part of William's life and the changes going on in the world.

RICHARDSON, GRACE. *Apples Every Day.* Har-Row, 1965, $3.95. When her mother remarries, thirteen-year-old Sheila is sent to a progressive boarding school with a sophisticated group of boys and girls. Utterly alone she begins the term reading, choosing not to attend classes. As Sheila begins to see that she alone must make the decisions concerning her education, she develops her own values.

ROBERTSON, DON. *The Greatest Thing since Sliced Bread.* Putnam, 1965, $4.50. Morris Bird, III, seeks "self-respect." He sets himself a goal, and in attempting to accomplish it, becomes a hero. The world of the 1940s is seen through the eyes of a nine year old as he struggles toward maturity and self-identity.

THOREAU, H. D. *Henry David Thoreau, A Man for Our Own Time.* ed. by James Daugherty. Viking Pr, 1967, $4.50. Selections from Thoreau's works, arranged by subject and beautifully illustrated by Daugherty, demonstrate the timeless ideas of this nineteenth-century New Englander. Thoreau's opinion about individual freedom and his love for an unspoiled natural environment will strike a most responsive chord with today's youth.

ULLMAN, JAMES RAMSEY. *Banner in the Sky.* Lippincott, 1954, $4.95 (P/WSP, $.60). Those in the little Swiss village think no one can climb the Citadel. Rudi, whose father had lost his life trying, joins the party of Captain Winter who believes the mountain can be conquered. The story shows a boy's struggle to develop independence and become a man.

* VAN DER VEER, JUDY. *Higher than the Arrow.*

WATSON, SALLY. *To Build a Land.* il. by Lili Cassel. HR & W, 1957, $3.27. Twelve-year-old Mia and her fifteen-year-old brother are sent from the postwar demoralizing slums of Naples to a camp for Jewish refugee children in Marseille, where they are taught Hebrew. After the British withdrawal the children are sent to Israel. Their adjustment to collective life against a background of Arab-Jewish conflict is vividly told.

WESTBROOK, ROBERT. *Journey behind the Iron Curtain.* Putnam, 1963, $3.50. This book presents impressions of Russia, Poland and Czechoslovakia gained during a summer tour for students. Observations and conversations provide an understanding of daily life, attitudes and occupations of youth living under Soviet rule.

WIBBERLEY, LEONARD. *Peter Treegate's War.* FS & G, 1960, $3.95. Peter Treegate, son of a Boston merchant and patriot and adopted son of a Scottish political exile living in the Carolina hills, tells of his part in the battles of Breed's Hill and Trenton. Interwoven in his accounts of the Revolutionary War, Peter narrates the conflicting loyalties he feels toward these two men who have raised him. In an exciting climax, he finally chooses the democratic world of his father over the semifeudal clan life of his foster father.

Senior

FORBES, KATHRYN. *Mama's Bank Account.* HBJ, 1949, $2.95 (P/HBJ, $.75). Mama, the lovable and resourceful mother of a large Scandinavian family in San Francisco, gives her children a sense of values and a feeling of security. She helps them adjust to new ways while maintaining the old.

* FRANK, ANNE. *Anne Frank: The Diary of a Young Girl.*

* HENTOFF, NAT. *I'm Really Dragged but Nothing Gets Me Down.*

HERSEY, JOHN. *The Child Buyer.* Knopf, 1960, $4.95 (P/Bantam, $.95). When the demands of scientific achievement can no longer be met by men trained in a normal fashion, a top secret organization is formed which seeks to purchase highly intelligent children for specialized training. *The Child Buyer* is the story of a child caught in the world of adults who seek to decide his future. The author does an excellent job of illuminating factors in politics, education, and adolescence.

————. *A Single Pebble.* Knopf, 1956, $4.95 (P/Bantam, $.75). A young American has grand ideas of building a vast power project on the Yangtze, the river the Chinese call "the Great." On his first surveying trip, traveling on a junk, he meets Su Ling, the wife of the junk owner, and Old Pebble, the head tracker (trackers pull the junks up the river). From Su Ling he learns the patience of the Oriental, the customs of China, and a part of the wisdom of that country. From Old Pebble he learns that if a man has pride in his work, his life has worth.

JOHNSON, ANNABEL AND EDGAR. *Count Me Gone.* S & S, 1968, (P/ several). Rion Fletcher, a misfit who rejects the values of his middle-class family, finds himself faced with the choice of jail or psychiatric treatment. When his big brother fails to come to his assistance, Rion is plunged into deeper confusion. Told in the first-person and in modern vernacular, this fast-moving flashback, at times humorous, at times pathetic, portrays a young man's search for meaning in a world that seems empty.

KENNEDY, JOHN F. *Profiles in Courage.* Har-Row, 1956, $5.00 (P/Har-Row, $.75). Eight men stand up for their principles although it may mean the end of their political careers. Here are examples of men who would rather leave the group than compromise with their consciences.

* KINNICK, B. J., AND JESSE PERRY. *I Have a Dream: Voices of Man.*

KNOWLES, JOHN. *A Separate Peace.* Macmillan, 1960, $4.95 (P/several). The boys in Devon School view the war as something remote. They have their own battles to fight, their own enemies to conquer. They are engaged in the struggle to find themselves, to find their place in the world. This is the story of two of these boys. One, the narrator, mistakes his fellow man as the enemy. Too late, he discovers that he is his own worst enemy. He is too late because he destroys his friend, the mistaken enemy. This is a moving story, remarkably well told, deep in understanding of the adolescent boy and his painful search for a sense of values.

LEE, HARPER. *To Kill a Mockingbird.* Lippincott, 1960, $4.95 (P/ Popular Lib, $.95). A young brother and sister in a small town in Alabama find themselves involved in adults' conflicting values. The central problem is the town's attitude toward Negroes. When their father, a lawyer, defends a Negro who has been charged with rape, they are forced to hold their tongues and their fists when taunted by the townspeople and their peers. During the trial, they discover that their father is braver than any other man they know and also much wiser.

LINDBERGH, ANNE MORROW. *Gift from the Sea.* Pantheon, 1955, $4.50 (P/Random, $1.65). The author has written these essays as musings while on a walk along the seashore. Using metaphors of the tides, shells, and waves, the author lyrically ponders the many patterns and relationships of life.

* MILLER, ARTHUR. *Death of a Salesman.*

NEWMAN, DAISY. *Mount Joy.* il. with photographs. Atheneum, 1968, $5.75. When Maris won the medieval history prize through intensive interest and scholarship but lost Jim over a moral question, she was confused as to what she really wanted in life. Rather than return to school, she embarked on a pilgrimage from Paris to Santiago de Compostela in Spain as pilgrims had done centuries before. Rich in artistic discovery and description of the country and architecture, this story illustrates how one girl discovers her own special goals.

SANSAN. *Eighth Moon: Autobiography of a Girl Growing up in Communist China.* ed. by Bette Lord. Har-Row, 1964, $6.95 (P/Har-Row, $.60). Memories of childhood and adolescence in Communist China. Sansan relates how she lived and how she felt about school, friends, family and the state's interference in her life. She discusses unpleasant aspects of life from the scarcity of food to assigned chores in summer work camps.

* Solberg, Gunard. *Shelia.*

Speare, Elizabeth George. *The Bronze Bow.* HM, 1961, $3.95. Daniel Bar Jemin has one all-consuming purpose in life: to help drive out the Romans, who killed his parents, from the land of Israel. He drags his family and friends to near-disaster in his tormented journey from blind hatred to his acceptance and understanding of love as he comes to know a rabbi called Jesus. This novel dramatizes the need to deepen and widen human understanding.

Stolz, Mary. *Some Merry-Go-Round Music.* Har-Row, 1959, $3.95. Miranda at nineteen has finished high school and has a dull job with no future; she finds little satisfaction in her family, their way of life, or the apartment in which they live. The book tells of a quest for a satisfying life.

Mature

Baldwin, James. *Nobody Knows My Name.* Dial, 1961, $4.95 (P/Dell, $.60). This well-known black author ponders the relationship between the races and the role of the writer in helping young blacks understand their roles in America.

Braithwaite, E. R. *To Sir, with Love.* P-H, 1960, $4.95 (P/several). At Greenslade School in the heart of London's slums life is explosive, often primitive, sometimes cruel. It takes a special kind of teacher to find the heart and intelligence of these slum children. The teacher, a Negro, fights not only ignorance and poverty, but also racial prejudice. In spite of all this, he helps his troubled teenage students find their dignity as human beings.

* Camus, Albert. *The Stranger.*

Hesse, Hermann. *Peter Camenzind.* trans. by Michael Roloff. FS & G, 1969, $5.95 (P/FS & G, $1.95). This book has captured the tragic beauty of bitter experiences in friendships, love, and death. Peter, a Swiss poet, discovers a deep appreciation of mankind in all things of nature. As he learns to climb the mountains of his country, so he learns to surmount the obstacles of life.

* ———. *Siddhartha.*

Hulme, Kathryn. *The Nun's Story.* Little, 1956, $5.95 (P/PB, $.95). A dedicated nurse and a courageous worker in the Belgian underground, Sister Luke makes a momentous decision that involves her personal integrity.

Malcolm X and Alex Haley. *The Autobiography of Malcolm X.* Grove, 1965, $7.50 (P/Grove, $1.25). Malcolm Little began as a straight-A student in Lansing, Michigan, and became known as "Detroit Red" in an infamous career before taking his final and well-recognized name, Malcolm X of the Black Muslims. His ideas and beliefs are described in this book.

* SALINGER, J. D. *Catcher in the Rye.*

SMITH, BETTY. *A Tree Grows in Brooklyn.* Har-Row, 1947, $6.95 (P/ several). During Francie Nolan's first sixteen years of growing up in a Brooklyn tenement district, her innate sense of proportion and gay spirit help her to rise above sordid experiences and surroundings.

TEAGUE, BOB. *Letters to a Black Boy.* Walker & Co., 1968, $4.50 (P/ Lancer, $.75). A father describes in detail his bitter experiences as a victim of racial prejudice with the hope of preparing his son for the indignities he may encounter. Written by a news commentator at NBC-TV for his two-year old son to be read by him at thirteen, this book affords insight into what it is like to grow up black, and the courage it takes to live in a biased world.

TOLSTOY, LEO. *Anna Karenina.* Dodd, 1966, $5.50 (P/several). Written between 1873 and 1877, this long novel with a double plot presents upper-class Russian society of the nineteenth century. Anna Karenina becomes involved in a love triangle which ends in her suicide. Konstantine Levin, the hero of the alternate tale, learns to appreciate the values of the peasants who toil on his estate. The contrast in moral values between Anna and Konstantine may be less apparent today than when this novel was written, but the lesson in value appreciation remains poignant.

LADDER 2

"Don't shoot!" he called out. *"I ain't the law.*
I'm yore kin." Well, even a one-eyed catbird
could see he wasn't the law; but he sure didn't
look like kin to the Fogles neither. *"My mammy*
were a Fogle from Chickasaw Creek. My pappy
were name of Bochamp. I is Lysander Bo-
champ."
Old Man Fogle came out from behind a
rock. He cocked his rifle slow. *"What do you*
want?" he said.
"My mammy taken sick and died last week,"
said the little fellow. *"I reckoned I could bide*
with you for a spell. I'll work for my keep
and I don't eat much."
"Where's yore pa?"
"He died too. A long time ago. No one left
but me. Yore all the kinfolk I got." *

LADDER 2

Living with Others

A most natural phenomenon is for men to belong to groups.
Throughout his early years, the child is profoundly involved in two
major pursuits: understanding his roles in his family and peer
group, and learning to perform the behaviors expected by each.
Nothing occupies more of the child's concern than his acceptance
in these groups. The books annotated in this second ladder focus
on the satisfactions and the problems of living with others, and
they should help young readers to walk the path of social responsibility with a lighter step.

In line with the young child's first concern, the books presented
initially in this category portray family relationships. A picture of a
happy, healthy situation has been created for the very young by
the Hobans in their books about Frances, a naughty badger. Many
realistic books, even for the young reader, cannot paint as perfect
a picture. *Did You Carry the Flag Today, Charley?* by Rebecca
Caudill presents a lovable Head-Starter eager for his first bit of
schooling. Although his family is very poor, his parents give Charley

* From *The Fiddler of High Lonesome* by Brinton Turkle. Copyright ©
1968 by Brinton Turkle. All rights reserved. Reprinted by permission of the
Viking Press, Inc.

much love and encouragement. Other stories show the strained relations that exist within some households as young people begin to see their parents as human beings with human weaknesses. *It's Like This, Cat* by Emily Neville revolves around a troublesome father-son relationship in a sophisticated city story.

In our culture and time, fewer children than formerly have opportunities for extended contact with their grandparents. Readers may keep in close touch with the wisdom of an older generation through some delightful books. Primary readers can enjoy Helen Buckley's *Grandfather and I;* intermediate-level readers may want to journey by dogsled through treacherous frozen arctic regions with Akavak and his grandfather in *Akavak: An Eskimo Journey* by James Houston. Senior and mature readers will be impressed with the difficult but sensitive family relationships found in the midst of poverty as life in Harlem is seen through the eyes of a grandmother in the recently re-issued *The Sweet Flypaper of Life* by DeCarava and Hughes.

Moving beyond immediate families to find special friends is an experience that is re-enacted in many worthwhile books and this becomes the second subcategory for this section. Mature readers will raise many questions in response to the sensitive relationship of two lonely boys in a New England prep school in *Good Times/Bad Times* by James Kirkwood. Their lives are shattered by an evil-minded headmaster who, through jealousy, permits one boy to die unattended and is killed himself in pursuit of the other boy who has left school.

Relationships within peer groups provide a third subcategory for this section. No normal young person escapes a mild "gang age," but for some youngsters, as for some characters in fiction, the experience is not a pleasant one. Peer group pressures often result in tensions for the individuals concerned. The young heroine in *Queenie Peavy* by Robert Burch finds it impossible to live peacefully in the shadow of her father's prison sentence and the poverty of her home. She thus reacts belligerently to those whom she would like to have as friends. In *The Greyhound* by Helen Griffiths, Jamie becomes deeply involved with a gang when he borrows money from the leader to buy food for his treasured dog.

The main characters in some books become involved with persons beyond the periphery of family and peers, and so a subcategory for these "other" relationships is provided. *Henry Three* by Joseph Krumgold is a perceptive look at what false values do to human relationships. Ester Wier in *The Loner* tells the story of a boy who literally had no one until Boss, a sheepwoman in Montana, befriended the boy and treated him as her own son. Older readers will be enchanted by the beautifully written story *The Sisters of the Angels* by Elizabeth Goudge. Here, characterizations move beyond a real and an adopted family to include an English girl's relationship with a talented painter. Their friendship creates a small miracle at the Christmas season.

A look at living with others would be incomplete if the more negative side were not shown, and a final subcategory deals with alienation, rejection, and conflicting values. Alienation from the total system of present-day values is one of the causes for youths' banding together and seeking their own solutions. This social reaction is being delineated in an increasing number of books for young readers. A touching story is that of a young boy who cannot find anyone to stand with him in his ideals. *The Fiddler of High Lonesome* by Brinton Turkle tells of Lysander Bochamp, who went to the Fogles to claim his kin after his father and mother died. When the Fogles refused to respect the lives of the "little critters of the mountains," however, Lysander decided that the men were no kin of his, and he, the little fiddler, wandered off as lonesome as before. *Sounder* by William Armstrong is a strong and forcefully written story of the alienation of black sharecroppers. Though Sounder is a coon dog, this story is of his master and especially of his master's young son. The boy's great love for both the dog and his father allows him to maintain a never-failing hope despite the indifference and cruelty of those who arrested his father and maimed his dog. *In a Beautiful Pea Green Boat* by J. M. Scott is the story of a man who tries to complete his sense of alienation by suicide but in so doing finds himself the protector of a little girl whose life depends upon his survival. Mature readers will find this a truly memorable book with a haunting ending. Warren Miller's *The Cool World* is set in Harlem and is the story of a gang, its activities, and the sentencing of its leader to reform school. It is concerned strongly with the alienation of the young in a narrow and often frightening world.

No book can take the place of real living, but young people can experience only a limited number of relationships in the "real world." Living with others vicariously in a balance of happy and problem-laden circumstances should lead young readers to a much enriched life, indeed.

E. Jane Porter and Dorothy MacDougall, SCN

Family Relationships

Primary

ARDIZZONE, EDWARD. *Sarah and Simon and No Red Paint.* Delacorte, 1965, $3.25. There is a painter who paints beautiful pictures, but no one buys them. He has a wife and three children, and although they are poor, they are very happy. When their poverty is about to overcome them, Simon and Sarah, the older children, help restore their family's fortune without realizing what they are doing.

AYARS, JAMES STERLING. *Happy Birthday, Mom!* il. by Elizabeth Donald. Abelard, 1963, $2.50. It is April, and Molly knows her mother's birthday is coming soon. She wants a present for her. Molly decides to give her mother petunias, but on her way to get them Molly sees some fluffy chicks she thinks her mother will love. As the chicks grow older they outgrow their pen and soon begin to perch on places where they are not wanted. Molly's family must find a place for the chicks where they will be happy. Warmth and understanding prevail throughout this family story.

BARCLAY, GAIL. *The Little Brown Gazelle.* il. by Kiyo Komoda. Dial, 1968, $3.95. This book presents a lovely and sensitive description of a small gazelle left alone by its mother. The fear and loneliness reflect a universal feeling of childhood.

BISHOP, CLAIRE H. *The Five Chinese Brothers.* il. by Kurt Wiese. Coward, 1938, $3.50. A tale of five clever brothers. Each of the brothers possesses an unusual talent; one can swallow the sea, one can stretch his legs great lengths, one has an iron neck, one cannot be burned, and one can hold his breath indefinitely. Each of these talents helps the brothers at just the right time.

BLUME, J. *The One in the Middle Is the Green Kangaroo.* Reilly, 1969, $3.95. The middle child has a more difficult time finding a place in the family than the other children. This book presents a delightful treatment of one adjustment to this problem.

BORACK, BARBARA. *Grandpa.* il. by Ben Shecter. Har-Row, 1968, $2.95. This book tells the story of the way a little girl sees her grandfather. The two have so much in common: when Marilyn dresses up in grandpa's shirt, her grandmother can't tell them apart. When company comes, they both hate it, but they sit quietly in the corner where the candy is—and eat it up!

BROWN, MARGARET WISE. *The Runaway Bunny.* il. by Clement Hurd.

Har-Row, 1942, $2.95. This is a repetitive tale of a bunny who threatens to run away. Each time he tells his mother what he will become, she answers with what she will become so that she can be near and care for him. Finally he decides he might as well stay home. The theme of a mother's love for her child becomes even more explicit in the "Song of the Runaway Bunny" at the close of the book.

* BROWN, MYRA BERRY. *Amy and the New Baby.*

BUCK, PEARL S. *The Little Fox in the Middle.* il. by Robert Jones. Macmillan, 1966, $3.95. The little fox in the middle is one of five baby foxes in a family, but he is always lonely because all the activities of the other little foxes are done in twos. One day the little fox in the middle runs away from home to find someone to play with. He meets some people who live in a house near the woods, among them a little boy. The little fox successfully makes friends with the boy and is surprised to learn people do not always cut off foxes' tails.

BUCKLEY, HELEN E. *Grandfather and I.* il. by Paul Galdone. Lothrop, 1959, $3.95. A young boy delights in taking walks with his grandfather because neither has to hurry, and they can stop and look at anything which interests them. It is a special relationship between two people who have the time to truly enjoy one another's company.

————. *Grandmother and I.* il. by Paul Galdone. Lothrop, 1961, $3.95. In childlike terms the book tells of a youngster's comfort in sitting on grandmother's lap as she rocks back and forth, humming a tune. The concept of a special love between grandmother and child is simply, yet fully, developed.

————. *Josie and the Snow.* il. by Evaline Ness. Lothrop, 1964, $3.78. After getting resistance from Dozy Cat, Buttercup, and Charles-the-Mouse, Josie goes with her mother, father, and brother for a happy time in the snow.

————. *My Sister and I.* il. by Paul Galdone. Lothrop, 1963, $3.50. A simple story of two sisters' appreciation of each other, this book is one which small children can understand and enjoy.

CARROLL, RUTH AND LATROBE. *Tough Enough.* il. by authors. Walck, 1954, $4.25. All of the Tatum family loves Tough Enough, Beanie's puppy, but the more he gets into things, the less he is loved. Finally only Beanie cares, and he is torn between his concern for the puppy and his belief that Tough Enough might be the one who has been killing chickens on the farm. Beanie tells his father and together they work out the problem. Throughout the story the family members show deep love and respect for one another. The illustrations reflect the emotions as well as the activities of the characters.

CAUDILL, REBECCA. *Did You Carry the Flag Today, Charley?* il. by Nancy Grossman. HR & W, 1966, $3.50 (P/HR & W, $1.65). That

Charley carries the flag, the reward for best behavior at school, becomes the daily concern of Charley's parents. However, Charley's intense imagination and curiosity seem always to get in the way of "good behavior." A number of comic episodes lead to the day Charley finally does carry the flag.

CLARK, ANN NOLAN. *In My Mother's House*. il. by Velino Herrera. Viking Pr, 1941, $3.00. The life and values of the Tewa Pueblo Indians in New Mexico are revealed in sensitive prose and illustrations.

* CLIFTON, LUCILLE. *Some of the Days of Everett Anderson*.

CLYMER, ELEANOR. *Belinda's New Spring Hat*. il. by Gioia Fiammenghi. Watts, 1969, $3.95. Belinda tries several new hats. Her mother notes that one looks like a lampshade and her aunt comments that another looks like a wastepaper basket. Only her father says the right thing. When he sees the flowerpot on her head he says, "There won't be another girl with a hat like that." This is a humorous book, depicting the warm feeling between father and daughter.

* DE JONG, MEINDERT. *Puppy Summer*.

DE REGNIERS, BEATRICE S., AND IRENE HAAS. *A Little House of Your Own*. il. by Irene Haas. HBJ, 1955, $2.75. This book describes and explains the need to be alone at times. Everyone must have a "house of his own," boys and girls, mothers and fathers. The many examples given help to explicate the idea and encourage respect for the privacy of family members and friends.

* DUNCAN, LOIS. *Giving Away Suzanne*.

* FISHER, AILEEN. *My Mother and I*.

FLACK, MARJORIE. *Ask Mr. Bear*. il. by author. Macmillan, 1958, $3.50 (P/Macmillan, $.95). Danny wants to give his mother a present for her birthday but does not accept the suggestions of a succession of animals whom he meets. Mr. Bear, however, provides the solution to Danny's problem—a Big Birthday Bear Hug. The simple repetitive plot and satisfying ending are appropriate for the young child.

FOX, PAULA. *Maurice's Room*. il. by Ingrid Fetz. Macmillan, 1967, $3.95. As a "collector," Maurice has a problem in his small room keeping things in order. His problem is solved when his family moves to the country where he will have a barn to keep his treasures.

GILL, JOAN. *Hush, Jon*. il. by Tracy Sugarman. Doubleday, 1968, $3.50. Jon is resentful of his baby sister, basically because her presence requires his silence, and there are only so many quiet activities one can pursue in a small apartment. However, he decides that she is growing up when he discovers that he can make her laugh.

* GOBHAI, MEHLLI. *Lakshmi, the Water Buffalo Who Wouldn't*.

* GODDEN, RUMER. *The Fairy Doll.*

HILL, ELIZABETH S. *Evan's Corner.* il. by Nancy Grossman. HR & W, 1966, $3.95 (P/HR & W, $1.45). Evan longs for a place to be alone, but as one member of a family of eight living in a two-room apartment, this is nearly impossible. When his mother gives him a corner of the living room, he decorates it, sits there, yet feels vaguely dissatisfied. Only when he begins to help his younger brother fix up another corner does he feel truly happy.

* HOBAN, RUSSELL. *A Baby Sister for Frances.*

————. *Bedtime for Frances.* il. by Garth Williams. Har-Row, 1960, $3.50. Frances, a badger with all the characteristics of a young child, uses many well-known ploys to keep from going to bed and staying there. Her understanding parents allow Frances several trips to their bedroom before father finally suggests the possibility of a spanking. This seems to be an effective sleep-inducer.

————. *A Birthday for Frances.* il. by Lillian Hoban. Har-Row, 1968, $3.50. Frances, a humanlike badger, suffers from an acute case of jealousy when her little sister Gloria has a birthday. Her parents demonstrate love and understanding as they adeptly cope with the situation.

————. *Bread and Jam for Frances.* il. by Lillian Hoban. Har-Row, 1964, $3.50 (P/Schol Bk Serv, $.75). Frances' philosophy of eating is that many different foods taste many different ways, but if she always has bread and jam, then she always knows what she is getting. Her parents cooperate by giving her only bread and jam. As expected, she tires of this menu and decides that she would rather eat a greater variety of foods.

————. *Harvey's Hideout.* il. by Lillian Hoban. Parents', 1969, $3.95. An argument begins over the noise Harvey Muskrat is making while his sister Mildred is trying to write a poem. The theme "it's more fun playing together than playing separately" comes through by the end of the book, especially since the muskrats seem so human!

————. *Nothing to Do.* il. by Lillian Hoban. Har-Row, 1964, $2.95. Walter Possum has nothing to do, so he continually asks his father for suggestions. Finally his father gives him a "magic something to do stone," which gives Walter ideas of things to do when he rubs it and thinks. He in turn gives his little sister a "play right here" stick, which keeps her from following him. The family relationships are portrayed with subtle humor, and the dialogue and situation will probably be familiar to many children.

JOHNSTON, JOHANNA. *Edie Changes Her Mind.* il. by Paul Galdone. Putnam, 1964, $2.75. Edie is a little girl who hates to go to bed. Every night when her mother says, "Time now," Edie opens her mouth and yells. One night her mother says: "We'll forget about bed." Mother takes away the bedclothes and Daddy takes the bed apart and carries it away piece by piece. After a while Edie changes her mind about bedtime.

KRAUSS, RUTH. *The Big World and the Little House.* il. by Marc Simont. Har-Row, 1956, $2.95. A family comes to live in a little house that is deserted and bare. They paint it and repair it, and it becomes their home, "because a home is the way you feel about a place, whether it is a house, a room, a corner, or the whole world."

* KROEBER, THEODORA. *A Green Christmas.*

LENSKI, LOIS. *Papa Small.* il. by Lois Lenski. Walck, 1951, $3.25. A very simple text describes the everyday activities of the Small family. Although their feelings are not expressed in the dialogue, they must be compatible as they do everything together.

LEXAU, JOAN. *Benjie.* il. by Don Bolognese. Dial, 1964, $3.95. Benjie is a very shy Negro youngster who refuses to speak to people. When his grandmother loses an earring which she has cherished for years, Benjie slips out to look for it. In the course of his search, he must speak to several people and thus overcomes his shyness.

――――. *Cathy Is Company.* il. by Aliki Brandenberg. Dial, 1961, $3.25. The anticipation and excitement of Cathy's first night away from home are realistically portrayed in this book for younger readers.

* ――――. *The Homework Caper.*

――――. *Me Day.* il. by Robert Weaver. Dial, 1971, $4.95. A simple affecting story told in black English and with sensitive drawings on every page.

――――. *Striped Ice Cream.* il. by John Wilson. Lippincott, 1968, $3.11 (P/Schol Bk Serv, $.60). School means five pairs of shoes, an expense which calls for working and saving by all five children as well as Mama who works in a button factory and as a part-time domestic to avoid going on welfare. In spite of family squabbles, there is evidence of respect for one another and delight over sharing a goodwill bag.

LONERGAN, JOY. *Brian's Secret Errand.* il. by Cyndy Szekeres. Doubleday, 1969, $4.50. From the window of their apartment, Brian watches his father go to work each morning, stopping at the newsdealer's to buy the morning newspaper. One day Brian's father is sick; he cannot go to work but he wishes he could get his daily newspaper. Brian takes some money he has saved and ventures secretly into the busy streets. The noise and the rushing of people, cars, and even animals bewilders Brian, but he has a successful adventure, and his father rewards him with a "big, smothering hug."

LOVELACE, MAUD HART. *Betsy-Tacy.* il. by Lois Lenski. TY Crowell,

1940, $3.50. Outgoing Betsy and shy Tacy have a variety of adventures from their first day at school in the "Baby Room," to climbing the "Big Hill," to meeting a new neighbor, Tib. Set in the early 1900s, this is a good story about two girls' friendship which should appeal to primary-age children.

McCLOSKEY, ROBERT. *Blueberries for Sal.* Viking Pr, 1948, $3.50 (P/ Viking Pr, $.65). Little Sal and her mother go out to Blueberry Hill to pick blueberries to store for the winter. Sal's mother, unaware that Sal has sat down to eat some berries, continues picking berries through the bushes. The same thing is happening on the other side of the hill with Little Bear and his mother. Sal and Little Bear follow the wrong mothers, but all ends well as Sal and Little Bear meet their respective mothers again.

* McNULTY, FAITH. *When a Boy Wakes up in the Morning.*

MARTIN, PATRICIA MILES. *The Rice Bowl Pet.* il. by Ezra Jack Keats. TY Crowell, 1962, $3.95. AhJim and his family live in crowded quarters in San Francisco's Chinatown. His mother tells him that he may have a pet provided it will fit in a rice bowl. His search for just the right-sized pet makes an exciting story enlivened by many engaging pictures of San Francisco.

MATSUNO, MASAKO. *A Pair of Red Clogs.* il. by Kazue Mizumura. World Pub, 1960, $3.95. A grandmother reminisces about the time she cracked her new red clogs as she played the weather game and almost did something dishonest so that her mother would buy her a new pair. This charming family story of Japan is told with warm sympathy and gentle humor.

MINARIK, ELSE H. *Little Bear.* il. by Maurice Sendak. Har-Row, 1957, $2.50. This easy-to-read book has four chapters in which Little Bear plays in the snow, makes "birthday soup" when he fears he may not get a cake, pretends to go to the moon, and talks with Mother at bedtime. The mother is warm and very understanding, and Little Bear expresses his feeling for her when he says, "You always make me happy."

* OLSEN, AILEEN. *Bernadine and the Water Bucket.*

POLITI, LEO. *Juanita.* il. by author. Scribner, 1948, $4.37. On her fifth birthday, Juanita receives a rose-colored dress from her mother and a white dove from her father. Juanita proudly carries her dove in the Blessing of the Animals procession, which winds through Los Angeles' Olvera Street on the Saturday before Easter.

REYHER, BECKY. *My Mother Is the Most Beautiful Woman in the World.* il. by Ruth Gannett. Lothrop, 1945, $3.50. This Russian folk tale is about a little lost girl who describes her mother as "the most beautiful woman in the world." To the children, "beautiful" means "much loved."

* SADOWSKY, ETHEL. *Francois and the Langouste.*

SCHICK, ELEANOR. *Peggy's New Brother.* il. by author. Macmillan, 1970, $4.50. Peggy wants a dog but gets a baby brother. As much as she tries to help, everything she does is wrong until one day she discovers that she has a special talent. She decides she doesn't mind waiting to have a dog—at least until she doesn't have so many important things to do.

* SCOTT, ANN HERBERT. *Sam.*

SENDAK, MAURICE. *Where the Wild Things Are.* il. by author. Har-Row, 1963, $3.95. Max is sent to his room without his supper because he has been misbehaving. He sails off in his own imaginary boat, through night and day, to where the wild things are, and becomes their king. Lonely, he decides to go back to where "someone loved him best of all." When he returns home, supper, still hot, is waiting for him.

SLOBODKIN, LOUIS. *Magic Michael.* il. by author. Macmillan, 1944, $4.95. Michael, the little brother in the family, gains attention by assuming the roles of all sorts of animals and things. His family scarcely gets used to one role when he tries out a new one. The arrival of a new bicycle on his birthday convinces him that being just plain Michael may be fun for awhile.

TAYLOR, MARK. *Henry Explores the Jungle.* il. by Graham Booth. Atheneum, 1968, $5.95. In this sequel to *Henry the Explorer* a boy and his dog set out on another "backyard" expedition.

TURKLE, BRINTON. *Obadiah the Bold.* il. by author. Viking Pr, 1965, $3.95. This story, with its setting in Nantucket about one hundred years ago, shows young Obadiah in the midst of a happy Quaker family. Brothers will tease, however, and when Obadiah wants to "play pirate" (in hopes of someday being one), he is not spared a little fright. An understanding father helps his son think about following in the footsteps of another kind of seafarer, his grandfather, Captain Obadiah Starbuck.

* UDRY, JANICE M. *Let's Be Enemies.*

———. *What Mary Jo Shared.* il. by Eleanor Mill. Whitman, 1966, $3.25 (P/Schol Bk Serv, $.60). Mary Jo wants to bring something very interesting and very unusual for the sharing period at school. Finally she decides on a precious, entirely unique possession—her father. The story is told with quiet humor, the problem of this young child being considered important by the rest of the family.

* WISE, WILLIAM. *The Cowboy Surprise.*

ZAVREL, STEPAN. *Salt Is Better Than Gold.* il. by author. Abelard, 1968, $3.95. This old folk tale tells the story of Princess Lidushka, a lovely young girl who was sent from the castle by her father, the king, with a small bag of salt. "Do not return until this salt is worth more than gold" are her father's parting words. The vibrant illustrations resembling children's art, are bound to be popular, making this a good read-aloud book.

ZOLOTOW, CHARLOTTE. *If It Weren't for You.* il. by Ben Shecter. Har-Row, 1966, $3.95. An older brother thinks of all the advantages of not having a younger brother; for example, he could "cry without anyone knowing." On the final pages he remembers that, "if it weren't for you, I'd have to be alone with the grownups" and this seems to outweigh all the disadvantages.

* ———. *Mr. Rabbit and the Lovely Present.*

———. *The Quarreling Book.* il. by Arnold Lobel. Har-Row, 1963, $2.50. Mr. James's forgetfulness makes Mrs. James cross; her crossness irritates Jonathan; and so the plot continues. The trend is finally reversed by a friendly dog.

———. *Someday.* il. by Arnold Lobel. Har-Row, 1965, $2.50. A little girl tells some of the highly imaginative things she would like to have happen, as well as some more feasible changes, such as having her brother introduce her as his sister rather than "the family creep." Amusing illustrations add to the enjoyment of this book of wishes.

———. *When I Have a Little Girl.* il. by Hilary Knight. Har-Row, 1965, $2.95. A little girl tells her mother all the things she will allow her own daughter to do, such as "touch the fur collars of ladies in front of her on the bus or train." The rules are all going to be different when she has a child of her own.

——— *William's Doll.* il. by William Pene du Bois. Har-Row, 1972, $3.95. William wanted a doll to love and take care of more than anything he could think of. His father, upset by this, bought William first a basketball and then an electric train, but William still wanted a doll. Finally his understanding grandmother bought him one because she realized how important this was to fill a small boy's needs.

Intermediate

AARON, CHESTER. *Better than Laughter.* HBJ, 1972, $4.75. Allan, aged 12, and his brother Sam, aged 10, feeling rejected and unloved, run away from home in search of a simple life with people who will love and understand them. Their escapade leads them to the county dump and its eccentric old caretaker who befriends them and in due course makes them realize they cannot run away forever. There is the inevitable confrontation with the parents. The breakdown in communication between the boys and their parents who have little time for them is especially well done.

ALCOCK, GUDRUN. *Run, Westy, Run.* il. by W. T. Mars. Lothrop, 1966, $3.95 (P/WSP, $.50). Eleven-year-old Westy has a long record of running away from his cramped city apartment. He is sent to a juvenile detention home when he steals money for his latest escape. An understanding juvenile officer helps Westy and his parents realize why he runs away and helps the family in its developing awareness of one another's needs.

ANCKARSVARD, KARIN. *Aunt Vinnie's Victorious Six.* trans. by Annabelle MacMillan. il. by William Hutchinson. HBJ, 1964, $2.95. Set in Sweden, six children stay with Aunt Vinnie while their parents are away. Their adventures depict realistic family relationships, including dissent and love.

————. *Doctor's Boy.* trans. by Annabelle MacMillan. il. by Fermin Rocker. HBJ, 1965, $3.50. Sensitively written, this award-winning Swedish book is an account of how a doctor helps his son learn about life. Jon learns to accept the friendship of Rickard, a boy from the slums, whose talents Jon envies. Rickard, in his turn, has been jealous of Jon's comfortable, secure life. The wisdom of the doctor helps the boys see that they are more alike than different and that each has special contributions to make to the people around them.

BAKER, MARGARET. *Home from the Hill.* FS & G, 1969, $3.75. Four of the six children of an impoverished but closely knit family are separated from their mother by a series of disasters. Determined to have the family together again, the four older children run away from the institutions where they have been living and look for a house. After many adventures, the family gets together again.

BARON, VIRGINIA OLSEN (ed.). *Here I Am: An Anthology of Poems Written by Young People in Some of America's Minority Groups.* il. by Emily A. McCully. Dutton, 1969, $4.95 (P/Bantam, $.75). Young people from Alaska, Utah, California, New Mexico, Oregon, Arizona, and New York wrote these poems, which tell what it is like to be black, Puerto Rican, Mexican, Indian, Eskimo, Cuban, Japanese—and American at the same time. The youngest poet is six years of age and the oldest are in their early twenties. All speak in a moving way about the human condition as felt and seen by one who belongs to a minority group.

BEHN, HARRY. *The Two Uncles of Pablo.* il. by Mel Silverman. HBJ, 1959, $3.00. Eight-year-old Pablo has two very different, antagonistic uncles. In this story contrasting farm and town life in Mexico, he learns to understand and appreciate both.

BELL, THELMA HARRINGTON. *The Two Worlds of Davy Blount.* il. by Corydon Bell. Viking Pr, 1962, $3.00. Davy, whose grandmother was from the mountains and grandfather from the sea, must decide which of these two worlds he likes best. This mild but satisfying story is unusually well written, with a remarkable feeling for nature and a warm approach to family relationships.

* BENARY-ISBERT, MARGOT. *The Ark.*

* BERRY, ERICK. *The Springing of the Rice.*

BLOCH, MARIE H. *Aunt America.* il. by Joan Berg. Atheneum, 1963, $3.50. Lesya thinks her uncle's cooperation with the Soviet government officials is better than her father's daring, independent ways. Lesya is ashamed that her parents had once been political prisoners. The visit of her American aunt Lydia—a rare and remarkable thing in itself—brings Lesya her first trip to Kiev, a strange and disturbing mixture of emotions, and finally real pride in being her father's daughter.

BRADBURY, BIANCA. *Andy's Mountain.* il. by Robert MacLean. HM, 1969, $3.50. For six generations the farm has been in the Wheeler family. Now it is about to be taken by the state for a four-lane highway. Gramps, determined that his grandchildren Andy and Ellen will inherit the land, stubbornly refuses all offers and orders. When all his plans fail, eleven-year-old Andy finally comes up with a plan to satisfy both Gramps and the state.

* ———. *Two on an Island.*

BRINK, CAROL RYRIE. *Family Sabbatical.* il. by Susan Foster. Viking Pr, 1956, $3.50. This humorous story tells of a six-month vacation of three children and their parents in France. Some episodes include an eccentric governess and a real princess.

* BUCK, PEARL S. *The Beech Tree.*

BURCH, ROBERT. *D.J.'s Worst Enemy.* Viking Pr, 1965, $3.50 (P/Viking Pr, $.75). D.J. constantly makes trouble for everyone in his family—especially his little brother Renfroe. Through the steady love and understanding of his family, D.J. begins to see that he is his own worst enemy. This humorous and sensitive book makes good use of the "country folk language" of Georgia.

———. *Renfroe's Christmas.* il. by Rocco Negri. Viking Pr, 1968, $3.50. Renfroe doesn't like being told he has a "selfish streak," but the remembrance of buying a more expensive pocketknife for himself than for his brother nags at his conscience. Finally he spontaneously gives away his watch, "the finest thing he'd ever owned," and experiences the deep satisfaction of bringing pleasure to another individual.

———. *Tyler, Wilkin, and Skee.* il. by Don Sibley. Viking Pr, 1963, $3.50 (P/Dell, $.75). Set in rural Georgia in the 1930s, this book presents twelve episodes in the lives of Tyler, Wilkin, and Skee Coley. The family members care so much for one another that these boys seem unaware of the poverty in which they are living.

BYARS, BETSY. *Summer of the Swans.* Viking Pr, 1970, $3.95. A beloved mentally retarded younger brother is lost and fourteen-year-old Sara is faced with the longest day in her life. Help comes from an unexpected source as she learns to understand herself and others a little better. A realistic, perceptive, nonsentimental story with a touch of romance.

————. *Trouble River.* il. by Rocco Negri. Viking Pr, 1969, $4.50. A young boy takes his grandmother forty miles down Trouble River to escape from Indians in the Old West. With the advice of his rather crotchety old grandmother to aid him, Dewey evades the enemy, fights wolves, and travels through rapids. A philosophy of not giving up amid hardships and a sense of real love and family solidarity predominate.

CARLSON, NATALIE SAVAGE. *The Half Sisters.* il. by Thomas di Grazia. Har-Row, 1970, $3.95. Luvena Savage longs to be accepted as "one of the girls." Luvvy finally achieves her desire by winning the respect of the older girls. This spirited, satisfying story of family life and growing up in Maryland in 1915 was drawn from the author's own childhood and has the ring of truth.

————. *Jean-Claude's Island.* il. by Nancy Burkert. Har-Row, 1963, $3.95. Whenever Jean-Claude misbehaves and is punished by his parents, he crosses the road to visit his Pepere and Memere, who comfort him, then send him home. When they go to France, he misses them terribly. However, by the time they return, Jean-Claude understands why his father, a grown man, listens to Pepere and how family members are dependent upon one another.

————. *The Letter on the Tree.* Har-Row, 1964, $3.95. Because his parents are poor, Bebert, a Canadian boy, attaches a note to a Christmas tree the family is selling. The buyer of the tree sends the family a check, and although it is returned, the buyer's son and Bebert become pen pals and eventually meet. With understanding and love from his parents, Bebert learns of the value of pride in work.

* ————. *Luigi of the Streets.*

CLEARY, BEVERLY. *Beezus and Ramona.* il. by Louis Darling. Morrow, 1955, $3.95. Beezus is continually exasperated by the antics of her younger sister Ramona, who somehow always manages to get her own way. However, Beezus begins to understand her feelings and accept them when her mother and aunt tell her of arguments they had as children, and that there were times when they did not love each other. Written in a light and humorous style, the book nonetheless has a deeper theme of family relationships.

————. *Ramona the Pest.* il. by Louis Darling. Morrow, 1968, $3.95. Ramona, the pesty kid sister of the *Beezus and Ramona* book, is going to kindergarten. Even more of a trial to her older sister than she had been earlier, Ramona keeps the reader delightfully entertained with her escapades.

CLEAVER, VERA AND BILL. *Lady Ellen Grae.* il. by Ellen Raskin. Lippincott, 1968, $2.95 (P/Dell, $.65). Ellen Grae's love for disarray and telling wild stories prompts Jeff, her divorced father, to send her to Aunt Eleanor's comfortable home in Seattle to learn the "big values." Ellen Grae plots not to leave the small Florida town she loves; once in Seattle, her homesickness nearly brings disaster. At last Jeff sends for her; he has decided that Ellen Grae belongs at home whether she learns to be ladylike or not. Humor and insight into unique child-adult relationships make this a memorable book.

CLYMER, ELEANOR. *My Brother Stevie.* il. by Estal Nesbitt (jacket design). HR & W, 1967, $3.50. Annie's and Stevie's mother leaves them with their grandmother after the children's father dies. Annie's mother says: "Take care of your brother." But at age eight Stevie throws stones at trains and breaks into candy machines. Grandmother is particularly impatient with Stevie, and whether this is the result of Stevie's behavior or whether his behavior resulted from harsh treatment remains a mystery to Annie. A new teacher at school, Miss Stover, shows Stevie love and understanding which change his life.

* CONE, MOLLY. *A Promise Is a Promise.*

* CRANE, CAROLINE. *Don't Look at Me That Way.*

* CRETAN, GLADYS YESSAYAN. *All except Sammy.*

DALY, MAUREEN. *The Ginger Horse.* il. by Wesley Dennis. Dodd, 1964, $3.50. Rob Murdoch's father takes it for granted that his sons will go to work in the mines of Dineen at an early age, just as he did. But Rob is different from most of the people of his village and when he meets Ginger Horse, a freedom-loving Shetland pit pony, he risks everything to bring about his escape. A sensitive story set in Scotland that resolves a breathtaking climax with a most satisfying ending.

DE ANGELI, MARGUERITE. *Skippack School.* il. by author. Doubleday, 1939, $2.95. Eli Shrawder and his family move into their new home in the Mennonite settlement on the Skippack. The fine family relationships and customs of this religious sect are well portrayed. Colloquial speech—such as "It wonders me now"—adds to the authenticity of the book.

DE JONG, MEINDERT. *Far out the Long Canal.* il. by Nancy Grossman. Har-Row, 1964, $3.95 (P/Har-Row, $.95). In the Dutch village of Weirom, Moonta is the only nine year old who has not yet learned to skate, and his impatience often makes him willful and disobedient. Luckily, his stern but loving parents have a sense of humor. This picture of a Dutch family in the early 1900s is one of warmth and security.

———. *Journey from Peppermint Street.* il. by Emily McCully. Har-Row, 1968, $4.95. Siebren, an imaginative little boy, finds great adventure in walking with his grandfather from their village by the North Sea to visit an aunt who lives inland. All the real and pretended dangers of his first real journey are climaxed by a tornado. Warmth and sensitivity characterize Siebren's relationship with each member of the family—his parents and sick little brother, his grandfather, the aunt who is immediately his friend, and the deaf and dumb uncle whom he at first fears.

ENRIGHT, ELIZABETH. *The Saturdays.* il. by author. HR & W, 1941, $3.50. When the four Melendy children pool their allowances and permit one child to use the whole amount for a Saturday on his own, the results are often startling and always amusing.

———. *Thimble Summer.* il. by author. HR & W, 1938, $3.95. When Garnet finds a silver thimble near the river just before a much needed rain, she thinks the thimble is an omen of a happy summer. Exciting things do happen: Garnet and a friend are accidentally locked in at the library; she hitchhikes to a town eighteen miles away; and she is trapped on a ferris wheel at the moment she is supposed to be showing her pig at the fair.

ERWIN, BETTY K. *Behind the Magic Line.* Little, 1969, $4.95. Residents of a New York ghetto, Dozie Western and her family are plagued with problems—a new baby, the disappearance of father, too little money, and an older brother in trouble with the police. In spite of everything, there is still love and solidarity between the members of the family. All ends on a hopeful note with father's return as the family sets out for the West Coast and a fresh start. Good characterizations and a realistic setting are the backbone of a compelling story.

ESTES, ELEANOR. *The Moffats.* il. by Louis Slobodkin. HBJ, 1968, $3.75 (P/HBJ, $1.25). An episodic plot has been used in developing the warm family relationships of the Moffats—Janey, Joey, Sylvie, and Rufus. The Moffats live with their mother in a yellow house on New Dollar Street in Cranbury, Connecticut, when trolleys and oil lamps are still common. A dance recital, an unexpected train ride, and a Halloween ghost are three of the humorous experiences shared by the four children.

———. *Pinky Pye.* il. by Edward Ardizzone. HBJ, 1958, $4.50. The Pyes' summer on Fire Island is more memorable than anticipated. The addition of Pinky, a remarkable cat, to the family menagerie, pet crickets and grasshoppers that continually disappear, and something strange about the cubbyhole under the eaves add suspense and interest to a story of warm family relationships.

FISHER, LAURA. *Amy and the Sorrel Summer.* il. by Sheila Greenwald. HR & W, 1964, $3.50. Amy and Berne spend their summer trying to earn money to buy a horse they admire.

————. *Never Try Nathaniel.* HR & W, 1968, $4.50. Life on an Idaho farm in the early 1900s is difficult for Nathaniel who is afraid of the farm animals and is overprotected by his mother, until an accident forces Nathaniel to take on responsibility and to make a decision that changes his life.

* FLORY, JANE. *One Hundred and Eight Bells.*

FOX, PAULA. *The Stone-Faced Boy.* il. by Donald A. MacKay. Bradbury, 1968, $3.95. Sensitive Gus has been the object of ridicule at school and of teasing at home for so long that he does not know when he first puts on his "stone face." What he now knows is that he can't smile or frown even when he wants to. Only his eccentric great-aunt Hattie seems to understand. Gus does some growing up and gains respect from his family when he braves a snowstorm in the middle of the night to free from a trap Serena's newly adopted stray dog.

* FYSON, J. G. *The Three Brothers of Ur.*

* GATES, DORIS. *Blue Willow.*

GRACE, NANCY. *Earrings for Celia.* il. by Helen Siegel. Random, 1963, $2.50. Mario is a little Mexican boy who prays to the Virgin Guadalupe to send earrings for his little sister Celia. His family lives in great poverty on a mountain slope. One day mother does not return home from the market and Mario has to take charge of his sister and the household duties. His prayers are answered, however, when mother returns with earrings for Celia.

* HAMILTON, VIRGINIA. *Zeely.*

* HARRISON, DELORIS. *The Bannekers of Bannaky Springs.*

* HEPPE, MARGARET, AND LULU HATHAWAY. *Especially Rosita.*

* HOUSTON, JAMES. *Akavak: An Eskimo Journey.*

INYART, GENE. *Jenny.* il. by Nancy Grossman. Watts, 1966, $3.50 (P/ WSP, $.60). Jenny calls the backyard of the house next door her "jungle." But one day the house is sold and the new family begins at once to clear the yard of its weeds. Jenny learns to enjoy her new neighbors and to understand and appreciate her new baby brother.

* JOHNSON, ANNABEL AND EDGAR. *The Grizzly.*

* LANSING, ELISABETH HUBBARD. *Liza of the Hundredfold.*

LATTIMORE, ELEANOR FRANCES. *The Bus Trip.* il. by author. Morrow, 1965, $2.75. Bettina's mother has just returned from the hospital with twin babies. The house is in confusion: meals have to be cooked, the twins require a great deal of attention, and Bettina's mother wonders how she can ever take care of the housework. It is decided that

Bettina and her little brother Kennie will spend the summer with their grandparents in Pennsylvania. As the long and exciting journey from Florida to Pennsylvania progresses, Bettina tries to get younger brother Kennie out of all the scrapes he gets into. Bettina's courage and independent nature are assets, but the reader rejoices with her as the eventful journey ends!

————. *Molly in the Middle.* il. by author. Morrow, 1956, $3.50. Molly, the middle child in a family of nine children, feels that her position gives her more than her share of problems. Her story is told through a series of episodes that show an understanding of children and family living.

* L'ENGLE, MADELEINE. *A Wrinkle in Time.*

* LENSKI, LOIS. *Shoo-Fly Girl.*

* LITTLE, JEAN. *Home from Far.*

MACPHERSON, MARGARET. *The New Tenants.* il. by Shirley Hughes. HBJ, 1968, $3.95. Liz Shearer and her family move from Glasgow to a small croft on the Isle of Skye. Increasingly suspicious of a neighbor whose advice always results in a monetary loss for the family, Liz finally intervenes by hiding six heifers so they cannot be sold. Her father is furious, and a family crisis arises.

* MARTIN, PATRICIA MILES. *Trina's Boxcar.*

* MEHTA, RAMA. *Ramu: A Story of India.*

MEYER, FRANKLYN. *Me and Caleb.* il. by Lawrence Beall Smith. Follett, 1962, $3.78. Me, in this warm and sensitive story of life in a small Ozark mountain town, is twelve-year-old Bud. Caleb is his younger brother. A moaning sound and a "stink" under the house in the middle of the night lead to calling the police to solve the mystery.

MEYERS, SUSAN. *The Cabin on the Fjord.* il. by Trina Schart Hyman. Doubleday, 1968, $3.50. Try as she might, Reidunn, a Norwegian girl, never seems as clever as her older sister Dagne Ranatta. But during the summer in the cabin on the Fjord, the nine year old learns that each person has her own special talents. She, Reidunn, doesn't have to be another Dagne Ranatta.

* MILLER, LUREE, AND MARILYN SILVERSTONE. *Gurkhas and Ghosts.*

* MOLNAR, JOE, ed. *Graciela: A Mexican-American Tells Her Story.*

* NESS, EVALINE. *Exactly Alike.*

NORRIS, GUNILLA B. *The Top Step.* il. by Richard Cuffari. Atheneum, 1970, $3.95. Asthma keeps Michael from doing all the rough-and-tumble things his father expects of him. To win his father's approval,

Michael attempts a really dangerous act with almost disastrous consequences. The story takes place in a modern Swedish city.

* PARKER, RICHARD. *Second Hand Family.*

* PARKINSON, ETHELYN. *Today I Am a Ham.*

PHIPSON, JOAN. *The Family Conspiracy.* il. by Margaret Horder. HBJ, 1964, $3.75 (P/HBJ, $.65). The father of the Barker family is not the best provider, but he is deeply concerned about his wife's health and his children's sense of values. The entire family must pitch in when their mother needs an operation.

———. *Threat to the Barkers.* il. by Margaret Horder. HBJ, 1965, $3.50. The Barker family, who raise sheep in Australia, is a close-knit group. When fourteen-year-old Edward gets involved with a gang of sheep thieves, he endangers the whole family.

* ———. *Good Luck to the Rider.*

* RAWLS, WILSON. *Where the Red Fern Grows.*

RENICK, MARION. *Seven Simpsons on Six Bikes.* il. by Gertrude Howe. Scribner, 1956, $2.75. Beany, next to the youngest in a family of five children, decides that instead of watching the adventures of others on television, he wants to find his own adventure. He involves the entire family in a search for a lost house and is accepted into the Home Guards Club regardless of the fact that he is the smallest and youngest.

ROBINSON, BARBARA. *Trace through the Forest.* Lothrop, 1965, $4.25. Jim Fraley goes with Colonel Zane to cut the road called Zane's Trace through the Ohio wilderness. Though hired as water boy Jim's real goal is to search for his father, who went into the wilderness a year earlier and never returned.

ST. JOHN, WYLLY FOLK. *The Christmas Tree Mystery.* il. by George Porter. Viking Pr, 1969, $3.95. Christmas for Beth and Maggie promises to be different this year because they are spending it with their new stepfather and his son, Trace. A surprise ending, brought on by a mysterious thief who steals tree ornaments, shows how the tragedy of a broken home can lead to a new search for love.

SAWYER, RUTH. *Maggie Rose, Her Birthday Christmas.* il. by Maurice Sendak. Har-Row, 1952, $2.75. Imaginative, eight-going-on-nine Maggie Rose, only industrious member of the nine Bunkers, raises money to celebrate her birthday Christmas. Her enthusiasm involves the whole family who at first merely watch Maggie with amazement. The Bunkers gain respect for each other, and the neighbors gain respect for the family.

SHEMIN, MARGARETHA. *Mrs. Herring.* il. by Robert Quackenbush. Lothrop, 1967, $3.95. Set in a Netherlands fishing village, this is a story of Pieter Tal's great desire to follow his ancestors as a herring fisherman. His grandmother, Mrs. Herring, refuses to allow Pieter to go to sea and instead apprentices him to a carpenter. The three Van Dam girls, on their annual visit to the Tal's find the usually happy family full of discontent. After Pieter runs away to sea, Jos Van Dam finds the solution to the problem as she tries to train Pieter's dog for city life. Her love for Wolf and her decision about him make her and Mrs. Herring realize one can't hold too tightly to loved ones.

* SNYDER, ZILPHA KEATLEY. *The Velvet Room.*

SORENSEN, VIRGINIA. *Lotte's Locket.* il. by Fermin Rocker. HBJ, 1964, $3.75. Lotte, age eleven, is the only one of all the family and friends of her mother who is unhappy when the announcement is made that her mother is going to marry Patrick and move to America. Lotte wants to stay in Denmark, live in the family farmhouse, and remain close to her heritage. She must resolve the conflict between love of her homeland and love for her mother.

————. *Miracles on Maple Hill.* il. by Beth and Joe Krush. HBJ, 1956, $2.95. The exciting first year on the farm is filled with many miracles of nature for Marly, who has been raised in the city. The most important miracle, however, is the change that country living works upon Marly's father, who is recovering from the experience of living in a prisoner-of-war camp. This is a beautiful story of changing family relationships.

SOUTHALL, IVAN. *Let the Balloon Go.* St. Martin, 1968, $3.95. A spastic child, stifled by his overprotective mother and friends, is determined to accomplish a feat which would tax the endurance of any boy. The result is nearly tragic, but John Summer's achievement makes a real difference in the way his parents respond to him.

* SPERRY, ARMSTRONG. *Call It Courage.*

SPYKMAN, E. C. *A Lemon and a Star.* HBJ, 1955, $3.50. The Cares family provides an interesting study of sibling relationships. Theodore, Jane, Hubert, and Edie each present unique characteristics as they interact in a well-staffed motherless household of the early 1900s.

STAPP, ARTHUR D. *The Fabulous Earthworm Deal.* il. by George Porter. Viking Pr, 1969, $4.13. Marshall Brown attempts to earn money raising earthworms. Marshall's father reacts with vigor to the fisherman who, having seen his son's sign, arrives at 3:00 a.m. to buy worms.

STEELE, WILLIAM O. *The Perilous Road.* il. by Paul Galdone. HBJ, 1958, $3.50 (P/HBJ, $.75). Eleven-year-old Chris Brabson thinks all Yankees are inhuman. He is torn with conflicts when his older brother joins the Union army and his parents seem to approve. Then he hears of a planned Confederate attack on a Union wagon train and his fear of the Yankees is overshadowed by his loyalty to and his concern for his brother who might be with the supply wagons. Family relationships and loyalties are realistically described.

* ———. *The Year of the Bloody Sevens.*

STEPHENS, PETER JOHN. *The Perrely Plight.* Atheneum, 1965, $3.95. Sturbridge, Massachusetts, in 1836 provides the setting for this mystery. Twelve-year-old Gib Martindale helps his family realize how foolish a family quarrel with the Perrelys is. In so doing, he helps to solve an unexplained barn burning and a robbery.

STEPTOE, JOHN. *Stevie.* il. by author. Har-Row, 1969, $3.50. Robert's mother takes care of Stevie while the younger child's mother works. Stevie demands and gets lots of attention, much to Robert's displeasure. Despite the fact that he resents Stevie's intrusion into his life, Robert misses him a great deal when Stevie's family moves away. The impact of the book is very strong and should appeal to any older child who has mixed feelings about sharing love with a younger one.

TAYLOR, SYDNEY. *All-of-a-Kind Family.* il. by Helen John. Follett, 1951, $4.95 (P/Dell, $.65). Although they have little money, five little Jewish girls and their parents find life rich and satisfying in New York's Lower East Side.

———. *A Papa like Everyone Else.* il. by George Porter. Follett, 1966, $3.95. Papa has gone to America to make enough money to send for his family in Czechoslovakia. As the years pass, Gisella's resentment grows towards a father she can barely remember who has left Mama to do a man's work and who would dare to take them to a strange land away from the home and friends she loves.

UCHIDA, YOSHIKO. *Hisako's Mysteries.* il. by Susan Bennett. Scribner, 1969, $3.50. Hisako lives with her grandparents in Japan. She, like all preteens, faces the problems of adolescence such as improving her failing grades in school and getting her tradition-oriented grandparents to accept modern ways. Hisako's greatest adjustment comes when she finally unravels the mysteries and discovers her father is alive when she had been told he was dead. The decision whether to stay with her grandparents or to go with her father requires much maturity and insight on her part.

———. *In-Between Miya.* il. by Susan Bennett. Scribner, 1967, $3.25. Twelve-year-old Miya builds her own set of values based on her experiences with her rural family, with their neighbors, and with her prosperous Tokyo relations and their friends.

WARD, MARTHA EADS. *Ollie, Ollie, Oxen-Free.* il. by Ralph J. McDonald. Abingdon, 1969, $3.25. Oliver Wellingham's lackadaisical father is so hard to understand that Ollie cannot feel really close to him. Ashamed of Pop on the night of the flood, he finally learns of his father's daring act of bravery at the levee. Respect from others brings Ollie's father a new sense of pride and a new ability to communicate with his son.

* WARREN, MARY PHRANER. *Walk in My Moccasins.*

WIER, ESTER. *The Long Year.* il. by Ursula Koering. McKay, 1969, $3.95. Thirteen-year-old Jesse Kingman is frustrated by his father's refusal to let him make his own decisions. The rule of the ranch is that the owner decides what is to be done with his animal, but Mr. Kingman has Jesse's pet cow dehorned without his consent, and then refuses to let his son keep a pet wolf. When Mr. Kingman finally begins to let Jesse have some responsibility, his son in turn gains new respect for his father.

———. *The Wind Chasers.* il. by Kurt Werth. McKay, 1967, $3.50. Jobidiah Klink, tired of "windchasing," returns to the Strip, a lonely section of Arizona, with his four boys. Benjy and Nate are happy to settle down and accept the harsh realities of the Strip. Their older brothers are not and finally go away, leaving young Benjy so overwhelmed by life that he withdraws into a dream of chasing wild horses in the canyons. When Benjy decides to make his dreams real and runs away to the canyons, Nate, searching for him, begins to realize that "windchasing" can also mean hope.

WILDER, LAURA INGALLS. *The Little House* (series). il. by Garth Williams. Har-Row. These universally loved stories picture the bravery, the hardships, and the joys of pioneer family life in the middle of the nineteenth century. Four of these are *Farmer Boy, Little House in the Big Woods, Little House on the Prairie* and *On the Banks of Plum Creek,* 1953, $4.95 each.

WILLARD, BARBARA. *Three and One to Carry.* il. by Douglas Hall. HBJ, 1965, $3.50. Rosanna Lodge is always rescuing helpless things, but when she brings Arthur home her younger sister and brother think she has gone too far. When whiny Arthur breaks his leg, Prue and Tiger feel responsible. Trying to care for Arthur, then being faced with the possible loss of part of their farm, makes Prue and Tiger more aware of their own responsibilities within their motherless family.

WILTON, ELIZABETH. *Riverboat Family.* FS & G, 1969, $3.75. The Angus family lives in Australia in the late nineteenth century. The four children and their cousin help Mr. Angus find work on his beloved river by raising and restoring an old paddlewheeler.

* YATES, ELIZABETH. *Carolina's Courage.*

———. *A Place for Peter.* il. by Nora S. Unwin. Coward, 1952, $3.95. Sensing his father's attitude that he is too young to do any of the important tasks on their New Hampshire farm, young Peter works hard to prove his value and earn his father's comradeship. The growth of the new father-son relationship as the boy slowly matures under the challenge is well developed.

Junior

* AARON, CHESTER. *Better than Laughter.*

* ALLAN, MABEL ESTHER. *The Dancing Garlands: The Ballet Family Again.*

ALMEDINGEN, E. M. *A Candle at Dusk.* FS & G, 1969, $3.75. Idrun's father, an eighth-century Frankish lord sees little need for learning letters but grants his son's desire after the boy heroically kills a wild boar and saves a servant girl's life. The skills learned by Idrun save his father's property. Following the Saracen invasion and destruction of the abbey where he is taught, Idrun finds a manuscript that is to be an important record of the past.

ARTHUR, RUTH M. *A Candle in Her Room.* Atheneum, 1966, $3.95. Dido, a wooden doll, causes three generations of a family in Wales to be haunted by evil. For a half century the family matures, ages, dies. New members are born, and all are overshadowed or influenced by Dido's strange fascination. This is a story of evil, of family, of life, and of the strength of love which finally breaks Dido's power.

* ———. *Portrait of Margarita.*

BARNWELL, ROBINSON. *Head into the Wind.* il. by Avery Johnson. McKay, 1966, $4.50. Toby Butler, an only child upset by his father's death, tries to find his role in a North Carolina farm family that includes his mother, his aunt, and his grandfather. His fourteenth year is one of confused feelings—about the new teacher, about the new neighbor girl, about his mother's romantic interest in an old family friend. His gradual acceptance of his mother's intention to remarry marks the beginning of Toby's understanding that life does go on.

* ———. *Shadow on the Water.*

* BARON, VIRGINIA OLSEN. *Here I Am: An Anthology of Poems Written by Young People in Some of America's Minority Groups.*

BARRETT, ANNE. *Midway.* Coward, 1968, $4.75. *Midway* is a perceptive and plausible story of a boy's struggle to understand himself and his family. Being just "ordinary" in a family of very clever and confident members, Mark feels very insecure. Mark gains confidence in his own worth and the respect of his own family with the help of Midway, an imaginary tiger, who appears at the appropriate moments to help him.

BROWN, PAMELA. *The Other Side of the Street.* il. by Nathan Mayer. Follett, 1967, $3.50. Linda Knight's main ambition is to get enough money to move her widowed mother, her brother, and two sisters out of the tenement house and into one of the private homes across the street. Her many money-making schemes, ranging from a house-keeping business to television quiz shows, end in success when the real estate agent marries her mother. This lively story contains sympathetic characterization and an accurate picture of lower middle-class London life.

BULL, ANGELA. *Wayland's Keep.* HR & W, 1967, $3.95. This mystery deals with the changing and developing relationship of young cousins Malinda, Sophie, and Anna and how they solve the one-hundred-year-old mystery concerning the ancient keep bought by their great-grand-father, Wayland, when he was only thirteen years old.

* BYARS, BETSY. *Summer of the Swans.*

* CHAPIN, HENRY, AND PETER THROCKMORTON. *Spiro of the Sponge Fleet.*

* CLEAVER, VERA AND BILL. *Where the Lilies Bloom.*

CORBIN, WILLIAM. *Smoke.* Coward, 1967, $4.95. This is a moving and realistic story of the relationship between a boy and the father who was forced upon him. Chris finds Smoke, a half-starved wild German shepherd dog, in the woods near his farm in Oregon. Smoke provides the opportunities for Chris to recognize and accept his stepfather's real love for him.

CRANE, CAROLINE. *Don't Look at Me That Way.* Random, 1970, $3.95. This is the story of Rosa Rivera, the oldest of seven fatherless children, living in the very poor section of New York's West Side. Situations arise which could end in a tragedy but are avoided through the kindness of people involved.

* DONOVAN, JOHN. *I'll Get There, It Better Be Worth the Trip.*

DOSS, HELEN. *The Family Nobody Wanted.* Little, 1954, $5.95 (P/Schol Bk Serv, $.60). Girls especially will enjoy this true story by a minister's wife who became mother to twelve adopted children—eleven of whom were considered unadoptable because of their mixed parentage: Oriental, American Indian, Spanish American, etc. A theme of accepting each person for his personal worth, regardless of background, is inherent in this story of a large, loving family.

EMERY, ANNE. *Mountain Laurel.* P/Schol Bk Serv, 1948, $.60. A mountain girl, Laurel finds her own place in life instead of always counting on her city friends who help her in the summer. Maintaining her five brothers and sisters in their motherless family, she wins for herself a sense of achievement through skill in mountain crafts.

FEAGLES, ANITA MACRAE. *Me, Cassie.* Dial, 1968, $3.95 (P/Dell, $.75). Cassie, growing up in a wacky suburban family augmented by cousins and foreign exchange students, begins to understand herself and her family through a series of amusing incidents.

FRIIS-BAASTAD, BABBIS. *Don't Take Teddy.* trans. by Lise S. McKinnon. Scribner, 1967, $4.50. Mikkel Grasbeth is a sensitive thirteen year old with an older brother who is mentally retarded. What the family has always feared happens one day. Teddy throws a rock and knocks out a boy's tooth. With echoes of "lock him up" and "call the police" in his ears, Mikkel decides to run away to protect Teddy. The long hard journey across the Norwegian countryside helps Mikkel to better understand his brother's needs and to do what would be best for him and for the whole family.

GEORGE, JEAN CRAIGHEAD. *Gull Number Seven Thirty-Seven.* TY Crowell, 1964, $3.50. Luke Rivers grows restless as he assists his ornithologist-father for the fifth summer in a lonely and exacting study of sea gull behavior. He cannot understand his father's passion for pure research; he longs for a practical, paying job. A plane crash caused by birds makes Dr. Rivers' work suddenly relevant. When Luke finds the courage to begin his own research on gulls, he gains new insight into his father's scientific convictions and new understanding of their relationship.

HEAPS, WILLARD. *Wandering Workers.* Crown, 1968, $4.95. This story of American migrant farm workers deals both with individual workers and their problems and with the major national problems posed by migrant workers as a group.

* HUNT, IRENE. *Across Five Aprils.*

HUNTLEY, CHET. *The Generous Years: Remembrances of a Frontier Boyhood.* Random, 1968, $4.95 (P/Fawcett World, $.75). A humorous account of growing up in simpler days at the beginning of the century in a Montana prairie town. The book recaptures the family relationships that seem to have passed with the small town.

JACKSON, SHIRLEY. *We Have Always Lived in the Castle.* Viking Pr, 1962, $3.95 (P/several). Two sisters retreat into the shell of a house, denying entrance to anyone from the village. Miss Jackson keeps the reader puzzled: Which of the gentle sisters is mad? What did happen to Uncle Julian? Why do the villagers feel guilty? This story explores the strange unbreakable ties that often bind sisters.

JOHNSON, ANNABEL AND EDGAR. *A Golden Touch.* Har-Row, 1963, $3.79. At thirteen, Andy begins a new way of life in the goldfields of California with a father he has never known. Andy's friendship brings together a strange assortment of people, and they begin a profitable mining venture. Then mystery and distrust threaten the friendships and the business.

———. *Torrie.* Har-Row, 1960, $3.95. Torrie Anders is bitterly resentful at leaving St. Louis to travel to California in a covered wagon. During the journey, Torrie reaches a new understanding of her parents' worth, and realizes that her own attitudes and values are in need of change.

KINGMAN, LEE. *The Year of the Raccoon*. il. by David Grose. HM, 1966, $3.50. Joel, fifteen, is the "normal, average" boy in a family with a nine-year-old scientific genius and a brilliant eighteen-year-old pianist. Joel's father, an aggressive, world-traveling businessman, tries to run the lives of his family with the efficiency of a factory. When conflict develops in the family, Joel's "normal" behavior is the responsible force that takes command.

* KREMENTZ, JILL. *Sweet Pea: A Girl Growing up in the Rural South.*

* KRUMGOLD, JOSEPH. *Henry Three.*

* LATHAM, JEAN LEE. *Trail Blazer of the Seas.*

* LEE, MILDRED. *The Rock and the Willow.*

* L'ENGLE, MADELEINE. *Camilla.*

LINDGREN, ASTRID. *Seacrow Island*. trans. by Evelyn Ramsden. il. by Robert Hales. Viking Pr, 1969, $5.95. A writer and his four children spend the summer in an old cottage on an island and grow to love the place and the people.

* MOLNAR, JOE (ed). *Graciela: A Mexican-American Tells Her Story.*

NEUFELD, JOHN. *Edgar Allen*. SG Phillips, 1968, $4.50 (P/NAL, $.60). Told from the viewpoint of a twelve year old, this is the story of a white, suburban minister's family that adopts a black baby. The large family is torn apart, faith in the father is jeopardized, and only a shaky truce is finally reached between father and son.

NEVILLE, EMILY. *It's Like This, Cat*. il. by Emily Weiss. Har-Row, 1963, $3.95 (P/Schol Bk Serv, $.60). Dave tells the story of the changes in his life after he brings Cat, a tiger-striped tom, home with him. Because of Cat, Dave meets Mary, a girl who lives near Coney Island with rather off-beat parents. Because of Cat, Dave meets Tom, a dropout from New York University. Because of Cat, Dave begins to communicate with his father, and as all these characters come together, he begins to know himself better.

* OGILVIE, ELISABETH. *Blueberry Summer.*

PARKER, RICHARD. *Second Hand Family*. il. by Gareth Floyd. Bobbs, 1966, $3.50. Orphaned, twelve-year-old Giles is sent to foster homes, accepted solely for the added income provided for his support. The changes which come about as a result of his move into the Maxwell family significantly affect his life. Sharing a bedroom with Martin and all the amplifiers and drums of the Minors, their rock group, Giles is gradually included in the group's future, and thanks to his interest they get their first job.

PEDERSEN, ELSA. *House upon a Rock*. il. by Charles Shaw. Atheneum, 1968, $4.50. Derrick Slocum's sixteenth birthday will be remembered as the day of the great Alaskan earthquake. The tidal wave destroys his family's hotel along with the rest of the waterfront in the small town of Fidalgo. As the townspeople react to the tragedy, Derrick's father finds new spirit in the challenge of rebuilding, and Derrick proves himself responsible enough for a coveted summer job aboard a fishing boat.

———. *Petticoat Fisherman*. il. by Charles Shaw. Atheneum, 1969, $4.95. Kent is afraid her father will discover that the car she has been given for graduation is already wrecked. She cannot explain to him that Robin, her boyfriend, is to blame, because her father disapproves of him. When her father finds out, he orders Kent to spend the summer working on his fishing boat. Her summer experiences lead to greater maturity as she becomes aware of what is expected of her in the adult world.

PHIPSON, JOAN. *Birkin*. il. by Margaret Horder. HBJ, 1966, $3.75. The grit and self-reliance of several children who attempt to bring up a motherless calf are portrayed in this light-hearted picture of village life in Australia.

* RINKOFF, BARBARA. *Name: Johnny Pierce.*

RUARK, ROBERT. *The Old Man and the Boy*. HR & W, 1957, $5.95 (P/ Fawcett World, $.95). A nostalgic, sometimes sentimental story of the friendship between a Southern boy and his grandfather which results in the boy's learning to hunt and to fish and to appreciate the beauty and terror of nature.

RUSSELL, ROBERT. *To Catch an Angel: Adventures in the World I Cannot See*. Vanguard, 1962, $4.95. In his account of accidental blinding in childhood, education at Hamilton, Yale, and Oxford, marriage to an English girl, fatherhood, and spiritual quest, Russell communicates a vigorous and joyful acceptance of life even in the midst of darkness and defeat.

SHERBURNE, ZOA. *Stranger in the House*. Morrow, 1963, $3.95. Kathleen's comfortable life with her father, brother, and devoted housekeeper is disrupted when her mother returns from a mental hospital after an eight-year absence. The whole family faces the tensions of mixed feelings and uncertain roles; slowly they learn more about the ties that make a group into a family.

* SMITH, GEORGE HARMON. *Wanderers of the Field.*

SOMMERFELT, AIMEE. *The White Bungalow*. il. by Ulf Aas. Criterion,

1964, $3.50. Lalu's hope of returning to the white bungalow of the medical missionaries in Agra, India, so he can study to be a doctor conflicts with his responsibilities to his family. Drought, the illness of his father, his family's need, and his association with his friend Ram help him make his decision.

* STEELE, WILLIAM O. *The Year of the Bloody Sevens.*

STOLZ, MARY. *Leap Before You Look.* Har-Row, 1972, $5.11. The shattering effect of her parents' divorce is seen through the eyes of a contemporary 14-year-old who fears the pace at which she is hurtling toward adulthood.

STUART, MORNA. *Marassa and Midnight.* il. by Alvin Smith. McGraw, 1968, $3.75 (P/Dell, $.75). A story of the great devotion between twin boys born into slavery. Separated when one is sold and taken to Paris, they are reunited as they take part in the black revolt in eighteenth-century Haiti.

SWARTHOUT, GLENDON AND KATHRYN. *Whichaway.* il. by Richard M. Powers. Random, 1966, $3.25. He is called "Whichaway" by the ranch hands because he always seems to be changing his mind. No one cares what he does or where he goes as long as he keeps the windmills greased in the summer. Enduring three days atop a windmill with both legs broken shows that Whichaway has the courage to face any situation and the maturity to talk with his unresponsive father about his future plans.

* VROMAN, MARY ELIZABETH. *Harlem Summer.*

WILKINSON, SYLVIA. *A Killing Frost.* HM, 1967, $4.95. The late autumn of Miz Liz's life is lovingly and understandingly detailed by her thirteen-year-old granddaughter, Ramie. The strong-willed, single-minded old lady is contrasted to the sensitive, artistic Ramie, revealed through her vivid perceptions and descriptions of the world of rural North Carolina.

WILLARD, BARBARA. *The Family Tower.* HBJ, 1968, $3.50. The many-branched Tower family is centered in an English town where their business, Tower Motors, is both the ambition and the passion of the boys and girls of the family. This is the story of the young Towers, mostly in their teens, whose patterns of friendship are disturbed by the arrival of Emily, a recently orphaned cousin from Ghana.

———. *Storm from the West.* il. by Douglas Hall. HBJ, 1964, $3.50. Molding two families into one is especially complicated when mother and two teenagers are British and father and four children are thoroughly American. A get-acquainted holiday in Scotland brings about such bitter squabbling that the parents go for a vacation of their own, leaving the six children under the care of neighbors to work out their own differences. The challenge of fending for themselves and facing inevitable minor crises enables them at last to refer to themselves as "The Clan."

———. *The Toppling Towers.* HBJ, 1969, $4.25. A sequel to *The Family Tower,* this book tells of the toppling of the family business in an industrial merger and the disturbing effects of two visitors from overseas—a cousin who returns from America as a Vietnam war widow, and Emily's good friend from Ghana who comes to study auto engineering.

WOJCIECHOWSKA, MAIA. *The Hollywood Kid.* Har-Row, 1966, $3.50. Fifteen-year-old Bryan Wilson, son of a famous movie actress, plans to leave Hollywood and go East to a school where his father teaches. Bryan suffers such conflict between loyalty to his mother and his desire to join his father that he suspects that he "is losing his mind."

Senior

AGEE, JAMES. *A Death in the Family.* G & D, 1963, $4.95 (P/Bantam, $.95). The father's death shatters the world of the close-knit Follet family. As the point of view shifts the reader sees the tragedy through the eyes of the loving, religious mother, the eyes of the relatives, and the eyes of young Catherine. Most often, however, it is six-year-old Rufus' troubled mind through which we look.

AUSTEN, JANE. *Pride and Prejudice.* Macmillan, 1962, $3.95 (P/several). Darcy's pride makes him unable to perceive any virtue in a small-town family. This pride prejudices the daughter Elizabeth against him. Before their problem is resolved many types of marriage relationships are examined.

BALDWIN, JAMES. *The Amen Corner.* Dial, 1968, $4.50. The play focuses on a storefront woman minister whose facade of perfection is destroyed when her parishioners learn of the harlotry of her youth. Her son, rebelling against his mother's strict religious upbringing, is startled to find his father did not leave her; rather, she left him.

* BAWDEN, NINA. *Tortoise by Candlelight.*

* BRADBURY, BIANCA. *The Blue Year.*

* ———. *Red Sky at Night.*

BRADBURY, RAY. *Dandelion Wine.* P/Bantam, 1964, $.75. This is the story of Douglas Spaulding's eleventh summer, when he learns what it means to "be alive." The idea of bottling up memories in the form of dandelion wine or as a happiness machine or in the patterns of an oriental rug is a dominant theme.

* CAPOTE, TRUMAN. *A Christmas Memory.*

* CATHER, WILLA. *My Antonia.*

* CLEARY, BEVERLY. *Sister of the Bride.*

DeCARAVA, ROY, AND LANGSTON HUGHES. *The Sweet Flypaper of Life.* Hill & Wang, 1967, $3.50 (P/Hill & Wang, $1.50). In a first-person account of life in Harlem, a grandmother describes her large family in a vividly colloquial, rhythmic narrative. The pattern of family life, their expectations, their values are sensitively portrayed in black and white photographs as well as words. The focus is not only on a particular ethnic group but on the universality of the experiences.

* FORBES, KATHRYN. *Mama's Bank Account.*

FROLOV, VADIM. *What It's All About.* Doubleday, 1968, $3.95. Sasha, a fifteen-year-old Russian boy, describes his struggle to cope with the knowledge that his mother, an actress, is an adulteress.

GALSWORTHY, JOHN. *A Man of Property.* W Collins, 1906, $2.45 (P/ several). The first and best of a trilogy, this book reveals the private and public world of the businessman between 1886 and World War I through the story of the close-knit Forsyte family. The smug, self-satisfied late Victorian world is crumbling for reasons that would seem very contemporary to young readers: the world of the man of property, interested only in material things, is threatened by a new set of values. Galsworthy details the conflicts and heartaches that occur when the stable values and guiding principles of a family are questioned.

GLOAG, JULIAN. *Our Mother's House.* S & S, 1963, $4.95 (P/PB, $.95). When their mother dies, seven children, fearing separation or being placed in an orphanage, bury her in the garden, build a temple over her grave, and create a kind of religion to hold them together. They are troubled by curious neighbors, their own quarrels, the dimming of memories, and the return of a lost father whose charm disarms them and ultimately leads to the discovery of their secret.

GODDEN, RUMER. *The River.* Viking Pr, 1946, $3.50 (P/Viking Pr, $1.65). This is the story of one winter in the life of an English girl growing up in India. The interactions of the various members of the family result in Harriet's developing an awareness of birth, death, and the kinds of love. As everything around her is changing, so, too, is she changing, for "you can't stop days or rivers."

* GOFF, GERALD M. *Voices of Man: Homecoming.*

GOLD, HERBERT. *Fathers.* Random, 1967, $7.95 (P/Fawcett World, $.95). This is the story of a Russian-Jewish immigrant boy's growing up in America, as well as a story of conflict and misunderstanding between two generations. The boy, so eager to find the American Dream that he changes his name to Gold, later produces a son he doesn't understand, an esthete unconcerned about money.

* GRIFFIN, JOHN HOWARD. *Black Like Me.*

* HART, MOSS. *Act One.*

HEAD, ANN. *Mr. and Mrs. Bo Jo Jones.* Putnam, 1967, $4.95 (P/NAL, $.75). July and Bo Jo, seniors in high school, marry hurriedly out of necessity. While concerned parents make the difficult marriage even harder, Bo Jo's menial bank job and July's struggle with domesticity spell a boredom that is suffocating. The couple finally learn to respect and love each other and succeed in establishing their independence from their families.

HORGAN, PAUL. *Things As They Are.* FS & G, 1964, $5.95 (P/Paperback Lib, $.95). Richard is an imaginative ten year old whose parents wonder when he will "see things as they are." In this novel which seems autobiographical, Richard's growing knowledge of himself is the beginning of his loss of innocence. Yet it becomes clear that while he will "see things as they are," he will also continue to view life in his own way.

KING, CORETTA SCOTT. *My Life with Martin Luther King, Jr.* HR & W, 1969, $6.95 (P/Avon, $1.50). Mrs. Martin Luther King, Jr., describes her life with Dr. King. The book is framed within the announcement of Dr. King as the recipient of the 1964 Nobel Peace Prize, the subsequent preparation for the award trip, and the Nobel award ceremony in Oslo. Using the flashback technique, Mrs. King discusses her childhood, the later courtship between her and Dr. King, and Dr. King's leadership after their marriage in the civil rights struggle.

MARQUES, RENE. *The Oxcart.* trans. by Charles Dilditch. P/Scribner, 1969, $1.96. Luis, attempting to make a better living, leaves an unproductive Puerto Rican farm for the city, going first to San Juan, then to New York. Luis is destroyed by false values of a mechanized society while his family is repeatedly humiliated until they return to the land.

NORTH, STERLING. *So Dear to My Heart.* Doubleday, 1968, $3.95 (P/several). Responsibility of caring for Danny, a pet lamb, enriches young Jeremiah's life. His relationship with his stern grandmother is strengthened when the lamb wins first prize at the state fair.

O'NEILL, EUGENE. *Ah, Wilderness* (in *Later Plays*). P/Modern Lib, $1.65. A nostalgic play about small-town Connecticut life in 1909. We see seventeen-year-old Richard's first encounter with a questionable lady, his first drink, and his straining to break away from the control of adults.

* PARKS, GORDON. *The Learning Tree.*

* POHLMANN, LILLIAN. *Sing Loose.*

* POTOK, CHAIM. *The Chosen.*

RICHTER, CONRAD. *The Waters of Kronos.* Knopf, 1960, $3.95. In a story reminiscent of *Our Town,* John Donner returns as an old man to the world of his youth. The novel explores the father-son relationship which John has never understood.

SAVAGE, ELIZABETH. *Summer of Pride.* Little, 1960, $5.95. The prosperous Oliver family has lived happily on their Idaho ranch for several generations, and the entire clan is aghast when Paul considers a career as a college teacher in preference to returning to the ranch. The results of this conflict make a lively, amusing account of family relationships.

* STEINBECK, JOHN. *The Red Pony.*

* STOLZ, MARY. *Leap Before You Look.*

* ———. *Some Merry-Go-Round Music.*

* STRACHAN, MARGARET PITCAIRN. *What Is to Be.*

TARKINGTON, BOOTH. *The Magnificent Ambersons.* P/Hill & Wang, 1957, $1.95. George Amberson Minafer, a spoiled only child and heir to the Amberson millions, is too proud of his mother's family name to marry a girl he feels to be below him. He also denies his adoring mother the love of a man of a lower class, an industrialist. The book is marred by a sentimental ending but at its best it powerfully explores a mother-son relationship.

* THOMAS, PIRI. *Down These Mean Streets.*

* THOMPSON, ERA BELL. *American Daughter.* (O.P.)

UPDIKE, JOHN. *Pigeon Feathers and Other Stories.* Knopf, 1962, $4.95 (P/Fawcett World, $.95). Nineteen stories, arranged from youth to early marriage, explore the small miseries of life as children, adolescents, and young adults try and so often fail to relate successfully to one another.

* VASQUEZ, RICHARD. *Chicano.*

WEST, JESSAMYN. *Friendly Persuasion.* HBJ, 1956, $4.95 (P/Avon, $.95). The Birdwells, a family of Irish Quakers living in Indiana at the time of the Civil War, typify the gentle ways of Friends. These sketches, with gentle humor, make real the inner tensions, the idiosyncrasies of members of the family, and the strain of going against conventions imposed by the community.

WILDER, THORNTON. *Our Town* (in *Three Plays*). Har-Row, 1957, $7.95 (P/Har-Row, $.65). Life in Grover's Corners, New Hampshire, in the early 1900s is portrayed through the routine daily events and the major moments in the lives of George Gibbs, Emily Webb, and their families. Through them the priceless value of even the most common and routine event becomes clear.

* WOLFF, RUTH. *Linsey, Herself.*

————. *A Trace of Footprints.* John Day, 1968, $5.95. Paul Scott, his marriage failing and his goals obscured, visits his grandfather, Mr. Sam. As he comes to understand the complicated and interrelated lives of the villagers and as he begins to see a trace of Mr. Sam's strength in himself, he is finally able to face up to his problems.

Mature

BAWDEN, NINA. *Tortoise by Candlelight.* Ballantine, 1963, O.P. In a strange household deserted by the mother, fourteen-year-old Emmie struggles to protect her aging grandmother, her drunken affable father, a nubile older sister, and a young brother, Oliver. Oliver is reminiscent of the amoral children in *High Wind in Jamaica,* with habits that hurt and harm, the face of an angel, and a sister who covers for him.

* BOOTH, ESMA RIDEOUT. *The Village, the City and the World.*

JAMES, HENRY. *Washington Square.* Modern Lib, $2.95 (P/several). In addition to being the classic portrayal of the plain rich girl courted by a wastrel, this book is also a poignantly etched portrait of the daughter of a domineering father.

JARRELL, RANDALL. *The Animal Family.* il. by Maurice Sendak. Pantheon, 1965, $3.50 (P/Dell, price not set). The hunter leads a solitary life until the mermaid joins him. In time the hunter brings home a bear cub, then a young lynx; these two "children" find and bring home the third, a shipwrecked boy. Basic family concepts are seen in this fantasy which outlines the individuality of those who share one roof, suggesting a bond stronger than blood holding them together.

LAWRENCE, D. H. *Sons and Lovers.* Viking Pr, 1968, $4.75 (P/several). Paul Morel is the favorite of his mother and despises his coal miner father. A sensitive boy with a talent for painting, he is attracted to two women, but his real affection always centers around his mother. Only after her death can he mature, impeded neither by her nor by his lover.

* LEE, HARPER. *To Kill a Mockingbird.*

MOODY, RALPH. *Little Britches.* P/Bantam, 1950, $.75. Not self-pity but pluck characterizes the experiences of a family struggling on a Colorado ranch in the early 1900s.

MORRIS, DESMOND. *The Naked Ape: A Zoologist's Study of the Human Animal.* McGraw, 1968, $5.95 (P/Dell, $.95). Zoologist Morris proposes that man's behavior patterns are inherited from his remote ape ancestors. Man still hunts for a living, establishes a pair-bond in marriage, indulges in extensive grooming practices, and claims and defends his territory.

O'NEILL, EUGENE. *A Long Day's Journey into Night.* Yale U Pr, 1956, $6.75 (P/Yale U Pr, $1.95). The terrible things that members of a family can innocently as well as deliberately do to each other are relentlessly and honestly portrayed in this tragic play about the four Tyrones, as drink and dope dull their painful futureless existence.

* TEAGUE, BOB. *Letters to a Black Boy.*

Friendships

Primary

* ANDERSON, NEIL. *Meet Sandy Smith.*

ANGLUND, JOAN WALSH. *A Friend Is Someone Who Likes You.* il. by author. HBJ, 1958, $2.50. A friend can be a boy or a girl, a cat or a dog. It can be a brook that "lets you sit quietly beside it" when you don't feel like speaking.

* BOYD, MARY E. *Joy.*

BROWN, MARCIA. *Felice.* il. by author. Scribner, 1958, $4.37. Gino, the gondolier's son, adopts a cat to accompany him on his travels through the canals of Venice. The charm and splendor of Venice is portrayed in vivid blues, lavenders, and pinks while the universal theme of a boy's love for an animal is quietly relayed.

* COHEN, MIRIAM. *Will I Have a Friend?*

DESBARATS, PETER. *Gabrielle and Selena.* il. by Nancy Grossman. HBJ, 1968, $3.25. Two friends, one black and one white, decide to trade places with each other. Their parents go along with the trade but each girl decides she likes her own home best.

FISHER, AILEEN L. *Listen, Rabbit.* il. by Shimin Symeon. TY Crowell, 1964, $3.50. A little boy tries through summer, fall, and winter to make friends with a wild rabbit. When spring comes, he hasn't exactly succeeded, but he has discovered a wonderful secret. He now has "five baby rabbits to watch grow up!"

FREEMAN, DON. *Corduroy.* il. by author. Viking Pr, 1968, $3.50 (P/

Viking Pr, $.95). One day Corduroy, a toy bear who lives in a big department store, discovers he has lost a button. That night he goes to look for it and in his search he sees many strange and wonderful things. He does not find his button, but the following morning he finds what he has always wanted—a friend, Lisa. Love and affection prevail through the friendship of Corduroy and Lisa, a pretty black girl.

GODDEN, RUMER. *The Mousewife.* il. by William Pene DuBois. Viking Pr, 1951, $3.00 (P/Viking Pr, $.65). Slowly a mousewife realizes how unhappy her friend the dove is, locked in his cage. She "could only think of it as a mouse, but she could feel as the dove could feel." She unlatches the cage, thus granting the dove his freedom, but losing the comfort of their conversations. Illustrations in soft gray match the gently worded text.

HOLMAN, FELICE. *Victoria's Castle.* il. by Lillian Hoban. G & D, 1966, $3.95. There must come a day when children are able to separate their fantasies from the world about them. That day comes for Victoria at the end of this book. An understanding mother and a bewildered father, who nevertheless gives Victoria support when she needs him, help this day to come in a normal, happy manner. The Victorian setting of the story adds to its charm.

HURD, EDITH THATCHER. *Who Will Be Mine?* il. by Georgia Longini. Golden Gate, 1966, $3.50. The photographs are so beautifully posed as to look unposed. The text, though slight, has a theme most children will recognize—the need for a friend of one's very own.

HUTCHINS, PAT. *Tom and Sam.* il. by author. Macmillan, 1968, $4.50 (P/Macmillan, $.95). Tom and Sam try to outdo one another in their garden and become temporary enemies.

* JOHNSTON, JOHANNA. *That's Right Edie.*

KEATS, EZRA JACK. *Goggles!* il. by author. Macmillan, 1969, $4.50 (P/Macmillan, $.95). This story shows the relationship between Archie and Peter, and the helpfulness of the dog Willie. The pictures themselves could readily tell the story and because there is little narration, a child can progress rather rapidly through the story of the peril of the young boys. Keats' characters are black and the inner city setting provides the young readers with a broadening experience. Peter and Archie seem so real that children will want to talk about them way past the last page of the book.

————. *A Letter to Amy.* il. by author. Har-Row, 1968, $3.95. Peter is planning a birthday party that at the moment is an "all-boy" party. When he expresses a desire to invite another friend, Amy, he is encouraged to do so by his mother; however, he isn't quite sure the fellows will understand his wanting a girl at the party. Peter begins to build some personal values of his own when he makes a decision, sticks by it, and is very pleased that he did.

KEITH, EROS. *A Small Lot.* il. by author. Bradbury, 1968, $4.25. Jay and Bob live in a great city and between their apartment buildings is a small lot. Every day the boys play "castle, jungle, or just anything" in the lot. When there seems to be danger that the lot will be used for some business purpose, Jay and Bob make their lot into a park. Imaginative pictures are in full color and realistic ones are in black and white—until "the park" becomes a reality!

* LEXAU, JOAN M. *I Should Have Stayed in Bed.*

* ———. *The Rooftop Mystery.*

LOBEL, ARNOLD. *Frog and Toad Together.* il. by author. Har-Row, 1972, $2.50. Continuing the saga of this rib-tickling twosome are five tales. In one of them, Toad makes a list of things to do. No. 1 on the list is "wake up." This book should wake up the reluctant reader.

* McGOVERN, ANN. *Little Wolf.*

* MANNHEIM, GRETE. *The Two Friends.*

PENE DU BOIS, WILLIAM. *Bear Circus.* il. by author. Viking Pr., 1971, $4.95. When grasshoppers demolish the bears' food supply, the kangaroos help their friends find a new home. The bears, after seven years' preparation, repay the favor by performing a circus. But the bears learn that "true friends never owe each other anything." The superb illustrations fill the book with dramatic sweeps.

SCHICK, ELEANOR. *Making Friends.* il. by author. Macmillan, 1969, $3.95. The story is told through pictures alone. The little boy accompanies his mother on a shopping tour and is continuously attracted by potential "friends" along the way. The response is most complete when he meets a real friend, and they run to the swings together.

SCHWEITZER, BYRD BAYLOR. *Amigo.* il. by Garth Williams. Macmillan, 1963, $4.95. Francisco wants a dog, but the only dog the family can afford is a prairie dog, for it finds its own food. The family is poor. The realism of the book turns into gentle fantasy as the prairie dog Amigo sets out to tame the boy!

SELZ, IRMA. *Katy, Be Good.* il by author. Lothrop, 1962, $2.75. This is a humorous story of a little Amish girl's visit to New York. When Katy visits her friend, she is introduced to TV, air conditioning, baby sitters, big stores, and escalators.

STEIG, WILLIAM. *Amos and Boris.* il. by author. FS & G, 1971, $4.50. Amos, a mouse, and Boris, a whale, become great friends when Boris rescues Amos from drowning. As Boris rides Amos toward shore on his back, they share their innermost secrets. They part promising never to forget each other and vowing to come to each other's aid should the need arise. Many years later Amos is able to repay Boris's kindness when the latter is tossed on shore by a tidal wave and stranded on a beach. The book points up the value of true and lasting friendship.

* TURKLE, BRINTON. *Thy Friend, Obadiah.*

UDRY, JANICE M. *Let's Be Enemies.* il. by Maurice Sendak. Har-Row, 1961, $2.50 (P/Schol Bk Serv, $.75). James and John have a rather superficial argument because, as John says, "James always wants to be the boss." The quarrel is resolved simply, and they continue their friendship. Sendak's illustrations are especially effective in portraying the emotions of the two boys, and one notes a change in the weather which corresponds to the change in the feelings of James and John.

VOGEL, ILSE-MARGARET. *Hello Henry.* il. by author. Parents', 1965, $3.95. Being lost in a supermarket can be fun, especially if you meet someone like you who's also lost. That's how the first Henry meets the second Henry, and they have a wonderful time being lost. More than that, they become friends.

WILL AND NICOLAS (WILLIAM LIPKIND AND NICOLAS MORDVINOFF). *Four-Leaf Clover.* il. by Nicolas Mordvinoff. HBJ, 1959, $3.00. Two boys, one white and one Negro, search for a four-leaf clover because they can use a little luck. Their search is successful, funny, and breathlessly exciting, but their greatest luck is that they are friends.

ZOLOTOW, CHARLOTTE. *The Hating Book.* il. by Ben Shecter. Har-Row, 1969, $2.95. A little girl tells of several instances of being rebuffed by her friend, ending with the comment, "I hated my friend." Finally, at the urging of her mother, she goes to see the friend and asks her why she's been so "rotten." The answer is that "Sue said Jane said you said I looked like a freak." The actual remark had been that she looked "neat." The point of the book is clear as the two friends make plans to play together the following day.

————. *My Friend John.* il. by Ben Shecter. Har-Row, 1968, $2.95. A brief but basic explanation of the friendship of two young boys is presented. Their knowledge of each other's strengths and weaknesses is stressed, and the book concludes with the idea that they like "everything that's important" about each other.

————. *The White Marble.* il. by Lilian Obligado. Abelard, 1963, $3.50. The friendship of a boy and girl, both about nine years old, who meet on a hot evening in the park as each is walking with his parents, is beautifully and poetically described. The blue and black illustrations have a soft quality reflecting the tenderness of the children's relationship.

Intermediate

BAWDEN, NINA. *The Runaway Summer*. Lippincott, 1969, $3.75. Mary, whose parents are getting a divorce, is sent to live with Grandfather and Aunt Alice in their English seaside home. Though resentful and determined to act hateful, Mary can't help being friends with Simon, who seems to believe her elaborate lies about her family. The arrival of Krishna, an Indian boy brought illegally into the country, leads Mary and Simon to cement their friendship in their efforts to hide him from the police. When Krishna's sudden illness forces them to get help, Mary begins to see that the only way to handle problems is to face them.

* BRINK, CAROL RYRIE. *Caddie Woodlawn.*

* ———. *Two Are Better than One.*

BURGWYN, MEBANE. *The Crackajack Pony.* il. by Dale Payson. Lippincott, 1969, $3.95. Cliff, a Negro boy, is surprised that he and Ted, a white boy, get acquainted so easily. Cliff is excited about the pony Ted is riding and Ted is so generous that the two boys soon become friends. Cliff wants to learn about ponies and most of all wants to own one. Ted's grandfather breeds ponies and encourages the two boys in their friendship which flourishes until Cliff misinterprets a remark of Ted's. Cliff finds that neither friendship nor ownership are easy responsibilities.

CALHOUN, MARY. *Honestly, Katie John.* il. by Paul Frame. Har-Row, 1963, $3.50 (P/Schol Bk Serv, $.75). Katie John, a tomboyish sixth grader, announces that she hates boys after being teased about them by some of her girl friends. Edwin, her special friend, overhears her and terminates their friendship. Katie John has several unhappy experiences as she attempts to understand her own feelings. At last she grows in maturity and once again establishes a friendship with Edwin. Girls who identify with Katie John will want to read two earlier books about her.

CARLSON, NATALIE SAVAGE. *Ann Aurelia and Dorothy.* il. by Dale Payson. Har-Row, 1968, $3.95 (P/Dell, $.75). Ann Aurelia's mother sends her to live with a variety of foster parents when she remarries. Staying with foster parents is an unhappy experience until Ann Aurelia comes to live with untidy but loving Mrs. Hicken. It is during her stay with Mrs. Hicken that Ann Aurelia meets Dorothy, a Negro girl who becomes her best friend. This is a refreshing change from the books in which a Negro child has all of the problems.

CHURCH, RICHARD. *The White Doe.* il. by John Ward. John Day, 1969, $4.50. The friendship of Billy Lander, a nobleman's son, and Tom Winter, the son of a woodman, is a firm one despite the social mores of England in 1910. Trouble arrives with Harold Sims, who respects neither the friendship of the other two nor their concern for the wild-life on the Lander estate. In the exciting climax Harold threatens a doe and fawn who are especially important to Tom. Tom must over-come his hostility to save not only the animals, but Harold as well.

DE ANGELI, MARGUERITE. *Bright April*. il. by author. Doubleday, 1946, $3.50. Set in Philadelphia during the 1940s, the story is about April Bright, a ten-year-old Negro girl. It tells of April's first encounters with prejudice when she attends an integrated school and belongs to a Brownie troop. The Bright family is a close-knit, happy one. Papa works as a letter carrier, Ken is in the army, Chris is studying to be a nurse, and Tom rattles and taps his drumsticks constantly.

* DOUGHTY, W. DYRE. *Crimson Moccasins*.

ENRIGHT, ELIZABETH. *Gone-Away Lake*. il. by Beth and Joe Krush. HBJ, 1957, $3.95. The discovery of an abandoned summer colony bordering a swamp leads to a vacation of glorious exploration and adventure for Portia and her cousin Julian.

* GAGE, WILSON. *Miss Osborne-the-Mop*.

GODDEN, RUMER. *Little Plum*. il. by Jean Primrose. Viking Pr, 1963, $3.50. Belinda and her cousin Nona watch the house next door being renovated and see the little girl, Gem, who moves in. However, their attempts at friendship fail, partially because Belinda is considered "too rough" by Gem's aunt and partially because Belinda herself sends some rather insulting notes. As Belinda learns more about Gem, she becomes more understanding, and a party for the Japanese dolls owned by all three girls brings them together.

* HAYWOOD, CAROLYN. *Eddie the Dog Holder*.

* HOFF, CAROL. *Chris*.

* HUSTON, ANNE AND JANE YOLEN. *Trust a City Kid*.

* JONES, ADRIENNE. *Sail, Calypso*.

KONIGSBURG, E. L. *(George)*. Atheneum, 1970, $4.95. Ben is a bright, gifted boy with problems—both family and school, compounded by (George). Up to now (George) and Ben had existed compatibly in the same body (Ben's), and in fact (George) probably had a great deal to do with Ben's brilliance. Now Ben feels the need for visible, peer acceptance and (George), in a huff, goes silent. Ben suffers suspicion of theft at school and cruel treatment by his stepmother. He finds a thought-provoking solution to his problems by assuming the blame and punishment for the crime he did not commit to spare an older boy who had been exploiting him. Some incidents and char-acters are unreal but the author's skill holds all together.

———. *Jennifer, Hecate, Macbeth, William McKinley, and Me, Eliza-*

beth. il. by author. Atheneum, 1967, $3.50. When you're lonely and bored as Elizabeth is, feet clad in Pilgrim shoes dangling from a tree and attached to a strange girl can mean the beginning of a friendship. Jennifer claims to be a witch and accepts Elizabeth as an apprentice. Secret meetings on Saturday, forbidden foods, watermelon on New Year's Day, and a very special toad acquired in the middle of winter are a few of the unusual elements in this story of a growing friendship. Both Elizabeth and Jenny grow into maturity when they put off the pretense of being witches and accept each other for what they are.

LITTLE, JEAN. *Take Wing*. il. by Jerry Lazar. Little, 1968, $4.95. Shy, sensitive Laurel is unable to make friends because of the demands made on her time by her seven-year-old retarded brother James. When her mother is hospitalized and an aunt comes to run the household the family acknowledges for the first time that James is "different." The family rallies and demonstrates that love and courage can help the handicapped boy while Laurie's determination wins her a friend.

MOSKIN, MARIETTA D. *With an Open Hand*. il. by Ann Grifalconi. John Day, 1967, $4.50. In this sequel to *The Best Birthday Party*, Jennie is upset when her best friend brings another girl to their secret club. Her anger increases when the new girl's idea instead of hers is chosen as their summer project. Jennie tries to demand loyalty and finds that she loses her friend completely. Through a series of events Jennie discovers the rights and responsibilities of friendship.

ORGEL, DORIS. *Next Door to Xanadu*. il. by Dale Payson. Har-Row, 1969, $3.95 (P/WSP, $.60). Patricia Malone is going to be ten years old soon, but she still has no special friend. Her two great wishes are that she find a friend and that she be thin so that Bill Wexler and Charlie Kriefer won't call her Fatsy Patsy any more. One day when Patricia comes home from school she finds that a family has moved in next door with a girl her own age. Friendship with Dorothy begins to change Patricia's life.

ROBINSON, JOAN G. *When Marnie Was There*. Coward, 1968, $4.25. Is Marnie real or imaginary? Lonely Anna doesn't know and doesn't care. Whenever she goes to the deserted Marsh house, Marnie is there and they have fun sharing secrets, playing on the beach, and exploring by boat. Then Anna realizes a family has moved into the Marsh house and knows that she will not see Marnie again. Fantasy is skillfully mixed with reality as Anna learns about friendship.

RYDBERG, ERNIE. *The Dark of the Cave*. il. by Carl Kidwell. McKay, 1965, $2.95. Ronnie is blind, so he doesn't know that Garth, the new boy next door, is black. However, he senses something odd in the behavior of other people who meet Garth. The two boys become good friends and spend a wonderful summer together, during which they explore a dangerous mysterious cave. After Ronnie has his operation, his suspicions about Garth are confirmed, but their relationship remains the same. Garth is still his best friend.

SHURA, MARY FRANCES. *Runaway Home.* il. by James Spanfeller. Knopf, 1965, $3.25. Mike, unhappy with his new home, takes a job tending goats to make money to run away. An accident occurs and Mike helps save a young girl. His new friends come to show their appreciation and he discovers home is not just a place but a place where friends are.

SIMPSON, DOROTHY. *A Lesson for Janie.* il. by Dorothy Bayley Morse. Lippincott, 1958, $2.95. When Myra, a city girl, moves to a pictur- esque Maine Island, Janie is expected to be friendly with her. Soon differences between them grow into a quarrel. Every day the two girls compete for the driftwood needed by their families, and new jealousies arise between them. An exciting and dangerous adventure helps each to learn what the other is really like.

* STERLING, DOROTHY. *Mary Jane.*

STOLZ, MARY. *A Dog on Barkham Street.* il. by Leonard Shortall. P/Dell, 1968, $.75. Edward Frost's life has one constant irritation—his neighbor, Martin. To Edward, Martin is simply a bully to be alter- nately avoided and teased. With his father's "encouragement," Ed- ward is made aware of Martin's needs and begins to understand an- other person's problems.

VAN DER VEER, JUDY. *Higher Than the Arrow.* il. by F. Leslie Mathews. Golden Gate, 1969, $3.95. Francie is a sensitive and talented twelve- year-old Indian girl living on a reservation in southern California. Her affection for a coyote and her desire to make a beautiful statue of St. Francis help the girl to learn deeper meanings of trust and friend- ship. Before this can happen, however, Francie has to accept the white girl, Lucy, who also has a special talent for art, and who, though she wants to be a friend, is at first perceived as a rival.

WHITE, E. B. *Charlotte's Web.* il. by Garth Williams. Har-Row, 1952, $3.95 (P/Dell, $.95). Fern, a little girl; Wilbur, a runt pig; and Charlotte, a spider, form a fast friendship. Wilbur becomes distraught when he discovers he is to be killed. The devoted spider spins mes- sages about Wilbur into her web in order to save his life. People come to see the messages and marvel at Wilbur. As a final act of love and friendship, Charlotte accompanies Wilbur to the fair even though she knows her life is nearly over. Her final message and Wilbur's ribbon assure his living. Wilbur's final act of love and friendship is to care for Charlotte's egg sac so her children can survive.

Junior

ARTHUR, RUTH M. *The Whistling Boy.* il. by Margery Gill. Atheneum, 1969, $4.50. Kirsty's stepmother is so much like her own mother that she finds it impossible to accept her. This leads the young English girl to take a fruitpicking job away from home. She finds an inner peace in the country, as well as a mysterious boy who whistles a strange tune she has heard somewhere before. Kirsty finds herself caring deeply for the boy, whose past is filled with many unanswered questions. This new concern plus a series of accidents at home help her to return to her stepmother with a new, more mature understanding of their relationship. A realistic story with an aura of fantasy.

BROWN, ROY. *The Viaduct*. Macmillan, 1968, $4.50. A sequel to *A Saturday in Pudney*. In this well-executed mystery set in contemporary England, young Phil Benson, last of a family of railroad people, inherits a trunk of apparently worthless papers that belonged to a miserly ancestor who was an engineering genius. Phil, his friend Andy, and old Mr. Felix unravel the mystery of codes and papers to reveal the miser's "hoard," a revolutionary locomotive design.

BURNFORD, SHEILA. *The Incredible Journey*. il. by Carl Burger. Little, 1961, $4.50 (P/Bantam, $.75). A very old bull terrier, a young Labrador retriever, and a Siamese cat make an almost incredible journey through 400 miles of Canadian wilderness to return to their old home. The remarkably well-written and absorbing story is told with great simplicity and understanding. The friendship and group feeling enjoyed by the three is a rare experience for children and young adults to share.

CAVANNA, BETTY. *Going on Sixteen*. il. by Morton Winslow. Westminster, 1946, $3.75. Daydreaming Julie finds herself a wallflower at the high school dance, because she is not able to meet either boys or girls easily. Through varied interests, entering and winning an art contest, and caring for her pets, Julie is able to adjust to her group and to achieve a better relationship with her father.

* CHESSMAN, RUTH. *Bound for Freedom.*

* CHURCH, RICHARD. *The White Doe.*

* DALY, MAUREEN. *Seventeenth Summer.*

DERLETH, AUGUST W. *The Irregulars Strike Again*. Hawthorn, 1964, $3.50. Steve and Sim, boy detectives, uncover deer poachers while camping out during a Wisconsin winter. The descriptions of the setting capture the feel of a northern winter.

FARJEON, ANNABEL. *Maria Lupin*. il. by James Hunt. Abelard, 1967, $3.75. Marie, a London schoolgirl burdened by her father's unexplained absence, her overworked and impatient mother, and boring days in school, finds her life changed when Ivan Abraham secretly gives her piano lessons. Because of her music and her friendship with Ivan and Sampson, Maria is able to solve her problems at home and at school.

FARMER, PENELOPE. *The Magic Stone.* il. by John Kaufmann. HBJ, 1964, $3.75. A magic stone draws two girls, Caroline and Alice, together; one is from the country and the other from the London slums. Their experiences with the stone help the girls to develop a deep friendship and a better understanding of both their families.

* HUNT, IRENE. *No Promises in the Wind.*

JONES, CORDELIA. *Nobody's Garden.* il. by Victor Ambrus. Scribner, 1966, $3.95. Not even the talkative and friendly Hilary can bring her friend Bridget, a lonely war orphan, out of her painfully quiet and reticent ways. Their "Secret Garden" in the bombed neighborhood of London becomes their hideaway and here Bridget, more spontaneous and natural, is eventually able to confront the unhappy secret of her war experience and face the future. This is a memorable book of friendship and understanding written with warmth, feeling, and humor.

* KONIGSBURG, E. L. (*George*).

* LAMPEL, RUSIA. *That Summer with Ora.*

LEVITIN, SONIA. *Journey to America.* il. by Charles Robinson. Atheneum, 1970, $4.25. As Jews are no longer safe in Hitler's Germany, Lisa and her family must abandon their home and go to America. Forced to wait in Switzerland while Papa earns their passage fare, the family courageously suffers poverty and loneliness, but they are able to survive with the help of new-found friends. This well-told and deeply moving story is both authentic and memorable.

NEUFELD, JOHN. *Lisa, Bright and Dark.* SG Phillips, 1969, $4.50 (P/ NAL, $.60). An unusual story of how three teenage girls attempt to help their friend Lisa, whose parents cannot be convinced that she needs psychiatric treatment. Tangled relationships and mounting frustrations finally frighten the parents into taking action.

* QUIMBY, MYRTLE. *The Cougar.*

STERLING, DOROTHY. *Mary Jane.* il. by Ernest Crichlow. Doubleday, 1959, $3.95. Mary Jane must enter seventh grade at newly integrated Wilson Junior High. During her first days at school she is either taunted or ignored by all the white students, except for Sally. The rescue of a half-grown squirrel leads to a bond between the two girls. Hiding and feeding Furry gives the girls a common cause and helps them to forget their differences, bringing about the first tentative gestures of friendship.

WALKER, DIANA. *An Eagle for Courage.* Abelard, 1968, $4.25. Trudy and Mary have been friends for years. When Trudy's cousin Tony flies into the Canadian wilderness to spend the summer with Trudy's family at the fire tower, Mary, fearing the loss of her friend, uses her

Indian heritage as an excuse to avoid Tony. Trudy, determined that the three should be close friends, is insensitive to Mary's behavior. The crisis of a forest fire finally forces the girls to examine their own feelings.

WALSH, JILL P. *Fireweed.* FS & G, 1970, $3.95. In London, during the blitz of 1940, a fifteen-year-old runaway who calls himself Bill meets Julie, a somewhat younger runaway. They cast their lot together and are so jubilant about being on their own that their friendship is almost gay, nearly untouched by the grim details of war around them. To escape detection, they move into a bombed-out cellar, where Julie is buried alive in fallen rubble. She survives, and Bill finally sees her reunited with her family. He realizes that their special feeling for one another, born of crisis, must inevitably end.

* WEBER, LENORA MATTINGLEY. *I Met a Boy I Used to Know.*

Senior

BRADBURY, RAY. *Something Wicked This Way Comes.* S & S, 1962, $5.95. A carnival comes to town and two boys discover a wax museum of living people, a mirror that steals souls, and a sinister carousel. One boy escapes from this weird incarnation of evil; the other almost succumbs. An understanding father shows the boys how easy it is to get on the "carousel," and how difficult it is to get off, and he demonstrates the need to be eternally alert to the "night people."

COHEN, TOM. *Three Who Dared.* Doubleday, 1969, $3.50 (P/Avon, $.75). Three young men—two white, one black—go south to participate in the civil rights movement. Henry Aronson plans to do only two weeks' legal work for the Mississippi Summer Project but instead gives up his job in Hartford and stays. John O'Neal gives up his dream of becoming a New York playwright in order to bring the Free Southern Theater to black people. Eric Weinberger endures abuse and mistreatment to give a poor black community dignity and a livelihood.

HENTOFF, NAT. *I'm Really Dragged but Nothing Gets Me Down.* S & S, 1968, $3.95 (P/Dell, $.60). As Jeremy Wolf struggles for identity, he is confronted with many choices related to drugs, sex, involvement in demonstrations, the draft, and the value of higher education. The book has no formal plot; it is a set of conversations capturing the fragmentation and disorientation felt by the young through chapters that depict Jeremy's world in contrast to that of his father.

* HILL, GRACE L. *A Patch of Blue.*

* JOSEPH, STEPHEN M. *The Me Nobody Knows: Children's Voices from the Ghetto.*

WESTHEIMER, DAVID. *My Sweet Charlie.* P/NAL, 1965, $.75. Marlene Chambers, seventeen, is the epitome of the Southern bigot. Forced to leave home when her father discovers she is pregnant, Marlene seeks sanctuary in a deserted summer house. This haven is soon invaded by Charles Roberts, an educated Northern black man who is fleeing the law after killing a man in a fight. Slowly their antagonism turns to mutual liking and respect, and Marlene comes to view Charles as a man and not as a Negro. The story may lack probability, but the situations are handled well and the plot moves at a good pace. Lessons in relationships between races emerge as the story develops.

Mature

HILL, GRACE L. *A Patch of Blue.* G & D, 1961, $2.50. Set in what appears to be the rural South, the story contrasts the life of Selina, a blind teenage white girl living with her prostitute mother and drunken grandfather, with a world of beauty as described by Selina's only friend, Gordon, a kind and gentle young black man.

STEINBECK, JOHN. *Of Mice and Men.* Viking Pr, 1937, $4.00 (P/several). The painful responsibilities of friendship are explored in this tragic story of the relationship between two migratory workers: George and Lennie. Lennie is a huge man of great strength and simple mind. Caring for Lennie becomes increasingly difficult for George. Lennie loves small animals, but because he is unable to control his strength, he often maims or kills them. When it is the matter of a girl's death rather than an animal's, George must mercifully kill Lennie to save him from a mob. The book is also available as a play.

Peer Relationships

Primary

AVERILL, ESTHER. *Jenny's First Party.* il. by author. Har-Row, 1948, $2.92. In this allegorical tale, a little black cat overcomes her timidity at her first party.

AYER, JACQUELINE. *Nu Dang and His Kite and A Wish for Little Sister.* il. by author. HBJ, 1959, $3.50. These two charming picture story books give a vivid picture of family living on the exciting *klongs* (Canals) of Bangkok, Thailand. The authentic sketches of the children, their friends, and families will make any reader feel he is there, chasing a kite with Nu Dang or helping Little Sister.

BEIM, JERROLD. *Swimming Hole.* il. by Louis Darling. Morrow, 1951, $3.78. This is a very pointed story in which Steve, a new boy in town, disagrees with the local practice of integrated swimming. Refusing to swim with boys who are "colored," he ties their clothes in knots while they are swimming. The white boys then refuse to swim with Steve because of his color, a bright sunburned red. Steve apologizes and they all go swimming together.

BEMELMANS, LUDWIG. *Madeline.* il. by author. Viking Pr, 1939, $3.50 (P/Viking Pr, $.95). The story of Madeline's individuality comes through the rhythmic verse in a steady beat. A scar from an appendectomy makes her the envy of all her peers.

* BLUE, ROSE. *I Am Here, Yo Estoy Aqui.*

* BONSALL, CROSBY. *The Case of the Hungry Stranger.*

CLEARY, BEVERLY. *Henry and the Paper Route.* il. by Louis Darling. Morrow, 1957, $3.95. Henry Huggins is too young for a paper route. Determined to show that he is ready for the responsibility, Henry helps Scooter, an older carrier, with his route and then takes over when Scooter is sick. His chance finally comes when Murph gives up his new route. Henry, now old enough, proves he can handle the job by outwitting Ramona, an imaginative four-year-old who has unusual ways of expressing her admiration for paper boys.

COOPER, ELIZABETH K. *The Fish from Japan.* il. by Beth and Joe Krush. HBJ, 1969, $3.75. Harvey wants a pet, but he is not even allowed to feed Karl's turtle at school. When an uncle in Japan promises to send Harvey a fish, he prepares for it and tells his friends about it. The fish comes at last, but it is only a paper fish, so Harvey hides it. Taking an empty jar to school, Harvey tells his classmates that the fish is transparent and can hardly be seen in the water. Some children claim to have seen parts of it and Harvey lets Karl feed the fish. After Harvey's fish is "eaten by a cat," Harvey and Karl feed the turtle together. A friendship has been formed!

* CRETAN, GLADYS YESSAYAN. *Run Away Habeeb!*

DAVIS, ALICE VAUGHT. *Timothy Turtle.* il. by Guy Brown Wiser. HBJ, 1940, $2.75. It takes all of his animal friends thinking and working together to help Timothy turn right side up again.

* EICKE, EDNA. *The Children Who Got Married.*

* JUSTUS, MAY. *New Boy in School.*

LIONNI, LEO. *Swimmy.* il. by author. Pantheon, 1963, $3.50. Swimmy shows the other little fish in the school that only by swimming in the shape of a large fish can they hope to be safe from the bigger fish.

* ORMSBY, VIRGINIA H. *What's Wrong with Julio?*

SCHICK, ELEANOR. *Katie Goes to Camp.* il. by author. Macmillan, 1968, $3.95. The action of the story—a first time at summer camp—shows peer relationships at their best. It is particularly through the pictures that the warmth of the story is conveyed. The need for security in unfamiliar surroundings is shown through Katie's doll. (The idea that the doll is the one who is first suffering is appropriate and will be pleasing to understanding children.)

YASHIMA, TARO. *Crow Boy.* il. by author. Viking Pr, 1955, $3.50 (P/ Viking Pr, $.95). This warm and sensitive story centers on the problems of a frightened, introverted country boy who is ridiculed by his classmates. A new teacher finds his special talents and brings them to the attention of the other children. Although Chibi never becomes part of the group, the children realize the wrong they have done him and regret it. A picture book in format, it will be most appreciated by the eight- to ten-year-olds.

Intermediate

BRODSKY, MIMI. *The House at 12 Rose Street.* il. by David Hodges. Abelard, 1966, $3.75 (P/WSP, $.60). Oaktown becomes involved in conflict when the Franklins, a Negro family, move into the house at 12 Rose Street. Bobby Myers is caught in the middle because he wants Will Franklin as a friend and as a member of his scout troop. The problem is that his best friend doesn't. The effect of a racially tense situation on the friendships within a group of boys is realistically portrayed.

* BUCHARDT, NELLIE. *A Surprise for Carlotta.*

CLEARY, BEVERLY. *Mitch and Amy.* il. by George Porter. Morrow, 1967, $4.25. Mitch and Amy Huff, nine-year-old twins, quarrel over everything from who gets the cereal box top to what TV program to watch. They do agree on the necessity to do something about the school bully who persistently bothers both of them.

———. *Otis Spofford.* il. by Louis Darling. Morrow, 1953, $3.95. This humorous book is an excellent one for reading aloud. Otis, a mischievous, fun loving boy, is always getting in and out of trouble. His mother, a dancing teacher, is busy earning their living and often leaves Otis on his own. This book tells of several episodes in Otis's life— from his sneaking vitamins to a white rat to "disprove" a diet experiment, to getting his final "come-uppance" when a trick on Ellen Tebbits backfires.

* COLMAN, HILA. *Classmates by Request.*

ESTES, ELEANOR, *The Hundred Dresses.* il. by Louis Slobodkin. HBJ, 1944, $3.95. A little Polish girl in an American school wants to win the acceptance of her classmates. Through her skill in art, shabby Wanda makes good her boast of having one hundred dresses and wins the acceptance she needs.

FITZHUGH, LOUISE. *Harriet the Spy*. il. by author. Har-Row, 1964, $3.95 (P/Dell, $.95). Harriet records in a notebook her reactions to and observations of various people who live in her New York neighborhood, because she wants to become a writer and writers must be good observers. When Janey and Sport, her best friends, discover the candor with which she has been writing, she is ostracized. Harriet then evaluates her friendships and develops some insight into the feelings and needs of herself and others.

FOLTZ, MARY JANE. *Nicolau's Prize*. il. by Brinton. McGraw, 1967, O.P. It is the year 1870. Nicolau Terra and his Portuguese family have lived for a year at a whaling station on Pigeon Point, California. The only time Nicolau doesn't wish to return to the Azores is when the whaling station is in full operation. When Nicolau smells of whale oil the school children make fun of him and hold their noses. Ownership of a carriage salvaged from the sea makes it possible for the lonely boy to accept his new home and to understand the words of the old saying, "A journey of a thousand miles begins with a single step."

FOX, PAULA. *How Many Miles to Babylon?* il. by Paul Giovanopoulos. D White, 1967, $3.95 (P/WSP, $.60). James Douglas lives in Brooklyn with his three great-aunts. He runs away from school one day in search of his mother. A gang of boys decide that they can use him in their racket of stealing dogs. James finally escapes and finds his mother sitting on his bed when he returns home. Although there is little hope at the end of this story for a better life for Jim, the reader will not soon forget him.

GRIFFITHS, HELEN. *The Greyhound*. il. by Victor Ambrus. Doubleday, 1964, $3.50. Jamie becomes deeply involved with a gang when he borrows money from the leader in order to buy food for his dog. Forced to help in robberies, his relationship with his mother becomes tense and strained. All ends well, but not without a struggle as Jamie attempts to determine which values should guide his actions.

HAYWOOD, CAROLYN. *Ever-Ready Eddie*. il. by author. Morrow, 1968, $3.75. Because of a delay in returning to school after a vacation, Eddie misses the opportunity to be a candidate for student council membership, but he does become campaign manager for Boodles Cary. Boodles has a formidable opponent in Anna Patricia Wallace and the competition develops a keen edge. Eddie is brought to some serious decisions as the generally light and funny book comes to a close.

HILDICK, E. W. *Manhattan Is Missing*. il. by Jan Palmer. Doubleday, 1969, $3.95 (P/Avon, $.75). Manhattan is a valuable Siamese cat who lives in an apartment in Manhattan. Twelve-year-old Peter Clarke from England assumes responsibility for Manhattan when the Clarke family sublets the apartment. When Peter discovers Manhattan has been stolen the family becomes frantic. All Peter's new friends join in organizing and conducting a search.

HODGES, MARGARET. *The Hatching of Joshua Cobb*. il. by W. T. Mars. FS & G, 1967, $3.25. A camp counselor bullies the boys in Cabin 13 and gives them all nicknames they hate. As the boys stick together they turn the summer vacation into a memorable, happy experience.

HULL, ELEANOR. *A Trainful of Strangers*. il. by Joan Sanden. Atheneum, 1968, $3.95. Eight children of various ethnic backgrounds are stranded for an hour on a subway train. During this hour, several memorable contacts are made—some pleasant, some not so pleasant; but all realistic.

KONIGSBURG, E. L. *About the B'Nai Bagels*. il. by author. Atheneum, 1969, $4.25. A warm and humorous story of a Jewish Little League team. Twelve-year-old Mark Setzer has problems: his mother is manager of the team; his brother is coach. This makes some sticky situations and "overlaps" in his life. And he has worries about losing his best friend. Mark matures, having to make some difficult decisions on his own.

* LAWSON, ROBERT. *They Were Strong and Good.*

MADDOCK, REGINALD. *The Dragon in the Garden*. Little, 1969, $4.50. When the family moves, Jimmy Stewart, who has been educated at home by his intelligent, artistic parents, is enrolled in the local school. Unversed in the ways of getting along with others, Jimmy learns to adjust, but the learning process is marked by the hostility of some of his classmates and even by violence. Adventure centers around Jimmy's find of a dragon fossil and the reformation of the local bully.

* MANN, PEGGY. *The Street of the Flower Boxes.*

MAYNE, WILLIAM. *Pit in the Middle*. il. by Mary Russon. Dutton, 1965, $3.50. Michael is initiated into a gang of boys because they need a navigator. The group works endless hours restoring an old barge on which they hope to sail to Holland. The barge, called the *Pig*, floats under an old deserted mill, full of hazards for the young people who climb regularly through its rafters. Each boy has his own reasons for wanting to leave England when they begin their task of restoration. When the old mill collapses and the barge is destroyed by fire, the boys are no longer certain of their goals but have learned much from working together.

MOLARSKY, OSMOND. *Where the Good Luck Was*. il. by Ingred Fetz. Walck, 1970, $4.25. The engaging story of four young city boys who are raising money to buy a pair of crutches for their friend. The friend cannot use them, and the boys give the crutches to a hospital so that someone else may be helped.

NEVILLE, EMILY CHENEY. *The Seventeenth-Street Gang.* il. by Emily McCully. Har-Row, 1966, $3.50. When Hollis moves into their block, the six children who play together in the Seventeenth-Street Gang label him a "flot"—imaginative Minnow's word for a stuffy adult— and lay plans for making him miserable. One scheme results in Minnow's fall into the East River, and it is Hollis who swims to her aid, making possible the first real overtures of friendship. The story explores the shifting loyalties within the group and reveals contrasts between group attitudes and individuals' feelings.

SANKEY, ALICE. *Music by the Got-Rocks.* il. by Fred Irvin. A Whitman, 1970, $2.95. Jerry and Ken decide to organize a musical combo and enter the school talent show. Despite opposition from a more talented and better equipped rival group, they are able to succeed by working together.

* SARGENT, SHIRLEY. *Yosemite Tomboy.*

SIMON, SHIRLEY. *Best Friend.* il. by Reisie Lonette. Lothrop, 1964, $3.50 (P/WSP, $.60). Jenny's best friend moves to another apartment building and becomes involved in new activities with a new "best friend," leaving Jenny hurt and resentful. Unwillingly at first, Jenny enlarges her own circle of friends and finds confidence and talents she had not known she possessed. Jenny learns about individuality from her family, too, particularly from Grandma, who is living proof of the joy of being one's self.

SNYDER, ZILPHA KEATLEY. *The Egypt Game.* il. by Alton Raible. Atheneum, 1967, $3.95. Melanie and April discover a common interest in reading and imaginative games. So begins the "Egypt game"—a re-creation of ancient rituals which comes to include Melanie's little brother, a new neighbor, and two sixth-grade boys. A murder in the neighborhood creates suspense for the exciting climax.

———. *Today Is Saturday.* il. by John Arms (photographer). Atheneum, 1969, $3.75. Friends, pets, and Saturday activities are the subjects of the poems in this collection. Black and white photographs enhance each poem.

SOUTHALL, IVAN. *Hills End.* St. Martin, 1963, $3.75 (P/WSP, $.60). Few ever missed the annual picnic of Hills End. This year, because of a fabricated tale of prehistoric drawings, seven children are not going. Instead they find themselves climbing up to the caves high above the town, led by their teacher, Miss Godwin, who had planned to explore alone. These events, however, combine to save the lives of the people of Hills End when a sudden, violent storm threatens to devastate the town, maroon their families, and trap the children in the caves.

SPEEVACK, YETTA. *The Spider Plant.* il. by Wendy Watson. Atheneum, 1965, $3.25 (P/WSP, $.50). Carmen Santos finds New York gray and dreary compared to the green landscape of her native Puerto Rico. Thus her new sixth-grade teacher's gift of a spider plant becomes Carmen's most prized possession. When urban renewal forces her family to an uptown high rise, Carmen is unhappy with the change and unable to make friends. The spider plant brings Carmen and her brother Pedro trouble with a policeman, but it also is the key to new friendships and to a new place in school and community activities.

STOLZ, MARY. *The Bully of Barkham Street*. il. by Leonard Shorthall. Har-Row, 1963, $3.50 (P/Dell, $.75). Eleven-year old Martin Hastings, large for his age, unattractive, and a bully, has trouble getting along with other young people. Several unpleasant incidents occur before he begins to realize that he may be at fault and that there are two sides to every issue. A perceptive study of a typical phase of growing up—feeling misunderstood.

* ———. *A Wonderful Terrible Time.*

WRIGHTSON, PATRICIA. *A Racecourse for Andy*. il. by Margaret Horder. HBJ, 1968, $3.75. The boys in the neighborhood play with Andy and protect him even though he is not able to keep up with them intellectually. They are furious with an old tramp who takes Andy's money and pretends he has "sold" him the racetrack. The protective allegiance of a group of friends distinguishes this story of a slow-learning child.

Junior

ALEXANDER, ANNE. *The Pink Dress*. Doubleday, 1959, $3.50. Sue Stevens admires the "in" crowd of the ninth grade. Then she has an opportunity to become a part of the crowd through her friendship with Dave, one of its leaders. When she discovers that the activities of the crowd involve stealing and vandalism, she must decide what her responsibilities are towards her family, friends, and school. Peer relations are portrayed accurately and sensitively, and the problems are relevant to today's teenagers.

ARMSTRONG, RICHARD. *The Mutineers*. il. by Rus Anderson. McKay, 1968, $4.50. Fifteen delinquent boys being transported to Australia for settlement hijack the ship and escape to an uninhabited island. They learn a new respect and need for each other and for the laws and rules of society as they struggle for both physical and emotional survival. The action is fast paced and realistic although the situation is somewhat reminiscent of *Lord of the Flies*.

BEIM, JERROLD. *Trouble after School*. il. by Don Sibley. HBJ, 1957, $3.50. Lee's mother decides to go back to work. Lee, an eighth grader, is thought mature enough to take care of himself; however, he begins to spend too much time with the wrong people. His grades slip, and he plays hooky. When the gang plans to wreck a high school recreation center, Lee realizes the wrongness of their action and talks the gang into working for a junior high center instead.

BERNA, PAUL. *Flood Warning.* il. by Charles Keeping. Pantheon, 1963, $3.54. A severe flood on the Loire in France threatens a boys' school. When six boys and an instructor are trapped in an old tower, their changing attitudes and heroism under stress come forth.

* BONHAM, FRANK. *Durango Street.*

————. *Mystery of the Fat Cat.* il. by Alvin Smith. Dutton, 1968, $3.95. Dogtown Boy's Club is threatened by the health authorities when Buddy is bitten by a rat in the swimming pool. Money is needed to keep the club open. Only the discovery of the death or continued existence of a wealthy cat whose heir is the Boys' Club offers a hope of acquiring the needed funds that can prevent a long, unbearable summer for the boys of Dogtown. The gang tackles the job with humor and realism.

BROWN, ROY. *A Saturday in Pudney.* Macmillan, 1968, $3.95. A jewel robbery involving the disappearance of three-year-old Willy who witnessed it moves his brother Dickie to organize a posse of friends to search for him. After several unexpected twists of events the junior sleuths solve the mystery.

* BURCH, ROBERT. *Queenie Peavy.*

BUTLER, WILLIAM. *The Butterfly Revolution.* Putnam, 1967, $4.95 (P/Ballantine, $.95). "There's going to be a revolution . . . against the butterflies . . . against the birdies, against the slow pace . . . marshmallows, tiddlywinks . . ." The story is told through the diary of Winston Weyn, a slight, bookish thirteen year old who becomes chairman of propaganda when the boys at Camp High Pines revolt, imprison the adults, and involve a neighboring girls' camp. Fun soon changes to fear when beatings and savage accusations occur.

CARSON, JOHN F. *The Twenty-Third Street Crusaders.* FS & G, 1958, $3.95. Some teenage hoodlums placed on probation for assault start to play basketball in the park and much to their surprise end up practicing in a church gymnasium. In making the transition from gang to basketball team, they find themselves idolized by a group of younger boys. In turn, they learn the meaning of responsibility and adult living.

DU JARDIN, ROSAMOND. *Wait for Marcy.* Lippincott, 1950, $3.70 (P/Schol Bk Serv, $.75). Marcy, a fifteen-year-old tomboy, secretly aided by her popular older brother Ken, enters the exciting world of teenage activities. This appealing and fast moving story portrays common problems in boy-girl relationships.

ESTES, ELEANOR. *The Alley*. il. by Edward Ardizzone. HBJ, 1964, $3.95. A fence-enclosed neighborhood of faculty homes on a small college campus in Brooklyn provides the setting for two burglaries. Connie and her friend Billy Maloon keep track of the clues and furnish evidence against two sets of thieves. Careful characterizations of the many children who play in the Alley combine to make a perceptive account of the group. The mystery element adds reader appeal.

* FITZHUGH, LOUISE. *Harriet the Spy*.

GOLDING, WILLIAM. *Lord of the Flies*. Coward, 1962, $5.95 (P/Putnam, $1.25). A group of English schoolboys marooned on a tropical island regress to ritual and savagery in their attempt to establish social order among themselves.

* GRIFFITHS, HELEN. *The Greyhound*.

* HAUGAARD, ERIK CHRISTIAN. *The Little Fishes*.

HAVREVOLD, FINN. *Undertow*. il. by Cathy Babcock Curry. Atheneum, 1968, $4.25. In spite of his parents' strong disapproval, fifteen-year-old Jorn spends a summer vacation on the Norwegian coast with his best friend, Ulf. Uneasy and suspicious of many of Ulf's ideas and actions, Jorn goes along with the more knowledgeable, self-assured older boy and becomes involved in a series of violent episodes. The intense love-hate relationship which develops between the two boys and Ulf's disregard for the law leads to a tragic climax which leaves Jorn saddened but newly appreciative of his parents' wisdom.

* HUNTSBERRY, WILLIAM. *The Big Wheels*.

KNOWLES, JOHN. *Phineas*. Random, 1968, $4.95 (P/Bantam, $.75). A book of six short stories, two of which, "Phineas" and "A Turn with the Sun," are about Devon, the boys' school of *A Separate Peace*. Both are stories of boys growing up in an all-boy world who have problems relating to their peers and understanding themselves.

LEE, MILDRED. *The Skating Rink*. Seabury, 1969, $3.95 (P/Dell, $.60). Tuck Faraday is a shy fifteen-year-old farm boy who, because of his awkwardness and stuttering, is accepted neither by his peers nor by his family. He becomes interested in a new skating rink which is being built near his home and is trained by the owner to be the star skater on opening night. His success brings courage, self-confidence, and self-respect, which lead not only to an improvement in his speech, but also in his relations with others.

* LIPSYTE, ROBERT. *The Contender*.

* MADDOCK, REGINALD. *The Pit*.

* ———. *The Dragon in the Garden*.

* PEYTON, K. M. *Flambards.*

PHIPSON, JOAN. *Peter and Butch.* HBJ, 1969, $4.50. Fourteen-year-old Peter tries very hard to establish his masculine role in a fatherless family by changing his name to Butch and seeking the notice of a gang of older boys. After the gang is arrested, he finds companionship with his peers at a boys' club. Association with members of the club helps Butch develop his own character as Peter.

* RICHARDSON, GRACE. *Apples Every Day.*

* ROBINSON, VERONICA. *David in Silence.*

* SOUTHALL, IVAN. *Hills End.*

STANKEVICH, BORIS. *Two Green Bars.* HBJ, 1967, $3.75. Leadership presents Howard Freeman with many problems the summer he is elected leader of his Boy Scout patrol by his two best friends. Howard shows his growing awareness of the responsibilities and qualities of a leader as he relates the experiences of the trio when a new boy joins their patrol just in time for camp.

* STRACHAN, MARGARET P. *Patience and a Mulberry Leaf.*

* SULLIVAN, MARY W. *Jokers Wild.*

* YOUNG, BOB AND JAN. *Across the Tracks.*

* ———. *Where Tomorrow?*

* ZINDEL, PAUL. *My Darling, My Hamburger.*

* ———. *The Pigman.*

Senior

* FREEDMAN, BENEDICT AND NANCY. *Mrs. Mike.*

GODDEN, RUMER. *An Episode of Sparrows.* Viking Pr, 1955, $5.50 (P/ Viking Pr, $1.45). The sparrows are the street children of a bombed section of London where the poor and the well-to-do touch but rarely meet. Thirteen-year-old Tim Malone is weaned away from his gang by Lovejoy Mason, an unusual eleven year old, when he aids her in creating a secret garden. They are discovered and brought to court for stealing soil from the square. The children find that "people need people."

* GREGORY, SUSAN. *Hey, White Girl!*

* HERZOG, MAURICE. *Annapurna: The First Conquest of an Eight Thousand Meter Peak.*

HUNTER, KRISTIN. *The Soul Brothers and Sister Lou.* Scribner, 1968, $4.50 (P/Avon, $.75). Louretta often wished that she had a place to go after school, "someplace where she could talk, and have fun, and be with her friends." Lou's efforts are responsible for the development of a recreation center for teenagers in the black ghetto on Chicago's South Side. Their singing comes to the attention of a recording studio and eventually brings them fame. A 1968 Council on Interracial Books Award winner.

* JOHNSON, ANNABEL AND EDGAR. *Pickpocket Run.*

KIDDELL, JOHN. *A Community of Men.* Chilton, 1969, $4.95. Hamish wrote the play. Bottle, David and Ann are the actors and production crew. The stage, in an unused building, belonged to a boys' home. The boys soon capture the hearts of the four college students, and when the authorities decide to close the home, the four use their time, financial resources, and ingenuity to keep it open.

* KNOWLES, JOHN. *A Separate Peace.*

LAWRENCE, MILDRED. *Once at the Weary Why.* HBJ, 1969, $3.75. Cammy Chase is so upset by her mother's remarriage that she rejects her old friends for the excitement of a new gang. Clothes, dates, and parties become so important and take so much of her time that she is unaware of her role as a member of a family and oblivious to the way the gang is using her. The loyalty of her former friends, an understanding stepfather, and the crisis precipitated when she is accused of shoplifting help Cammy face reality.

* LOTT, MILTON. *Backtrack.*

MATTHEWS, JACK. *Hanger Stout, Awake.* HBJ, 1967, $3.95. Clyde Stout, an eighteen year old, works contentedly at a gas station, interested only in his car and his girl. Then he discovers he can hang by his hands for 2-3-4 minutes and a gambler starts making a book on him. During practice on the grease rack he sometimes has visions and his friends urge him to "awake"—to what the gambler, the girl, and his world are doing to him. As Holden Caulfield is the verbal adolescent, Hanger is the inarticulate youth.

* MAUERMANN, MARY ANNE. *Strangers into Friends.*

MAYERSON, CHARLOTTE LEON. *Two Blocks Apart: Juan Gonzalez and Peter Quinn.* HR & W, 1965, $3.95 (P/Avon, $.60). Juan Gonzalez and Peter Quinn, both seventeen, live two blocks apart in New York City. Their lives are very different but their aspirations are surprisingly similar. The book is a compilation of edited tapes but because of the selected details it seems more fiction than fact. The book delineates the problems of relating to family and peers in both worlds.

* ROSE, KAREN. *A Single Trail.*

WALTON, BRYCE. *Cave of Danger.* TY Crowell, 1967, $4.50 (P/WSP, $.75). Competition between Matt and Spotty and the other senior boys in the search for a cave causes Matt to ignore all the rules of spelunking. The suspense and danger of cave exploration in the Ozarks are succinctly described when Matt is trapped underground. Matt and Spotty and their main rival Kurt exhibit changes in their attitudes toward each other as the severity of the situation increases.

Mature

FARRELL, JAMES T. *Studs Lonigan* (trilogy). Vanguard, 1935, $7.50 (P/NAL, $1.50). During the six months following graduation from St. Patrick's grammar school, fifteen-year-old Studs gains the leadership of one gang and fights the leader of another, hitches rides, steals candy and fruit, baits the Jews and Negroes in the neighborhood, explores sex, but fails to get a job. Studs is not the product of the slums but he does reveal a sense of moral and spiritual decay that seems very contemporary. This is the story of *Young Lonigan: A Boyhood in the Chicago Streets,* the first book in the trilogy.

KIRKWOOD, JAMES. *Good Times/Bad Times.* S & S, 1968, $5.98 (P/ Fawcett World, $.95). Eighteen-year-old Peter Kilburn writes to his lawyer from jail where he is imprisoned for murdering the headmaster of a fashionable prep school. Peter, a sensitive, lonely boy, has longed for a special friend. In Jordan Legier he finds one. Because of an earlier scandal in the school and because of his own warped nature, headmaster Hoyt fears a homosexual relationship between the two boys. The good times are menaced by increasing tension and terror.

* SANDBURG, CARL. *Always the Young Strangers.*

Relationships with Others

Primary

BEIM, LORRAINE AND JERROLD. *Two Is a Team.* il. by Ernest Crichlow. HBJ, 1945, $3.25. Two young boys find that two can accomplish things that neither can alone. Only through the illustrations is it apparent that one boy is Negro and one is white.

BENNETT, RAINEY. *The Secret Hiding Place.* il. by author. Hale, 1960, $3.12. Little Hippo, the pet of the herd, is tired of always being petted and fussed over. He searches for a place where he can be alone but then is afraid. All ends well when he finds a secret hiding place where he can be alone but "not too alone." Even children past the picture book stage will appreciate Little Hippo's predicament.

BLUE, ROSE. *A Quiet Place*. il. by Tom Feelings. Watts, 1969, $3.95. The vivid drawings of Tom Feelings bring to life nine-year-old Matthew, a foster child in a big city, for whom the library satisfies a real need.

COHEN, MIRIAM. *The New Teacher*. il. by Lillian Hoban. Macmillan, 1972, $3.95. The first grade teacher has left to have a baby. Who will take her place? Jim and his classmates know she will be big, she will holler and have smoke coming out her "mean, green nose." They tell typically first grade jokes as they anxiously await her arrival, but their fears are unfounded for the new teacher turns out to be a really "good guy." A perfect book for the child who is entering school for the first time and is apprehensive about what his teacher will be like. The illustrations are delightful and add considerably to the book.

COLVER, ANNE. *Bread and Butter Indian*. il. by Garth Williams. HR & W, 1964, $2.95. Based on an actual happening, this story tells of a young girl, Barbara, living in the Pennsylvania wilderness in the late 1700s. An Indian whom Barbara has befriended saves her when she is kidnapped by a hostile Indian tribe.

* DAVIS, CHRISTOPHER. *Sad Adam—Glad Adam*.

ETS, MARIE HALL. *Play with Me*. il. by author. Viking Pr, 1955, $2.50 (P/Viking Pr, $.75). The meadow animals run away when the little girl tries to catch them. But when she comes and sits quietly by the brook, they come out, one by one.

EVANS, KATHERINE. *A Bundle of Sticks*. il. by author. A Whitman, 1962, $2.95. A rug maker gives his business to his three sons. One makes the patterns, one mixes the dyes, one works the loom. When a prize is offered for the most beautiful rug, they quarrel. With a bundle of sticks their father teaches them a lesson. In the end the prince says, "The prize is yours. You have won it by working together."

* KOREN, EDWARD. *Don't Talk to Strange Bears*.

LEXAU, JOAN M. *Benjie on His Own*. il. by Don Bolognese. Dial, 1970, $3.95. When his grandmother is not at school to meet him Benjie fearfully tries to find his way home alone. He watches for familiar landmarks, all the time wondering where his grandmother is. He discovers her at home, too ill to come out of her room, so she asks Benjie to run for help. This is a charming story, well-developed, with good characterization, full of suspense, and beautifully written. The illustrations enhance the telling of the story, a good sequel to the first book about Benjie.

* LITTLE, JEAN. *Spring Begins in March*.

* McDonnell, Lois Eddy. *Stevie's Other Eyes.*

* McGovern, Ann. *Black Is Beautiful.*

* Molarsky, Osmond. *Song of the Empty Bottles.*

Raskin, Ellen. *Franklin Stein.* il. by author. Atheneum, 1972, $4.95. Franklin called his ingenious Rube Goldberg contraption "Fred." To Franklin, Fred was the friend he always wanted. All others found Fred "awful, evil or wicked." The police noted him as an "atrocious, ferocious, ghastly giant monster." But everyone sings a different tune when the judge awards Fred the prize as the most unusual pet in the pet show.

Sauer, Julia. *Mike's House.* il. by Don Freeman. Viking Pr, 1954, $2.75 (P/Viking Pr, $.75). Robert attends story hour at the public library and hears *Mike Mulligan and His Steam Shovel,* which becomes his favorite book. His sense of belonging at the library helps him in a time of need.

Van Leeuwen, Jean. *Timothy's Flower.* il. by Moneta Barnett. Random, 1967, $3.50. "Timothy's block has everything," including a candy store, barbershop, and laundry—and their respective owners. Timothy attempts to grow a flower he brings home from the park. When this project fails, Mrs. Valdez shares her flower box with him. Very little plot but the inner-city illustrations should involve non-readers and beginning readers with familiar settings worth discussing.

Yashima, Taro. *Youngest One.* il. by author. Viking Pr, 1962, $3.50. It's not always easy to make new friends. Bobby tries many times to see who lives on the other side of a large hedge growing by his house, but when Momo comes near to speak, Bobby backs away and closes his eyes. Only after many tries does Bobby open his eyes to meet the smiling face of a new friend.

Intermediate

Baudouy, Michel-Aime. *The Boy Who Belonged to No One.* HBJ, 1967, $3.50. Hans is only twelve years old at the time of this story, but he lives in a world of adults. When he is an infant two uncles take him to a construction site. The boy touches the lives of many and for some, especially the tough-acting boss Karl, he helps to keep alive both hope and compassion.

Biesterveld, Betty. *Run, Reddy, Run.* il. by E. Harper Johnson. Nelson, 1962, $2.95. Eleven-year-old Henrilee Fenton, daughter of a migrant worker in Ohio, finds Reddy, a baby fox that she wants desperately to domesticate and keep as a pet. She has numerous conflicts with Jiggers, a boy from a neighboring farm, who belittles her because her father is a migrant worker. Jiggers also threatens to kill Reddy because he thinks the fox is killing his family's chickens. The two children eventually learn to get along, the fox is released, and all ends well.

BRAGDON, ELSPETH. *That Jud!* il. by Georges Schreiber. Viking Pr, 1957, $3.00. As an orphan living with old Captain Ban, Jud's life is a lonely one. His secret camp on an island off the coast of the remote Maine fishing village fills his empty days. The arrival of two summer visitors brings adventures that help Jud gain self-respect and the admiration of the whole village.

BULLA, CLYDE ROBERT. *Benito.* il by Valenti Angelo. TY Crowell, 1961, $3.50. Because his father has left and his mother is dead, Benito must live with his Uncle Pedro, doing farm work and sleeping in the barn. His aunt and uncle do not let him draw, but after meeting an artist in town he begins secretly to prepare first a drawing, then a piece of sculpture. The sculpture is accepted for use in the Treasure Chest, an art collection sent to various schools. Benito gains the courage to demand time for his art and time for school.

BURCH, ROBERT. *Skinny.* il. by Don Sibley. Viking Pr, 1964, $3.50 (P/ Dell, $.75). Skinny is eleven going on twelve, without a family and unable to read. Miss Bessie takes him in and gives him odd jobs at her hotel, but now he must be placed in an orphanage. Life in a small southern town during the 1930s is well described as Skinny tries various ruses in order to stay with Miss Bessie.

BYARS, BETSY C. *The Midnight Fox.* il. by Ann Grifalconi. Viking Pr, 1968, $4.50 (P/Viking Pr, $.75). Tom reluctantly spends a summer on a farm while his parents tour Europe. The boy has learned that he can never live up to his athletic father's expectations of him, but Tom's picture of himself is changed when he realizes he alone can save the black fox from his uncle's gun.

CARLSON, NATALIE SAVAGE. *A Brother for the Orphelines.* il. by Garth Williams. Har-Row, 1959, $3.79 (P/Dell, $.75). Twenty orphan girls living in a village near Paris want to keep an infant boy who was left at their orphanage. Just when he is about to be sent to the boys' orphanage, a photographer and newsman print the story including details of the deplorable condition of the building. As a result, the two orphanages are to be combined and the children may stay together. The book presents a loving atmosphere, and the determination displayed by Josine may remind some readers of their younger brothers or sisters.

———. *The Family under the Bridge.* il. by Garth Williams. Har-Row, 1958, $3.95. An old Parisian hobo, Armand, finds that his special place under a bridge has been appropriated by three children. They convince him that he should stay there too and be their grandfather. Armand finds it impossible to continue his façade of gruffness, and a deep relationship develops between Armand, the children, and their mother.

CHASTAIN, MADYE LEE. *Magic Island.* il. by author. HBJ, 1964, $3.50. Barbados in the 1850s is a magic island for frail ten-year-old Angel Thorne. Angel, Lissa Spenlow, and two friends are sent by Grandfather Spenlow to the Jolly family of Barbados to recover from a cold, damp New York winter. A cave adventure, intrigue in a sugar cane mill, smugglers, and the closely knit Jolly family help Angel and Lissa realize it "isn't how big or little you are, but what's in the heart that counts."

* CLEAVER, VERA AND BILL. *Grover.*

COATSWORTH, ELIZABETH. *The Cave.* il. by Allan Houser. Viking Pr, 1958, $3.50. Jim, a young Navajo, senses that all is not well as he sets out with his sheep for summer pastures. Fernando, the sheepherder in charge, lost twenty-seven sheep the year before, and he resents Jim's presence on the trip. Jim finally wins Fernando's confidence and friendship while at the same time overcoming his own fears.

————. *Jon the Unlucky.* il. by Esta Nesbitt. HR & W, 1964, $3.50. Bad luck follows Jon to Greenland where in a few years both parents die. Lost in a snowstorm, Jon wanders inland where he saves the life of a strange boy. The friendship that grows as the two return to the boy's home is so strong that each is prepared to die for the other. However, the boy's people permit no strangers to live who might carry back the location of their secret paradise. Jon's ability to read and write saves his life, for when he haltingly reads the history of this remnant of an early settlement, his life and that of his new friend are spared. For the first time in his life, his luck has changed.

COHEN, PETER ZACHARY. *The Muskie Hook.* il. by Tom O'Sullivan. Atheneum, 1969, $4.25. The three muskie fishermen resent having to accept Aaron Rennin as a guide in place of his father and Aaron resents having to guide. Relationships between the fishermen and Aaron worsen as Aaron floods the motor, nearly swamps the boat, snags the net, and threatens to return home when the fishermen remove their life jackets. The day on the lake is not a total loss to Aaron, for he gains new insight into his father's job and the feelings of men who fish for muskie.

* COOK, OLIVE R. *Serilda's Star.*

CORCORAN, BARBARA. *A Row of Tigers.* il. by Allan Eitzen. Atheneum, 1969, $4.25. Eleven-year-old Jackie runs away from home, unable to accept her father's death or to get along with her mother. On the road she meets Gene Locke and discovers that he, an adult with a curved spine making him a deformed dwarf, is also running away. She persuades him to return home with her, where she introduces him to her friends: Windy, the manager of the dump; Lucky, the manager of the ranch; and Old Lady Beavertail from the Indian reservation. As friendships develop both Jackie and Gene are better able to understand themselves, their limitations, and their capabilities.

DARINGER, HELEN FERN. *Adopted Jane.* il. by Kate Seredy. HBJ, 1947, $3.25. Jane's one wish is that some day she will have a chance to leave the James Ballard Memorial Home and live with a real family. When she is invited to two different homes for the summer, she is overjoyed. Remembering her experiences in making new friends and in living with each family helps Jane as she decides which family she will live with permanently.

DE JONG, MEINDERT. *The Wheel on the School.* il. by Maurice Sendak. Har-Row, 1950, $2.92. Six Dutch children encouraged by a sensitive schoolmaster search for a wheel to place on the schoolhouse roof as a nesting place for storks. Their efforts and ultimate success lead to better understanding among the children and closer ties to older members of the community.

* FENISONG, RUTH. *Boy Wanted.*

* FITZHUGH, LOUISE. *Harriet the Spy.*

FOX, PAULA. *Portrait of Ivan.* il. by Saul Lambert. Bradbury, 1969, $4.50. Ivan, a lonely boy whose mother has died and whose father is too busy for him, comes to a series of sittings while he has his portrait painted. The young painter and Mrs. Manderby, the old woman the painter has hired to read to his restless subjects, open up a whole new world for Ivan—helping him make and explore new relationships as well as talk about his mother whom he never knew. A warm, sensitively written story.

GAGE, WILSON. *Big Blue Island.* il. by Glen Rounds. World Pub, 1969, $4.95 (P/WSP, $.50). Darrell, who has always lived in Detroit, is orphaned and sent to live with his great-uncle on a lonely island in the Tennessee River. He is first intent on running away, but after his great-uncle has an accident, Darrell begins to understand himself and finds that he has a home at last.

* GRAY, ELIZABETH JANET. *I Will Adventure.*

GREENE, CONSTANCE C. *A Girl Called Al.* il. by Byron Barton. Viking Pr, 1969, $3.95 (P/Viking Pr, $.95). Written in an amusing first-person style, this is the story of a friendship between two seventh grade girls. Al (short for Alexandra) and the unnamed narrator of the story learn much from Mr. Richards, the elderly assistant superintendent of their apartment house, as he helps build their self-confidence and reveals his own ability to accept life's problems as well as its joys.

* GUILLOT, RENE. *Fonabio and the Lion.*

HAMILTON, VIRGINIA. *The Planet of Jr. Brown*. il. by author. Macmillan, 1971, $4.95. The story of a crucial week in the lives of two black, eighth grade dropouts who have been spending their time with the school janitor. Each boy is presented as a distinct individual. Junior is a 300-lb. musical prodigy as neurotic as his overprotective mother. Buddy has learned to live by his wits in a world of homeless children. Buddy becomes Jr. Brown's protector and says to the other boys, "We are together because we have to learn to live for each other."

* HOUSTON, JAMES. *The White Archer: An Eskimo Legend*.

HUNTER, EDITH. *Sue Ellen*. il. by Bea Holmes. HM, 1969, $3.50. Sue Ellen is a slow learner and runs into many difficulties in a regular school. She is usually in the way and in the wrong. With an invalid mother and a father who works seven days a week, Sue Ellen and her five brothers and sisters do not have an easy time. A special class for children with severe learning problems changes her concept of herself and her life experiences.

JOHNSON, DORIS. *Su An*. il. by Leonard Weishard. Follett, 1968, $3.50. Su An's mother leaves her in a Korean orphanage when she can no longer care for her, but the little girl wants no mother other than her own. This book presents the thoughts of Su An as she arrives in America to meet her new mother and father. She is introduced to them at the airport; they give her a doll with black hair like her own, and for the first time in many months, Su An smiles.

* KEY, ALEXANDER. *The Forgotten Door*.

* KINGMAN, LEE. *The Secret Journey of the Silver Reindeer*.

* KONIGSBURG, E. L. *From the Mixed-up Files of Mrs. Basil E. Frankweiler*.

* LAMPMAN, EVELYN SIBLEY. *Tilted Sombrero*.

LITTLE, JEAN. *One to Grow On*. il. by Jerry Lazare. Little, 1969, $4.50. Janie Chisholm finds it much easier to make up stories than to tell the truth. Her family never knows when to believe her and neither do her friends. When summer comes, her godmother Tilly takes her camping. With Tilly's wise help Janie begins to better understand herself and her friends.

* McDONNELL, LOIS EDDY. *Susan Comes through the Fire*.

MAURIAC, FRANCOIS. *The Holy Terror*. il. by Ingrid Fetz. Funk & W, 1967, $3.95. Ernest is a little boy so spoiled that he terrorizes everyone around him. Neither Ernest's father, grandmother, nor nurse can make him behave. When he needs something he shouts and threatens the whole household until he gets what he wants. Ernest has had seventeen governesses in three years but none will stay because Ernest is uncontrollable. However, the day comes when Ernest finally meets a governess who is his match, and she succeeds in making Ernest a happy and well behaved boy. The early twentieth-century French setting gives a quaint air to the book.

* NEWMAN, SHIRLEE PETKIN. *Yellow Silk for May Lee.*

OLSEN, JOHANNA. *Stray Dog.* Criterion, 1968, $3.95. Erling, Mangus, and the dog are all strays looking for a real home. A long holiday spent in forests of western Norway leads to a series of varied adventures for all three. The last adventure results in unexpected fortune— homes and love for all.

* ORMONDROYD, EDWARD. *Time at the Top.*

RINKOFF, BARBARA. *Member of the Gang.* il. by Harold James. Crown, 1968, $3.50. Because he wants to be a respected member of Leroy's gang, Woodie agrees to play hooky and to "front" for the gang in a store stickup. When one boy is knifed in the fracas, Woodie stays with him, is "busted," tried, and put on probation. An honest and realistic treatment of boys seeking easy prestige and of their handling by understanding personnel representing authority.

SACHS, MARILYN. *Veronica Ganz.* il. by Louis Glanzman. Doubleday, 1968, $3.95 (P/WSP, $.60). Thirteen-year-old Veronica's automatic response to being teased about her height is to bully the teaser. One day she realizes that Peter actually admires her and instead of bullying him, she giggles. The story is complicated by the fact that Veronica and her sister live with their mother and stepfather and visit their father with decreasing frequency.

SEREDY, KATE. *A Brand New Uncle.* il. by author. Viking Pr, 1961, $3.00. An orphan from the training school finds a friend when a retired gentleman fills his butterfly net with the boy's kittens. The boy learns that one never solves a problem by running away from it.

SIMPSON, DOROTHY. *A Matter of Pride.* Lippincott, 1959, $3.95. This story of a seventh grade girl ashamed to tell the substitute teacher that she is too poor to have new shoes for another two months describes quite clearly the child's reactions to the teacher's attempts to give her individual help. Life in a small school on a small island is appealingly pictured.

* STEVENSON, WILLIAM. *The Bushbabies.*

STOLZ, MARY. *Juan.* il. by Louis Glanzman. Har-Row, 1970, $4.43. A beautiful character study of an eight-year-old Mexican orphan who daydreams that his parents will someday come to reclaim him. The poverty of the orphanage, both physical and spiritual, is clearly expressed by Juan, who longs for a party so he will have good things to eat. He also craves a pair of red rubber boots but after beguiling a rich American couple into buying some for him, he finds that there are drawbacks in being the only orphan to receive such a present.

STUART, JESSE. *The Beatinest Boy.* il. by Robert Henneberger. McGraw, 1953, $2.75. David, a small orphaned boy, finds a real home with his grandmother who lives in the mountains of Kentucky. The understanding, esteem, and love that evolve between the two culminate in David's successful struggle to earn the money to buy a Christmas present for his grandfather.

* TREFFINGER, CAROLYN. *Li Lun, Lad of Courage.*

* UNITAS, JOHNNY, AND ED FITZGERALD. *Pro Quarterback: My Own Story.*

WARREN, MARY PHRANER. *A Snake Named Sam.* il. by Beth and Joe Krush. Westminster, 1969, $4.50. Corky has just moved to the city of Portland from rural Oregon. Neither he nor his collection of snakes can get used to the city. Through Sam, his four-foot snake, Corky develops fast friendships with an unusual teacher, a school principal, and several classmates. Sam helps catch a robber, gets caught adrift in a houseboat during a storm, and serves in a secret club's initiation.

WIBBERLEY, LEONARD. *Journey to Untor.* FS & G, 1970, $3.95. The journey from Colorado to Untor takes only an instant. The trip to meet the governor of the planet involves many days of hard travel in a land where time no longer exists as it does on Earth. Uncle Bill and his six nieces and nephews learn the value of the many senses human beings possess and especially the importance of love and concern for others. Deep philosophical understandings of people and their relationships with each other are imbedded in this delightful fantasy.

* WIER, ESTER. *The Loner.*

Junior

BAKER, BETTY. *Walk the World's Rim.* Har-Row, 1965, $3.95. Fourteen-year-old Chakoh, an Indian, travels with four Spanish survivors of an exploring party to Mexico. He becomes a close friend of the black slave Esteban, a man who displays great courage on the expedition through Indian territories. Chakoh discovers that Esteban is a slave, but the Indian learns, through his friendship with Esteban, that the institution of slavery, not the slave himself, is to be despised.

BALL, ZACHARY. *Bristle Face.* Holiday, 1962, $3.95 (P/Schol Bk Serv, $.60). Neither Jase nor the dog Bristle Face seem to belong anyplace until they stop one day at a country store run by Lute Swank. Lute persuades them to stay. Jase and Bristle Face hunt, meet the widow, and help Lute campaign for the sheriff's job. After Bristle Face dies, Jase runs away, and only then does he realize how much he has grown to love Lute and the widow.

BENNETT, JACK. *Mister Fisherman*. Little, 1965, $4.95. When a boat engine fails off the coast of Africa, a rich, unpleasant young white man and a tough old black boat owner are forced to learn to get along with each other. Arrogant young Farradey finally sees the old man as a human being as well as a protector. He is unable, however, to free himself from the values of the narrow world to which he returns.

BONHAM, FRANK. *The Nitty Gritty*. il. by Alvin Smith. Dutton, 1968, $3.95 (P/Dell, $.75). Charlie Matthews from Dogtown must earn a lot of money fast so he can leave the area with his Uncle Baron. He clears a vacant lot of tons of bricks and bottles, collects ladybugs, and takes part in a boxing match with a buddy. All the money-raising schemes have some drawbacks and Uncle Baron deserts him in the end, but Charlie has learned a great deal about himself and his friends in Dogtown.

———. *Viva Chicano*. Dutton, 1970, $4.50 (P/Dell, $.75). In this story, Joaquin "Keeny" Duran struggles to rise above the influences of the urban, Mexican-American ghetto where he lives. Unjustly accused of pushing his brother out of the window, Keeny runs away and takes refuge in an abandoned police station. The book passes almost into the realm of fantasy when Keeny and his gang, the Aztecs, are given advice by a cardboard model of Emiliano Zapata which Keeny has stolen. The voice is later explained as being Keeny's conscience. The book returns to strict realism in the end.

* BUTLER, BEVERLY. *Light a Single Candle*.

BUTLER, MARJORIE. *The Man Who Killed a Bear with a Stick*. il. by Jack Gaughan. Criterion, 1967, $3.95. Despite Gerry Miller's academic success, his ambitions are in Wyoming, where his widowed mother runs their cattle ranch. Boys will understand Gerry's wanting to prove himself by working for a summer in the cow camp in the rough country. Although in his first few days he makes too many mistakes to earn the unqualified respect of the experienced hands, it is a measure of his worth that he allows the credit for his first real act of bravery to go to a fading old mountaineer known as "the man who killed a bear with a stick."

CAMERON, ELEANOR. *A Spell Is Cast*. il. by Beth and Joe Krush. Little, 1964, $3.95. When Cory Winterslow first sees Tarnhelm, the house where her grandmother and uncle live, she thinks it enchanted. Her initial reaction is strengthened as she discovers there is something strange about her mother's failure to adopt her, about her unicorn necklace, and about her uncle's wood carvings. New friends, the warm understanding of Fergie and Andrew, the Scottish couple who work at Tarnhelm, and the desire to make Tarnhelm her home help Cory unravel the mysteries.

FALL, THOMAS. *Canalboat to Freedom*. il. by Joseph Cellini. Dial, 1966, $3.50 (P/Dell, $.95). Young Benja Lown comes from Scotland as an indentured servant and is made a "hoggee" boy on a canalboat. He has no defense against the cruelty of his owner-captain except for Lundius, the deckhand, a free Negro who is strong in body and spirit. When Benja discovers Lundius's involvement with the underground railroad, he offers to help. Benja thinks that Newt, the fugitive slave, is a coward and is bitter as well as grieved when Lundius is killed while helping him. The love and respect which Lundius has taught Benja help him to see Newt in a different way and to think clearly about his own future.

* GREENE, CONSTANCE C. *A Girl Called Al.*

* HAMILTON, VIRGINIA. *The Planet of Jr. Brown.*

HARRIS, CHRISTIE. *Forbidden Frontier.* il. by E. Carey Kenney. Atheneum, 1968, $4.50. This story of the Pacific Northwest frontier deals with gold rushes, fur brigades, and overland expeditions as well as the Indians' rebellion against the white man's cruel treatment. Allison, half Indian and half white, makes a pact with Ross, also a half-breed, to stand up to the white man's abuses. Eventually both come to accept the reality of changing conditions without sacrificing their sense of values. The book is written with deep sympathy for the Indians.

KEY, ALEXANDER. *The Forgotten Door.* Westminster, 1965, $3.50 (P/ Schol Bk Serv, $.60). Little John is discovered in a mossy cave by a kind family, the Beans. As they care for him they discover that he cannot speak English but can communicate with animals and humans. Little John, after some breathtaking experiences, takes his new friends through the forgotten door into the world where humans are friends with the animals as well as with one another.

* LEE, MILDRED. *Honor Sands.*

L'ENGLE, MADELEINE. *The Young Unicorns.* FS & G, 1968, $3.95. Josiah Davidson, seventeen, is seen in relation to many others—Emily, the blind piano prodigy; the Austins, who are his only real family; the Alphabats, a teenage gang whose power he is trying to escape; and the dean of the great cathedral where much of the action is set. An exciting climax emphasizes the theme of the importance of free will; even good cannot be forced on others.

MOREY, WALT. *Home Is the North.* il. by Robert Shore. Dutton, 1967, $4.50. Fifteen-year-old Brad and his malamute dog Mickie are taken in by Captain Ed Bishop and his wife "Stampede" Annie when Brad's grandmother dies. He learns to shoot with Annie's directions, signs on as a member of Captain Ed's salmon crew, and finally completes a sixty-mile trek cross-country in an effort to escape having to return to Seattle with his aunt.

———. *Angry Waters.* il. by Richard Cuffari. Dutton, 1969, $4.95. Dan, a fifteen-year-old city boy, is sentenced to a year's probation on the

Edwards' Oregon dairy farm. Dan hates farm life and resents the Edwards family's overtures of friendship. When he is given a calf to care for, he begins to change his attitude. Later, during a raging flood, he meets some of his former companions and has the courage to stand up against them for the sake of the Edwards family.

MOSKIN, MARIETTA D. *A Paper Dragon.* John Day, 1968, $4.50. When her father's job takes him out of the country, sixteen-year-old Karen Stevens reluctantly moves to New York to live with her grandmother and her older sister, Wendy. Favoritism towards Wendy and restrictions placed on Karen cause Karen to think of her grandmother as a dragon. Relations with an adopted aunt and the family of a new friend help Karen grow in her understanding of her grandmother and sister.

NOBLE, IRIS. *Megan.* Messner, 1965, $3.50. In 1902, seventeen-year-old Megan arrives in western Alberta, Canada, as the hired girl for an immigrant family from Wales. During her first two years in Canada, she searches for a place to belong, a family, and someone she can love and who will return her love. Through experiences with other immigrants she develops a growing loyalty to Canada and the idea of being a Canadian, and discovers the meaning of belonging to a family.

* RINKOFF, BARBARA. *Member of the Gang.*

* SAMS, JESSIE. *White Mother.*

SHALER, ELEANOR. *Gaunt's Daughter.* Viking Pr, 1957, $3.37. A promising young actress at seventeen, Cordelia faces the decision of accepting her first big part in a play that stars her father, a famous actor who deserted Cordelia and her mother when Cordelia was a young child. Cordelia works out the problems of parental rejection and finally stabilizes her strong conflicting values.

* SIMPSON, DOROTHY. *A Matter of Pride.*

SOUTHALL, IVAN. *Ash Road.* il. by Clem Seale. St. Martin, 1965, $3.95. The heat on January 13 near Tinley, Australia, is oppressive and the threat of a bush fire greater than in many years. When the fire comes the adults leave their homes on Ash Road to help near the front lines. Only five children, Grandpa Tanner, and three strange teenage boys are left. As each person faces the reality of the approaching fire and the problem of survival he learns about himself and his relationship with others.

* STUART, JESSE. *The Beatinest Boy.*

* SUTCLIFF, ROSEMARY. *Warrior Scarlet.*

* TUNIS, JOHN R. *His Enemy, His Friend.*

* WEAVER, STELLA. *A Poppy in the Corn.*

WERSBA, BARBARA. *The Dream Watcher.* Atheneum, 1968, $3.95. Anti-hero Albert Scully doesn't seem to fit in anywhere, either at home or at school. Thoroughly convinced that he is destined for failure in life, he meets an eccentric, aging actress who teaches him that there is nothing wrong with being different.

WIER, ESTER. *The Barrel.* McKay, 1966, $3.50. Until he is twelve, Chance Reedy lives only in foster homes. Then he is sent back to his home in the Florida back country. There he begins to take part in a new life with his granny and his older brother, Turpem. Turpem takes every opportunity to test Chance's courage and to show him that he is as fearless as their father had been. A storm and an accident demand courage and cooperation from both boys and this leads to real understanding and friendship.

Senior

AUSTEN, JANE. *Persuasion.* Dutton, $3.95 (P/several). Though more sentimental than *Pride and Prejudice* or *Jane Eyre*, this story appeals to the same readers. The plot concerns the revival of Anne Elliot's romance with Captain Wentworth whom she has been persuaded not to risk marrying unless he has money. The novel considers how all men are inclined to cling to their persuasions (their prejudices) and how it is only in relating to others that one can avoid narrow-minded opinions.

* BARRETT, WILLIAM. *Lilies of the Field.*

BAWDEN, NINA. *A Little Love, A Little Learning.* Har-Row, 1966, O.P. Kate, a member of a doctor's family living in London's slums, is both good and evil. Her attempts to cope with adult problems such as the justification of abortion nearly ruin Dr. Boyd's reputation. Kate's world is shattered briefly when she discovers that her mother and Dr. Boyd are not legally married. However, a little love and a little learning help Kate cope with her many problems.

CATHER, WILLA. *Death Comes for the Archbishop.* Knopf, 1927, $5.95 (P/Random, $1.95). Two French priests come with faith and zeal to the Indians of New Mexico. While influencing many to accept the Christian way of life, they must themselves adjust to the people they meet.

CRANE, CAROLYN. *Wedding Song.* il. by Kurt Werth. McKay, 1967, $3.75. The summer romance of April Waterson and Fen Graham becomes a secret marriage in the fall. When the secret is out, April faces expulsion from high school, her parents' dismay, and—worst of all—

the growing realization that life with Fen will be dull and unrewarding. The problems of teenage couples are realistically if somewhat grimly portrayed.

ECKMAN, FERN MARJA. *The Furious Passage of James Baldwin*. M Evans, 1966, $4.50 (P/Popular Lib, $.75). This story of James Baldwin, Negro novelist and essayist, shows the arduous struggle of a black man to become a writer and to find his identity and worth as a person in American society. While not definitive, it is an interesting and informative biography.

FRANK, PAT. *Alas, Babylon*. Lippincott, 1963, $5.95 (P/Bantam $.95). What might happen if the United States were subjected to a nuclear attack? A small Florida town surviving the blast rebuilds because of the leadership of Randy Bragg and the relationships which develop under pressure and out of necessity among the surviving citizens. Some survivors commit suicide; some become highwaymen; but many follow Randy and learn to live.

GOUDGE, ELIZABETH. *The Sister of the Angels*. il. by C. Walter Hodges. P/Popular Lib, 1967, $.60. Foremost among the rich themes of this Christmas story set in England at the turn of the century is the value of learning to accept help. There are glowing characterizations of Henrietta, her famous but irresponsible father, the elderly churchman and his wife, and the talented but unfortunate painter who, with Henrietta's inspiration, works a most satisfying and believable miracle on the walls of the chapel.

* GREENE, CONSTANCE C. *A Girl Called Al.*

HILTON, JAMES. *Goodbye, Mr. Chips*. Little, 1934, $3.95 (P/several). A sentimental, nostalgic portrayal of a classics teacher in an English boarding school who becomes a figure of affection to the hundreds of "old" boys who come under his influence.

HUNTER, EVAN. *Blackboard Jungle*. Dell, O.P. A first-year English teacher refuses to accept that the students in a tough city school can't be taught but must just be kept under control. His persistent attempts to understand and help one black student pay off when his life is saved in a classroom scuffle. The book deals with many contemporary questions.

LAING, FREDERICK. *A Question of Pride*. Schol Bk Serv, 1967, $3.50. Two first-person narratives tell the story of a young musician and his high-school sweetheart. Lisa reveals herself as a sensitive girl who cannot quite admit her feelings. Larry's story shows his own fierce pride and accounts for the misunderstanding which has kept them apart. Suspense hinges on whether Larry, now a known entertainer, will come home to play for a school dance.

* McCullers, Carson. *Member of the Wedding.*

* Mather, Melissa. *One Summer in Between.*

Moray, Ann. *The Rising of the Lark.* Morrow, 1964, $5.95. Wales and all its magic affects young Catty as she grows up in the early 1900s. The countryside and community, her governess, tutor, and housekeeper play different roles in helping her to understand herself and others.

Nathan, Robert. *Portrait of Jennie.* Knopf, 1940, $4.95 (P/Popular Lib, $.60). In this romantic short novel, artist Eben Adams comes to love Jennie Appleton, who appears and disappears in space and time, growing from a child to a young lady. The tragic ending is inevitable. The story emphasizes the timelessness of lovely things, including feelings for other people, and raises philosophical questions about man's relationship to other men and to his Creator.

* Naylor, Phyllis Reynolds. *Dark Side of the Moon.*

* Peck, Richard (ed.). *Sounds and Silences.*

Richter, Conrad. *A Country of Strangers.* Knopf, 1966, $4.50. Stone Girl, a captive of the Indians, is returned unwillingly to her white family. Mother of an Indian child, she journeys with her son through a country of strangers: first, from one Ohio tribe to another, then to French Detroit, and then to the antagonistic world of colonial Pennsylvania. Rejected by family, her child brutally killed, she follows into exile True Son, whose similar story is told in *The Light in the Forest.*

Solberg, Gunard. *Shelia.* HM, 1969, $4.95. This is the love story of Wayne Divine, a confused and troubled young white student, and Shelia Smith, a beautiful black girl. Wayne cannot completely submerge those voices of his white past which forbid him to cross the color line. Shelia cannot accept the middle-class values of her doctor father who does everything in his power to deny his origins in the rural South. The two flee to Chicago underground bars, experience a brush with the police, and in their runaway attempt have a violent encounter on a lonely highway. Yet for all they have shared, they are strangers.

* Sommerfelt, Aimée. *My Name is Pablo.*

* Sutcliff, Rosemary. *The Mark of the Horse Lord.*

* Walker, Margaret. *Jubilee.*

Wolff, Ruth. *The Space Between.* John Day, 1970, $5.95. The characters are the most memorable part of this chronicle of a family that falls apart. Sensitive Kate, the elder daughter, is left to fill the long spaces between events in her life by writing new poems in the notebooks she had started as a child. Love comes late for her, and real recognition for her writing even later.

Mature

* BRAITHWAITE, E. R. *To Sir, with Love.*

FAULKNER, WILLIAM. *The Reivers.* Random, 1962, $6.95 (P/several). Initiation into the adult world is the result of eleven-year-old Lucius Priest's four-day visit to Memphis in the company of two unconventional adult companions. He meets gamblers, visits a brothel, tangles with the law, and gets involved in an amazing horse race. Beautifully written, the language and some of the episodes indicate a mature audience.

FORSTER, EDWARD M. *Passage to India.* HBJ, 1949, $2.95 (P/HBJ, $1.95). The friendship of Dr. Aziz, a sensitive and intelligent young Moslem, and Cyril Fielding, principal of Government College, Chandnapore, cannot survive the pressures and tensions between the races in colonial India. A trip to the strange Marabar Caves ends in tragedy. The echoing laugh of the caves seems to mock those British and Indians who try to understand one another.

* FURUYA, MIYUKI. *Why, Mother, Why?*

HESSE, HERMANN. *Demian.* Har-Row, 1965, $4.95. The story of a unique relationship between Emil Sinclair and Max Demian which has been described as "a primeval blood-tie among men of similar destiny" rather than a traditional friendship. The title is *Demian* but Sinclair tells the story about his "trying to live in accord with the promptings which come from my true self."

* ———. *Narcissus and Goldmund.*

SCHAEFER, JACK. *The Canyon.* Ballantine, 1953, O.P. Little Bear, a Cheyenne Indian, "holds the pipe upright according to custom. He passes it unsmoked." He is a stranger to his tribe for he opposes the warpath as a way of life; he retires to a hidden canyon to find his own way. When his bride loses her child and longs for the companionship of women, he must reluctantly face the fact that he needs other men, and he leaves the canyon convinced that "one man can live with a tribe and not let it change him too much."

WHARTON, EDITH. *Ethan Frome.* Scribner, 1911, $4.50 (P/Scribner, $1.65). Ethan tries to escape the stultifying world of Starkfield, Massachusetts, but he is prevented from doing so by his obligations first to his parents, then to his hypochondriac wife Zeena, and finally by an accident which injures him and a young cousin Mattie to whom he is attracted. In an ironic twist, Mattie becomes the querulous invalid and Zeena cares for both Mattie and Ethan.

Alienation and Rejection

Primary

GAG, WANDA. *Millions of Cats.* il. by author. Coward, 1938, $3.50. The little old man and little old lady want a cat for their family, and the little old man sets out to find the most beautiful cat in the world. He asks the cats to decide among themselves which is the prettiest and they devour each other. One bedraggled kitten survives the melee because she knows that she is not pretty. She is loved and fed by the little old man and lady and becomes the most beautiful cat in the world. Children will enjoy participating in the repetitive refrain.

LIONNI, LEO. *Little Blue and Little Yellow.* il. by author. Astor-Honor, 1959, $4.50. Simple abstract figures convey the universal idea of rejection because one is different from others. In this case, Little Blue and Little Yellow become Little Green, and their families no longer know them.

PIATTI, CELESTINO. *The Happy Owls.* il. by author. Atheneum, 1964, $4.95. Here is a legend which will perhaps never be heeded perfectly in reality but which needs to be told over and over. Children may understand the wisdom of the owls better than many adults can. At least, they should hear this barnyard story of peace and happiness.

SEUSS, DR. (THEODER GEISEL). *Horton Hears a Who!* Random, 1954, $2.95. Big Horton, the elephant, tries to protect the settlement of small Whos which he discovers.

Intermediate

* AARON, CHESTER. *Better than Laughter.*

AGLE, NAN HAYDEN. *Joe Bean.* Seabury, 1967, $3.95. Joe Bean, an eleven-year-old Negro boy living with his married sister, always seems to find himself in trouble for rebelling against unkindness and injustice. Becoming a ward of Mr. Tipper, a warm, kind, and empathic person who loves horses, makes Joe feel wanted for the first time. Practicing with members of the Maryland Amateur Jousting Club provides friendship and a satisfying outlet. Eventually, Joe is mature enough to return to his sister and to help with his nephew.

* ARMSTRONG, WILLIAM H. *Sounder.*

* BUCK, PEARL S. *Matthew, Mark, Luke and John.*

* CUNNINGHAM, JULIA. *Dorp Dead.*

* FRANCHERE, RUTH. *Stampede North.*

* FRIEDMAN, FRIEDA. *Ellen and the Gang.*

* GEORGE, JEAN. *My Side of the Mountain.*

HARNDEN, RUTH. *The High Pasture.* il. by Vee Gutherie. HM, 1964, $3.25. This sensitively written book tells the story of Tim's stay with Aunt Kate on a Colorado ranch while his mother is dying in a city hospital. Tim resents being sent away when he wants so much to be near his mother. But as the boy makes friends with Lobo, a handsome German shepherd dog turned wild, he comes to learn about animals, people, and life itself.

HARVEY, JAMES O. *Beyond the Gorge of Shadows.* Lothrop, 1965, $4.25. In prehistoric times in the southwestern United States, a young boy travels with two companions beyond their tribe's home to prove the existence of other men. The central theme is the contrast between an open mind and a closed one.

* HAUGAARD, ERIK CHRISTIAN. *Hakon of Rogen's Saga.*

HOLMAN, FELICE. *The Blackmail Machine.* il. by Victoria DeLarrea. Macmillan, 1968, $4.95. With several children aboard, Oggy Clay's tree house suddenly takes off from its maple stump and flies over the town. The flying house becomes a "blackmail machine" when the children blackmail adults into good behavior and make pleas for conservation, sense, and peace.

KENDALL, CAROL. *The Gammage Cup.* il. by Eric Blegood. HBJ, 1959, $3.95 (P/HBJ, $.65). This excellent fantasy of the nonconforming minnipins versus the Establishment seems to be particularly appropriate now. The understated commentary on the false values of society and on the need for both tradition and innovation is timeless.

* KONIGSBURG, E. L. *(George).*

KRUMGOLD, JOSEPH. *Onion John.* il. by Symeon Shimin. TY Crowell, 1959, $4.50 (P/Apollo, $1.65). Andy, twelve, and his father, a small-town hardware dealer, are in conflict about Andy's vocational and educational plans and about his friendship with Onion John, the town's odd-job man. Onion John, a middle-European immigrant who has never learned English, lives close to nature and finds in the supernatural answers to all his questions. A high spot comes when the two Andy loves best, his father and Onion John, begin to understand each other.

MACKEN, WALTER. *The Flight of the Doves.* Macmillan, 1968, $4.50 (P/ Macmillan, $.95). Finn Dove and his little sister Derval run away from their cruel stepfather to seek love and security with their grandmother in Ireland. Always on the run, they get help from gypsies, a kindhearted thief, and a dedicated policeman. Adventure, suspense, pathos, and humor are combined to make a memorable book.

PRINCE, ALISON. *The House on the Common.* il. by W. T. Mars. FS & G, 1970, $3.50. The old German couple who live in the small town near London are thought to be spies by many of the townspeople. Derek and Jane set out to prove this to be true. Their ineptness at spying plunges them into a strange situation during an air raid as they learn the truth about the inhabitants of the house on the common. Young readers will learn something of the way the British, young and old, reacted to food rationing, blackouts, and especially the nightly air raids during World War II.

TURKLE, BRINTON. *The Fiddler of High Lonesome.* il. by author. Viking Pr, 1968, $3.50. Sud, Deet, Hunk, and Old Man Fogle live at the top of High Lonesome. Lysander Bochamp goes there to claim his kin when his mother dies, for his "mammy were a Fogle from Chickasaw Creek." The boy decides that the Fogles are no kin of his, however, when they refuse to respect the lives of the "little critters" of the mountains. The book retains the flavor of the oral tale, and the timelessness of an important literary theme shows through the author's simple plot and style.

* UCHIDA, YOSHIKO. *The Promised Year.*

VANCE, MARGUERITE. *Willie Joe and His Small Change.* il. by Robert MacLean. Dutton, 1959, $2.50. Willie Joe, eleven years old, is the son of a gentleman planter. His family thinks Willie Joe odd because he loves to work and save money. Even though different from the rest of his family, Willie Joe finds that he cannot ignore their love and demands.

VARGA, JUDY. *The Magic Wall.* il. by author. Morrow, 1970, $3.95. King Frederick finds that he doesn't need walls of stone and high watchtowers to protect his castle; he has walls which only his enemies could see. King Bertram "wondered how one built such a wall made of love and trust." The values of love and trust are triumphant. The question the young reader will find himself asking is: Can't this happen today?

WOODS, HUBERT C. *Child of the Arctic.* il. by Doris Reynolds. Follett, 1962, $3.48. The stark beauty of Eskimo village life is authentically portrayed in the story of twelve-year-old twins, Tooruk and Kumalik, the latter a deaf mute. Only Tooruk and Dr. John at the trading post realize Kumalik's potential. Their faith helps the boy to live beyond his silent world.

YOUNG, MIRIAM. *The Dollar Horse.* il. by William M. Hutchinson. HBJ, 1961, $3.25. Keery Jamison is bitterly disappointed to receive an envelope containing a dollar for his tenth birthday when he expected a horse! However, with the dollar he starts off on a series of business ventures that eventually bring him his heart's desire. He also learns that more is to be gained by giving than by getting.

Junior

* Aaron, Chester. *Better than Laughter.*

Armstrong, William H. *Sounder.* il. by James Barkley. Har-Row, 1969, $3.95. A strong and forcefully written tale of the alienation of the black sharecropper of a century ago, *Sounder* is also the story of an enduring family relationship of father, mother, and son: the father who steals food for his hungry family and is imprisoned; the mother who toils quietly on to provide for her son; and the boy who searches constantly and maintains his hope for his father's return.

Behn, Harry. *The Faraway Lurs.* il. by author. World Pub, 1963, $4.95 (P/Avon, $.60). Heather Goodshade and her tribe are remnants of the Stone Age. Wolf Stone and his tribe are a part of the Bronze Age. When their cultures clash in Denmark, the two teenagers are torn between family loyalties and customs and their love for each other.

* Cavanna, Betty. *Going on Sixteen.*

* ———. *Jenny Kimura.*

Clark, Marvis Thorpe. *The Min-Min.* Macmillan, 1969, $4.95. Sylvie Edwards cannot let her brother Reg be sent to reform school so both run away from home. They travel on foot through many miles of the desolate country of inland Australia and face hardships and danger in their attempt to gain meaning for their lives. The strong terse prose vividly pictures the harsh Australian outback and the people and wild things that survive there.

Cunningham, Julia. *Dorp Dead.* il. by James Spanfeller. Pantheon, 1965, $3.50. In this highly symbolic story, orphan Gilly Ground describes his deliberately lonely life. He shuns friendships, disguises his intelligence, is glad to leave the orphanage to be the solitary apprentice of Kobalt the ladder maker. The security of Kobalt's routine soon becomes stifling, however, and Gilly discovers that he is, in fact, to become a prisoner. Helped by the dog Mash, with whom he has shared affection, Gilly escapes to the promise of freedom.

Franchere, Ruth. *Stampede North.* Macmillan, 1969, $4.95. When the news of the Klondike gold strike spreads, Charlie is seized with gold fever. Yet when his father agrees to take him there it is merely to take pictures, not to pan gold. Through the fierce privation of the Klondike winter Charlie and his father resolve their conflicts about gold and photography, independence and responsibility. Excellent prose, characterization, and dialogue contribute to make this an exciting adventure story.

George, Jean. *My Side of the Mountain.* il. by author. Dutton, 1959, $3.95. Sam Gribley feels closed in by the city and his large family so he runs away to the Catskills and the land that had belonged to his grandfather. He tells the story of his year in the wilderness—the loneliness, the struggle to survive, and the need for companionship.

GRANGER, PEG. *Canyon of Decision.* Criterion, 1967, $3.95. Jo Scott, seventeen and confused, struggles between conflict with her parents and social acceptance by her peers. Banished to her uncle's home in Jagged Canyon after a serious automobile accident, Jo is forced to think about the safety and welfare of others and thus begins to grow up. In the emergency of a forest fire Jo suddenly sees the world without "phony blinders" and learns to respect the "real" Jo that she finds.

* HARNDEN, RUTH. *The High Pasture.*

* HARRIS, CHRISTIE. *Forbidden Frontier.*

HUNT, IRENE. *No Promises in the Wind.* Follett, 1970, $4.95. At the height of the Depression, fifteen-year-old Josh Grondowski leaves home to escape a cruel, irritable father. His travels looking for work force him to assume adult responsibilities. When he finally returns home, he has come to understand the other people better and has even learned to love his father.

* JOHNSON, ANNABEL AND EDGAR. *Torrie.*

JOHNSTONE, PAUL K. *Escape from Attila.* il. by Joseph A. Phelan. Criterion, 1970, $4.00. Walter Alferson is a free Frank fighting with Attila the Hun. He and Hilde were offered to Attila as hostages when they were young children and though they live and fight with the Hun, they never forsake their own country or religion. Walter becomes a favorite of Attila for his courage and fighting prowess and Hilde is betrothed to Attila's son, but neither wishes to lose his identity as a Frank. When word reaches them of plans to march westward and conquer their homeland, the two escape and return home to warn their countrymen. The story tells of the hardships of that journey and also of the conflicting values of the two worlds in which Walter and Hilde have lived.

JONES, WEYMAN. *Edge of Two Worlds.* il. by J. C. Kocsis. Dial, 1968, $3.95 (P/Dell, $.75). Calvin Harper is on his way to law school when his wagon train is ambushed by Comanches and he is the only survivor. He meets an old Indian, Sequoyah, the Cherokee who invented an alphabet for his tribe. Neither trusts the other and for days they travel together mainly for survival, but as they learn more about each other their trust and friendship grow. Both are on the edge of two worlds: the boy is on the edge of manhood and the Indian, because of his alphabet, feels alienated from both Indian and white men. When they part company both their lives have been changed.

* KENDALL, CAROL. *The Gammage Cup.*

* McGRAW, ELOISE JARVIS. *Moccasin Trail.*

* MACKEN, WALTER. *The Flight of the Doves.*

MACPHERSON, MARGARET M. *The Rough Road.* il. by Douglas Hall.
HBJ, 1966, $3.95. Jim Smith is always hungry. His foster parents
begrudge him the little food they have. These are the Depression
years of the 1930s. Into the Scottish highlands comes a man who
sees Jim as a source of willing help and for whom Jim works whenever he finishes his chores at his foster home. The security of his new
friendship makes Jim an apt pupil and he learns much about life and
the ways of cattle from Alastair McAlister.

MONTGOMERY, JEAN. *The Wrath of Coyote.* il. with woodcuts by Anne
Siberall. Morrow, 1968, $4.75. The story is told as a flashback by
Chief Marin of the Miwok Indians who once lived where San Francisco is now located. Slowly the Spanish encroach on Indian lands
to spread their civilization. But from Chief Marin's point of view,
they bring only disease, slavery, war, and eventual extinction to his
once powerful tribe.

RICHTER, CONRAD. *The Sea of Grass.* Knopf, 1937, $4.95 (P/Bantam,
$.95). Feminine but strong-willed Lutie comes to the Southwest to
marry domineering cattleman Jim Brewster. Her sympathy for the
homesteaders ("nesters"), her involvement with the nesters' lawyer,
Chamberlain, the inevitable clash of wills and values between Lutie
and Brewster results in Lutie's departure. This is complicated by the
question of young Brock Brewster's parentage: he resembles all three.
The passage of time and tragedy finally unite Lutie and Brewster.

SCHULMAN, L. M. (ed.). *The Loners: Short Stories about the Young and
Alienated.* Macmillan, 1970, $4.95. The stories in this collection deal
with those aspects of the human condition that relate specifically to
the young and alienated—disillusionment, anger, rebellion, and lone-
liness.

* SWARTHOUT, GLENDON AND KATHRYN. *Whichaway.*

WOJCIECHOWSKA, MAIA. *Shadow of a Bull.* il. by Alvin Smith. Atheneum, 1964, $4.25. Manolo's father was a great bullfighter. The peo-
ple of the village and his mother have decided that Manolo must
follow in his father's footsteps. The boy's inner conflict as he tries
to resolve the differences between his aspirations and the expectations
of the community has been realistically and sympathetically described.

* ———. *A Single Light.*

Senior

BORLAND, HAL G. *When the Legends Die.* Lippincott, 1963, $4.95 (P/
Bantam, $.75). Tom Black Bull, a Ute Indian boy "civilized" against

his will, finds reservation life impossible. He is also rejected by the
whites. He is driven to success in the rodeo arena by his consuming
hatred of the white man's ways. It is only while recuperating from a
serious injury in the mountain home of his youth that Tom undergoes an experience which helps him to understand both himself and
his world.

* CANZONERI, ROBERT. *I Do So Politely.*

* DUBERMAN, MARTIN B. *In White America.*

* EMERY, ANNE. *Carey's Fortune.*

* MEANS, FLORENCE CRANNELL. *Our Cup Is Broken.*

MILLER, ARTHUR. *Death of a Salesman.* Viking Pr, 1949, $3.50 (P/
Viking Pr, $1.45). Willy Loman, a salesman, accepts the denatured
ideals of American society, not the highest values but those which
are the most publicized. Because of his misplaced values Willy cannot accept the defeat life gives him in his sixty-third year when he
is suddenly unemployed. *Death of a Salesman* is as moving as it is
significant.

RICHTER, CONRAD. *The Light in the Forest.* Knopf, 1953, $4.50 (P/
several). True Son, a white captive, is raised by an Indian chief. He
develops deep loyalties to his adopted father and the tribe. New
treaties mean that True Son must return to his home. His attempt to
reconcile his feelings of alienation and rejection as he moves from
one culture to another and his search for some meaning in his own
life are relevant today.

* SALINGER, J. D. *Catcher in the Rye.*

* SCHULMAN, L. M. (ed.). *The Loners: Short Stories about the Young and
Alienated.*

* STEELE, MARY Q. *Journey Outside.*

WALLACE, IRVING. *The Man.* P/Fawcett World, 1971, $1.50. An incred-
ible chain of events results in the succession of a Negro to the presi-
dency of the United States. The well-developed characters are dis-
turbingly believable, but most inspiring is the strength of the Man
as he rises above his own doubts and fears.

WOJCIECHOWSKA, MAIA. *Tuned Out.* Har-Row, 1968, $3.95 (P/Dell,
$.50). Sixteen-year-old Jim discovers that his brother Kevin, a college
student, is on drugs. In this novel, written in the form of a journal,
Jim tries to understand by sharing a drug experience; then, shedding
the influence of his brother, he realizes he must make it on his own.

Mature

ANDERSON, SHERWOOD. *Winesburg, Ohio.* Viking Pr, 1960, $4.50 (P/ Viking Pr, $1.45). The sense of isolation and alienation that haunts twentieth-century man is explored in a small-town setting. Only for very mature students.

FAULKNER, WILLIAM. *Intruder in the Dust.* Random, 1948, $6.95 (P/ Modern Lib, $1.45). Laid in Faulkner's mythical Yoknapatawpha County, the story tells of Lucas, a black falsely accused of murder, and of the search for the truth by Chick, a white sixteen-year-old, and Aleck, his black friend. Chick is torn between his conscience and tradition. Yet he seeks the truth, finally, because "somebody had to and nobody else would."

HEINLEIN, ROBERT A. *Stranger in a Strange Land.* Putnam, 1961, $6.95 (P/Berkley Pub, $1.25). Valentine Michael Smith is the only survivor of the first Mars probe. By ancestry he is a man; by education and instinct, a Martian. Heinlein wittily and cynically comments on man's values and mores as Michael learns of and is appalled by man's ways. Mike forms a new sect based on the principle of mutual love of and respect for members of a "nest."

HOOPES, NED E. *Who Am I: Essays on the Alienated.* P/Dell, 1969, $.75. The twenty-seven essays in this collection examine many of the various kinds of alienation which afflict our modern world: being a member of a minority, being too young or too old, being among the most or the least talented, being criminal or insane. A depersonalized, mass society makes human relations with others more and more difficult for virtually everyone.

MALAMUD, BERNARD. *The Assistant.* FS & G, 1957, $5.95 (P/several). Frank Alpine holds up a Jewish grocer in the Bronx and, then, feeling a sense of guilt, returns to become the grocer's assistant. The story is about Frank's search for self-discipline: "how often he had wished for better control over himself." Frank soon takes to stealing from the kind and honest grocer. Then he begins to desire the grocer's daughter. Finally, however, the positive relationships break through the almost hopeless pattern of his existence and Frank finds the strength he seeks.

MILLER, WARREN. *The Cool World.* Little, 1967, $5.95 (P/Fawcett World, $.75). Told from the point of view of a fourteen-year-old Harlem boy who assumes leadership of a gang, leads a rumble, kills another boy, and is sent to reform school. The boy is given a chance for a better future when he is sent to a farm. It is a true portrayal of a frighteningly narrow world. The accurate dialect does not slow the pace of this story.

SCOTT, J. M. *In a Beautiful Pea Green Boat.* Chilton, 1969, $4.95. Vacationing Jonathan Bordas is desperate: plans for his own bookshop have bankrupted him; his inability to relate to others has left him utterly alone. He swims miles from the Portuguese coast, intending suicide, but instinct forces him to clutch a rubber raft which drifts within his reach. Inside is seven-year-old Bonnie, whose dependence on Bordas forces his own survival, both physical and emotional. Their adventure on the sea has both beauty and violence; its dramatic conclusion is a haunting one.

* STEELE, WILLIAM O. *Wayah of the Real People.*

UPDIKE, JOHN. *Rabbit, Run.* Knopf, 1960, $5.95 (P/Fawcett World, $.95). Rabbit Angstrom, a former basketball hero, is unable to cope with his vulgar and dull life and the responsibilities of a pregnant wife. He deserts her and finds solace with Ruth; the book comes full circle when he deserts a pregnant Ruth, too. Rabbit personifies the immature American pursuing the myth of success and happiness without responsibility or effort. He is "floundering in the deadly flypaper of life" and those from whom he seeks advice are as confused as he. He retreats to the nostalgia of basketball and to a dependence on sex.

LADDER 3

There is a great deal of pathos, suffering, and emptiness among those who live in the culture of poverty. . . . A Puerto Rican up here has a hard time finding a job and a safe place to live. If you're a Puerto Rican you can apply in 20,000 places without getting a job . . . in the best places you find only Americans, never a Puerto Rican.*

"Yes, we are citizens," his mother said angrily. "I come here a citizen and have to learn to speak all over again. And we must live by the clock as if we are machines. . . . And your teacher tells me I do not even know the name of my son, because she does not care how many names he has in the middle, he has to go by his last name." The teacher had been new and it was hard for her to understand that the last name was the name of the mother, and the name in the middle was that of the father.†

LADDER 3

Appreciating Different Cultures

Learning to accept and respect the diverse cultures in our pluralistic society involves more than recognition of differences in diet, family custom, and language pattern. Literature which goes beyond a mere acknowledgment of difference to an appreciation of the richness of cultural differences leads to a "people knowledge" and feelings of empathy. Activity, the inherent quality of empathy, allows an individual to span barriers of race, color, and religion which keep people apart. Books can provide this knowledge and sensitivity, and it is only through a book that many of us have the opportunity to enter the heart and mind of one who is different. In this way a book can be a richer experience than life itself. Books

---

* From *La Vida* by Oscar Lewis, p. iii. Copyright 1966 by Random House, Inc. Reprinted by permission of the publisher.

† From *Jose's Christmas Secret* by Joan Lexau. Copyright 1963 by The Dial Press. Reprinted by permission of the publisher.

which enhance appreciation for different cultures can lead to pride in the pluralism of our society.

Books in this ladder were chosen and organized in four categories of cultural differences: ethnic, religious, regional, and world. The first three lie within the geographic boundaries of the United States while the last category provides some understanding of world cultures in contrast to our own.

An area of primary concern in contemporary society is ethnic diversity as we focus attention on the needs of minority groups. An effort has been made, therefore, to include numerous books depicting children and families that represent different ethnic backgrounds. Children as well as adults can unknowingly hurt another person whose customs, physical appearance, or language are obviously different. The expectation of a stereotyped personality often causes one to "put down" another. This feeling is vividly revealed in *Wigwam in the City* by Barbara Smucker. A Chippewa Indian and his daughter, traveling from the reservation to Chicago, have the following encounter with a food vendor:

> "Speaka English?" he asked and then waited.
>
> Father said nothing and looked straight ahead. Susan's face flushed. She did not want the man to think they could not speak English. She wondered why he had asked. . . . He stopped at the next row of seats where people laughed. . . .
>
> "The Indians back there don't speak English. I don't know what they'll do when they get to Chicago."
>
> "Maybe they'll hunt bears at Lincoln Park Zoo," a woman with a high voice giggled.
>
> Father spoke quietly in the language of the Chippewa. "They must think we do not live in America."

The Outsiders, by teenager, S. E. Hinton, provides insight into the lives and feelings of boys who, like Pony Boy, know what it is like to be called "greasers." He protests:

> "It ain't fair!" I cried passionately. "It ain't fair that we have all the rough breaks!"
>
> I didn't know exactly what I meant, but I was thinking about Johnny's father being a drunk and his mother a selfish slob, and Two-Bit's mother being a barmaid to support him and his kid sister after their father ran out on them, and Dally—wild, cunning Dally—turning into a hoodlum because he'd die if he didn't, and Steve—his hatred for his father coming out in his soft, bitter voice and the violence of his temper.

. . . Sodapop . . . a dropout so he could get a job and keep me in school; and Darry, getting old before his time trying to run a family and hang on to two jobs and never having any fun—while the Socs had so much spare time and money that they jumped us and each other for kicks, and beer blasts and riverbottom parties because they didn't know what else to do. Things were rough all over, all right. All over the East Side. It just didn't seem right to me.

Freedom of religion will exist in actuality in our country only with understanding. Included in this ladder, therefore, is a group of books designed to provide knowledge of various religious beliefs as represented in fiction. The story of Ruthy in *A Promise Is a Promise* by Molly Cone offers a unique presentation of Jewish values. The customs of the religious services and holidays are carefully interwoven into this story for elementary children. Older students will derive a deeper understanding of Jewish beliefs through reading of the relationship of two boys and their fathers in *The Chosen* by Chaim Potok. Some students may identify with the ten-year-old Mennonite girl in *Hannah Elizabeth* by Elaine Rich as she recognizes and faces conflicting values and customs of her family and the outside world. Lois Lenski's vivid story of *Shoo-Fly Girl* leads the reader to a quiet understanding of an Amish family in Pennsylvania. Older students may find the ideas of Buddhism in *Siddhartha* by Hermann Hesse appealing or identify with the conflicts that Corey Tremaine, a young Mormon girl, faces in *Wilderness Bride* by Annabel Johnson.

A third aspect of developing appreciation of different cultures is understanding of regional variation within the American culture. The picture books of Leo Politi have consistently portrayed customs in the lives of people who live closely together in urban settings. In his picture book *Mieko* one immediately feels the importance of the Japanese summer festival held during Nisei Week as a part of the cultural environment of Little Tokyo. Harper Lee's *To Kill a Mockingbird* depicts life in a different setting in a small southern town with all its prejudices. In teaching his children, Atticus Finch tried to promote understanding for all: "You never really know a man until you stand in his shoes and walk around in them." The authentic and vivid series of regional books by Lois Lenski, such as *Coal Camp Girl, Strawberry Girl, Cotton in My Sack,* offers insights into the lives of American children in a variety of localities. Students who face the problem of "straddling" two cultures will understand Su-Lin's comment in *Moon Guitar* by Marie Niemeyer: "I knew very well that the well-brought-up Chinese girl Grandfather wanted me to be would not answer back. That was the trouble. I didn't want to be that girl any more."

The American culture exists in a world composed of other diverse cultures. It will be helpful, therefore, for the student to gain some understanding of cultures other than his own as he learns to live freely in a world where people differ in many ways. Students will discover differences and, at the same time, many similarities. The autobiographical *Diary of Nina Kosterina*, for instance, demonstrates the universality of adolescent problems as the Russian girl tells of her life in Moscow.

As students are introduced to this ladder and to a variety of aspects of contemporary culture, both within the United States and in other countries, they will become more aware and search out books. How many books must a person read to gain full understanding? There is no set answer. One continues to grow as one reads and relates to people in reality. Certainly one book is only a beginning as the reader perceives the problems, the lives, the reality of those who represent other cultures. He must have time to read and time to think about what he reads. Only through continued effort will he grow from the recognition of differences, gain insights, develop understanding, and ultimately attain appreciation of cultural diversity.

Iris M. Tiedt and Maude Edmonson

Appreciating Different Ethnic Cultures

Primary

ANDERSON, JUANITA B. *Charley Yee's New Year.* il. by Dave Bhang. Follett, 1970, $1.95. Before the New Year's festival in San Francisco's Chinatown ends, seven-year-old Charley Yee must pay his debt of $3.15, or face disgrace according to an old Chinese custom. Charley searches for a chance to earn money and finally finds an unusual way to solve his problem.

* ARUEGO, JOSE. *Look What I Can Do.*

BAKER, BETTY. *Killer-of-Death.* Har-Row, 1963, $3.95. Killer-of-Death, son of an Apache chief growing to manhood toward the close of his tribe's freedom, knows that the ever-increasing demands of the white man will bring war. As friction increases between the Apaches and the whites, so does the tension between Killer-of-Death and his rival. They appease their hatred for one another to stand together for their tribe. The author's knowledge of Apache customs and lore is evident in the unforgettable story of a fierce, proud, and doomed world.

BANNON, LAURA. *Manuela's Birthday.* Whitman, 1972 (Revised), $3.75. This long-time favorite tells how a little girl in a Mexican village is surprised on her birthday by a special doll.

BLUE, ROSE. *I Am Here, Yo Estoy Aqui.* Watts, 1971, $3.95. Luz, who speaks no English, is lonely and frightened in kindergarten, until a Spanish speaking aide and her teacher help her to understand how to exchange words with the other children.

* BUCK, PEARL S. *The Chinese Story Teller.*

CLIFTON, LUCILLE. *The Black BC's.* il. by Don Miller. Dutton, 1970, $3.95. A short poem and a page of prose for each letter of the alphabet set forth the ways in which black people and black culture have contributed to our American heritage. The book talks of soldiers and politicians, teachers and writers, scientists and sportsmen—such people as Frederick Douglass, Harriet Tubman, Malcolm X, Martin Luther King, Jr., Mohammed Ali, Julian Bond, and Edward Brooke. Tempera drawings enhance the text.

FEAGUE, MILDRED. *The Little Indian and the Angel.* il. by DeGrazia. Childrens, 1970, $3.50. The Little Indian has "a very special friend who did whatever he did and went whenever he went." He is never alone. The angel is always with him. This rhythmical, charming text with its delicate, sparkling, and uncomplicated illustrations captures the quiet beauty of some of the activities of the little Navajo Indian and his friend through the seasons.

FEELINGS, MURIEL. *Moja Means One: A Swahili Counting Book.* il. by Tom Feelings. Dial, 1971, $4.50. Written to familiarize other children with East African life, this picture book also teaches them to count from 1 to 10 in Swahili. A map shows where Swahili is spoken.

GIOVANNI, NIKKI. *Spin a Soft Black Song.* il. by Charles Bible. Hill and Wang, 1971, $5.50. A beautifully illustrated book of poems about black children for children of all ages. The poems tell what childhood and growing up is all about as seen through the eyes of the very young. There are poems about mommies and daddies, about going to bed and out to play and to the supermarket, about having friends and about being afraid and just wanting a chance to grow up and meet the world. Simple in theme but a very moving collection nonetheless.

GREENE, CARLA. *Manuel, Young Mexican-American.* il. by Haris Petie. Lantern, 1969, $3.50. Young Jimmy learns through his friend Manuel about many Mexican-American customs and values: the making of tamales by watching Mrs. Perez, Manuel's mother, cook this popular food; the celebration or fiesta held on September 16, Mexican Independence Day, with all of its singing and dancing and the accompanying parade; the breaking of a piñata at a birthday party. This easy-to-read story includes a description of Jimmy's visit to Olvera Street, the oldest street in Los Angeles and one that remains as it was when the city was a small village.

HOOD, FLORA. *One Luminaria for Antonio: A Story of New Mexico.* il. by Ann Kirn. Putnam, 1966, $2.68. The importance of a religious saint's celebration, the preparation of the customary Christmas luminaries, are reflected in this simple beginning-to-read-story. Antonio, a small boy from a village in New Mexico, receives an unusual blessing because he is industrious and determined to celebrate Christmas.

KEATING, NORMA. *Mister Chu.* il. by Bernarda Bryson. Macmillan, 1965, $3.95. Mr. Chu, a shop owner in Chinatown, and Johnny, a six-year-old orphan living with Mr. Lee, another Chinese merchant, are very close friends. Mr. Chu demonstrates his interest and love for the boy in many ways: taking him on trips to many parts of the city, cooking Chinese suppers for him, explaining some of the Chinese food customs, playing and singing Chinese songs, having Johnny as his guest at the New Year's festival. The easy-to-read story, a descriptive account of the activities and warm friendship of an old man and a little boy, presents and explains aspects of the Chinese culture for the young reader.

* MILES, MISKA. *Annie and the Old One.*

PERRINE, MARY. *Nannabah's Friend.* il. by Leonard Weisgard. HM, 1970, $3.75. Those who prized *Salt Boy* will welcome this equally straight-forward and unsentimental story of a small, gentle Indian girl who faces loneliness and conquers it.

PRICE, CHRISTINE. *One Is God: Two Old Counting Songs.* Warne, 1970, $4.95. This very special book has lyrics and music of two old religious songs. "Green Grow the Rushes, Oh" is from the British Middle Ages and is illustrated with Christian religious symbols. "Who Knows One?" is a Hebrew song with lyrics in both English and Hebrew and Judaic symbols. There is a brief history of the song and an explanation of the symbols at the end of each song. Color illustrations on every page give the effect of stained glass windows. Type and design are handsome.

WRIGHT, M. W. *A Sky Full of Dragons.* Steck, 1969, $3.25. A Chinese boy in San Francisco is not included in the ritual to spring—the game of marbles—because he does not own any marbles. His grandfather helps him and his friends understand that kite flying is the Chinese welcome to spring. Through this story young children may see how all children love games even though their toys and equipment vary.

Intermediate

ATWOOD, ANN. *Haiku: The Mood of the Earth.* il. with photographs. Scribner, 1971, $5.95. The author asks whether or not it is possible by using Haiku, to combine verse and photography in order to go "inside nature" and see it from "one's head." The answer in this book is surely, "Yes."

BARNOUW, VICTOR. *Dream of the Blue Heron.* il. by Lynd Ward. Dell, 1969, $4.50 (P/Dell, $.75). Wabus, at twelve, is torn between loyalty to Chippewa customs and the desire to obtain an education so as to serve on the white men's councils. In school a web of events that he cannot understand or cope with almost causes him to give up. Wabus' sacred dream of the blue heron, symbolizing his future, finally helps him make peace with himself and the white man's world.

BUFF, MARY AND CONRAD. *Dancing Cloud.* il. by author. Viking Pr, 1957, $3.95. This recently revised story of Dancing Cloud and Lost Tooth, two Navajo Indian children, and their families gives the reader a perspective of some of the activities and values of these Arizona people. Separate episodes that center on such activities as weaving, shearing sheep, and herding are arranged in chapter form.

* BULLA, CLYDE. *Indian Hill.*

* BURCH, ROBERT. *D.J.'s Worst Enemy.*

* Castellanos, Jane. *Tomasito and the Golden Llamas.*

* Clark, Ann Nolan. *Medicine Man's Daughter.*

————. *Paco's Miracle.* il. by Agnes Tait. FS & G, 1962, $3.50. The miracle of love enriches the life of Paco, an orphaned boy of ten, and the families of a New Mexico village, who have befriended him now that his elderly guardian, Old Pierre, has fallen ill. Paco has always lived in seclusion in the remote mountain area with the Old One until he has to find help for hospitalizing his friend. A young villager, Thomas, welcomes the lonely boy into his home and later marries, and Paco remains as a third member of the family. This warm sensitive story, filled with detailed descriptions of the Spanish colonial culture of this area, the traditional wedding, La Posada Christmas festival, attitudes and values, will not only stimulate interest but help readers gain insights and understanding.

Clark, Electa. *Cherokee Chief: The Life of John Ross.* Macmillan, 1970, $3.95. The story of John Ross and the Cherokee Indians is told simply, in a direct, concise style. Like many tribes, the Cherokees were deceived, misused, and murdered. Their conscious, deliberate efforts under far-sighted leaders to save themselves by adopting the white man's ways did not prevent their being dispossessed of their lands on the eastern shores. Those who survived the Trail of Tears to Oklahoma in 1838 built new homes only to see them ravaged during the Civil War. The story is told with such dispassion and objectivity that the reader is affected more by the resiliency with which the Cherokees adapted to adversity than the tragedy of the injustice they suffered. The full-page charcoal drawings add much to the appeal of the story.

* Clifton, Lucille. *The Black BC's.*

* Crowell, Ann. *A Hogan for the Bluebird.*

De Gerez, Toni. *2 Rabbit 7 Wind: Poems from Ancient Mexico.* il. by Jorge Enceso. Viking Pr, 1971, $4.75. The fragments of three ancient Aztec texts reflect both the culture and the feelings of this ancient people. At the same time they appeal to the emotions of all peoples. The quality of the telling, the beauty of the format, and the informative introduction combine to produce an outstanding volume.

Doughty, W. Dyre. *Crimson Moccasins.* Har-Row, 1966, $3.95. Quick Eagle, an adopted son of Blue Heron, a Miami Indian chieftain, faces agony and pain in his manhood testing, only to learn that he is not an Indian, but a white boy. Confused, he begins to question his true worth as a future chieftain and his ability to uphold all the rich Indian culture in which he has been raised. The story of Revolutionary War times depicts the strong influence of tribal beliefs and customs. Eventually Quick Eagle returns to his family and bridges the gap between his two worlds.

FITCH, BOB AND LYNNE. *Soy Chicano, I Am Mexican-American.* il. with photographs. Creative Ed., 1971, $4.95. The story of a young Mexican-American girl living in the Central Valley of California. One of a family of nine children, Lupe tells of her day-to-day life, her family, her school, her friends and of the problems which face the Mexican-American farmworkers. Two things that come through very strongly are the unquestioned authority of the father as head of the family and the great allegiance of the Mexican-Americans to the United Farm Workers Union and to the Huelga (the strike).

* GRAHAM, LORENZ. *Every Man Heart Lay Down.*

————. *A Road Down in the Sea.* il. by Gregorio Prestopino. TY Crowell, 1971, $3.95. The story of Moses is retold in the words and thought patterns of a modern African boy. Mr. Graham says, "Behold a new vision with sharper images, sway with the rhythm of the storyteller, feel the beat of the drums."

HAUGAARD, KAY. *Myeko's Gift.* il. by Dora Ternei. Abelard, 1966, $3.95. Myeko, a Japanese girl newly arrived from Osaka, does not like the frightening world of the United States. Her mother, not wanting to deny their own culture, continues to encourage celebrating holidays in the ways of their homeland and uses some Japanese foods and clothes, while at the same time beginning to take on new ways. Myeko finds that she cannot deny her former culture and is surprised and pleased to discover that her American friends envy her having this opportunity.

* HOUSTON, JAMES. *Eagle Mask: A West Coast Indian Tale.*

JAMES, HARRY C. *Ovada: An Indian Boy of the Grand Canyon.* il. by Don Perceval. Ritchie, 1969, $3.95. The daily activities of Ovada, son of one of the thirty-four families of the Havasu Indian tribe, are described in this brief, informational narrative. Through the quiet, simple story and the orange silhouetted illustrations, one begins to build an understanding of the relationship between the Havasu's way of life and the Colorado River Canyon environment.

* JOHNSON, JAMES WELDON AND ROSAMOND. *Lift Every Voice and Sing.*

JONES, HETTIE (comp.) *The Trees Stand Shining.* il. by Robert Andrew Parker. Dial, 1971, $4.95. Beautiful watercolor paintings illustrate this selection of poetry which originally came down through the oral tradition of the Native Americans. There is a real depth to the songs which talk of the things that are most important to the Indian culture: the physical world and living creatures about them and above them, and the world of yesterday, today and tomorrow. For these people there seems to be a marvel in each new day's dawning.

KOHN, BERNICE. *Talking Leaves: The Story of Sequoyah.* il. by Valli. Hawthorn, 1969, $4.25. This well-researched biography is made more vivid by Valli's detailed illustrations. Sequoyah, though small and crippled, toiled for years to develop a syllabary and thus gave the Cherokees a written language.

LAMPMAN, EVELYN SIBLEY. *Go up the Road.* il. by Charles Robinson. M. K. McElderry, 1972, $5.50. A Chicano girl's dream of finishing grade school is made almost impossible because of her family's annual journey north from New Mexico to harvest crops in Oregon and Washington. This is a sensitive portrayal of the life of the migrant farm worker.

* ———. *Half-Breed.*

* LEWITON, MINA. *Candita's Choice.*

LEXAU, JOAN M. *Jose's Christmas Secret.* il. by Don Bolognese. Dial, 1963, $3.50. Pride in not accepting welfare in strange, foreign New York while struggling to earn a meager living on their own is a strong value held by ten-year-old Puerto Rican Jose, his younger brother, and his mother.

* MARTIN, PATRICIA MILES. *One Special Dog.*

———. *Trina's Boxcar.* il. by Robert L. Jefferson. Abingdon, 1967, $3.25. Trinidad Gonzales (Trina) and her family live in a boxcar at the edge of a small Wyoming town. She wants very much to have friends and feel that she is part of this small community. Her father works for the railroad and the family has traveled so much she has never felt as if she belongs anywhere. Trina's inability to speak English makes her problem even more acute.

* MILES, MISKA. *Annie and the Old One.*

NEWMAN, SHIRLEE PETKIN. *Yellow Silk for May Lee.* il. by Leslie Goldstein. Bobbs, 1961, $3.25. May Lee, daughter of a San Francisco Chinatown restaurant owner, faces, sometimes with difficulty, the differences between the older Chinese generation and the somewhat Americanized members of her family.

NIEMEYER, MARIE. *The Moon Guitar.* il. by Gustave E. Nebel. Watts, 1969, $3.50. Twelve-year-old Su-Lin is American; she does not want to be sent to Taiwan to become "a proper Chinese girl." But Grandfather thinks she ought to be brought up in the old established ways —the ways of the family which once owned the long-lost and beautiful moon guitar. Su-Lin and her American friend Tracy search San Francisco's Chinatown for the family treasure. The result is exciting and changes the attitudes of both Grandfather and Su-Lin.

* OAKES, VANYA. *Willy Wong: American.*

O'DELL, SCOTT. *Island of the Blue Dolphins.* HM, 1960, $3.75 (P/Dell, $.95). An Indian girl is forced to spend eighteen years alone on a harsh, bleak island off California. Courageously she makes the best of circumstances, forages for food, makes animals her companions, and relies upon herself during her growing years. She is a young woman when rescued and taken to the mainland.

* POULAKIS, PETER (ed.). *American Folklore.*

ROCKWELL, ANNE. *The Dancing Stars.* il. by author. Crowell, 1972, $3.95. In easy language and pleasing illustrations the author, who has spent several years on an Indian reservation, tells one of the most moving legends of Native Americans. The mythical story of the creation of a familiar constellation is embodied in the human and poignant story of the deep and lasting love among seven brothers.

* SCHAEFER, JACK. *Old Ramon.*

* SHECTER, BEN. *Someplace Else.*

SMUCKER, BARBARA C. *Wigwam in the City.* il. by Gil Miret. Dutton, 1966, $3.95. Twelve-year-old Susan Bearskin and her family leave their Chippewa reservation in Wisconsin to live in Chicago. Susan is told to always be proud she is Chippewa and encouraged to learn in school the ways of the white man in order to someday return home to help her people. However, her seventeen-year-old brother feels that Indians will never rise above poverty if they keep their Indian ways. Therefore, Jim Bearskin changes his name and severs his Indian ties in his efforts to become white. The conflicts of minority-group children are convincingly presented.

TABRAH, RUTH M. *Hawaiian Heart.* Follett, 1964, $3.48. Dr. Fergus and his family, including twelve-year-old Emily, her nine-year-old brother, and their mother, arrive in Hawaii to live on a large sugar plantation for a year. All are eager to learn about Hawaii and become *kamaaina* (true islanders at heart). With such attitudes and eagerness, their desire becomes reality as they enjoy learning about the diverse cultures and people who inhabit the islands. The family goes on archaeological explorations, participates in the Bon Dance at the Buddhist temple, and enjoys other activities characteristic of island life.

THOMPSON, VIVIAN L. *Aukele The Fearless: A Legend of Old Hawaii.* il. by Earl Thollander. Golden Gate, 1972, $4.50. With smooth-flowing continuity, the author has woven the legends of Aukele into a rousing tale that should appeal to those with an interest in Polynesian folk literature. Aukele is the eleventh and favorite son of a rich and powerful aging chief, who is descended from the gods and who is further allied with them through marriage. The jealousy and tyranny of the oldest brother lead Aukele into a series of Jason-like adventures which bring about the death of the ten brothers and Aukele's marriage to a sorceress. Unlike Medea, the wife is everlastingly won over by his power, fearlessness and generosity, and with her help he is able to restore his brothers to life. The illustrator, with very attractive pen and ink wash, creates a mood just right for the legend. There are a list of characters, explaining relationships, and a glossary of Hawaiian words that strengthen the story. Sources are credited and the legend is seemingly well researched.

————. *Hawaiian Tales of Heroes and Champions.* il. by Herbert Kawainui Kane. Holiday, 1971, $4.95. The authors knows and respects Hawaiian legend, and has always shown integrity in her retelling. This collection is her best yet. The subject matter also has great appeal, dealing with kupua, or supernatural beings, who roam the islands and do great deeds. The element of exaggeration adds to the excitement and entertainment in these tales. The illustrations give an authentic feeling of the islands. Glossary and excellent bibliography included.

WALTRIP, LELA AND RUFUS. *Quiet Boy.* il. by Theresa Kalab Smith. McKay, 1961, $2.95. Before Quiet Boy's father is killed in military service during World War II, he advises his son, a young Navajo living on an Arizona reservation, to study and learn as much as he can about the white man's ways and language. Attending a government school, carrying the responsibilities as man of the house, facing conflicts of ideas between generations even within his family, and serving his people by working with government pilots during a heavy storm, make an intriguing story centered around Quiet Boy. Many aspects of culture, such as the beliefs and lore that surround the use of turquoise; the foods and clothing; and the meeting of change, all depict the feelings, beliefs and everyday life of the Navajo of today. Readers have an excellent opportunity to sense the conflicts and to heighten awareness of these people.

WARREN, MARY PHRANER. *Walk in My Moccasins.* il. by Victor Mays. Westminster, 1966, $3.75. Twelve-year-old Melody, a Sioux Indian girl, and her younger brothers and sisters are adopted by a childless white Montana couple. The many and trying adjustments include learning the family patterns and living in an "everything-in-its-place-home" and a "dishes-can-wait-home."

WYNDHAM, ROBERT. *Tales the People Tell in China.* Messner, 1971, $4.95. A collection of stories, fables, and proverbs that reflects many facets of Chinese culture, including a People's Republic version of "Mai Liang and his Magic Brush."

WYSS, THELMA HATCH. *Star Girl.* il. by John Pimlott. Viking Pr, 1967, $3.95. The Bannock Indians relate a historical legend filled with vivid, authentic accounts of their customs and arts. The story centers on Star Girl who is mysteriously taken to the Cheyenne of the Sky and forgets her earthly past in the Snake River country of Idaho. Star Girl, adopted by the Cheyenne grass root woman, is taught the secrets of healing with roots and herbs. Indian herbal medicine practices are often traced to Star Girl's daughter who brought this knowledge to her people.

Junior

ADLER, MORTIMER J. *The Negro in American History,* 1972 edition. Encyclopaedia Britannica, 1972, $24.50 per set. This 3-volume set contains 186 selections by 134 different authors covering a period of 400 years of American history. It is reprinted in reverse chronological order, with Volume 3 containing a complete index: Volume 1, Black Americans, 1928-1971; Volume 2, A Taste of Freedom, 1854-1927; Volume 3, Slaves and Masters, 1567-1854. These volumes, updated through 1971, give a detailed documentary history of the Afro-American by black and white authors who voice a personal view of the relationship between the Afro-American and white American life and culture during these 400 years.

ADOFF, ARNOLD (ed.). *Black Out Loud: An Anthology of Modern Poems by Black Americans.* il. by Alvin Hollingsworth. Macmillan, 1970, $4.95. Black poets of all ages—many under thirty—tell of the black experience in America. Adding much to the reading pleasure is the organization of the book into six theme areas, each poem complementing others within the group. Few modern collections seem so promising for classroom sharing in single or in choral readings.

———. *I Am the Darker Brother: An Anthology of Modern Poems by Negro Americans.* il. by Benny Andrews. Macmillan, 1968, $4.95 (P/Macmillan, $1.25). These poems, by accomplished authors such as Langston Hughes, Richard Wright, and Gwendolyn Brooks, have been selected to reveal how the Negro feels about his condition in America.

———. (ed.) *It Is the Poem Singing into Your Eyes: An Anthology of New Young Poets.* Har-Row, 1971, $4.50 (P/Har-Row, $1.95). A fine collection of poems written by young adults mostly in their late teens, all Americans from every ethnic and economic background. Many poems show the influence of modern poets, e.g., Ezra Pound, E. E. Cummings. One poet who seems to be finding her own voice is Laura Nagan whose four contributions are strong and individual.

ALEXANDER, RAE PACE (comp.) *Young and Black in America.* Random, 1970, $3.95. Selections from the writings of eight black Americans, the majority of whom came from humble beginnings in the South and fought against great odds to gain recognition not only for themselves but for their people. Determined, angry young men and women, they could no longer accept the position they held in society. This book serves as a good introduction to the complete works of these people who contributed so much to the black heritage of America today.

* Atwood, Ann. *Haiku: The Mood of the Earth.*

* Barnouw, Victor. *Dream of the Blue Heron.*

* Bartholomew, Carol. *My Heart Has Seventeen Rooms.*

Bonham, Frank. *Durango Street.* Dutton, 1965, $3.95 (P/Schol Bk Serv, $.75). In order to survive, Rufus Henry violates the terms of his parole and joins the Moors, one of the rival gangs in the Durango Housing Project. Rufus fights his way to leadership and establishes a territory that no one dares challenge. This book gives insight into the lives of teenagers who must resort to violence in order to survive and tells of the frustrations of those who try to help them.

* ———. *Viva Chicano.*

Clark, Ann Nolan. *Medicine Man's Daughter.* il. by Donald Bolognese. FS & G, 1963, $3.50. Her heritage and devotion to the Navajo way of life guide Tall-Girl through years of grooming to become Medicine Woman for her people. Prompted by a ritual experience, she gradually realizes that she must leave the reservation and attend a white man's school. After facing many obstacles, Tall-Girl is finally assured of her "modern medicine" education.

* Clark, Electa. *Cherokee Chief.*

* Colman, Hila. *A Girl from Puerto Rico.*

Davis, Russell, and Brent Ashabranner. *The Choctaw Code.* P/ McGraw, 1961, $.60. Fifteen-year-old Tom finds it hard to understand the law of the Choctaw nation in Indian Territory, now Oklahoma. His young Indian friend, Jim, who teaches him to hunt and trap, must surrender to the law and uphold Choctaw honor because of an accidental killing.

* De Gerez, Toni. *2 Rabbit 7 Wind: Poems from Ancient Mexico.*

Dodson, Owen. *When Trees Were Green.* P/Popular Lib, 1951, $.60. Coin Foreman is a nine-year-old Negro boy from the Brownsville section of Brooklyn. This is his year of growing up, the year when he finds out that "nigger" means "a bad person."

* Doss, Helen. *The Family Nobody Wanted.*

* Douglass, Frederick. *The Mind and Heart of Frederick Douglass: Excerpts from Speeches of the Great Negro Orator.*

Emery, Anne. *Tradition.* Vanguard, 1946, $3.50. Students may enjoy this novel about the impact a Japanese family has on the all-white community it moves into during World War II. The Japanese children excel in school, including sports, and thus represent a threat to the hometown students. When the neighbors learn the Nisei family's oldest son has been killed in action defending, coincidentally, a boy from the new neighborhood, hope for the community rises.

* FITCH, BOB AND LYNNE. *Soy Chicano, I Am Mexican-American.*

GRAHAM, LORENZ. *South Town.* Follett, 1958, $3.95 (P/NAL, $.60). Young David Williams yearns to become a doctor and help his Southern Negro neighbors. However, even daily existence becomes a fearful problem when some white citizens try to keep the Negroes "in their place." The improving status of the Negroes threatens those whites who need to feel superior to others.

HAZELTON, ELIZABETH BALDWIN. *Tides of Danger.* Scribner, 1967, $4.50. This story set in northern Mexico concerns Trinidad Delgado, a fourteen-year- old boy who vows to rescue his family from peonage. Trin dreams of happy times on the peaceful island where his father had been a pearl diver and decides that he too will be a diver and find a great pearl that will pay for his family's ransom.

* HINTON, S. E. *The Outsiders.*

HOUSTON, JAMES. *Songs of the Dream People.* il. by author. M. K. McElderry Books, Atheneum, 1972, $5.95. This collection by a distinguished Canadian author and artist arranges by regions the chants and poems by North American Indians and Eskimos.

* ISSLER, ANNE ROLLER. *Young Red Flicker.*

* JONES, HETTIE (comp.) *The Trees Stand Shining.*

* JONES, WEYMAN. *Edge of Two Worlds.*

* LAMPMAN, EVELYN SIBLEY. *Go up the Road.*

* LESTER, JULIUS. *To Be a Slave.*

LEWIS, RICHARD (comp.) *I Breathe a New Song: Poems of the Eskimo.* il. by Oonark. S & S, 1971, $5.95. An effective, representative collection of Eskimo poetry. Most of the pieces are anonymous but are identified by Eskimo group or geographical origin, and the book is illustrated with primitive drawings by an Eskimo artist. Combining forcefulness with simplicity, the poems include songs of joy, love, fear, and death. Anthropologist Carpenter's introduction explains Eskimo beliefs and manner of expression.

LIVANT, ROSE A. *Julie's Decision.* Washburn, 1969, $3.95. Julie, a fifteen-year-old Negro girl from Georgia, moves to an integrated housing project in the North. Not only must she adjust to a new way of life, but also to a mother and sister she has never known. How Julie adjusts is the theme of this perceptive, well-written, and fast moving story. The subtle contrasts between Negro life in the North and South are well done.

McDOWELL, ROBERT E. AND EDWARD LAVITT. *Third World Voices for Children.* il. by Barbara Kohn Isaac. Viking Pr, 1971, $4.95. An anthology of stories, folktales, and poems for all children divided into four sections containing stories from Africa; the other three, stories from the West Indies, the United States and Papua-New Guinea point up the great influence of African folklore on cultures throughout the world. The same characters and concerns turn up repeatedly under different guises. Many of the stories included are traditional and many were written by contemporary authors.

MARRIOTT, ALICE. *Indian Annie: Kiowa Captive.* McKay, 1965, $3.75. At the age of ten Annie Donovon is taken from her family in Texas by Kiowa Indians. Her captor Sahnko and his wife treat her kindly and Annie grows up as a member of the Kiowa tribe. After many years, she finds her own family.

MELTZER, MILTON. *Tongue of Flame: The Life of Lydia Maria Child.* TY Crowell, 1965, $3.95. Lydia Maria Child, leading writer of the 1830s, was also one of the humanitarians in the abolitionist, later the civil rights, movement. She founded the first children's magazine, wrote a history of women, was an editor and syndicated newspaper columnist, and wrote the first book to attack slavery.

* MONTGOMERY, JEAN. *The Wrath of Coyote.*

NEWELL, HOPE. *A Cap for Mary Ellis.* Har-Row, 1952, $3.50. Mary Ellis and her friend Julia feel that they must accept an invitation to attend an all-white nursing school to pave the way for other Negro students. Although suffering from homesickness for Harlem, Mary Ellis has many new exciting experiences during her first year of training.

———. *Mary Ellis, Student Nurse.* Har-Row, 1958, $3.50. Mary Ellis undertakes her second year of nurses' training, as eager as ever to help anyone in distress.

NEWLON, CLARKE. *Famous Mexican Americans.* il. with photographs. Dodd, 1972, $3.95. Mexican-Americans were building the Southwest long before the Pilgrims landed. This and other overlooked facts come to light in this collective biography of twenty Chicanos who have become known for their accomplishments. It contains a foreword by a Chicano psychiatrist, a list of source materials, and an index.

* O'DELL, SCOTT. *The Black Pearl.*

* ———. *Island of the Blue Dolphins.*

* OJIGBO, A. OKION, (comp.) *Young and Black in Africa.*

PEARE, CATHERINE O. *Mary Macleod Bethune.* Vanguard, 1951, $3.95. Raised in poverty, Mary Macleod Bethune was fired with determination to learn to read and thereby help her people. She was educated through prayer, sacrifice, and scholarships. With $1.50 and faith in

God, she founded a Negro college in Florida, now Bethune-Cookman College. She became a national Negro leader and held positions in the National Youth Administration, the National Urban League, the N.A.A.C.P., and the United Nations.

PECK, IRA. *The Life and Words of Martin Luther King, Jr.* P/Schol Bk Serv, 1968, $.60. This biography outlines the life of Dr. King, his accomplishments and his trials, including the indignities to which he and his followers were subjected. Many extracts from Dr. King's speeches indicate the major points for which he labored.

RASMUSSEN, KNUD (ed.) *Beyond the High Hills: A Book of Eskimo Poems.* il. with photographs by Guy Mary-Rousselierre. World Pub, 1961, $4.95. Containing poems collected from among the Eskimos in the Hudson Bay region and in the Copper Country and illustrated with many fine contemporary photographs, this book gives great insight into the Eskimo way of life and thinking. It depicts them in times of joy and sorrow, plenty and need. Several poems tell of their fishing and hunting exploits, and of death and the hereafter in the world "beyond the high hills."

* SHECTER, BEN. *Someplace Else.*

SOMMERFELT, AIMÉE. *Miriam.* Criterion, 1963, $3.95 (P/Schol Bk Serv, $.60). In Oslo during World War II, Hanne's family moves into the house from which Miriam's family has been forced to flee because they are Jews. The two girls meet; their friendship lasts through the terrors of German occupation and Miriam's years as a refugee in Sweden. The Nazi purge brings death to Miriam's father, sister, and brother-in-law; but her final despair is that the end of war does not bring an end to prejudice.

STERNE, EMMA GOLDERS. *Benito Juarez: Builder of a Nation.* Knopf, 1967, $3.95. Benito Juarez, a poor Indian in Oaxaca state in the early nineteenth century, had to struggle to earn a living and gain an education. Entering politics during the crucial period of Mexico's emergence as a democratically self-governing nation, he helped shape the destiny of Mexico.

* THOMPSON, VIVIAN L. *Aukele The Fearless: A Legend of Old Hawaii.*

TINKER, BARBARA WILSON. *When the Fire Reaches Us.* Morrow, 1970, $6.95 (P/Curtis, $.95). Danny Sands, a product of the Detroit ghetto, looks back on his life immediately after the riots of 1967. He pictures —despite his disillusionment with white America and his years of poverty, injustice, and bitterness—his world on Pine Street with a bitter-sweet humor.

* VOSS, CARROLL. *White Cap for Rechinda.*

* VROMAN, MARY ELIZABETH. *Harlem Summer.*

* WENTWORTH, ELAINE. *Mission to Metlakatla.*

* WIBBERLEY, LEONARD. *Island of the Angels.*

* WONG, JADE SNOW. *Fifth Chinese Daughter.*

YATES, ELIZABETH. *Amos Fortune, Free Man.* il. by Nora S. Unwin. Dutton, 1950, $3.95. At fifteen, a boy was captured and enslaved. Taken to America, he tried to hold on to his proud ideals. Earning his freedom, he became a useful and worthwhile citizen of New England, also purchasing the freedom of several others. He was a quiet-living, unassuming man of whom few knew; yet, when Amos Fortune died in 1801 in Jaffrey, New Hampshire, he had reason to be proud of the life he had led.

YOUNG, BOB AND JAN. *Across the Tracks.* Messner, 1958, $3.50 (P/WSP, $.60). Third-generation Mexican-American, Betty Ochoa is an active senior student at Bellamar High School. Elected against odds as Activities Commissioner, she plays a major role in developing better relations between Mexican-Americans and the middle-class whites who live in Northridge on the "right side" of the tracks. Betty also comes to appreciate her own heritage.

Senior

* ADLER, MORTIMER J. *The Negro in American History,* 1972 edition.

* ADOFF, ARNOLD (ed.). *Black on Black: Commentaries by Negro-Americans.*

* ———. (ed.). *Black Out Loud: An Anthology of Modern Poems by Black Americans.*

* ———. *I Am the Darker Brother.*

* ———. (ed.) *It Is the Poem Singing into Your Eyes: An Anthology of New Young Poets.*

* ALEXANDER, RAE PACE (comp.) *Young and Black in America.*

ALLEN, TERRY. *The Whispering Wind: Poetry by Young American Indians.* Doubleday, 1972, $1.95. These poems reflect the young Native Americans' dreams, hopes, yearnings, and flashes of insight, and are sensitive and vivid expressions of a valued but little known facet of American Literature.

* ANDERSON, WILLIAM ASHLEY. *Angel of Hudson Bay.*

* ASTROV, MARGOT. *American Indian Prose and Poetry.*

* ATWOOD, ANN. *Haiku: The Mood of the Earth.*

* Baldwin, James. *The Amen Corner.*

* Bartholomew, Carol. *My Heart Has Seventeen Rooms.*

Bierhorst, John (ed.). *In the Trail of the Wind: American Indian Poems and Ritual Orations.* il. with engravings. FS & G, 1971, $4.95 (P/ FS & G, $2.45). Poetry, prayers, incantations, myths, and omens gathered from the oral tradition of many native American tribes of both North and South America (including Eskimo). Includes poems of creation, life and death, poems about love and war, fear and courage, and poems of dreams, omens and prophecies of life to come. A glossary of tribes and language as well as notes for each poem contribute greatly to the collection.

Bontemps, Arna (ed.). *American Negro Poetry.* Hill & Wang, 1963, $4.95 (P/Hill & Wang, $1.75). A fine collection of poems by Negro poets who express the desires, the fears, the struggles of the black man. Included are poems suitable for use from upper elementary grades through college levels.

* Borland, Hal G. *When the Legends Die.*

Bothwell, Jean. *The Silver Mango Tree.* HBJ, 1960, $3.50. Barbara Tennant returns reluctantly to India after four years at an American college. Her father is a mission administrator in Rajahpur, but Barbara had hated India on an earlier visit. She finds herself caught up in local Indian affairs and is even wooed by a handsome young Indian prince. She grows to love India, but must also decide whether she can give up her American heritage and learn to live as a Hindu in a mixed marriage.

* Boyle, Sarah Patton. *The Desegregated Heart.*

Brooks, Gwendolyn. *Maud Martha* (in *The World of Gwendolyn Brooks*). Har-Row, 1971, $7.95. A series of vignettes tells of Maud Martha, a Negro girl who wants "to be cherished." The story tells about Maud from the age of seven through the school years, and into marriage and the birth of her first child. Although life does not fulfill her dreams, Maud Martha continues to feel a great joy in being alive.

Canzoneri, Robert. *I Do So Politely.* HM, 1965, $4.00. A Mississippian examines relations between Negroes and whites in his native state. Based primarily upon personal experiences, this book comments upon the author's hypocrisy and inability to face the reality which he finds.

* Cather, Willa. *Death Comes for the Archbishop.*

David, Jay (ed.). *Growing up Black.* Morrow, 1968, $6.50 (P/several). A collection of excerpts from the writings of Negro authors who describe their experiences in childhood and adolescence. The selections are divided into three sections—Growing up Black; The Nineteenth

Century: A Time of Upheaval; and the Twentieth Century: The Bitter Legacy.

* DeCarava, Roy, and Langston Hughes. *The Sweet Flypaper of Life.*

Demby, William. *Beetlecreek.* P/Avon, 1969, $.95. Old Bill Trapp lives for many years near the black section of a West Virginia town. This recluse, who chases away those who try to come near his home, gradually learns that people are important in his life. As he opens up to them, however, he is exposed to the prejudice of both blacks and whites.

Duberman, Martin B. *In White America.* P/NAL, 1964, $.60. Except for introductory narratives, this play is based entirely on documents, diaries, and speeches pertaining to the historical plight of black people in America. It starts with comments concerning desegregation of schools in 1964 and continues by moving backward in time through the period of the slave trade. The Civil War, Reconstruction, World Wars I and II, and the experience of a lone black girl in Arkansas in 1954 are some topics.

* Fuller, Iola. *The Loon Feather.*

Graham, Lorenz. *Whose Town?* TY Crowell, 1969, $4.50. David Williams, a black high school student living in North Town, inadvertently gets into trouble involving some whites. The incident ends in the shooting of one of his friends.

Hansberry, Lorraine. *Raisin in the Sun.* Random, 1959, $5.50 (P/NAL, $.75). An insurance check for $10,000 is what World War II veteran Mr. Younger left for his wife and two children who live on Chicago's south side. Walter, the son, is eager to use the money to buy a business, but his wife and mother are more concerned about a house where they can live decently. Although he loses two-thirds of the money to an untrustworthy friend, Walter "comes into his manhood" when he faces the white man who tries to discourage the family from moving into a white neighborhood.

Hoffine, Lyla. *Carol Blue Wing.* McKay, 1967, $4.50. Having just finished her junior year at college, Carol Blue Wing returns home for the summer. She is struck anew by the beauty of the Indian ways and by her grandmother's ability to unite the old and new. Yet she hopes to teach white children rather than children on the reservation. This leads to conflict between Carol and the man she loves, who wants to help the Indians.

* Houston, James. *Songs of the Dream People.*

Hughes, Langston. *Black Misery.* il. by Arouni. Erickson, 1969, $2.50. This humorous, satirical portrait lends some insight into the problems of the black child growing up in America.

————. *Simple's Uncle Sam.* Hill & Wang, 1967, $3.95 (P/Hill & Wang, $1.75). These forty-six new stories by Langston Hughes are told in the words of Jesse B. Semple, known as Simple, the sage from Harlem. His wise witticisms cover all topics, for example: "If I was of a mind to give a Christmas gift to the Devil . . . I would give him Mississippi, the whole state of Mississippi, police dogs and all."

* HUNTER, KRISTIN. *The Soul Brothers and Sister Lou.*

JORDAN, JUNE. *Who Look at Me?* il. with twenty-seven paintings. TY Crowell, 1969, $5.95. "We do not see those we do not know. Love and all varieties of happy concern depend on the discovery of one's self in another. The question of every desiring heart is, thus, WHO LOOK AT ME?" So writes the poet-author of this sensitive portrayal of the black man in poetry and painting.

* KISSIN, EVA H. (ed.). *Stories in Black & White.*

KROEBER, THEODORA. *Ishi in Two Worlds: A Biography of the Last Wild Indian in North America.* U Cal Pr, 1961, $5.95 (P/U Cal Pr, $2.25). Ishi is the last of the California Indians. Robbed of his home and bereft of his people, in final desperation he turns to the white man, his enemy. Yet it is with the white man that he lives out his final years. In gentleness and peace, he lives in the white man's city, taken with the great wonder of the modern world.

* ————. *Ishi, Last of His Tribe.*

* LEWIS, RICHARD (comp.) *I Breathe a New Song: Poems of the Eskimo.*

* LIVANT, ROSE A. *Julie's Decision.*

* McDOWELL, ROBERT E. AND EDWARD LAVITT. *Third World Voices for Children.*

MADDUX, RACHEL. *Abel's Daughter.* Har-Row, 1960, O.P. An Army officer and his wife learn about racial problems in a small southern town. The problem of white people who accept and want to be accepted by a Negro group as "people" rather than as "white people" is complicated by rules established by groups beyond their control.

* MARQUES, RENE. *The Oxcart.*

* MARRIOTT, ALICE. *Indian Annie: Kiowa Captive.*

* MEANS, FLORENCE CRANNELL. *Our Cup Is Broken.*

* MELTZER, MILTON. *Tongue of Flame: The Life of Lydia Maria Child.*

* MOMADAY, N. SCOTT. *House Made of Dawn.*

* MORIN, RAUL. *Among the Valiant.*

* NEWLON, CLARKE. *Famous Mexican Americans.*

OJIGBO, A. OKION, (comp.) *Young and Black in Africa.* Random, 1971, $3.95. The author believes that "if a non-African truly wants to understand Africans he should listen to what Africans have to say about their own way of life." In this book eight young Africans from six different countries write simply and with feeling of their struggle for education and independence, recognizing the clash that exists between the old world and the new. Educated mainly abroad, the majority have since returned to their native countries to continue their work.

PARKS, GORDON. *A Choice of Weapons.* Har-Row, 1966, $6.95. This is the autobiography of the prominent black photographer for *Life* magazine who learned about prejudice firsthand as a pullman porter and as a photographer in World War II.

* ———. *The Learning Tree.*

PECK, RICHARD (ed.). *Sounds and Silences.* Delacorte, 1970, $4.50 (P/ Dell, $.60). An anthology of contemporary poems which deal with such topics as family, childhood, love, war, self-concept, etc.

* RASMUSSEN, KNUD (ed.) *Beyond the High Hills: A Book of Eskimo Poems.*

* RICHTER, CONRAD. *A Country of Strangers.*

RODMAN, BELLA. *Lions in the Way.* Follett, 1966, $3.95 (P/Avon, $.60). Five years after the U.S. Supreme Court outlawed racial segregation in the public schools, eight black students are admitted to fictitious Fayette High School in a southern border town. The opposition is strong, but sixteen-year-old Robert Jones and his friends courageously make the effort that helps to establish equal educational opportunities for members of their race.

SCHULTZ, JAMES W. *My Life as an Indian.* Hawthorn, 1957, $3.00 (P/ Fawcett World, $.95). The author, who as a youth indulged in adventure-fantasies, left New England to live among the Blackfeet, experience the rhythm of their lives, and learn to relate to their culture. He recounts the tribe's history and his day-to-day acculturation.

SILBERMAN, CHARLES E. *Crisis in Black and White.* Random, 1964, $5.95 (P/Random, $1.95). This objective analysis probes the Negro problem, tracing the transformation of the heroic African into the submissive slave. The crux of the present-day Negro problem is seen not as discrimination, but as apathy born of self-hatred due to the Negro's lack of power to help himself.

SMITH, LILLIAN E. *Strange Fruit.* HBJ, 1944, $4.95. (P/NAL, $.95). Tracy Deen and Nonnie Anderson love each other as they grow up together. Tracy is white and Nonnie is black. Each feels the pressure of the racial barriers of the South.

* SOMMERFELT, AIMÉE. *My Name Is Pablo.*

STEINBECK, JOHN. *The Pearl.* Viking Pr, 1947, $3.50 (P/several). This old Mexican folk tale is simple, but moving. Kino the fisherman, his wife Juana, and their baby Coyotito have an indestructible closeness as they face the events following Kino's discovery of a priceless pearl. Portrayed poignantly is the people's superstition, which is supported by illiteracy and ignorance. The love of family and the patriarchal family structure are vividly described, as is the feeling of the Mexicans toward those who rule the village.

STYRON, WILLIAM. *The Confessions of Nat Turner.* Random, 1967, $7.95 (P/NAL, $1.25). A Negro preacher, Nat Turner, led the only partly effective revolt in the annals of American Negro slavery. An educated man, he felt divinely ordained to free the blacks of Virginia.

THOMAS, PIRI. *Down These Mean Streets.* Knopf, 1967, $5.95 (P/NAL, $1.25). This autobiography is set in the streets of Spanish Harlem where every form of human depravity seems commonplace. Rejected by his father because of his dark skin, Piri turns rebelliously to the street, which is a battleground where he earns his rights. Piri fights, steals, becomes a drug addict, and finally goes to prison after shooting a policeman. He survives drug withdrawal and the physical and mental degradation of prison.

VASQUEZ, RICHARD. *Chicano.* Doubleday, 1970, $6.95. This absorbing novel traces the Sandoval family through several generations. In a Mexico torn by revolution, Hector Sandoval dreams of a better life and flees with his family to *Los Estados Unidos,* where they must work as itinerant farm workers, facing the prejudice, discrimination, and police harassment all too common to Chicanos.

VOSS, CARROLL. *White Cap for Rechinda.* Washburn, 1966, $3.75. Rechinda is torn between loyalty to her Indian reservation and her love for the hospital world. Each time Rechinda becomes discouraged with her attempts to adjust to the white man's customs, intern Ross Two Moon goads her into trying harder. Eventually Ross shows Rechinda that it is possible to live successfully as a member of both worlds.

WALKER, MARGARET. *Jubilee.* HM, 1966, $6.95 (P/Bantam, $.95). This powerful narrative of the Civil War is told through the central character, Vyry, daughter of a white father and a Negro slave mother. This remarkable woman, even after she endured unbelievable physical mistreatment as a slave and cruel harassment of herself and her family by the Ku Klux Klan, could still say, "God knows I ain't got no hate in my heart for nobody." Vyry was the maternal great grandmother of the author. This novel is a Houghton Mifflin Literary Fellowship Novel.

* WALLACE, IRVING. *The Man.*

WATERS, ETHEL, AND CHARLES SAMUELS. *His Eye Is on the Sparrow.* P/Pyramid Pubns, 1951, $.75. This autobiography by Ethel Waters tells of an unhappy, unloved, and sordid life in the black tenements. Born out of wedlock, Miss Waters refused to be kept down by her environment. She started out as a shimmy shaker, created a name as a blues singer, and became an established Broadway actress and movie star. Yet, never did she lose touch with the black people.

WONG, JADE SNOW. *Fifth Chinese Daughter.* Har-Row, 1950, $5.95. Although Jade Snow and her family live in San Francisco, her strict parents demand that she conform to Chinese customs. Jade Snow's opinions are not highly regarded in her home until she goes away to college and learns the American way of life. As Jade Snow grows in independence, she earns the respect of her family, and is able to help them to cope with the problems arising from the conflict of cultures.

* YOUNG, BOB AND JAN. *Across the Tracks.*

Mature

* ALLEN, TERRY. *The Whispering Wind: Poetry by Young American Indians.*

AZUELA, MARIANO. *The Underdogs.* P/NAL, 1962, $.75. This book is a translation of *Los de Abajo,* considered the greatest novel of the Mexican revolution. Demetrio Macias, the young hero, is forced to side with the rebels to save his family. In the course of the battle he becomes a compulsive militarist and emerges a general. The brutality of the revolution is manifested through every character.

BROWN, CLAUDE. *Manchild in the Promised Land.* Macmillan, 1965, $6.95 (P/NAL, $1.25). Autobiographical in approach, the book deals with ghetto life in Harlem. Claude Brown, former dope pusher completely enmeshed in ghetto misery, finally realizes that he is an example for no man. He finally extricates himself, becoming a law student at one of America's leading universities.

CLARK, ANN NOLAN. *Journey to the People.* Viking Pr, 1969, $4.50. *Journey to the People* is a collection of essays by Ann Nolan Clark telling of her experiences in teaching and living with children of the Zuni, Navajo, Pueblo, and other Southwest Indian nations. Although about children, this book is probably more valuable to teachers and others who seek a deep insight into the lives, cultures, and aspirations of the Indians.

CLEAVER, ELDRIDGE. *Soul on Ice.* McGraw, 1968, $5.95 (P/Dell, $.95). Primarily autobiographical, this collection of essays and letters written while Cleaver was in prison describes those relationships and events which shaped his life: Catholicism, Muslims, the death of Malcolm X, and his own "healed spirit."

* DAVID, JAY (ed.). *Growing up Black.*

* DUBERMAN, MARTIN B. *In White America.*

ELLISON, RALPH. *Invisible Man.* Random, 1952, $7.50 (P/NAL, $1.25). "I'm an invisible man and it placed me in a hole—or showed me the hole I was in, if you will—and I reluctantly accepted the fact," summarizes a black who struggled from the South to the North in his search for identity. Educated in a black college, he becomes a spokesman for blacks in Harlem. But he speaks against race riots and so continues to be the invisible man, whom people look at but do not see. This story portrays the tragedy of a black man in America.

FADERMAN, LILLIAN, AND BARBARA BRADSHAW (eds.). *Speaking for Ourselves: Contemporary Ethnic Writing.* P/Scott F, 1969, $5.25. This excellent anthology of ethnic writing features contemporary authors, many of whom have never been widely published. The six chapters focus attention on Spanish, Negro, Oriental, Jewish, Indian, European, and Near-Eastern Americans.

FANON, FRANTZ. *Black Skin, White Masks.* Grove, 1967, $5.00 (P/Grove, $.95). Frantz Fanon, famed author of *Wretched of the Earth*, analyzes the black's psychology in a white world. Fanon's in-depth analysis of this multifaceted problem is drawn from personal experience as well as from training in psychiatry, emphasizing the black's conscious and subconscious reactions to world-wide racism and colonialism.

* GIOVANNI, NIKKI. *Spin a Soft Black Song.*

GREGORY, DICK. *Nigger: An Autobiography.* Dutton, 1964, $5.95 (P/PB, $.95). The autobiography of Dick Gregory, the well-known comedian, depicts his struggle to success. The book stresses those people and events that helped him to achieve his goal.

HERSEY, JOHN R. *White Lotus.* Knopf, 1965, $6.95 (P/Bantam, $1.50). China conquers the United States and makes slaves of the whites. A young girl's experiences depict the familiar patterns of prejudice, discrimination, racist myths, quixotic rebellions, liberalism, and conflicts of radical solutions against patient nonviolent protests. More than a mere transformation of the white vs. black racial conflict, the novel is a serious, completely developed portrayal of the universal elements of slavery in all cultures.

JONES, LEROI. *Tales.* Grove, 1967, $4.50. *Tales* is a book of stories, the titles of which are indicative of the suggestiveness and the clarity of message. "A Chase" and "Uncle Tom's Cabin: Alternate Ending" are only two examples. The basic issue in each tale is that of black consciousness, either in black or in white America.

LEWIS, OSCAR. *La Vida*. Random, 1966, $12.50. This story of a low-income Puerto Rican slum family in San Juan and New York depicts a style of life which is common in many of the deprived and marginal groups in our society but which is largely unknown to or ignored by most middle-class readers. Lewis presents the culture of poverty and the individuals who live within it.

LITTO, FREDRIC M. (ed.). *Plays from Black Africa*. Hill & Wang, 1968, $5.95 (P/Hill & Wang, $1.95). Here are six plays written by modern African dramatists. Written in English by Negro authors, these plays present Africa and its problems, some of which prove to be universal.

* MILLER, WARREN. *The Cool World*.

* STYRON, WILLIAM. *The Confessions of Nat Turner*.

Appreciating Different Religious Cultures

Primary

BRECHT, EDITH. *Ada and the Wild Duck*. il. by Charlotte Erickson. Viking Pr, 1964, $3.00. Clyde the duck is hatched as spring comes to the Mennonite farm in the Pennsylvania Dutch countryside. Ada loves him from the moment she first sees him. As he grows, Ada carefully explains to him the customs and traditions of the Mennonites.

DE ANGELI, MARGUERITE. *Yonie Wondernose*. il. by author. Doubleday, 1944, $3.50. Young, Pennsylvania Dutch Yonie Wondernose earns his name because he is unusually curious. Left in charge of his family's Lancaster County farm, his curiosity pays off. In sharing Yonie's feelings children will learn of the Amish customs and see the family life described in the language of the region.

————. *Thee, Hannah!* il. by author. Doubleday, 1940, $3.50. Hannah, a little Quaker girl, longs to wear the bright-colored clothes and beribboned bonnet which Cecily, her friend next door, wears. The value of her Quaker bonnet is proved when a fugitive slave recognizes it and asks for help. The story of Hannah is a delightful picture of the happy simple life of a family of Friends living in Philadelphia just before the Civil War.

RICH, ELAINE SOMMERS. *Hannah Elizabeth*. il. by Paul Edward Kennedy. Har-Row, 1964, $3.79. Hannah Elizabeth, a ten-year-old Indiana Mennonite girl at the time of the Civil War, recognizes and faces conflicting values between her family beliefs and customs and the "out-side" world.

ROWLAND, FLORENCE WIGHTMAN. *Amish Boy.* il. by Dale Payson. Put-nam, 1970, $3.29. Jonathan Lapp, a ten-year-old Amish boy anxious to help and please his family, demonstrates his ability to assume re-sponsibility when lightning strikes, the barn burns, and the Amish neighbors cooperate in a barn raising.

SELZ, IRMA. *Wonderful Nice!* il. by author. Lothrop, 1960, $3.50. Alison, from New York City, accidentally meets and makes friends with Katy Zook and her father, Pennsylvania Plain People. Riding in the black buggy back to the Amish farm, listening to an unfamiliar language, learning about the hex signs on the barns, and eating Amish style foods are all new experiences for this little girl. The illustrations and brief story introduce the reader to a group of people living as their forefathers lived.

Intermediate

CONE, MOLLY. *A Promise Is a Promise.* il. by John Gretzer. HM, 1964, $3.25. Ruthy Morgen develops a self-conscious attitude because she is Jewish. The neighborhood homes celebrating Christmas, the invita-tion to a party at the church, and the hidden feelings she holds about her brother's Bar Mitzvah all naturally intensify her desire to be like everyone else. The descriptions of Ruthy's perceptive inner thoughts and of exchanges with her gentile friend Sandra about religion, rituals, and customs contribute to her growing pride in her own heritage.

* DE ANGELI, MARGUERITE. *Skippack School.*

FYSON, J. G. *The Three Brothers of Ur.* il. by Victor Ambrus. Coward, 1966, $3.95. Haran, the youngest of the three sons of the greatest merchant of Ur, accidentally breaks a statue of their household god, thus depriving the family of divine guidance. The story culminates in the oldest brother's dawning belief in one God. The simple, vigorous style of writing, rich in biblical allusions, unfolds terrifying experi-ences which are interwoven with the religious, mercantile, and artistic life of the ancient Mesapotamian city. Also outstanding is its sequel, *Journey of the Eldest Son,* which exhibits the same compassionate awareness of mankind.

GARLAN, PATRICIA WALLACE. *Orange-Robed Boy.* il. by Pan Oo Thet. Viking Pr, 1967, $4.50. Aung Khin, Burmese boy of twelve, has his head shaved, puts on the customary orange-colored robe, gives up his name, and enters a monastery to learn the precepts of Buddhism. The reader gains insight and respect for this religion through the de-scriptions of the induction ceremony and the chief tenets of the beliefs.

Some of the thoughts and questions of Aung Khin as he ponders whether to stay in the monastery or return home are given in verse.

ISH-KISHOR, SULAMITH. *Master of Miracle.* il. by Arnold Lobel. Har-Row, 1971, $3.95. A beautifully written fantasy based on the Jewish golem legend is set in the 16th century Prague ghetto as was the author's previous *Boy of Old Prague.* Gideon, a lonely orphan of uncertain parentage, is entrusted with controlling the golem, a huge clay humanoid fashioned by "the master of miracle," the venerated High Priest of Prague, in order to save the ghetto population from a pogrom. In his excitement, Gideon forgets to deactivate the golem when the task is completed and so faces punishment. The background is skillfully done and Gideon is a well-developed character.

JORDAN, MILDRED. *Proud To Be Amish.* Crown, 1968, $3.50. Katie Zook wrestles with the realities of the modern world and her Pennsylvania Dutch conscience. Her love of beauty and childlike desire for fun conflict with her deep loyalty to her Amish training. Sacrifice and trust in those nearest her enable Katie to find a happy direction for her young life.

LENSKI, LOIS. *Shoo-Fly Girl.* Lippincott, 1963, $4.29. Suzanna, Pennsylvania-Amish girl nicknamed Shoo-Fly, lives a confined, controlled life, yet a happy one. Curiosity about the non-Amish "English" neighbors leads her to question, "Why do we wear bonnets?" "Why do we wear black aprons?" The answer is that it has always been done this way and the Amish do not change. One gets a vivid glimpse into the inner life of the "Plain People," a religious sect who live close to the teaching of the Bible.

* RICH, ELAINE SOMMERS. *Hannah Elizabeth.*

UNRAU, RUTH. *Who Needs an Oil Well?* il. by Jan Gleysteen. Abingdon, 1968, $4.50. The Depression meant many things to many people: shortage of money, hard luck, unrealized dreams. But to Matt Rempel, a Mennonite farm boy, it seems to mean an end to his education. From his deep religious strength, Matt gains the determination to go to school, despite his father's belief that education is evil. With the aid of Grandfather Enns, he finally convinces his father that schooling will help rather than destroy the faith of the church.

Junior

* BAKER, BETTY. *Killer-of-Death.*

* FYSON, J. G. *The Three Brothers of Ur.*

* ISH-KISHOR, SULAMITH. *Master of Miracle.*

JOHNSON, ANNABEL AND EDGAR. *Wilderness Bride.* Har-Row, 1962, $3.95. Corey, fifteen and a Mormon, is engaged to a young Englishman,

Ethan, who is traveling westward on the Mormon train. Corey is disconcerted to discover that Ethan does not hold to the Mormon faith and is bent on becoming a physician. Eventually both Corey and Ethan find the courage to act according to their own convictions.

KARMEL-WOLFE, HENIA. *The Baders of Jacob Street.* il. by Paul Bacon. Lippincott, 1970, $6.95 (P/Popular Lib, $.95). The Baders return to Krakow during the German occupation. Halina, a young teenage girl, rebels against her Jewish heritage and against her parents' submission to German control. She sees the terrors and agonies of her neighbors and friends, and watches as they're systematically deprived of their freedom and eventually forced into a closed ghetto. Her final decision to remain with her family in the ghetto is an indication of her acceptance of her own identity. An excellent evaluation of the European Jewish tragedy as seen through the eyes of a young girl facing the frustrations of growing up.

LAMPEL, RUSIA. *That Summer with Ora.* trans. by Stella Humphries. Watts, 1967, $3.50. Eleanor, an American Jew, goes to spend the summer with a Jewish family in Israel. The differences in outlooks between Eleanor and Ora, an Israeli, lead to many misunderstandings. Through the pages of Ora's diary a sensitive story unfolds of two girls from seemingly opposed cultures who gain in their understanding of each other and of their heritage. Awarded the 1966 German Children's Book Prize for treatment of a contemporary problem.

MALVERN, GLADYS, *Secret Sign.* Abelard, 1961, $3.75. When Stephanus, a handsome young actor in ancient Rome, learns the meaning of the sign of the Cross, the love of the new brotherhood for mankind and their God becomes the governing influence on his behavior.

* NEVILLE, EMILY CHENEY. *Berries Goodman.*

NIELSEN, VIRGINIA. *The Road to the Valley.* McKay, 1961, $2.95. The Mormons were a group with a purpose in 1848 as they left Nauvoo, Illinois, for the West. This is the story of the young teenagers on the trip, especially Ellen Barlow and Chris, who was not a Mormon.

ROSE, KAREN. *There Is a Season.* Follett, 1967, $3.25 (P/Avon, $.60). Katie Levin, a fifteen-year-old Jewish girl, is growing into womanhood with questions about herself and her religion. She meets James, almost eighteen and a devout Catholic. The relationship between them is confusing as feelings heretofore unknown are discovered. Jamey decides to fulfill his long-time ambition—to enter the priesthood. This decision and involvement in family problems help Katie develop into a mature woman.

Senior

ALDRIDGE, JAMES. *My Brother Tom—A Love Story.* Little, 1967, $4.95. Fierce-tempered Tom Quale is caught in an Australian small-town web of prejudice and opposing view when he falls in love with the daughter of his father's arch enemy. This intense love story exposes the bitterness and bigotry that existed in Australia in the late thirties. The conflicts and frustrations of a youth entering manhood are depicted with ironic humor and deep insight.

BARRETT, WILLIAM E. *Lilies of the Field.* Doubleday, 1962, $3.50. Homer Smith, an easy-going yet hard-working Negro, is "trapped" by Mother Marie Marthe into building a chapel for the convent. Mother Marie Marthe thinks that God sent Homer to do the job. Despite initial conflicts and obstacles, he agrees to do the work and the chapel is constructed, followed by reconciliation between Homer and the nuns.

* FIEDLER, JEAN. *In Any Spring.*

* FREEDMAN, BENEDICT AND NANCY. *Mrs. Mike.*

* HESSE, HERMANN. *Siddhartha.*

HOWELL, BETH PRIM. *Lady on a Donkey.* Dutton, 1960, $4.50. Lillian Trasher, an intensely religious child, grew up on a Georgia farm. Just before her wedding day, she decided she should do more with her life than become a housewife. From that day on, as a missionary in Egypt, she filled her life with work, love, and service to others. The orphanage she founded and fought to maintain turned no one away, though often she did not know where the funds were to come from to maintain life for her children.

LIGHTWOOD, TERESA. *My Three Lives.* Dutton, 1960, $3.95. The author of this book began a life dedicated to serving people by becoming a Catholic missionary nun in Thailand, where for fourteen years she taught school, weathered earthquakes and floods, and learned to love people. Ill health and a desire to leave the mission resulted in her choice of a career as a nurse in England and later led to love, marriage, and living in India.

MEANS, FLORENCE CRANNELL. *Emmy and the Blue Door.* HM, 1959, $3.00. Emmy spends a summer as a participant in a Quaker work camp in Mexico where she finds her ideals considerably strained by the realities she encounters.

* MICHENER, JAMES A. *Hawaii.*

POTOK, CHAIM. *The Chosen.* S & S, 1967, $4.95 (P/Fawcett World, $.95). A portrayal of two young Jewish boys, *The Chosen* tells the story of Danny Saunders, whose father is a Hasidic rabbi, keeper of an ancient tradition, and Reuven Malter, whose father is an Orthodox rabbi, despised by the Hasidim. An accident brings the boys into unexpected contact. They experience the strains of ending adolescence and the conflicts between each boy and his father. The beauty of the novel lies in the expression of humanity, the demonstration of love and respect between father and son, and the transmitting of religious and intellectual traditions.

————. *The Promise.* Knopf, 1969, $6.95 (P/Fawcett World, $1.25). This sequel to *The Chosen* describes the lives of the two boys who are now men. Reuven Malter studies to be a rabbi while Danny Saunders is a clinical psychologist. "All around us everything was changing in the order of things we had fashioned for ourselves."

* SAVAGE, ELIZABETH. *Summer of Pride.*

* SPEARE, ELIZABETH GEORGE. *The Bronze Bow.*

WIBBERLEY, LEONARD. *Stranger at Killknock.* Putnam, 1961, $3.75. Who was the stranger? Did the stones on the mountaintop really walk down to drink from the lake every November? Could Mairin go flying on the wind? Here is a tale of Irish mysticism set in a lonely fishing village where the age-old Celtic superstitions still flourish, and one stays close to one's own hearth on dark, blustery nights.

Mature

CAMUS, ALBERT. *The Stranger.* Knopf, 1946, $4.95 (P/Random, $1.65). Here is a translation of the French novel about a man living a life like any other, until he commits a senseless murder. Though convicted of the crime, he has no fear of death; for what is death after all but the opportunity to begin life over again.

HESSE, HERMANN. *Siddhartha.* trans. by Hilda Rosner. New Directions, 1951, $5.00 (P/New Directions, $1.75). Siddhartha is a soul-searcher who meets the Buddha, a manifestation of the ultimate good. Siddhartha must find the ultimate good on his own; so he abandons his friends, rejects the teachings of his elders, and goes to the city to "learn" the life of man. After numerous experiences, he accepts the final renunciation and achieves self-knowledge. A particularly significant book for students interested in Oriental philosophy.

HONE, RALPH E. (ed.). *The Voice out of the Whirlwind: The Book of Job.* P/Chandler Pub, 1960, $3.50. This collection of essays presents interpretations of the Book of Job from religious and philosophical points of view, ranging from Calvin to Niebuhr. Topics include discussions of the meaning of the book, problems related to evil and suffering, and studies contrasting the ancient book with Archibald MacLeish's contemporary version.

MACLEISH, ARCHIBALD. *J.B.* HM, 1958, $4.95 (P/HM, $1.75). The Book of Job has been modernized in this play in verse of the age-old dilemma of trying to reconcile the image of a just God with the senseless reality of human suffering. Two carnival vendors, both former actors, begin by spoofing the parts of God and Satan. They find themselves caught up in an ageless reality that transcends their temporal reality as they are made to view the life of a modern Job.

MALAMUD, BERNARD. *The Fixer.* FS & G, 1966, $6.95 (P/Dell, $.95). Yakov Bok, a simple Russian peasant of Jewish descent, is wrongly accused and convicted of murdering a boy. The setting is the city of Kiev in tsarist Russia during a period of violent antisemitism. Bok becomes a hero because he refuses to confess to a crime he did not commit.

MICHENER, JAMES A. *Hawaii.* Random, 1959, $10.00 (P/Bantam, $1.95). This is the story of Abner and Jerusha Hale and their four children, but more important, it is the story of missionaries and their influence on life in Hawaii. The natives come to Hale's church, but in times of crisis they revert to the traditional pagan rites. It is Abner's son, Hoxworth Hale, who sees the day when East and West can be united in the "new Hawaii."

* POTOK, CHAIM. *The Chosen.*

* ———. *The Promise.*

READ, KATHERINE L., AND ROBERT O. BALLOU. *Bamboo Hospital.* Lippincott, 1961, $4.95. The Burmese brought their problems of health and religion to the wise and understanding Hendersons, whose daughter tells the story of their service.

Appreciating Different Regional Cultures

Primary

CREDLE, ELLIS. *Andy and the Circus.* il. by author. Nelson, 1971, $3.95. Andy, another Appalachian Mountain character drawn well by Miss Credle, longs to go to the circus. Earning his way involves nonsense and mounting suspense.

FRASER, JAMES. *Las Posadas: A Christmas Story.* il. by Nick De Grazia. Northland, 1968, $2.75. The colorful Christmas festival Las Posadas, celebrated in South American countries, is described in simple text with gay illustrations. During each of the nine days before Christmas, friends walk through the streets from house to house, carrying candles, streamers, or flowers. They sing the traditional requests to enter, searching for the night's lodging. Thus they enact the Holy Family's search for shelter.

GREENBERG, POLLY. *Oh Lord, I Wish I Was a Buzzard.* il. by Aliki. Macmillan, 1968, $4.95. A Southern Negro's wishes, thoughts, hardships, feelings of despair, and joy are vividly revealed both through the dramatic illustrations and the language pattern. The repetitiveness of the refrain, "We picked and we picked and we picked and we picked," creates a vivid picture of a day in a cotton field.

LENSKI, LOIS. *We Live in the Southwest.* il. by author. Lippincott, 1962, $3.50. Tomaso, a Spanish-American boy living in a New Mexico mountain village, wants to be a wood-carver like his grandfather. Sara, living in a hogan on the dry plains of Arizona, gives up her precious blue turquoise necklace to help her family during a financial crisis. Nancy and Jim in Jerome, Arizona, a copper mining town, face problems of adjustment when the mine closes down.

MORROW, SUZANNE STARK. *Inatuk's Friend.* il. by Ellen Raskin. Little, 1968, $3.50. Inatuk's family faces a severe shortage of food. The difficulty of finding seal meat forces this modern Eskimo family to move to Point Barrow. Inatuk reluctantly says goodbye to the life of hunting and fishing and to his best friend Soloquay. A piece of soapstone, given as a gift of encouragement, is carved by Inatuk for his "new-found" friend, his younger brother. The simple, stark, blue and brown illustrations reinforce the drama of the story.

POLITI, LEO. *Mieko.* il. by author. Golden Gate, 1969, $4.95. Mieko, the small daughter of a Japanese-American couple, works diligently to learn the traditional Nisei arts, hoping that she will become queen of the annual Ondo Parade, a festival held during Nisei Week in Little Tokyo, a section of Los Angeles. Descriptions of the paper-mache monster and the gorgeous floats of the parade, the tea ceremony, and the Japanese flower arranging are all carefully woven into the story.

———. *Moy Moy.* il. by author. Scribner, 1960, $4.37. Chanking Street in Los Angeles provides the setting for the Chinese New Year of Moy Moy, a small Chinese-American girl. The lively colorful illustrations are filled with detailed aspects of the Chinese New Year: the dancing lion collecting coins for gifts, and the colorful excitement of the dragon parade.

WATSON, CLYDE. *Father Fox's Pennyrhymes.* il. by Wendy Watson. TY Crowell, 1971, $4.50. Good Father Fox in his stout work overalls is as American as barley corn. His exuberant rhymes and jingles inspired by life on a Vermont farm sing with the ring and the twang of a square-dance fiddler. The black line and watchcolor illustrations are in keeping with the wit and language of the Pennyrhymes.

WATSON, NANCY DINGMAN. *Sugar on Snow.* il. by Aldren A. Watson. Viking Pr, 1964, $3.00. The maple-sugaring coincides with Cammie's birthday, and Cammie's party turns out to be a sugar-on-snow party. The descriptions and illustrations of tapping trees and the collecting and boiling of sap are vivid.

Intermediate

ADOFF, ARNOLD. *Malcolm X.* il. by John Wilson. TY Crowell, 1970, $3.75. This is a very strong, positive but balanced, engrossing, straight-forward biography of Malcolm X for third and fourth graders (or perhaps useful for reluctant junior high readers). Malcolm X really comes to life in this biography which is not an in-depth study but which manages to cover the highlights of his life.

BUCHARDT, NELLIE. *A Surprise for Carlotta.* Watts, 1971, $4.95. This story is of a third-grade Puerto Rican girl who lives in the city. She feels alienated from her family, and when her class acquires a duck, she finds an outlet for her love. Funny, perceptive vignettes involving school and Puerto Rican family life brighten this story of growing pains.

* BURCH, ROBERT. *Skinny.*

BURLESON, ELIZABETH. *Middl'un.* il. by Don Asumussen. Follett, 1968, $3.91. A picture of the times and the people of Texas at the turn of the century, the story centers on tomboy Hannah's growing up and her search for cattle rustlers.

* CARLSON, NATALIE SAVAGE. *The Empty Schoolhouse.*

FRANCHERE, RUTH. *Cesar Chavez.* il. Earl Thollander. TY Crowell, 1970, $3.75. In this biography the author presents a sympathetic picture of the harsh life of migrant workers in California, both past and present. This tells about the man whose name is constantly in the media as he continues striving to obtain more consideration for the farm workers.

GARTHWAITE, MARION. *Mario: A Mexican Boy's Adventure.* il. by Ronni Solbert. Doubleday, 1960, $2.95. Mario longs to return to his home, a small friendly village in Mexico. His thoughts turn to a series of earlier events: his grandmother's illness, Doctor Gabriel's arrangements for her to be flown to a Tijuana hospital, the incomplete arrangements for Mama to meet an aunt in Tijuana, and his being "befriended" and imported illegally with "wetbacks" into California to pick cotton. Alone and frightened, Mario is helped by a rancher and Miss Hallie, a truant officer, who had once met the young boy in his own village. Reading this story one gets a realistic view of the grim conditions facing individuals who, like Mario, cross the border to pick cotton.

GATES, DORIS. *Blue Willow.* il. by Paul Lantz. Viking Pr, 1945, $3.50 (P/Viking Pr, $.75). Having to move from one migrant camp to another intensifies Janey Larkin's desire for a permanent home, friends, and school. The only beautiful possession the family has is a blue willow plate handed down from generation to generation. It is a reminder of happier days in Texas and represents dreams and promises for a better future. Reading about this itinerant family's ways of life, often filled with despair and yet always hopeful, leaves little room for the reader's indifference.

JULINE, RUTH BISHOP. *A Place for Johnny Bill.* il. by Georgiann Helms. Westminster, 1961, $2.95. Johnny Bill Mason and his family are migrant workers. They live in shacks or tents, stay in one place only a short while, but are always hoping for a permanent home. Attending school regularly as other boys and girls do, making new friends and keeping them until at last they are old friends, is Johnny Bill's greatest wish. The sensitive story reveals human problems of poverty and change.

JUSTUS, MAY. *Eben and the Rattlesnake.* il. by Carol Wilde. Garrard, 1969, $2.39. While hoeing the cornfield, Eben kills a huge "granddaddy" rattlesnake. His hoe handle grows to the size of a fence post and then to the size of a log, all supposedly from the rattlesnake "pizen." Eben and Pappy build a corncrib from the log, and the tale spreads far and near. No-End Hollow is soon crowded with visitors. The family's plan to stop the "curious folks" from coming to see the building made from the famous hoe handle and a surprise shrinkage of the corncrib make this Tennessee mountain story an amusing one. It introduces the reader to the folk speech, some details of life in the Smokey Mountains, and one of their tall tales or bits of folklore.

————. *It Happened in No-End Hollow.* il. by Mimi Korach. Garrard, 1969, $2.39. These three short stories, filled with the colorful language of the Smokey Mountain folk, provide insight into the lonely life, the customs, and the superstitions of isolated communities.

LENSKI, LOIS. *Coal Camp Girl.* il. by author. Lippincott, 1959, $4.82. The story of nine-year-old Tina, daughter of a West Virginia coal miner, is filled with vivid descriptions of the hazardous and uncertain lives of the coal miners: their hopes, fears, and needs. Readers can gain insights into segments of culture that are closely tied to occupational and regional living. In the foreword of the book the author reveals her own appreciation and feelings for the "coal camp" children.

————. *Cotton in My Sack.* il. by author. Lippincott, 1949, $4.82 (P/ Dell, $.65). Joanda Huntler with other members of her sharecropper family picks cotton in the fields of Arkansas. She assumes many family responsibilities for overcoming the everyday hardships faced by the field workers. Joanda looks forward to the Saturday night pleasures in town when cotton-picking is good, even though it often means having little or no money for the next week. The colorful and descriptive language of this region reflects a cultural aspect of a way of life. Young readers have the opportunity to see how the joys, hopes, and beliefs of a group of people are closely interwoven with their means of earning a living and their environment.

————. *Lois Lenski's Christmas Stories.* il. by author. Lippincott, 1968, $3.95. The stories in this collection, gathered largely from nine of the author's well-known books about regions, enrich the reader's understanding of regional customs.

————. *Strawberry Girl*. il. by author. Lippincott, 1945, $4.50 (P/Dell, $.75). Birdie Boyer, "Strawberry Girl," seems as real to today's readers as she was to Lois Lenski when she first saw her plowing in a Florida field. With her many insecurities, Birdie faces adversities by dreaming of the future. The story contrasts the lives of the Boyer family with that of their "shiftless" neighbors in the backwoods of Florida. Readers can gain insights into life in this region with its dialect and traditions.

* MERRILL, JEAN. *The Pushcart War.*

* MEYER, FRANKLYN. *Me and Caleb.*

MOLNAR, JOE (ed.) *Graciela: A Mexican-American Tells Her Story.* Watts, 1972, $4.50. One of ten children in a migrant Chicano family, 12-year-old Graciela describes the annual trip to pick produce in Michigan. She is candid about the prejudice her people face but does not dwell on it. Rather she comments on her family's efforts to improve their financial and educational condition. It is a good family story.

MORSE, EVANGELINE. *Brown Rabbit: Her Story.* il. by David Hall Martin. Follett, 1967, $4.98. Leaving their lifelong home in Mississippi for a large industrial city in the North is a challenge in many ways for the Browns. Ceretha learns that being a friend means having friends, and that friends are more important than status.

RAWLS, WILSON. *Where the Red Fern Grows.* Doubleday, 1961, $4.95. Billy Colan, who lives on Cherokee land in the heart of the Ozarks, wants a dog more than anything. He finally is able to buy two coon dogs, Old Dan and Little Ann. By training the brawn of Old Dan and the brains of Little Ann to work as one, he wins the coveted gold cup in the annual coon contest.

ROBINSON, BENELLE H. *Citizen Pablo.* il. by Jean M. Porter. John Day, 1959, $3.69. Drought in Mexico forces young Pablo and his family to migrate to the United States. The new life in migrant camps leads only to the death of Pablo's younger sister Rose and his learning to run from the border patrol.

RUSHMORE, HELEN. *The Magnificent House of Man Alone.* il. by Frank Vaughn. Garrard, 1968, $2.39. In the early 1900s, Man Alone, an elderly Osage Indian, tries in vain to prevent his tribe from allowing the white man to drill for oil on Indian land. In speaking to his fellow tribesmen about the transaction he says, "A man cannot follow two paths at once. He cannot follow the white man's path and still remain true to his Indian ancestors." This sometimes humorous, sometimes tragic story of the mixing of old and new cultures was written by a woman who spent her childhood playing and going to school with the Indians.

SHOTWELL, LOUISA R. *Roosevelt Grady.* il. by Peter Burchard. World Pub, 1963, $3.95 (P/several). The life, hardships, and desires of nine-year-old Roosevelt, son of a migrant family who earn their living by following the crops, are vividly described.

* SMITH, ERIC B., AND ROBERT MEREDITH. *Pilgrim Courage.*

SMITH, GEORGE HARMON. *Bayou Belle.* il. by Albert Orbaan. John Day, 1967, $3.96. Civilization in the form of a paper mill and the development of a recreational area envelop the environment of sixteen-year-old Willie Potter and his aging grandparents who live in a shanty in the bayou country of Louisiana. Willie knows their only chance for survival is to change with the times. The colorful and descriptive dialect and the trials of swamp living are revealed in the story of Willie's experiences earning money so that he can cope with and resolve the problems facing him.

————. *Bayou Boy.* Follett, 1965, $3.48. Offshore oil drilling and new roads into the Louisiana swamp force Papa LeBlanc to leave the bayou to seek work, leaving fourteen-year-old Jean to take care of the family. Jean learns to deal with the dangers of the swamp and the problems of the new and different way of life ahead of him.

————. *Wanderers of the Field.* il. by Albert Orbaan. John Day, 1966, $3.96. The vernacular of the rural southeastern United States pervades this warm novel of a small migrant family consisting of Jack, his mother, his young sister, and his dog. His father's death has left seventeen-year-old Jack the responsibility of driving the old truck, his family, and their meager belongings from crop to crop.

SNYDER, ZILPHA KEATLEY. *The Velvet Room.* il. by Alton Raible. Atheneum, 1965, $3.95. The Depression forces Robin's family to sell their dairy in central California and live a migratory life following the crops. In their circuitous travels, the old Model-T breaks down near the McCurdy ranch. Mr. Williams luckily finds immediate work in the surrounding apricot orchards, and eventually a permanent job. Robin escapes to a tranquil, book-lined "velvet room" in a nearby abandoned mansion to free herself from the harsh thoughts of schoolmates' attitudes and remarks about her and other farm labor children and from the realities of her noisy, crowded, poverty-stricken life. Ensuing events of a deep friendship and mystery compel Robin's acceptance of reality.

* STUART, JESSE. *The Beatinest Boy.*

* TAYLOR, THEODORE. *The Children's War.*

WALTRIP, LELA AND RUFUS. *White Harvest.* il. by Christine Price. McKay, 1960, $2.95. Susan Mathis, whose family has been forced to follow the cotton harvest, yearns to stay in one place long enough to make friends and attend school. Bad luck causes Mr. Mathis to lose faith in others, until his family has the opportunity to work for the generous, kindly, and religious Mills family. Susan encourages her father, who begins to show renewed faith in others, to try for a homestead in the new Southwest. A realistic view of the pervading desire for permanency unfolds as the family gets the opportunity to realize their dreams.

* WATSON, CLYDE. *Father Fox's Pennyrhymes.*

Junior

* ALDRICH, BESS STREETER. *Lantern in Her Hand.*

* AMES, FRANCIS. *That Callahan Spunk.*

* BURCH, ROBERT. *Queenie Peavy.*

CLARKE, TOM E. *Puddle Jumper.* Lothrop, 1960, O.P. Arne has the special knowledge and skills needed to fly a plane in the mountains of Alaska plus the courage which enables him to cope with the dangerous situation in the manner of a mature and experienced flyer.

CLEAVER, VERA AND BILL. *Where the Lilies Bloom.* Lippincott, 1969, $3.95. When Roy Luther dies it is Mary Call, his fourteen-year-old daughter, who must assume the responsibility for the lives of her brother and two sisters in a broken-down house in the Appalachian Mountains.

DEAL, BORDEN. *The Least One.* Doubleday, 1967, $5.95 (P/Curtis, $.95). "Boy" Sword is a youth searching for identity, an identity symbolized by the Christian name he has never been given. The Swords are desperately poor cotton farmers in the deep South during the Depression. Although they undergo many misfortunes, there is humor as well as pathos in the account of this family's struggle to maintain its pride and individuality.

* FRANCHERE, RUTH. *Cesar Chavez.*

* HOUSTON, JAMES. *Songs of the Dream People.*

KREMENTZ, JILL. *Sweet Pea: A Girl Growing up in the Rural South.* HBJ, 1969, $4.50. This picture story was photographed and written by Jill Krementz, *Time* photographer, who met Sweet Pea's sister while photographing a Job Corps training camp in Maine in 1968. She later spent several weeks with the Anderson family gathering material for this book. As Margaret Mead points out in the foreword, this book provides vivid insight into a cultural pattern in the rural South.

LEWITON, MINA. *Elizabeth and the Young Stranger.* McKay, 1961, $3.44. Drawn to her new classmate, a Hungarian refugee who has known the horrors of war, Elizabeth finds she has much in common with him. But Elizabeth's feelings are not shared by her father nor some of the snobbish New Englanders who are her friends and neighbors. The problems involved in their friendship are the same faced by many newcomers to our country.

MIERS, EARL SCHENCK. *Pirate Chase.* il. by Peter Burchard. HR & W, 1965, $3.95. Fifteen-year-old Timmy Baillee, from Jamestown, Virginia, is on his way to England when he is captured by Captain Bluebeard and forced to serve in the pirate crew. This vigorous tale gives a glimpse of early America from an unusual viewpoint.

* PEDERSEN, ELSA. *House upon a Rock.*

PORTIS, CHARLES. *True Grit.* S & S, 1968, $4.95 (P/NAL, $.95). Fourteen-year-old Mattie Ross of Yell County, Arkansas, sets out with the help of a renegade lawman to avenge her father's murder. Mattie is a marvelously spunky and determined young lady, with a forthright, practical manner of dealing with all eventualities, such as being in a cave with a dead man and a bunch of rattlesnakes.

STEELE, WILLIAM O. *The Wilderness Tattoo: A Narrative of Juan Ortiz.* HBJ, 1972, $4.95. A compelling narrative of Juan Ortiz's adventures among the Temucuan Indians of Florida in the 16th century. He served as an interpreter with Hernando de Soto's expedition.

STREET, JAMES. *Good-Bye, My Lady.* Lippincott, 1954, $5.95. Skeeter tracks down a wonderful laughing dog in the wild swamps of Mississippi. Between them a relationship grows that is deep and rare, an unspoken communication of love and fellowship. The life of the simple swamp folk, their loyalty to their neighbors regardless of color, and their amazing knowledge of their land are clearly drawn in this heart-warming tale of a boy and his road to manhood.

TAYLOR, THEODORE. *The Children's War.* il. by author. Doubleday, 1971, $3.95. Set during World War II, this story focuses on 12-year-old Dory, his gun, his wolf pup and hunting trips with the old Eskimo Bakutan. He and his navy family live in a tiny Alaskan village which is briefly captured by the Japanese. Dory and his pacifist teacher become personally involved in the realities of warfare. In the process, Dory's ideas about war and patriotism are affected. As in *The Cay,* the power of the novel is in the shifting relationships and changing values of the characters.

TERZIAN, JAMES P. *Mighty Hard Road: The Story of Cesar Chavez.* Doubleday, 1970, $3.50 (P/Doubleday, $1.45). An interesting and readable account of the life of the dynamic leader of the Mexican-American farm workers. Emphasis is placed on his deep spiritual convictions and his adherence to nonviolence. At the same time the book gives the reader much information on the mechanics of his labor tactics and their repercussions.

THALER, SUSAN. *Rosaria.* McKay, 1967, $3.50. Rosaria's family comes to New York from Puerto Rico to start a new life. Her father, unable to get a plumber's job, gradually becomes discouraged. The hard-working family finally gets opportunities that open the door to happiness.

* WIER, ESTER. *The Loner.*

Senior

ANNIXTER, PAUL. *Swiftwater.* Hill & Wang, 1950, $3.50 (P/several). Those Calloways are the queerest folks in the Maine woods. They shun the townsfolk's doings, run wild, spare trees, and protect the wild geese. Against the derision of the community, Cam and his son Bucky cling to their solitary, outdated way of life. Their close relationship shows a rare and beautiful courage. Their desperate struggles culminate in the establishment of a wild geese sanctuary.

BARRIO, RAYMOND. *The Plum Plum Pickers.* il. by author. P/Canfield Pr, 1971 (reprint of 1969 ed.), $2.45. In this novel about migrant Mexican fruit pickers in the Santa Clara valley of California, Barrio portrays the anguished life of people he knows well. He writes of the loves and hates, the passions and pathos of Lupe, Manuel, Margarita —children living in shacks, finding rare moments of gaiety in Sunday gatherings, searching for hope, and dreaming of a little place of their own. Barrio is an art teacher in Santa Clara and a promising regional writer. He brings the vernacular of the Chicanos to the non-Spanish speaking reader with skill. He conveys the message clearly: how is it that men can be stripped of dignity and reduced to an animal existence? For most readers, he will succeed in opening hearts and minds.

BRECK, VIVIAN. *Kona Summer.* Doubleday, 1961, $2.95. Sixteen-year-old Lani entertains Priscilla, a cousin from the mainland, for the summer in Hawaii. Prill's adjustment to an atmosphere of racial tolerance helps Lani gain a broader tolerance herself.

* COHEN, TOM. *Three Who Dared.*

GILES, JANICE HOLT. *Shady Grove.* HM, 1968, $4.95. A rollicking good tale about Kentucky mountaineers with their own code of morality, a code which was "heathenish" in the new preacher's opinion. The preacher approved of the mountaineers' "pickin' and singin'," however, and was eager to record their folk songs.

HAGEDORN, HERMANN. *The Hyphenated Family.* Macmillan, 1960, $5.00. The unwillingness of an immigrant German father to give up his loyalty to his native country and to adapt himself wholeheartedly to the groups of his adopted country works disastrously upon his wife and children, who are torn between two countries all their lives.

* HOUSTON, JAMES. *Songs of the Dream People.*

* LEE, HARPER. *To Kill a Mockingbird.*

* LOTT, MILTON. *Backtrack.*

* MCCULLERS, CARSON. *Member of the Wedding.*

STRACHAN, MARGARET PITCAIRN. *Trouble at Torrent Creek.* Washburn, 1967, $4.25. A first-year teacher from the city goes to Appalachia to teach in a one-room schoolhouse. During the year, she succeeds in convincing the deprived families that school consolidation would benefit the entire community.

SWITZER, GLADYS. *Betwixt and Between.* Follett, 1959, $3.78. At the turn of the century, there were still many immigrant families coming to farm in the Midwest. Eighteen-year-old Olivia started her first year of teaching amidst such families. Frustrated by ignorance, bigotry, and racial "clannishness," she tries to knit the different families together into a more congenial community. Her job is complicated by an interest in two men of varying backgrounds.

Appreciating Different World Cultures

Primary

ANDERSON, JOY, AND JAY YANG. *Hai Yin, the Dragon Girl.* il. by author. HBJ, 1970, $3.50. Hai Yin of Taipei, Taiwan, is different and lucky because she was born in the Year of the Dragon. Her brother Wu thinks she is silly and accuses her of daydreaming when she says she will become famous, but Hai Yin is determined. Her plans for proving herself come true at the Lantern Festival when she, as a result of long secret hours of pasting and cutting during the New Year holiday, reveals her beautiful dragon lantern. Amid the festival fireworks, the mayor awards the prize to the first girl winner, Hai Yin.

BALET, JAN B. *Joanjo.* il. by author. Dell, 1967, $4.50. Joanjo, living in a fishing village by the sea, decides he is tired of the taste and smell of the everyday diet of fish in this Portuguese village. Traditionally the men in his family were all fishermen, but this small boy falls asleep and vividly dreams of another life. Vibrant, colorful illustrations show the activities when the fishermen set out to sea and when they return home.

BARRY, ROBERT. *The Musical Palm Tree: A Story of Puerto Rico.* il. by author. McGraw, 1968, $3.95. Readers will have a gay time following Pablito on a tour of San Juan, Puerto Rico. As he counts the shiny quarters he earns as a guide, he dreams of the beautiful Spanish mantilla he wants to give his mother in time to wear to the Fiesta Patronal. A page of Spanish vocabulary is included.

BIALK, ELISA. *Tizz at the Fiesta.* il. by Hildegard Lehmann. Childrens, 1970, $3.00. When Tracy and Don visit their grandparents in Mexico they have the opportunity to learn firsthand about the all-day drama-tization of Mexican history held on the Tuesday before Lent. The Americanos and two small Mexican friends act out a bullfight with all of its language and routine in which they star Tizz, Tracy's Palo-mino pony, as El Toro. Later, Tizz and Tracy are so carried away with the drama of the fiesta, that they unconsciously join in the chas-ing of bandits far down the street, much to the enjoyment of the crowd. Details of some aspects of modern life in Mexico are revealed in an easy-to-read text.

BRADLEY, DUANE. *Meeting with a Stranger.* il. by E. Harper Johnson. Lippincott, 1964, $3.75. Through the eyes and innermost feelings of Teffera, an Ethiopian boy, the customs and beliefs of shepherds in a village far from Addis Ababa are shown. Teffera, anxious to pre-serve his way of life, fears the "ferangi," the strangers who come with new ideas to improve the livestock.

BUDD, LILLIAN. *Tekla's Easter.* il. by Genia. Rand, 1962, $3.47. Eight-year-old Tekla and the many generations of her family share the fun, gaiety, and excitement of Easter as it is traditionally celebrated on one of the western islands of Sweden. Easter fires, witch burning, dec-orated eggs, and dressing for the ride in the church boat are all in-cluded in the story.

CAMILLE, JOSEPHINE AND ALBERT. *Carlos and the Brave Owl.* il. by Albert Camille. Random, 1968, $3.50. Poor Carlos, a little Mexican boy, has no pet; then, by chance he finds a young owl with an in-jured wing. But his Papa says the owl is useless. "He does nothing but sleep, sleep, sleep." While the Blessing of the Animals goes on in the daytime Buho the owl is always asleep. How can an animal who is asleep be blessed? The solution is exciting.

CARIGIET, ALOIS. *Anton the Goatherd.* il. by author. Walck, 1966, $7.00. Anton, a little goatherd, daily leads the village goats up the high Swiss Alps and tends them during grazing.

CHONZ, SELINA. *A Bell for Ursli.* il. by Alois Carigiet. Walck, 1967, $7.00. Young Ursli and his family in the Engadine Mountains of Switzerland hold dear their herds of cattle. In March, boys find the largest cowbell they can carry and march through the village in a procession to celebrate the end of winter, a time when cattle are housed in sheds.

CRETAN, GLADYS YESSAYAN. *Run Away, Habeeb!* il. by Robert L. Jefferson. Abingdon, 1968, $3.00. Although his family has saved money for his education and even moved from the countryside to Tangier, Habeeb feels strange among new faces and runs away on his first day of school. At his disappointed family's suggestion, he tries to work as an apprentice for a number of craftsmen: a tailor, the wool dyer, and the camel merchant. Upon receiving a letter from his grandfather advising him to use his chance to learn, Habeeb returns to school and finds his friendliness is returned with friendliness from his peers. The story is enhanced by the descriptions of the culture and crafts of northwest Africa. A glossary of less familiar words is provided.

———. *A Gift from the Bride.* il. by Rita Favo Fegiz. Little, 1964, $3.25. In spite of tradition, Mari, a small girl in an Armenian village, is resolute in her determination to go to school and learn to read. The pageantry and customs of the Armenian people, the wedding rituals, the foods and festivities are vividly described as Annig, the new bride-to-be who had been away to college, prepares for her wedding. The bride persuades Mari's father that "It is the wondering and the finding out that separates us from the barbarians."

ECONOMAKIS, OLGA. *Oasis of the Stars.* il. by Blair Lent. Coward, 1965, $3.25. Abu, with his nomad family, wanders through the desert from oasis to oasis; the constant search for water, the loading of camels and donkeys, and hot days, all make Abu long for a real home in one place. His intense desire to find as many drops of water as there are stars in the sky, gives him strength to dig at his well night after night.

EISMAN, ALBERTA. *Candido.* il. by Lilian Abligado. Macmillan, 1967, $4.25. Candido is a three-year-old white llama, fully grown, overprotected, and dearly loved by Paco, a small Peruvian boy. Paco devises an original plan to hire rather than force his pet into carrying his share of the burden.

ETS, MARIE HALL, AND AURORA LABASTIDA. *Nine Days to Christmas.* il. by author. Viking Pr, 1959, $3.50. Ceci, now old enough to participate in the Posadas, the festive Mexican parties given for the nine nights preceding Christmas, has difficulty choosing a special piñata. Her sadness at the thought of her star piñata being broken is overcome by the sight of the real Christmas star. The illustrations and sensitive story, filled with myriad details, will supplement the reader's appreciation of Christmas life in Mexico.

FENNEMA, ILONA, AND GEORGETTE APOL. *Dirk's Wooden Shoes.* il. by Georgette Apol. HBJ, 1970, $4.25. Dirk's father, a Holland clog-

maker, promises to carve him a pair of "magic shoes" from two pieces
of wood with a curious grain that looks like eyes. However, amid the
rush of making clogs and all kinds of wooden shoes for tourists, Dirk's
two blocks of wood are accidentally carved and sold to an American
woman for her grandson. Deeply disappointed, Dirk begins a search
for the buyer.

FERN, EUGENE. *Lorenzo and Angelina*. il. by author. FS & G, 1968,
$3.75. Angeline Garcia and her donkey Lorenzo share marketplace
experiences and a dangerous mountain adventure to build a close
and sometimes humorous relationship between them. The alternating
points of view of Angeline and her stubborn donkey add interest.
The South American countryside and its family and village life are
concisely depicted by the artist-author.

FEUSTEL, GUNTHER. *Jose: A Tale from South America*. il. by Hans Balt-
zer. Delacorte, 1968, $3.95. Jose leaves the Bolivian Andes, driven
by hunger to the city to search for work and food. On the way he
is joined by a one-eared donkey who, like Jose, has met trouble and
rejection. With humor and pathos the book gives insight into life
as it is for the poor of South America.

GOBHAI, MEHLLI. *Ramu and the Kite*. il. by author. P-H, 1968, $4.95.
Sankranth, the first day of kite season in India, is a joyous holiday
when young boys have kite battles. Ramu, old enough to take part,
chooses a purple kite with a sharp edge. On the festive day, Ramu,
with practice and his father's encouragement, cuts down a blood-red
rival kite. A few moments of victory precede a white kite defeating
Ramu's purple one.

————. *Lakshmi, the Water Buffalo Who Wouldn't*. Hawthorn, 1969,
$4.25. Gokul tends Lakshmi and swims with her, but she only per-
mits his mother, Hansa, to milk her. When Hansa falls ill, the family
resorts to subterfuge and the reluctant father wears Hansa's bracelets
and red headcloth so that the milking can be accomplished.

GOETZ, LEE A. *A Camel in the Sea*. il. by Paul Galdone. McGraw, 1966,
$2.95. In one of the driest summers that the Somali village can re-
member, ten-year-old Mohamed longs for someone to play with. The
weather grows worse and the locusts come. The people seek the
oldest villager's advice on how to make it rain. He tells them that
when a camel can be led into the sea, the rain will start. A mother
camel and her baby are purchased for this purpose. The furry baby
Kali and Mohamed become close friends. The men of the village try
in vain to lead the mother camel into the water, but it is Mohamed
who is finally successful in fulfilling the old prophecy.

GUILLAUME, JEANETTE, AND MARY LEE BACHMANN. *Amat and the Water
Buffalo*. il. by Kurt Wiese. Coward, 1962, $2.75. It seems to Amat,
a small Indonesian boy, that he will never be old enough to go to

school or ride a water buffalo. Without telling his family, he persuades a neighboring farmer to let him care for his water buffalo and then ride it home to convince his parents that he is "big" enough. Numerous family activities, watching the planting of rice and using the water buffalo, making Wajang puppets similar to those used in the native shadow plays, playing games, visiting the busy marketplace, along with references to customs and foods, reveal a segment of present-day Indonesian culture.

* HAWKINSON, LUCY. *Dance, Dance, Amy-Chan!*

KAY, HELEN. *Henri's Hands for Pablo Picasso.* il. by Victor Ambrus. Abelard, 1965, $3.50. Henri lives in the small mountain community of Vallauris, France, whose famous pottery kilns have been cold and idle for years. Grandpere wants Henri to become a potter; his baker-father is anxious for him to follow his trade; and Henri wants to make his own decision when he is older. When Pablo Picasso, the great and famous artist, helps revitalize the village pottery industry, Henri is torn between his interest in pottery making and baking. He proves his artistry when he molds bread dough into croissants that became known as "Picasso's Hands."

————. *An Egg Is for Wishing.* il. by Yaroslava. Abelard, 1966, $3.75. If Nikolas, the very young Ukranian boy, is to be given one of the elaborately decorated eggs, an Easter gift of love, he must overcome his fear of chickens. He so wants a pysanka, a decorated egg, that he gains enough confidence to take an egg from the cuckoo, the owl, the duck, the goose, and the stork. His mother decorates each egg and includes on the largest egg paintings of hens and roosters, symbols that stand for wishes. Nikolas is able to overcome his fear, and the hen's egg holds a special surprise for him. This easy-to-read story is supported with illustrations that extend the text. The book will enable the reader to compare the Ukranian Easter with that of the United States.

LEWIS, JANET. *Keiko's Bubble.* il. by Kazue Mizumura. Doubleday, 1961, $2.50. Keiko believes that she will be given a doll, something she longs for, on Girl's Day, the day of the Festival of Dolls. Her father, a Japanese fisherman, can only afford to give Keiko a glass float, something he needs for his fishing net. The float, called Keiko's bubble, is cherished, brings the family good luck, but eventually is lost at sea. The doll that Keiko receives one year later never quite seems to replace the lost bubble. The story can give the young reader a glimpse into some of the customs of modern Japan.

LIANG, YEN. *Happy New Year.* il. by author. Lippincott, 1961, $3.93. Throughout the narrative, description and detailed illustrations take precedence over any action of the two Chinese children, Dee-Dee and Boo. The text, although concise, depicts with authenticity the preparations, foods, decorations, gifts, beliefs about gods, duty toward debts, fireworks, and naming of the year. The book enables readers to know and to understand how celebrations play an important part in the feelings and heritage of a people.

LUMN, PETER. *Great Day in China, the Holiday Moon.* il. by Peter Thompson. Abelard, 1963, $2.75. New Year's Day is especially important to Lao Tien, a small Chinese boy, as he finally gets a chance to fly his very own dragon kite, which soars the highest of all the kites in the new year's celebration.

MARTIN, PATRICIA MILES. *Friend of Miguel.* il. by Genia. Rand, 1967, $2.95. Miguel stops every day to watch horses drinking at the river while on his way to shine tourists' shoes in the small Mexican village. The boy becomes very fond of one special horse, Santiago, owned and driven daily to market by the vegetable man. When Santiago's owner must leave for Mexico City, Miguel, in his concern and love for the horse, searches for someone to buy him. When there is no buyer, the owner leaves his faithful horse to Miguel, remembering his friendship with Santiago. The gay and bold illustrations extend the light story to enable the reader to see village life and a young Mexican boy's love for an animal.

O'NEILL, MARY. *Ali.* il. by Juan C. Barberis. Atheneum, 1968, $3.95. Tunisian beliefs and customs are richly interwoven in the story of Ali, a Tunisian boy, and his family facing the conflicts of change. Ali wants to retain the old ways, while his wise Bedouin father encourages his son to attend school before choosing a way of life.

PALMER, C. EVERARD. *The Cloud with the Silver Lining.* Pantheon, 1967, $3.95. This poignant story of two Jamaican brothers deeply devoted to their invalid grandfather tells how they plan to earn money at the Christmas festival in order to bring their grandfather back into the mainstream of village life.

PATERSON, A. B. *Waltzing Matilda.* HR & W, 1972, $5.95. Well-illustrated edition of an Australian song that has become almost a legend for that country.

POLITI, LEO. *Lito and the Clown.* il. by author. Scribner, 1964, $3.25. Everyone is happy that the carnival has come to the Mexican village, everyone except Lito who is sad because his kitten Paquita is lost. The tallest clown in all Mexico, Payaco, offering to help, rescues Paquita from the ferris wheel after the kitten makes a brief appearance on the carnival puppet stage, amusing the audience who think it is the funniest show they have ever seen.

——. *Rosa.* Scribner, 1963, $4.95. Rosa, a Mexican girl, realizes her wish for a doll with the arrival of a baby sister at Christmas.

PRIOLO, PAULINE. *Piccolina and the Easter Bells.* il. by Rita Fava. Little,

1962, $3.25. This is a legend of a very small Sicilian girl, Piccolina, and the problems she faces because of her size and her intense desire to grow in the ceremony of the bells, a Sicilian custom held one day before Easter. Traditionally it is a time when all village children are lifted high into the air by their tallest relative so that they will grow tall. The illustrations of the village square supplement the story.

SADOWSKY, ETHEL. *Francois and the Langouste*. il. by Herbert Danska. Little, 1969, $3.75. Francois has great trouble arriving at school on time. He almost makes it one day, his last chance to earn his right to go on a school trip, but finds a giant crawfish (langouste) big enough to make many meals for his family. Francois hurries home with his catch and tries to get to school on time. Martinique residents of many occupations are seen in many settings as Francoise journeys to and from school.

SHANNON, TERRY. *And Juan*. il. by Charles Payzant. A Whitman, 1961, $2.75. Juan, youngest in a family of potters, lives in Metepec, Mexico. His job is to work the clay with his feet while the other male members of the family shape the pottery. When the father introduces his potter sons, he always pauses before saying, ". . . and Juan." Juan, wanting his father's recognition, forms a clay figure by himself. For assurance, he has it blessed at the Blessing of the Animals before taking it to the city to sell. Now when Papa tells the buyer that his sons are potters, he does not pause before naming Juan. Young readers will discover varied aspects of the Mexican culture.

SOTOMAYOR, ANTONIO. *Khasa Goes to the Fiesta*. il. by author. Doubleday, 1967, $3.25. Playing a panpipe and marching in the Fiesta of the Virgin of Copacabana just like his uncle was Khasa's ambition. In the fields among the llamas in the Andes Mountains of Bolivia, Khasa practices daily and overcomes his problem of playing the panpipe with his front teeth missing. Temporarily separated from his uncle, he takes a gay boat trip on Lake Titicaca and finally participates in the festivities.

* STINETORF, LOUISE A. *A Charm for Paco's Mother*.

* ———. *The Treasure of Tolmec*.

SURANY, ANICO. *The Burning Mountain*. il. by Leonard Everett Fisher. Holiday, 1965, $3.95. Jose lives in a tiny village at the foot of an everthreatening volcano in El Salvador. In a niche carved in the side of the volcano stands a statue of San Cristobal, the village's patron saint. Two days before the feast day of the saint, the volcano sends down a river of lava that could destroy the village. As the families prepare to flee, Jose contrives a desperate plan to save the statue. His efforts plus the miraculous halting of the lava flow make the fiesta possible after all. This story depicts life in a little-known coffee-growing area in Central America.

————. *Ride the Cold Wind.* il. by Leonard Everett Fisher. Putnam, 1964, $3.69. In the Lake Titicaca country of Peru, small Paco grows tired of shepherding his herd of stubborn llamas. Daily he watches his father and other fishermen "ride the cold wind" and dreams of catching the famous fish, El Rayo de Oro, Golden Lightening. Eventually he secretly sails with the aid of his sister onto the treacherous lake. Paco encounters a heavy storm and hooks the mysterious fish.

SUTHERLAND, EFUA. *Playtime in Africa.* il. by Willis E. Bell. Atheneum, 1962, $3.75. Both primary- and middle-grade children will be interested in the clear photographs which cover the page and in the spritely descriptive text showing what the childern of Ghana do for amusement.

VAVRA, ROBERT. *Pizorro.* HBJ, 1968, $3.95. Pizorro, an eight-year-old Mexican boy, works from early morning until late in the day helping his father on a rancho north of Mexico City. The rancho is owned by a patron. The family is poor and their life is simple and pleasures few. One day Pizorro is delighted to receive a baby burro from the patron. Pizorro and the burro become great friends. They work together and take siestas together. But one day the burro runs away and Pizorro finds him at the market. He takes him home and promises him that as soon as the burro is big enough for him to ride they will go to San Miguel every Sunday. Perhaps some day they may even go to Mexico City.

WATTS, MABEL. *Yin Sun and the Lucky Dragon.* il. by H. Tom Hall. Westminster, 1969, $3.75. The five "uncles" or guardians responsible for Yin Sun, a young Chinese orphan, are determined that this boy of Hong Kong will follow, according to ancient customs, one of their five trades—fisherman, tailor, bookseller, grocer, or curio shop owner. However, Yin Sun dreams only of being a kite maker. While he is busy flying his dragon kite, the Honorable Uncles agree that Yin Sun must learn each trade and one year later he is to reveal his choice. The young boy succeeds in each. Then, he tactfully persuades each uncle of the importance of becoming a kite maker.

WEIL, LISL. *Eyes So-o Big.* HM, 1964, $3.25. It was a fish that started Isabel and Clara on their painting spree. It was a fish that gave the girls their white dresses, angel wings, and a place in the festival parade. This is a story of the warmth and friendliness of a Portuguese coastal village.

WYNDHAM, ROBERT (compiler-editor). *Chinese Mother Goose Rhymes.* il. by Ed Young. World Pub, 1968, $5.95. Poetry and nursery rhymes are found in most countries and are suprisingly universal. According to the author there seems to be a common thread of themes: counting toes and fingers, animals, flowers, good and bad children, and many others. The verses in this collection include both new and old translations from China and from this country.

Intermediate

* ABRAHAMS, ROBERT D. *The Bonus of Rendonda.*

ARORA, SHIRLEY L. *What Then, Raman?* Follett, 1960, $3.95. Raman is the first boy in his village to learn to read. His desire for knowledge is thwarted when family circumstances make it impossible for him to continue his education. Later, when he begins teaching his former friends to read, he realizes the responsibilities that come with the privilege of learning.

BARUCH, DOROTHY W. *Kobo and the Wishing Pictures.* il. by Yoshi Noguchi. CE Tuttle, 1964, $3.75. Kobo is the small son of a Japanese artist who paints for the springtime Wishing Day. At this time people hang illustrations symbolizing their wishes on the temple walls. Kobo is not able to make up his mind about his own wish, and his father, so busy with other people's paintings, finds no time for his own family's wishing pictures.

* BEHN, HARRY. *The Two Uncles of Pablo.*

BERRY, ERICK. *The Springing of the Rice.* il. by John Kaufmann. Macmillan, 1966, $3.24. The importance and intertwining of the rice culture with the strong values and beliefs of the Thai rural folk is shown as Tam, a Thai boy, and his family tend the rice fields from planting to harvest. The absorbing story concludes with a procession of thanksgiving, followed by offerings to the temple and a feast attended by all the festively dressed villagers.

BERTOL, ROLAND. *The Two Hats: A Story of Portugal.* il. by Allan Bitzen. TY Crowell, 1969, $3.75. Although Antonio has a natural way with animals and handles the most stubborn team of oxen, he yearns to sail the sea as a fisherman like his father and wear a barrete. In Portugal a man's hat indicates his work. When a storm threatens the fishing fleet, Antonio earns the right to replace his flat-brimmed farmer's hat with that of a fisherman.

BLOCH, MARIE. *The Two Worlds of Damyan.* il. by Robert Quackenbush. Atheneum, 1966, $3.95. Damyan, growing up in the Ukraine, is torn between two worlds. At school he speaks Russian and never questions what his teacher says or what he reads in books; at home he and his grandmother speak Ukrainian and she tells him many things he does not repeat. To realize his dream of becoming an Olympic swimmer he must join the Komsomol. If he joins he will lose the warm relationship with his grandmother and friends. Damyan must make the difficult choice himself.

* ———. *Aunt America.*

* BUFF, MARY AND CONRAD. *Magic Maize.*

* CARLSON, NATALIE SAVAGE. *Jean-Claude's Island.*

———. *Luigi of the Streets.* il. by Emily Arnold McCully. Har-Row, 1967, $3.95. In the fascinating setting of Marseilles, young Luigi tries to remove what he is convinced is a gypsy curse upon his family. Neither prayers, nor candles in the Cathedral, nor the offering of his mother helps his sister Doro walk again. Finally his efforts, combined with those of his mother and their numerous friends, bring forth two "miracles."

———. *Befana's Gift.* il. by Robert Quackenbush. Har-Row, 1969, $3.95. One chilly December afternoon, Cesare, a carriage driver on the way home to the poorest section of Rome, gives a ride to an old woman. She looks so much like the legendary Befana who brings gifts to Italian children at Christmas that he jokingly asks her to bring him a grandson. How Befana answers Cesare's wish provides a warm and colorful story that reveals the daily life of a close-knit Italian family.

CASSEDY, SYLVIA, AND KUNIHIRO SUETAKE. *Birds, Frogs, and Moonlight.* il. by Vo-Dinh and Koson Okamura. Doubleday, 1967, $3.95. These haiku celebrate the child's experiences with animals. Pictures and calligraphy inform the reader that writing and slippers in Japan are different but poems inform the readers that kittens, birds, spiders, frogs, and feelings are delightfully the same.

CATHERALL, ARTHUR. *Camel Caravan.* il. by Joseph Rapin. Seabury, 1968, $3.95. The camel men travel across the African desert twice a year carrying precious salt from the mines to Timbuktu. Twelve-year-old Youba and his younger sister Fedada become separated from the rest of the caravan while protecting a newborn camel, Amr'r. Problems are compounded when the stranded children attempt to aid a wounded old man. This adventurous suspense story includes many of the desert's dangers: the lack of water and food, a raid by desert marauders, the hazards of a desert storm, and the capture of the children by the marauders.

———. *Duel in the High Hills.* Lothrop, 1969, $4.25. Temba and his father, a rugged Himalayan trader, leave for a lowland market with their sheep and goats laden with produce to sell. Along the trail their train is attacked by a snow leopard who kills a sheep and two of their best dogs, and seriously injures Temba's father. Temba must secure help for his father. The trip is near catastrophe when two Hindu thieves almost steal all the family wealth. How Temba saves the family fortune and proves his manliness is portrayed against the life, beliefs, and customs of the mountain people.

* CLARK, ANN NOLAN. *Secret of the Andes.*

* COATSWORTH, ELIZABETH. *The Lucky Ones: Five Journeys toward a Home.*

————. *The Noble Doll.* il. by Leo Politi. Viking Pr, 1961, $3.00. Dona Amalia, formerly a wealthy lady, lives in what had once been her own fine house, earning a very meager living by serving. The daughter of a former servant learns of the old lady's failing eyesight and brings her own little girl, Luisa, to care for her. Dona Amalia unpacks a valuable heirloom doll and refuses an offer to sell the beloved keepsake in spite of needing the money. Detailed illustrations give the reader a vivid sense of the daily activities, life, and festivities of Christmas in Mexico.

COLLINS, RUTH P. *Hubba-Hubba, A Tale of the Sahara.* il. by Harold Berson. Crown, 1968, $3.50. Musa, a desert boy from the Sahara, loves his baby camel named Hubba-Hubba. Hubba-Hubba, which means trouble, is a real nuisance to everyone in the village, until the village is threatened by a hungry lion and visited by a caravan.

* DE JONG, MEINDERT. *Journey from Peppermint Street.*

* ————. *Far Out the Long Canal.*

* ————. *The House of Sixty Fathers.*

DILLON, EILIS. *The Sea Wall.* il. by W. T. Mars. FS & G, 1965, $2.95. This book introduces the family customs, the language rich with humor, and the colorful storytelling of the people of Inisharcain. The Irish islanders' seemingly complacent attitude about the unmended sea wall and the dangers of a tidal wave do not deter Pat's belief in a prediction. Aided by his grandmother, the sage village prophet, Pat and his friend John overcome the island people's reluctance to accept outside help for rebuilding the sea wall.

FANTE, JOHN, AND RUDOLPH BORCHERT. *Bravo, Burro!* il. by Marilyn Hirsh. Hawthorn, 1970, $4.50. A small burro, courageously defying a cougar, is aided by Manuel, a young Mexican boy, taken home, and appropriately named El Valiente, the valiant one. Life in the hacienda, where Manuel lives with his self-pitying, ex-bullfighter father, Juan, is not a pleasant one. The bond of love and friendship with El Valiente gives Manuel the courage to face problems of great responsibility.

FENISONG, RUTH. *Boy Wanted.* il. by Lili Cassel-Wronker. Har-Row, 1964, $2.95. Abused, unhappy ten-year-old Ron, a Bahamian orphan, plans and executes his escape from his cruel "aunt" and "uncle," finding a new home with Miss Flora and Mr. Thorne on Piper Cay. This story is rich with native dialect, foods, customs, superstitions, and home life.

* FEUSTEL, GUNTHER. *Jose: A Tale from South America.*

FIEDLER, JEAN. *Call Me Juanita.* McKay, 1968, $3.75. Johanna Gilbert does not want to go to Mexico to live even though her father has been offered a professorship there. Once in Mexico Johanna puts up

a losing battle against the fascination of things Spanish and is completely drawn into the colorful life and culture of the people she
meets.

FIFE, DALE. *A Stork for the Bell Tower.* il. by Alain. Coward, 1964,
$3.50. Storkheim in Alsace awaits the return of the spring migration
of storks, but with little hope, for they have not come back for several
years. Eight-year-old Seppala helps the villagers see that they make
their own good luck and persuades them to prepare for the customary
festival honoring the storks' return.

* FLORY, JANE. *One Hundred and Eight Bells.*

FUKADA, HANAKO. *Wind in My Hand.* il. by Lydia Cooley. Golden Gate,
1970, $4.95. Based on the autobiography of Issa, celebrated Japanese
haiku poet, this story recreates his lonely childhood, his early life in
Tokyo, his recognition as a poet after years of struggle, his wanderings
across the length and breadth of Japan, and his final homecoming to
his friends, the children. Poems included illustrate his deep love of
nature and of the hearty, simple things of life, and they depict the
love and reverence which the Japanese feel for their artists. "The first
firefly, swept away, leaving the wind in my hand."

GRAY, ELIZABETH JANET. *The Cheerful Heart.* il. by Kazue Mizumura.
Viking Pr, 1959, $3.50. Eleven-year-old Tami gives courage and
hope to her family as they rebuild their lives and home in Tokyo
following World War II bombing. Many customs; foods and their
preparation; festivals, such as the one held on New Year's day with
kite flying; and family relationships are vividly described in this warm
and human story. Black and white illustrations heighten the feeling of
life in Japan.

GUILLOT, RENE. *Fonabio and the Lion.* il. by W. F. Phillips and J. P.
Wriel. Watts, 1966, $3.95. Fonabio, an orphaned African bushboy
living with the aged witch doctor Ziemoko, inherits all of his friend's
treasures and mystic powers. Fonabio also has a strong desire to become a part of the household of another friend, the white planter
Marlow. The story revolves around Fonabio's friendship with and devotion to a cub lion which he raises. The story is rich in the fascinating
customs and folklore of the bush natives. Further insights into the life
and rituals are portrayed through strong black and white water-color
illustrations.

HALLIN, EMILY WATSON. *Moya and the Flamingoes.* il. by Rus Anderson.
McKay, 1969, $3.50. The flamingoes are the sacred totem of Moya's
Kenya clan and when naturalists come to the area to study the birds,
the tribe is unfriendly to them. Moya saves the life of the boy Peter,
about his own age, by using the medicine man's magic. Making Peter
his blood brother makes many special things possible for Moya.

———— AND ROBERT KINGERY BUELL. *Follow the Honey Bird.* il. by Larry Toschik. McKay, 1967, $3.50. The Masai are herdsmen with proud traditions and Ori must help his older brother tend the cattle, a tedious task. Ori adopts a baby honey badger, which leads to difficulties in the family. He and his pet are alternately culprits or heroes in the events that follow, but the friendship endures.

HAYWOOD, CHARLES. *Folk Songs of the World.* il. by Carl Smith. John Day, 1966, $10.95. Folk songs, often spontaneous and improvised, describe or tell about a particular culture: the activities and feelings of people. The anthology contains songs representing one hundred and nineteen countries, with extensive descriptive commentaries on the musical culture, instruments, and dances. Chord suggestions and lists of folk song records are also included. Teachers and librarians will find this a valuable resource.

HODGES, MARGARET. *The Wave.* il. by Kent Blair. HM, 1964, $3.50. Through the story of Ojusan, a rice farmer, and his little grandson Tada, the reader pictures the old Japanese way of life and gains an understanding of the conflicts between age and youth and a realization of the dignity of man and his ability to fight natural disaster. The illustrations are especially suited to the story, for they show both the delicacy and the strength of old Japan.

HOUSTON, JAMES. *Akavak: An Eskimo Journey.* il. by author. HBJ, 1968, $3.25. A grandfather and his grandson make a treacherous journey over miles of frozen land to fulfill a promise. The wisdom of the old man and the physical endurance of the boy, coupled with the moral courage of both, enable them to reach their destination.

IK, KIM YONG. *Blue in the Seed.* il. by Arthur Marokvia. Little, 1964, $3.95. The blue eyes of Chun Bok, a Korean boy, distinguish him from the usual dark-eyed people of his country. The frustrations and suffering of being different cause Chun to be rebellious for a time, until his schoolmates finally accept him.

ISHII, MOMOKO. *The Doll's Day for Yoshika.* il. by Mamoru Funai. Follett, 1966, $3.50. Each year on Doll's Day, Yoshika feels sure she will receive a set of the real O-hina dolls. Her mother has frequently told the ten-year-old girl of her own cherished set, given to her by Yoshika's great-grandmother, and how they had been destroyed during the bombing of Tokyo. The memory of this beautiful set of dolls carved with unusual craftsmanship is so vivid in the mother's mind that she cannot bear to buy Yoshika a gaudy modern set. The young girl's burning disappointment is relieved when she discovers the real reason for the delayed purchase.

* JENKINS, ALAN C. *Wild Swans at Suvanto.*

JENNESS, AYLETTE. *Gussuk Boy.* il. by author. Follett, 1967, $2.95. "Gussuk Boy" means "white boy" in Eskimo and that's just what

Aaron is—the son of one of two white families in an Eskimo village in Alaska. Little by little Aaron consciously and happily adjusts and learns to appreciate a culture different from his own. The author draws her information from her life as an anthropologist's wife.

KINGMAN, LEE. *The Secret Journey of the Silver Reindeer*. il. by Lynn Ward. Doubleday, 1968, $3.50. Told in a style similar to that of a legend or folk tale is the fascinating story of Aslak, a fifteen-year-old Lapp boy, who proves to himself and the village elders his ability to care for his younger brothers and sisters and the family herd of silver reindeer. Through his secret journey to the Cave of the Great Hunters, the family burial ground, we learn of the ancient Lapp culture and customs, which are nearly extinct.

LAMPMAN, EVELYN SIBLEY. *Tilted Sombrero*. il. by Ray Cruz. Doubleday, 1966, $3.95. Nando, thirteen-year-old son of a wealthy Mexican Creole plantation owner, leaves home after his father is killed participating in a *coleada*, a Mexican sport. He has another reason for leaving also: his older brother is ashamed of his resemblance to the mestizos or Indians. Alone and penniless on his way to Mexico City, Nando makes many interesting friends and becomes involved in the terrifying beginnings of Mexico's War of Independence.

LAST, JEFF, AND U. P. TISNA. *The Bamboo School in Bali*. il. by Albert Orbaan. John Day, 1969, $4.29. Bontot, son of a Balinese farmer, dreams of becoming a teacher. A new school in the mountain village and the opportunity for advanced work in the city bring the fulfillment of his dream.

LEWIS, RICHARD (comp.) *Miracles: Poems by Children of English-Speaking Countries*. S & S, 1966, $4.95. This selection of poems was written by children from English-speaking nations throughout the world. Through the eyes of these children, the reader realizes that no matter where they live or what their backgrounds may be, children have many of the same interests, the same reactions to fears and joys, ask the same questions, and wonder at the same things.

MASTERS, ELAINE. *Ali and the Ghost Tiger*. il. by author. Westminster, 1970, $4.25. In Amin, a tiny village in Indonesia, Ali is obsessed with thoughts of the terrible ghost tiger that brings fever and death to his people. Ali plans for the day when he will kill the ghost tiger, malaria, and rid the villagers of its deadly power. Ali's friendship with Min, a young engineer, influences his aims and helps him understand how best he can destroy the deadly terror and help his people.

MEHTA, RAMA. *Ramu: A Story of India*. il. by W. T. Mars. Tri-Ocean, 1966, $3.95. Ramu, son of Kalu Ram, a maker of sweets, lives in a mud-plastered earthen-floor village house in India. He participates in the activities in preparation for the Diwali, a Festival of Lights believed to bring blessings, comfort, and wealth to the family. Insights into present day Indian life may be gained through reading about ancient village customs.

MILLEN, NINA. *Children's Festivals from Many Lands.* il. by Janet Smalley. Friend Pr, 1964, $3.95. Almost all societies have some form of ritual and ceremony and periodically interrupt their daily routine with times of relaxation. The keeping of festivals is an imbedded and cherished part of the cultural pattern of people. Some festivals arise from religious beliefs and folklore. Dressing-up regalia and using preferred foods are unique characteristics of social occasions. This text, a collection of festival descriptions, is an excellent resource for students, teachers, or community groups interested in promoting the understanding of the cultural heritage of other people. Some practical suggestions for using the material with children are offered.

————. *Children's Games from Many Lands.* il. by Allan Eitzen. Friend Pr, 1965, $2.75. This anthology is a survey of two hundred fifty-eight children's games from sixty-four countries. Readers will find games reflecting the music and language of people, the way people earn a living, daily customs and common foods from various countries. They may also discover the universality of games and game patterns. Each geographical section of the book is introduced with comments noting the main characteristics of games of this area.

MILLER, LUREE, AND MARILYN SILVERSTONE. *Gurkhas and Ghosts.* il. by Marilyn Silverstone. Criterion, 1970, $4.95. Masina wants to become a gurkha (Nepali soldier) but is discouraged because he is so small. He and his friend Purna go on a walking trip far from home to a village where Masina finds a gurkha who tells him, "It is not the length of your stride but the courage in your heart that makes you a man." Advised that his courage will be proven if he makes the journey to his home village alone, Masina bravely goes back. Excellent photographs, filled with details and coordinated with the story, augment this narrative of the people of the Himalayas.

MITCHISON, NAOMI. *Friends and Enemies.* il. by Caroline Sassoon. John Day, 1968, $4.50. Petrus lives in South Africa. When his schoolteacher brother is arrested and sentenced to ten years in prison for questioning apartheid, Petrus must flee to his cousin's home in Botswana, once known as Bechuanaland. He learns what it is like to sleep on the floor of a thatched hut, always feeling hungry, and to stand helplessly while crops wither and die from drought. In this insightful story of the lives and culture of the people of Mochude, Petrus learns to grow and think like a man in a free country.

NICKERSON, ELIZABETH. *Celebrate the Sun.* il. with art by children from many lands. Lippincott, 1969, $6.95. People of all cultures have ways of celebrating important events, moments, holidays, and seasons. This attractive text is a collection of stories capturing the festive celebrations of many lands and peoples.

* NORRIS, FAITH, AND PETER LUMN. *Kim of Korea.*

OTTLEY, REGINALD. *Rain Comes to Yamboorah.* il. by Robert Hales. HBJ, 1968, $3.50. The book presents the Australian outback aborigine, his beliefs and seemingly inborn knowledge of his wild and drought-stricken land. The drama of the Australian outback isolation and its effect on men, the emu egg hunts, and aborigine "walkabouts" are supported in this sequel to the other Yamboorah tales of *Boy Alone* and *Roan Colt.*

PATTON, WILLOUGHBY. *Manuel's Discovery.* il. by William Hurchinson. McKay, 1970, $2.95. Manuel, a thirteen-year-old native Bermudian, member of a family of immigrants from the Azores, has difficulty accepting his Portuguese background and scorns the traditional family customs of his heritage. Unwillingly, he accompanies his grandfather to the Azores, gradually developing understandings that allow him to return to Bermuda with pride in his people and in himself.

RANKIN, LOUISE. *Daughter of the Mountains.* il. by Kurt Wiese. Viking Pr, 1948, $3.50 (P/WSP, $.60). Momo, a twelve-year-old Tibetan girl, hungers for a dog of her own. Finally, she acquires a pet terrier, Pempa, brought to her from Lhasa, the holy city. Devotion to Pempa and faith that she will be guided by Buddha prompt Momo to go to Calcutta to find her dog which has disappeared. The long, dangerous journey; her courage in facing grave problems; and her conviction that she will get Pempa back make for a story fully textured with customs, beliefs, feelings, and descriptions of the Tibetan way of life.

REGGIANI, RENEE. *The Sun Train.* Coward, 1966, $3.95. Through the La Rosa family the poverty and oppression in Sicily is revealed. The struggle against bondage to a privileged class brings death to Saro, a popular hero and trade unionist. The La Rosas go to the mainland at the invitation of an uncle, only to find that prejudice against "southerners" keeps them second-class citizens. Resourceful Agata becomes the family breadwinner and finds friends who share her ambitions for Sicily. Sicilian tradition and rich historical background enrich the contemporary setting.

RHOADS, DOROTHY. *The Corn Grows Ripe.* il. by Jean Charlot. Viking Pr, 1956, $3.77. The corn grows ripe this year because of Dionisio, a twentieth-century Mayan Indian boy living in Yucatan. Dionisio's parents understand his childlike ways, but his great-grandmother is sure he is lazy. Due to his father's injury, the young boy becomes the sole provider for his family. Still farming in the ancient tradition, making animal sacrifices, following the old beliefs in raising corn, yet getting modern answers to questions in school, Dionisio skillfully blends the old and the new with reverence and dignity.

RUTHIN, MARGARET. *Elli of the Northland.* Ariel, 1968, $3.50. Elli, living a nomadic life with a Lapp family, must make a difficult decision when her unknown father in Helsinki finally locates her. Her true identity is finally revealed. Influences of Lapp family traditions on Elli are colorfully portrayed in the person of Grandmother Kirsti.

SCHATZ, LETTA. *Bola and the Oba's Drummers.* il. by Tom Feelings. McGraw, 1967, $4.50. Bola, a little village boy in Nigeria, dreams of becoming a drummer for the Oba (king). He becomes acquainted with two little boys who are in the Oba's musical group and whose father is the Head Royal Drummer. Bola learns to understand the drums and to play well enough to become one of the Royal Drummers.

STEVENSON, WILLIAM. *The Bushbabies.* il. by Victor Ambrus. HM, 1965, $3.50 (P/Bantam, $.75). Thinking she has misplaced her permit slip allowing her to take Kamau, her pet bushbaby, out of Africa, Jackie decides to leave the ship and return the tarsier to his natural environment. On the wharf she finds Tembo Murumbi, her father's former assistant, and seeks his aid and protection for this improbable journey. Unfortunately authorities believe Tembo a kidnapper and issue orders to shoot him on sight. Additional hazards magnify their danger, for prolonged drought has upset the wildlife and caused forest fires. Then comes the deluge of rains ending in floods. As the reader joins the three on their journey, he learns about the life of inner Africa, the tribal beliefs and superstitions, the types of shelters, the food habits, the love and deep devotion of native friendships, and the strong cultural ties with nature necessary for survival in this bush country.

STINETORF, LOUISE A. *A Charm for Paco's Mother.* il. by Joseph Escourido. John Day, 1965, $3.86. Paco and his blind mother learn to adjust their lives to the handicap. However, when an Americanos Los Ruristos suggests an operation to restore his mother's sight, Paco decides to turn to his religion for help. The story of his arduous pilgrimage to the great Stone Cross to pray on Christmas Eve is a stirring one. Here is a tale with deep insights into the religious faith and customs which govern the lives of these Mexican-Indian people of Oaxaca.

————. *Manuel and the Pearl.* il. by Joseph Escourido. John Day, 1966, $3.86. Old Papacito, a pearl fisherman, has brought up the Pink Lady, a very large and exquisite pearl, from the cold waters of the Gulf of California. Now it is lost, and Papacito, discouraged and ill, is accused of the theft. How his son Manuel saves the family honor makes lively reading.

————. *The Treasure of Tolmec.* il. by Ann Grifalconi. John Day, 1967, $3.86. This story is one of action and mystery set in the country of the Tarascan Indians in Michoacan, Mexico. Though the padron system no longer exists in this Indian village, the closeness of the people in the community to their padron and their willingness to love and care for him reveal the interrelationships of these people in rural Mexico.

* TAYLOR, SYDNEY. *A Papa Like Everyone Else.*

* UCHIDA, YOSHIKO. *Hisako's Mysteries.*

* ———. *In-Between Miya.*

———. *The Sea of Gold and Other Tales from Japan.* il. by Marianne Yamaguchi. Scribner, 1965, $3.95. A collection of traditional Japanese folk tales with delightful indigenous characters, animals, goblins, ogres, and customs. They are enhanced by imaginative illustrations in charcoal. While the characters and folk motifs are distinctly Japanese, many themes are universal: kindness, honesty, and perserverence pay off in the end.

VAN STOCKUM, HILDA. *Mogo's Flute.* il. by Robin Jacques. Viking Pr, 1966, $3.50. Mogo, Kikuya boy of Kenya, cannot participate in the usual children's games and adult and family activities. The villagers believe that the boy has had a spell, or "thahu," cast on him, which leaves him frail and useless. The love of his younger sister Njoki and the recognition of his talent for flute playing by the Mundo-Mugo help the young East African overcome his handicap.

WESTWOOD, GWEN. *Narni of the Desert.* il. by Peter Warner. Rand, 1967, $3.50. Narni, a young boy of a nomadic tribe of African bushmen on the Kalahari Desert, wants more than anything to be old enough to hunt with the older boys and men. During drought season when animals are scarce and there are few rains, Narni's efforts to help the tribe secure food win him the coveted status of hunter. This quiet story in large print and simple writing style will appeal to less mature readers.

WILSON, CARTER. *On Firm Ice.* il. by William A. Berry. TY Crowell, 1970, $3.95. Netsilik Eskimo legends and beliefs about life and death emerge as Ukpik overcomes the sadness caused by his father's unusual death.

* WOODS, HUBERT C. *Child of the Arctic.*

WYCKOFF, CHARLOTTE CHANDLER. *Kumar.* il. by Robin Jacques. Norton, 1965, $3.69. Following his father's death in 1945, Kumar leaves Madras, India, and with his sister and mother goes to live in the country. Village life and customs are conveyed, as is the observance of religious holidays associated with the Hindu religion. Kumar has heard much of Gandhi and his teachings and is disturbed by the unfairness and inconsistencies of the caste system. Young Americans might see a parallel between our process of integration and the attempt to abolish the caste system in India.

Junior

ABRAHAMS, ROBERT D. *The Bonus of Redonda.* il. by Peter Bramley. Macmillan, 1969, $4.50. Bonus, a thirteen-year-old orphan living with

his "King" of the fishermen gran'pa on the island of Nevis in the West
Indies, tells in a language rich in dialect of his dream to become the
ruler of the nearby deserted island of Redonda. Local customs with
their charm, calypso music and its beat, religion and superstitions that
influence the island people are colorfully revealed through the humorous adventures of Bonus. The personal narrative includes the words
of native songs.

ALMEDINGEN, E. M. *Fanny.* il. by Ian Ribbons. FS & G, 1970, $3.95.
Fanny is Frances Hermione de Poltoratsky, a turn of the century
novelist and historian, and aunt of the author. Based on sketches written in 1911 by Fanny, the book is rich in the adventures of her childhood in Russia, France, and England as daughter of a wealthy Russian
landowner and writer father and an English mother. It is also the
story of a writer growing up and her sensitivity to life about her.

BAUDOUY, MICHEL-AIME. *More than Courage.* trans. by Marie Ponsot.
HBJ, 1961, $3.50. Several boys from different social levels in a French
town work together to overhaul an old motorcycle and enter it in a
cross-country race.

CAVANNA, BETTY. *Jenny Kimura.* Morrow, 1964, $4.50. Jenny Kimura
Smith goes to Kansas City to visit the American grandmother she has
never met. Raised in a westernized Tokyo home with the shared cultures of East and West, sixteen-year-old Jenny finds America and
Americans a confusing intrigue. Dating, social customs, and racial
bigotry are all met and faced.

CHAPIN, HENRY, AND PETER THROCKMORTON. *Spiro of the Sponge Fleet.*
il. by Bertil Kumlein. Little, 1964, $3.75. On Easter Sunday, the
people of the Greek island of Kolymnos participate in the impressive
religious ceremonies of the Greek Orthodox church. They make a
great circle by the wharf to watch the blessing of the sponge fleet
in preparation for its six month journey across the Aegean and Medi-
terranean Seas to the North African coast. Sixteen-year-old Spiro is
anxious to go and be a sponge diver like his older brother and father,
while his mother tries to keep the sixteen-year-old at home. Eventually,
Spiro goes on the trip, not as a diver, but as a deck boy. When the
fleet returns, new government safety regulations and new methods of
diving with oxygen tanks convince his mother to permit his choice
of career. The story helps one see how the islanders' occupation influences the attitudes, dreams, and aspirations of the people.

DE JONG, MEINDERT. *The House of Sixty Fathers.* il. by Maurice Sendak.
Har-Row, $2.95 (P/Dell, $.75). The river rises, and young Tien Pao,
alone on his family sampan, is swept downriver into Japanese-occupied
China. With only his little pet pig for a companion, Tien Pao makes
his way back to find his family. All the terrors of a country at war
are felt by the bewildered boy, whose unfaltering faith in his family
pushes him forth against all odds.

DOBIER, MAURICE. *Benjy Boone.* Dial, 1967, $4.95. When fifteen-year-old Benjy Boone arrives in Philadelphia to join his famous actor father, he discovers that Mr. Boone has been accused of murder and has disappeared. Benjy joins a warm-hearted theatrical group and travels to the Mississippi frontier in search of his father. Benjy succeeds in unraveling the mystery of the murder, finds and frees his father, and in the process, becomes an accomplished actor himself.

FENTON, EDWARD. *An Island for a Pelican.* il. by Dimitris Davis. Doubleday, 1963, $2.75. When a lost pelican makes his home on a tiny Greek isle in the Aegean, the villagers are delighted to have another tourist attraction in addition to their 366 unique churches. He becomes Vassili's pet and is christened Petros. Jealous neighboring islanders kidnap Petros, setting into action some exciting and humorous events. Vassili takes matters into his own hands when adults fail to solve the problem. Young readers should gain an appreciation for life in a Greek village.

* HEAPS, WILLARD A. *Wandering Workers.*

JENKINS, ALAN C. *Wild Swans at Suvanto.* il. by Robert Frankenberg. G & D, 1965, $3.95. An old Lapland legend tells how wild swans bear summer on their wings, and if ever the swans should not return, the legend warns, there will be no more summer. To fifteen-year-old Jouni, the swans mean even more, for the birds are his secret talisman. As this insightful story unfolds, Jouni is torn between shooting one of his beloved wild swans to win the favor of Marjatta and preserving these beautiful creatures that bring summer to Lapland. Herein is revealed a vivid picture of a little known land and a peaceful people.

KALNAY, FRANCIS. *Chucaro, Wild Pony of the Pampa.* il. by Julian de Miskey. HBJ, 1958, $3.25. Chucaro is a pink and white pony belonging to Pedro, a boy of the Argentine pampa. Because of his unique color and his swiftness, Chucaro is also desired by the rich patron's son. The plot and characterizations are rather stilted and cartoonlike. However, the book is very good as an elementary narrative-type explanation of Argentine gaucho life.

KRAVETZ, NATHAN. *The Way of the Condor.* il. by W. T. Mars. Crown, 1970, $3.95. Young Carlos Bernal longs to leave his Peruvian village in the Andes for Lima and the "world beyond." Ultimately his wish is fulfilled and he becomes a chulillo on the bus El Condor Dorado. Life away from the little village is filled with new adventures, a new way of living, but is short-lived. Family changes push him to a decision of returning to his home to assist his father, tend the land, and help in the village school whose staff includes two Peace Corps workers. Many facets of ancient culture and modern Peruvian life are skillfully blended in this story. A glossary of Spanish words is included.

LEWIS, ELIZABETH. *To Beat a Tiger, One Needs a Brother's Help.* HR & W, 1956, $3.59. The horrors of the Japanese invasion of China are vividly told in this novel of the search for values in a war-torn world. These boys from entirely different backgrounds and social classes are thrown together as part of a gang in Shanghai. Their very existence depends on their quick wits, nimble fingers, and fast feet. They experience disease and starvation, witness violent death, which they never become accustomed to, and through common needs become close friends. These experiences force quick maturation of emotions and values.

* Lewis, Richard (comp.) *Miracles: Poems by Children of English-Speaking Countries.*

Loisy, Jeanne. *Sierra Summer.* trans. by Irene Salem. Follett, 1965, $3.25. Isabel is the rather spoiled thirteen-year-old daughter of a sheep rancher in Spain. Her ambition is to accompany the flocks and the herders' families to the high mountains for the summer. While there, a mystery develops when some sheep disappear. Isabel's diary reveals her growth in maturity.

Mirsky, Reba Paeff. *Nomusa and the New Magic.* Follett, 1962, $4.98. Nomusa, whom readers have come to know and admire in the earlier books about this endearing Zulu girl, *Thirty-One Brothers and Sisters* and *Seven Grandmothers,* now goes to live with the nurse Buselapi to learn how to become a nurse herself. Readers are able to see the contrast between the old and the new ways of Nomusa's people.

* Nickerson, Elizabeth. *Celebrate the Sun.*

* Noble, Iris. *Megan.*

* Ojigbo, A. Okion, (comp.) *Young and Black in Africa.*

Sanford, David E. *My Village, My World.* il. by Gustave Nebel. Crown, 1969, $4.25. Nikos feels intense loyalty to his father and to the way of life in their small Greek village, but a conflict arises when Nikos has the opportunity to leave the village to continue his education. Nikos is confused by the confrontation of the traditional with the progressive, the provincial with the sophisticated, but he finds a solution to his problem that is satisfactory to all.

Serraillier, Ian. *Escape from Warsaw.* il. by Erwin Hoffman. P/Schol Bk Serv, 1968, $.60. When the Nazis overran Poland during World War II, many families were separated. Some members were sent to prison camps, others to work camps, and many others were left to scavenge a living or starve to death. This story relates a true account of a journey four children take from Warsaw to find their parents in Switzerland. Guided by nothing but a dim hope and a silver sword, they survive insurmountable odds.

Seymour, Alta Halverson. *Toward Morning: A Story of the Hungarian Freedom Fighters.* Follett, 1961, $3.48. A group of courageous

Hungarian teenagers join a rebellion against the Russian rulers who have taken over their homeland. The young people participate in the riots until all supplies are exhausted, then undertake the harrowing experience of escaping across the border. Their loyalty and concern for each other, as well as their devotion to their country, make this a moving story.

* SOMERFELT, AIMEE. *The White Bungalow.*

* STEELE, MARY Q. *Journey Outside.*

STRACHAN, MARGARET P. *Patience and a Mulberry Leaf.* Washburn, 1962, $3.00. This is the story of a young Chinese girl and her friends as they attempt to understand and combat prejudice. Mabel Doug is a senior in high school in Seattle, Washington, during the Korean War. The incidents of prejudice and what the girls do about them make interesting reading.

STUCLEY, ELIZABETH. *Family Walk-Up.* il. by Lawrence Beall Smith. Watts, 1960, $2.95. The Berners family has plenty of storms and stresses in its crowded London flat at the top of the long stairs. It is Mum's cheerfulness, diplomacy, and common sense that keep the family going. Tenderness and toughness mingle in this realistic story of a London working-class family.

TENNANT, KYLIE. *All the Proud Tribesmen.* St. Martin, 1960, $2.95. A native Australian writes of adventures experienced by natives in escaping from a volcanic island eruption.

THOGER, MARIE. *Shanta.* trans. by Eileen Amos. il. by Marvin Friedman. Follett, 1968, $3.50. Shanta, who lives a life of extreme poverty in a small village in India, has the promise of comfort, security, and education when she is betrothed to a wealthy cousin. The plague changes Shanta's plans, but she courageously perseveres and proves that hardship can cause a girl to mature quickly into a woman able to take on the responsibility for her whole family.

TRIPP, ELEANOR. *To America.* HBJ, 1969, $3.95. An interesting account of nine different groups of people who migrated to America, with good descriptions of the circumstances which prompted the migrations. The groups emerge as living people with personal problems who are forced to abandon homes and friends to seek more tolerable conditions in an alien land. This book deals primarily with events before these groups came to America.

* WATSON, SALLY. *To Build a Land.*

WEAVER, STELLA. *A Poppy in the Corn.* Pantheon, 1960, $4.29. A thirteen-year-old war orphan comes to live with an English family and finds herself the "outsider." The oldest children accept her and the smallest boy adores her, but Anna is jealous of this poised stranger. Strained relations develop when the children are unexpectedly left alone. In this picture of a small Cornish coast community and its people, characterizations and interrelationships between the children and newcomer are especially well done. The story is told with insight and with understanding of family relationships.

WHITNEY, PHYLLIS. *Secret of the Tiger's Eye.* il. by Richard Horowitz. Westminster, 1961, $2.95. South Africa is the setting for this teenage mystery story about a widowed American journalist who takes his fourteen-year-old daughter, a younger son, and the teenage son of a friend with him on an assignment to Capetown, South Africa. There the group faces many problems, including adjusting to new surroundings and new friends and South Africa's unjust policy of apartheid.

* WIBBERLEY, LEONARD. *The Island of the Angels.*

ZIEGLER, ELSIE REIF. *The Face in the Stone.* il. by Ray Abel. Longmans, 1959, O.P. Dushan Lukovich, an immigrant to America, comes from a long line of Serbian master stonecutters whose craft and artistry are known throughout the world. In the Chicago of the 1890s he struggles to find a place in American industry, to avenge his father's murder, and to win the girl he loves. He meets frustration on every side until he searches his soul and finds himself. Only then does he forge ahead.

Senior

* ALDRICH, BESS STREETER. *Lantern in Her Hand.*

ANDERSON, WILLIAM ASHLEY. *Angel of Hudson Bay.* Dutton, 1961, O.P. A true story of Maud and Jim Watt and their lifelong struggle in the arctic wilds of Canada to help the Indians adapt to and survive with civilization. Working for the Hudson's Bay Company and sometimes even against it, the Watts fight prejudice and governmental policies. Together they endure bitter hardships, deprivations, and danger in a land where few white men had ever traversed.

* BRADDON, RUSSELL. *When the Enemy Is Tired.*

BURGESS, ANTHONY. *A Clockwork Orange.* Norton, 1962, $3.95 (P/several). Unfolding like a nightmare, this shocking fantasy shows England's young hoodlums in power. The characters, like oranges, are organic, but their grotesque violence has a clocklike mechanical quality that leeches it of its emotional impact. The plot centers around the antihero Alex, who is temporarily rehabilitated through conditioning that robs him of free will.

CONRAD, JOSEPH. *Heart of Darkness.* Eriksson, 1969, $5.00 (P/several). Conrad takes the reader on a psychological journey into the mystical depths of man's darkest nature. Marlow's journey into the heart of

Africa pierces into the most primitive and unconscious levels of man's being. He goes in search of a man who has sold his soul for the price of ivory. Here is a tale of horror, of despair, of man in his heart of darkness.

DOOLEY, THOMAS A. *The Edge of Tomorrow.* FS & G, 1958, $5.95 (P/ NAL, $.60). Tom Dooley, the remarkable young American doctor, tells how he and a small group of men started a jungle hospital to help the villagers of the remote areas of Laos who, without previous medical help and victimized by political assassins, learned to know and trust the Americans, to help themselves, and to help others.

EARL, LAWRENCE. *She Loved a Wicked City: Story of Mary Ball, Missionary.* Dutton, 1962, $4.50. In 1925, Mary Ball, a young English nurse, found herself in the city of Tatung on the Mongolian border of China, where, in a mission hospital she spent most of the rest of her life helping the sick, the foolish, the wicked, any who came to her needing help. She lived through the horrors of war, Japanese occupation, and Communist control. Her wisdom and determination in the face of unbelievable obstacles reveal a woman of limitless courage and devotion.

FANON, FRANTZ. *Toward the African Revolution.* P/Grove, 1969, $1.25. These essays, written over several years by a noted black psychiatrist, move from the particular problems of living as free people in West India and Algeria toward a general discussion of the requisite condition for African liberty. The treatment of both practicality and theory, together with the prophetic chords struck at the close of this collection, cast an informative light on the search for values among today's socially disinherited.

FIEDLER, JEAN. *In Any Spring.* McKay, 1969, $3.95. Unusual in that true love does not win out, this book tells of a college girl's love for a man from India. Kapur returns Laura's love, but is unable to marry her because of an arranged betrothal that he feels he must honor.

GERSON, NOEL B. *I'll Storm Hell.* Doubleday, 1967, $4.95 (P/Curtis, $.75). "Mad Anthony" Wayne's childhood fascination with military strategy served him well when he was called to command troops in the American Revolution. His men both feared and loved him, and leaders like Franklin and Washington respected and admired him. Wayne's military triumphs, however, could not compensate for his personal tragedies.

* GOFF, GERALD M. *Voices of Man: Homecoming.*

GOTTLIEB, ROBIN. *That Summer in Paris.* Funk & W, 1961, $2.95. Amy Benton goes to Paris for a summer of study at the French Center, lives with an attractive French family, and enjoys visiting the Tuilleries Gardens, the opera, the Comedie Francaise, Notre Dame, and many other historic spots with her French pupil, Jacques. Here are Paris and the French people seen through the eyes of a sensitive adolescent who discovers much about herself as she discovers much about the French.

* HERSEY, JOHN R. *A Single Pebble.*

HEYERDAHL, THOR. *Kon-Tiki.* Rand, 1960, $4.95 (P/several). Six scientists cross the Pacific from Peru to Polynesia to substantiate the theory that the islands were populated from South America. Sailing 4300 miles on a raft on an open ocean, these Scandinavians encounter storms, monsters of the sea, and shipwreck. The courage and determination on the part of the voyagers to make the expedition scientifically accurate and to achieve their goal is a tribute to the adventurous spirit of the group.

HOLMBERG, AKE. *Margaret's Story.* Viking Pr, 1961, $3.00. This story of nineteen-year-old Margaret, an orphan on her own, and the breaking of her self-built protective crust gives an idea of Swedish middle-class homes and customs.

HUXLEY, ELSPETH. *The Flame Trees of Thika, Memories of an African Childhood.* P/Apollo, 1959, $1.95. In an oxcart loaded with their provisions, the Huxleys set out for Thika, Kenya. It was 1913 and the Huxleys were farming pioneers on "the dark continent." Their adventures in the strange land with its native inhabitants are vividly evoked in the childhood memories of Elspeth Huxley. It is a haunting tale of leopard hunts, witch doctors, and people struggling against the elements and trying to carve out a new life in a new land.

JOY, CHARLES R. *Young People of West Africa.* Hawthorn, 1961, $3.75. Poignant and lively are these stories of real young people who will shape the future of several newly evolving countries of West Africa.

KAMM, JOSEPHINE. *The Hebrew People: A History of the Jews.* McGraw, 1968, $4.50. Briefly and clearly, Mrs. Kamm traces the Hebrews from their early roots as a nomadic tribe, through the Diaspora, to their present position in today's societies. A final chapter outlines the achievements of numerous contemporary Jews.

* KINNICK, B. J., AND JESSE PERRY. *I Have A Dream: Voices of Man.*

KOSTERINA, NINA. *The Diary of Nina Kosterina.* trans. by Mirra Ginsburg. Crown, 1968, $3.95. The inner turmoil of a vital, rebellious girl going through adolescence is described in the diary of Nina Kosterina, a loyal Russian during Stalin's dictatorship. While political events overshadow Nina's life, the diary basically is an account of Nina's relationships with her family and her friends, and of her involvement in the culture of her native city, Moscow.

* LEDERER, WILLIAM J. *A Nation of Sheep.*

———— AND EUGENE BURDICK. *The Ugly American.* Norton, 1958, $4.95 (P/several). These vignettes of Americans living in Asian countries show both good and bad representatives. The intent is to shake American complacency. Although characters are imaginary, the authors testify that many of the stupid and tragic incidents typify American ineptness in foreign relations. The Ugly American, introduced late in the book, is an engineer who develops a practical water pump powered by a bicycle. He works with a Sarkhanese who aids him in helping the local people help themselves.

MAUERMANN, MARY ANNE. *Strangers into Friends.* Washburn, 1969, $3.95. Karen faces her senior year with dread. Shy and retiring with a fear of failure in anything, Karen has never belonged in the high school crowd. When her father becomes an exchange teacher to England, Karen is overjoyed to get away from Seattle. She finds, however, that she cannot escape the problem of finding herself.

MEANS, FLORENCE. *But I Am Sara.* HM, 1961, $3.50. Sara is unwilling to return to her father's home in Mexico. When she does, her sense of values regains perspective. This story of an American girl in Mexico reveals significant aspects of Mexican life and values.

* MEDEIROS, V. *The Eyes of Love.*

MORRIS, EDITA. *The Flowers of Hiroshima.* Viking Pr, 1959, $4.95. A short, moving account of the after-effects of the atomic attack on Hiroshima.

* NATHAN, ROBERT. *Portrait of Jennie.*

* OJIGBO, A. OKION, (comp.) *Young and Black in Africa.*

POLISHUK, NANCY, AND DOUGLAS LOCKWOOD. *Four against the River.* Dutton, 1962, $3.95. Although Nancy Polishuk has lived all her life in Australian cities, she sets off with her American husband and a two-year-old child to live in Australia's wild and primitive outback land. Dangers come from many sources—crocodiles, sharks, poisonous snakes, the river—yet the family survives.

REMARQUE, ERICH M. *All Quiet on the Western Front.* Little, 1929. $4.95 (P/Fawcett World, $.75). The journal of a young German man forced to serve in the German army during World War I. Written after his war experiences, he expresses his hate of war and love of mankind. As his many friends die, he becomes a broken man, wondering about the futility of life.

RUHEN, OLAF. *Corcoran's the Name.* FS & G, 1968, $3.50. Sixteen-year-old Bob Corcoran decides that what he wants to learn isn't taught by books but is learned through experience. As he roams Australia as a cattle driver, he becomes closely acquainted with his country and its people.

VON HOFFMAN, NICHOLAS. *We Are the People Our Parents Warned Us Against.* Quadrangle, 1968, $5.95 (P/Fawcett World, $.95). The hippie world of the Haight-Ashbury district of San Francisco during its first year of growth (1967-1968) is depicted. Sundry clippings from a variety of newspapers are interspersed in the text, suggesting the worldwide import of the subject at hand.

* WIBBERLEY, LEONARD. *Stranger at Killknock.*

YOORS, JAN. *The Gypsies.* S & S, 1967, $6.95 (P/S & S, $1.95). This firsthand account of the gypsy life in Europe is told in a lively, enjoyable style. Jan Yoors runs away from home to join a group of gypsies. Although he returns to his home and understandingly permissive parents, Jan frequently returns to live with his gypsy friends whom he loves. The lore of the gypsy is presented with an indubitable ring of authenticity.

Mature

BELLOW, SAUL. *Henderson the Rain King.* Viking Pr, 1959, $6.00 (P/ several). An allegorical novel which tells of an older man's search for the meaning of life. His travels take him to a remote village in Africa where he becomes the friend of the chief who helps him to face the primitive elements of life and to overcome his fears.

BUCK, PEARL. *The Three Daughters of Madame Liang.* John Day, 1969, $6.95 (P/PB, $.95). Educated in America, the three daughters of this heroic woman love China, but only one can accept the tenets of modern Communist China. Here is an enlightening picture of the past, present, and future of China.

* BURGESS, ANTHONY. *A Clockwork Orange.*

CONTON, WILLIAM. *The African.* Little, 1960, $4.00. Kisimi Kamara, a child of the African bush, is chosen as one to be educated. His intelligence leads to a scholarship and further contact with the ways and people of the white world. Thus he becomes a man who lives between two worlds. In his desire to help his own people, he returns to Africa to live as an African and to achieve the leadership that later places him in a powerful position to assist his people in their search for freedom and equality in a world of black and white.

DE JESUS, CAROLINA MARIA. *Child of the Dark: The Diary of Carolina Maria de Jesus.* P/NAL, 1964, $.95. Carolina, an unmarried black woman, lives from day-to-day, gathering garbage to support her three children. The favela, the poorest section in Sao Paulo, Brazil, is haunted by hunger. This uneducated woman has a drive to write, to record her observations of life—daily search for food, loneliness, the desire for love, and the urge to survive and to raise her children. It is her diary that lifts her and her children out of desperate poverty.

DEL CASTILLO, MICHEL. *A Child of Our Time.* Knopf, 1958, $5.95. A young Spanish refugee in France is rounded up early in World War

II and sent to a concentration camp, to remain there until liberated by the Allies. The grim details of camp life are vividly portrayed. Although many people in the camp degenerate under the bestial conditions, the young refugee and others act nobly and heroically. In the latter part of the book, the young refugee returns to Spain and attempts to adjust to the institutions and the people there. This is rewarding reading for mature readers.

* Hersey, John. *A Single Pebble.*

Lewis, Oscar. *The Children of Sanchez.* Random, 1961, $12.50 (P/Random, $2.95). Each member of a typical lower-class family of Mexico City recounts his life and brings into dramatic focus the great problem of urban poverty, under which a billion of the world's population live today.

Luthuli, Albert. *Let My People Go.* McGraw, 1962, $5.95 (P/World Pub, $3.45). The author of this book, winner of the 1962 Nobel Peace Prize, is a thirty-year-old South African leader of the African National Congress. Despite being continually surrounded by the doctrines of prejudice and hate, the indignities of apartheid, this complex man is not driven by injustice to meet hate with hate. With wisdom and maturity, Luthuli writes about his people and those unwilling to let his people emerge.

Pasternak, Boris. *Doctor Zhivago.* Pantheon, 1958, $7.95 (P/NAL, $1.25). Spanning a broad panorama of Russian history, this Nobel Prize-winning novel is the story of Doctor Zhivago who cannot suppress his passionate belief in humanity although it would be politically expedient to do so.

Paton, Alan. *Cry, the Beloved Country.* Scribner, 1948, $3.95 (P/Scribner, $1.65). The confusion, poverty, and delinquency of crowded Johannesburg are contrasted with the quiet, rural life in the plantation area.

———. *Tales from a Troubled Land.* Scribner, 1961, $3.95 (P/Scribner, $2.25). Probably no one has so well interpreted apartheid and the struggles of both the Negroes and the whites in South Africa as has Alan Paton in this group of realistic stories.

Spencer, Cornelia. *Claim to Freedom: The Rise of the Afro-Asian Peoples.* John Day, 1961, $3.50. Through the story of a young Indian who works in the post office of Nairobi and of the mail that goes through this hub, one gets the complex story of awakening Africa and Asia told in human terms.

* Turnbull, Colin M. *The Lonely African.*

Vining, Elizabeth Gray. *Return to Japan.* Lippincott, 1960, $5.95. Elizabeth Gray Vining, who went to Japan after World War II to tutor the crown prince and came to know, love, and understand the Japanese, relates her experiences on her return there after ten years. She gives an honest and penetrating interpretation of modern Japan, its people, and its problems.

LADDER 4

I doubt that I would ever have gone into Tad's room alone. With Mama it was easier somehow. It's funny how you have to learn little simple things for the second time—looking at a room, gazing through a window, walking through a door, coming back home—things you've been doing all your life. I must have been like a crippled person learning to walk again, or a blind person with sight restored and learning to see the trees and clouds and stars once more. When a person dies, there's certainly a lot more to it than being sad. Lots more.*

If you're young, smart, and a born leader, you have to be involved in the issues erupting in the streets of your city—especially when its East Los Angeles, California. And especially in the springtime, a time of restlessness. If your friends depend on you to lead a strike, naturally you're going to lead a strike.†

LADDER 4

Coping with Change

If children and young people are to be effective individuals, they need to learn how to cope with a world that will not stand still. Human existence is not a static state; people and the conditions that affect them are continually changing. In addition to developing a healthy self-image, learning to live with others, and appreciating different cultures within and outside our society, children and young people need to learn to deal constructively with a dynamic, changing world.

The books listed in this ladder are concerned with three kinds of change that affect individuals: personal, social or economic, and political.

All individuals eventually face the reality of personal change.

* From *Another Part of the House* by Winston M. Estes. Copyright © 1970 by Winston M. Estes. Reprinted by permission of J. B. Lippincott Company.

† From *You Can't Make It by Bus* by James L. Summers. Copyright © 1969 by James L. Summers. Reprinted by permission of the Westminster Press.

Such situations may be pleasant or unpleasant, but they do demand individual adjustment. The birth of a new baby in a family changes the pattern of family life. Sometimes children react with mild resentment as does Frances in *A Baby Sister for Frances* by Russell Hoban; sometimes children react more strongly as does Laurie in *Laurie's New Brother* by Miriam Schlein.

Moving to a new neighborhood and leaving old friends and familiar surroundings behind can be especially difficult for children. Moving is reflected in books for younger children in a variety of ways. In *Sad Day, Glad Day* by Vivian Thompson, the trauma of moving is intensified for Linda because her favorite doll is left behind. Thomas, in Charlotte Zolotow's *A Tiger Called Thomas*, is preoccupied with what the people in the new neighborhood think of him. Santiago, in Pura Belpre's *Santiago*, makes a big move from Puerto Rico to New York City and has much difficulty adjusting. Books for older children also depict problems faced when families move. In *Up From Appalachia* by Charles Raymond, the Cantrells are ridiculed and called "hillbillies" when they move to Chicago.

Pearl Buck in *The Beech Tree* explores the changes caused when a grandfather comes to live with a family. Jean Little in *Mine for Keeps* presents a realistic picture of the dramatic changes in the life of Sally Copeland. Sally had lived nearly as long as she could remember in a special boarding school for physically handicapped children, but she suddenly finds herself home attending a regular school—not an easy adjustment for a child with cerebral palsy. Similar problems face Mark Mansfield in Kathryn Vinson's *Run with the Ring*. Mark, accustomed to success in athletics, suffers a track accident which leaves him permanently blind.

In *The Blue Year* by Bianca Bradbury, Joan has difficulty adjusting to her parents' divorce. In *Linsey, Herself* by Ruth Wolff, a junior high school girl's father dies suddenly. Other books in this ladder reflect children seeking or suddenly finding themselves in radically different family circles, or children or youth caught in a maze of problems caused by growing up.

Some changes that affect individuals can be directly traced to changing historical, social, or economic conditions. Biographies sometimes help readers to understand the issues involved when history forces change upon individuals, as in Etta DeGering's *Wilderness Wife: The Story of Rebecca Bryan Boone* or Milton Meltzer's *Langston Hughes*. Historical novels sometimes show characters caught up in changing events. Two such books, *The Undergrounders* by Bianca Bradbury and *By Secret Railway* by Enid Meadowcroft, give insight into the underground railway and other methods of helping slaves to freedom.

Other books center on problems of changing social and economic conditions. In *Soo Ling Finds a Way*, June Behrens tells the story of a young girl who discovers a laundromat being installed directly across the street from her grandfather's Chinese hand laundry. *Goodbye, Dove Square* by Janet McNeill is one of many books which deal with changing neighborhood patterns. Other stories are concerned with problems of youth who must face changing social or economic conditions. *The Talking Leaf* by Weyman Jones deals with the decisions faced by a young Indian American concerned for his people. In *Breakthrough to the Big League,* Jackie Robinson tells of the problems he faced as the first Negro in big league baseball. Information books, too, tell of social and economic change. *This is Automation* by Carl Hirsh explains briefly the phenomenon of automation and the impact of the computer on today's economic life and suggests changes which are in store for tomorrow's working force.

War stories, contemporary and historical, are vivid examples of how political events can affect individuals. *The Grist Mill Secret* by Lillie Albrecht, set at the time of the American Revolutionary War, and *The Winged Watchman* by Hilda Van Stockum, set in Holland at the time of World War II, show the reality of change due to political events. *The Endless Steppe* by Esther Hautzig is a gripping, personal account of the five years one girl spent in Siberia during World War II.

Other Sandals by Sally Watson, is set in the politically volatile Middle East of today. Alki Zei's *Wildcat under Glass* pictures the fascism in Greece in the late 1930s. Arna Bontemps' dramatic short biography of *Frederic Douglass* pictures the struggles of this fighter for freedom.

Books that bring the reality of change dramatically to life for children and young people have the potential of helping them understand that life is not static. It is changing and men must move with, adjust to, as well as influence, change. When incidents in books deal with a change that a child has already experienced, he may feel a sense of relief to find his experience is not entirely unique. When books deal with change situations a child sees his friends or others going through, he may gain additional insight or knowledge and may have greater capacity for empathy. Some incidents in books are vivid slices of life useful at specific times for discussion purposes. But perhaps the greatest value of these books to children who know them is that the books may help to bring an underlying realization that change itself is very much an element of life that must be faced. Some changes that come are predictable, some are not. But only those children, youth, and adults who learn to face and accept change creatively will be able to cope with the demand for rapid adaptation in the seventies and beyond.

ROBERT MARSHALL AND DONALD J. BISSETT

Coping with Personal Change

Primary

ABBOTT, SARAH. *Where I Begin*. Coward, 1970, $3.75. A quiet book intended to develop the concept that parents were once children, too. As a small girl looks through a family album, she discovers the many changes time brings in its wake.

ALEXANDER, MARTHA. *Nobody Asked Me If I Wanted a Baby Sister*. il. by author. Dial, 1971, $3.50. A fine book for the older brother or sister who feels a bit neglected after the arrival of a younger sibling. In this book Oliver, disgusted at all the to-do being made over his new sister, decides to give her away. Then he discovers he is the only one who can make the baby stop crying. With this he decides she's pretty smart after all.

* BELL, GINA. *Who Wants Willy Wells?*

BELPRE, PURA. *Santiago*. il. by Symeon Shimin. Warne, 1969, $3.95. Santiago, a young Puerto Rican boy, wants to take his stereoscope to school to show pictures of his pet hen which he had to leave behind in Puerto Rico. When his classmates finally see his pictures, they view Santiago differently. Beautiful, sensitive pictures show an integrated classroom and help tell of Santiago's adjustment to a new environment.

BOUCHARD, LOIS. *The Boy Who Wouldn't Talk*. il. by Ann Grifalconi. Doubleday, 1969, $3.50. Carlos, who comes from Puerto Rico, is frustrated by the problems of adjusting to a new city and a new language. To the distress of his family, his friends, and his teacher, Carlos decides to stop using words at all until he becomes friends with Ricky, who is blind and cannot read Carlos' signs and gestures. A sensitive "boy's eye" view of the problems of a child facing a new urban environment.

BRENNER, BARBARA. *Nicky's Sister*. Knopf, 1966, $3.25. Nicky has a new baby sister over whom a great fuss is made. Nicky is disgusted; he would rather have a hamster. When the baby breaks his plastic Indian Nicky decides to run away, but he confronts McGillicuddy, the neighborhood bully, and he decides to stay to protect his sister, declaring that brothers and sisters should stick together.

BROWN, MYRA BERRY. *Amy and the New Baby*. Watts, 1965, O.P. Amy waits for her mother to come home from the hospital. She watches mother change, nurse, and bubble the baby. She likes to help her mother with Ricky, but doesn't think he will stay long. When mother takes Amy on her lap and explains that Ricky is now a part of their family and daddy takes her for a pony ride, Amy realizes that her parents love her just as much as ever.

————. *First Night Away from Home.* il. by Dorothy Marino. Watts, 1960, $3.75. Packing to sleep away from home for the first time, Stevie remembers his airplane and rock collection, but his mother has to remind him to pack his pajamas. On the way, he asks each neighbor child if he has ever slept away from home. Stevie and his best friend spend a nice evening, but somehow Stevie cannot fall asleep until the doorbell rings and Stevie is given the one thing that he can hug to make him feel at home—his teddy bear. A simply written account of an event important to many children—that first night away from home.

————. *Pip Moves Away.* il. by Polly Jackson. Golden Gate, 1967, $3.75. For first-grader Pip, the prospect of moving to a new house in a new neighborhood with a new school is frightening. But "even birds have to move away" so he settles down to watching the movers empty the house and pack the van. When the Potters arrive at their new home, Pip discovers a new friend who offers to walk to school with him the next day.

* CASTELLANOS, JANE. *Tomasito and the Golden Llamas.*

CAUDILL, REBECCA. *A Certain Small Shepherd.* il. by William Pene Du Bois. HR & W, 1965, $3.50 (P/HR & W, $1.45). When Jamie was born, his mother died. The situation is difficult for all the family to face, and Jamie grows up unable to speak his first words.

COHEN, MIRIAM. *Will I Have a Friend?* il. by Lillian Hoban. Macmillan, 1967, $3.95 (P/Macmillan, $.95). While Pa is taking him to school for the first time, Jim asks if he will have a friend. Jim goes through the day watching other children playing with their friends until Paul shows him a car with doors which really open. Jim promises he will bring his gas pump the next day and goes home secure in the knowledge that he has a friend. The charming illustrations include black and white children and a black teacher.

FREEMAN, DON. *Fly High, Fly Low.* Viking Pr, 1957, $3.50. Syd and Midge, two pigeons, are happy with their nest in the B of the sign over the Bay Hotel. When the building is being demolished, Midge stays with the nest as the B crosses town to be a part of another sign. Syd does not know where Midge and the nest have gone. The illustrations show Syd's frustration as he tries to find his family.

HOBAN, RUSSELL. *A Baby Sister for Frances.* il. by Lillian Hoban. Har-Row, 1964, $3.50. Frances, a badger who acts like a little girl, has a baby sister who gets an inordinate amount of attention. Frances decides to run away under the dining room table, but is enticed back because "everybody misses her and wants to hug and kiss her." A gentle story interspersed with Frances' original poems. Good to use with children of families with new babies, or those who can remember when a new baby came.

HOLLAND, VIKI. *We Are Having a Baby.* il. with photographs. Scribner, 1972, $5.50. Based on a true life experience, this is the story of four-year-old Dana Pratt who very much wanted a baby brother or sister. However, she found that things were different when her baby brother came home from the hospital and she couldn't understand why. Daddy comes to the rescue, a friend comes to play, Dana helps with the baby's bottle and all of a sudden things fall into place. The photographs show what happens at the hospital as well as at home. A good book to help overcome the problem of sibling jealousy.

HOLT, MARGARET. *David McCheever's 29 Dogs.* il. by Walter Lorraine. HM, 1963, $3.25. On the way home from the market David McCheever couldn't have been more surprised to find that the meat he has bought for mother has fallen through the bag and is being eaten by all the neighborhood dogs. One thing leads to another and before long, 29 dogs followed by children, parents, the school band, and a policeman parade through the streets with David as their leader! David comes to feel important and well-liked in his new neighborhood. A humorous treatment of adjusting to a new house in a different neighborhood, presented in an easy reading format.

HURD, EDITH T. *The Day the Sun Danced.* il. by Clement Hurd. Har-Row, 1966, $3.50. A new approach to the age-old theme of the coming of spring sees changes in the positive sense. Mr. Hurd's woodcuts are outstanding in cold blue, white, and black in winter, and in the soft colors of spring. Mrs. Hurd's text has almost a poetic quality in her description of the earth's awakening, as well as of the cold, frozen times of winter. Honor winner, 1966 Spring Book Festival.

KEATS, EZRA JACK. *Peter's Chair.* Har-Row, 1967, $3.95. Peter is unhappy because all of his baby furniture is being painted pink and being given to his baby sister. He takes his chair, his dog, his toy crocodile, a picture of himself when he was a baby, and runs away to settle in the front of his house. He finds his chair is too small and ends up helping his father paint it pink. The Caldecott Award-winning author-illustrator creates a meaningful dramatization of the "new baby" problem with a black boy as the central character.

KEEPING, CHARLES. *Joseph's Yard.* il. by author. Watts, 1970, $4.95. Joseph's back yard consists of a brick wall, a wooden fence, and stone paving. It contains some rusty old iron objects—but no living things. One day Joseph trades the iron pieces for a plant to grow in his yard. In caring for the delicate flower he eventually learns that sharing is best, for it brings beauty and life into his once bleak back yard.

KROEBER, THEODORA. *A Green Christmas.* il. by M. Gordon. Parnassus, 1967, $3.50. "Santa cannot find us here," say two children who have moved west from Colorado to California. A good family relationship saves the day when they awake to the surprise of their first green Christmas.

* KUSKIN, KARLA. *The Bear Who Saw the Spring.*

LEAF, MUNRO, AND ROBERT LAWSON. *The Story of Ferdinand.* trans. by Pura Belpre. il. by Robert Lawson. Viking Pr, 1936, $2.95 (P/Viking Pr, $.75). A peace-loving bull is forced into the bull ring. He adjusts to the situation by reverting to his true nature. This Caldecott Award-winning book is excellent to introduce Spain and bullfighting and to read just for fun.

LIPKIND, WILLIAM, AND NICOLAS MORDVINOFF. *Chaga.* HBJ, 1945, $3.50. Chaga, an elephant, is the largest animal in the jungle. He trumpets so loudly that every small animal scampers in panic from him. When Chaga eats some sweet grass, he shrinks to a very small size. Before he is restored to his normal size he learns what it means to be small in this world.

LOVELACE, MAUD HART. *The Valentine Box.* il. by Ingrid Fetz. TY Crowell, 1966, $3.50. Janice suffers all of the pangs of being the new girl in the classroom. The traditional exchange of cards on Valentine's Day makes her adjustment even more difficult. An understanding teacher, a windy snowstorm, and a good deed by Janice all combine to make the outcome of this story pleasant and natural.

McCLOSKEY, ROBERT. *Make Way for Ducklings.* il. by author. Viking Pr, 1941, $3.50 (P/Viking Pr, $.85). In this Caldecott Award-winning book, Robert McCloskey, using only brown and white illustrations, tells of a mother and father mallard finding a home for their children on an island in the Charles River in Boston. They adjust to a new life in the city, and the people of the city adjust to them.

———. *Time of Wonder.* il. by author. Viking Pr, 1957, $3.95. A family experiences the changes of nature in their vacation home. Along with the beauty of the storm comes destruction which the family has to deal with and adjust to. The award-winning illustrations help to dramatize the family's reaction to weather and seasonal changes.

* McGOVERN, ANN. *Black Is Beautiful.*

MANN, PEGGY. *That New Baby.* Coward, 1967, $2.97. Jenny does not like the idea of a new baby coming into her life, but eventually comes to realize that for Mommy and Daddy the baby is more work, but for her the baby is "extra fun."

* MASON, MIRIAM E. *The Middle Sister.*

* RASKIN, ELLEN. *Spectacles.*

* REESINK, MARYKE. *The Fisherman's Family.*

ROUNDS, GLEN. *Wild Horses of the Red Desert.* il. by author. Holiday, 1969, $4.95. The world with all its delights is a dangerous place for a colt growing to yearling in the high barren Badlands. This story unfolds simply in words and beautiful action pictures of the band of horses. Man is one of the dangers in this world.

SCHLEIN, MIRIAM. *Laurie's New Brother.* il. by Elizabeth Donald. Abelard, 1961, $3.50. A wise mother helps Laurie accept and adjust to the changes in her life that a new baby in the family makes. Instead of wanting to be a baby again herself, Laurie becomes glad that she is a big girl and looks forward to the day when John will be big enough to do things with her.

THOMPSON, VIVIAN L. *Sad Day, Glad Day.* Holiday, 1962, $2.95. Moving from her familiar surroundings is bad enough, but when Linda leaves her favorite doll behind the situation seems even worse. Eventually she understands life will go on and be much the same even though the surroundings will be different.

ZOLOTOW, CHARLOTTE. *A Father like That.* il. by Ben Shecter. HarRow, 1971, $3.50. A small boy, left fatherless at a very young age, imagines what it would be like to have a father and what the two of them would do together in the course of a day.

――――. *A Tiger Called Thomas.* il. by Kurt Werth. Lothrop, 1963, $3.95. Children who have experienced the fear of not being liked when they move into a new neighborhood will identify with Thomas who refuses to leave his porch for fear of not being liked or accepted. By hiding behind a tiger costume at Halloween, Thomas gains the courage to venture out trick or treating into the neighborhood. To his amazement and delight he finds that all the neighbors know who he is. He returns home happy and secure in the belief that new people like him and that he is going to like them too.

Intermediate

ALBRECHT, LILLIE V. *The Spinning Wheel Secret.* il. by Joan Balfour Payne. Hastings, 1965, $2.95. Joan would rather swim and fish than spin and knit. Mother is indulgent and lets her go "if she must," while other girls during the colonial period learn necessary housekeeping skills. During an Indian raid, Mother is carried away and Joan is left with an ailing grandfather. Helpless to aid him, Joan recognizes the importance of learning the skills she has avoided.

* ANDERSON, LONZO. *Zeb.*

* ARORA, SHIRLEY L. *What Then, Raman?*

BACHMANN, EVELYN TRENT. *Tressa.* Viking Pr, 1966, $3.50. For Tressa, moving to West Texas is frightening because everything is overwhelmingly big and strange. Through courage, she makes friends, and even learns to like horses.

BARNES, NANCY. *The Wonderful Year.* il. by Kate Seredy. Messner, 1946, $2.50. When Ellen and her parents move from a Kansas town to a Colorado ranch, Mother makes the move an adventure. Hard work and new neighbors make the year a memorable one. Set near the turn of the century, it is a family story concerned not only with adjustments to moving, but with Ellen's growing up, her romantic interests, and her increasing awareness of and ability to deal with her role as a young woman.

* BOLTON, IVY. *Wayfaring Lad.*

BRADBURY, BIANCA. *Two on an Island.* il. by Robert MacLean. HM, 1965, $3.25 (P/Schol Bk Serv., $.60). Two children are marooned on a tiny island just off shore from a large city on the Atlantic Coast. Hunger, thirst, exposure, fright, and courage are all ingredients of a three-day ordeal during which Trudy and Jeff learn much about themselves and each other.

————. *Lots of Love, Lucinda.* Washburn, 1966, $3.95. Corry's family decides to sponsor Lucinda, a southern Negro, to live with them for her senior year. When Lucinda arrives, Corry finds it difficult to make friends with her. Corry's reactions to Lucinda's presence and Lucinda's reactions to her strange new home and school first lead to conflict, later to understanding.

BUCK, PEARL. *The Beech Tree.* John Day, 1955, $3.50. A whole family is faced with the adjustment of grandfather's coming to live with them. Mother is unhappy about the situation, feeling it would be best for all if he went to a nursing home, but Mary Lou explains how grandfather is like the beech tree, giving life to the little trees around it. Mary Lou also notes that grandfather is the only one who has time for her. An extremely sensitive and realistically drawn portrayal of a serious social problem.

————. *The Big Wave.* John Day, 1948, $3.29 (P/Schol Bk Serv, $.60). The Japanese boys, Kino, son of a mountain-side farmer, and Jiya, son of a fisherman, are only friends until the day a tidal wave sweeps away Jiya's family and village, and Jiya is alone. Kino's family helps Jiya through his grief, and the boys grow up as brothers. The lure of the sea is stronger for Jiya, and when grown, he returns to build again on the ocean's shore.

BUFF, MARY AND CONRAD. *Magic Maize.* il. by author. HM, 1953, $4.00. A young Guatemalan boy plants a few seeds of the white man's corn and overcomes his father's distrust of the gringos and modern farming. The outstanding illustrations capture the spirit of the people and the country.

BULLA, CLYDE ROBERT. *New Boy in Dublin: A Story of Ireland.* il. by Jo Polseno. TY Crowell, 1969, $3.75. Coady wants to earn enough money to replace his mother's lost gold wedding ring. When Cousin Michael offers him an opportunity to work in Dublin, he is willing to leave the farm. He has a great deal of difficulty adjusting to his new life in the city with Aunt Kate and his cousin. He finds it is not easy to earn the money that he will need and almost gives up to return home. Finally, as he helps a new boy learn to be a page at the hotel, Coady realizes that he can learn to adjust to life in the city.

CASTELLANOS, JANE. *Tomasito and the Golden Llamas.* il. by Robert Corcy. Golden Gate, 1968, $4.25. Tomasito Chavez, a Peruvian boy, comes to California with his sister Teresa and her husband Jack Mc-Gerraghty, to make his home. Accompanying them are his four golden llamas, with which he hopes to earn money for his support. In his struggle for understanding, acceptance, and learning, Tomasito is confronted with prejudice and near defeat. His determination to succeed is restored by his friend, his Uncle Joe, and a teacher, Miss Ramiriz.

CLARK, ANN NOLAN. *Secret of the Andes.* il. by Jean Charlot. Viking Pr, 1952, $3.50 (P/Viking Pr, $.75). A young South American Indian boy searches for his destiny, eventually realizing that he wants to be a llama herder just as he has been trained to do. Interwoven into the story is the history of the Spanish conquerors and the value of continuing the ancient Incan traditions.

CLEAVER, VERA AND BILL. *Grover.* il. by Frederic Marvin. Lippincott, 1970, $3.50. No one tells Grover anything during the time of his mother's emergency surgery. No one even hints that she might not recover. Following her suicide and funeral there is a long, empty summer during which neither his grieving father nor the clergyman who fails to answer his questions about life and death can comfort him. Despite the grim situation, the book is not wholly depressing. Comic incidents and dialogue serve to heighten and lighten the story somewhat.

* COATSWORTH, ELIZABETH. *Jon the Unlucky.*

* COLES, ROBERT. *Dead End School.*

* DARINGER, HELEN F. *Adopted Jane.*

FLEISCHMAN, SID. *By the Great Horn Spoon.* il. by Eric von Schmidt. Little, 1963, $4.50 (P/Avon, $.60). In 1849, Jack Flagg and his loyal butler Praiseworthy set out from Boston for California to make their fortune and save Jack's Aunt Agatha from financial ruin. Throughout the eventful sea voyage and search for gold, Praiseworthy more than deserves his name. Aunt Arabella follows them to California and they end up a real family. Delightful hero story with line drawings that help to enliven the action of mastering a new environment.

FRY, ROSALIE K. *September Island.* il. by Margery Gill. Dutton, 1965, $3.75. Martin Roberts unexpectedly becomes the explorer of a newly created island one September afternoon. In an attempt to save his sister Alex from certain death as she sails down the rain-swollen river clinging to the uprooted pear tree, he climbs into the leaky boat with his sister Linda, six, and Benbow, their dachshund. The boat entwines with the tree, eventually becoming a breakwater for their own sandbar island suddenly created in the middle of the river. Stranded on the temporary island each child has an opportunity to demonstrate his resourcefulness.

GARDNER, JEANNE LE MONNIER. *Mary Jemison: Seneca Captive.* il. by Robert Parker. HBJ, 1966, $3.50. This is a true story of Mary Jemison, a fifteen-year-old white girl captured by a band of Shawnee Indians. It is an excellent characterization and account of a youngster's adjusting to an entirely different culture, family, and role.

GARST, SHANNON. *Cowboy Boots.* il. by Charles Hargens. Abingdon, 1946, $3.95. Bob Benton goes to Wyoming to spend the summer on his Uncle John's cattle ranch. Bob wants very much to be a real cowboy and work with the rest of the cowboys on the ranch. Montana, the foreman of the ranch, is assigned the task of breaking Bob into ranch life. Realizing that a cowboy's life is much more difficult than he had thought, Bob soon finds himself hard pressed to meet the rugged standards. Failure takes on a new meaning but in the end the boy earns his cowboy boots and a feeling of accomplishment.

GATES, DORIS. *Sensible Kate.* Viking Pr, 1943, $3.50 (P/Viking Pr, $.75). Kate, a ten-year-old orphan, regrets that her portion in life is not to be cute and pretty, but to be sensible. Having been shifted from one relative to another, Kate has grown into a very practical "little woman," but has not learned to laugh and be a little girl. The Tuttles, with whom she lives; the Clines, who have "no sense" but much love; the Corsattis, who become her friends, all help Kate to begin to grow up, accept herself more graciously, and enjoy her life.

GODDEN, RUMER. *Miss Happiness and Miss Flower.* il. by Jean Primrose. Viking Pr, 1961, $3.25. Miss Happiness and Miss Flower, two Japanese dolls, are sent to live with a family in England, hoping they will encounter a girl who will understand them. The two dolls are received by Nona, who knows very well what it is like to feel lonely and uprooted for she also has been sent to live in London. An interesting variation on the theme of adaptation to a different environment.

* HAUGAARD, KAY. *Myeko's Gift.*

* HICKOK, LORENA A. *The Story of Helen Keller.*

JACKSON, JACQUELINE. *The Taste of Spruce Gum.* Little, 1966, $3.95. Libby and her mother return to Vermont after Libby's father's death. Libby, recently left nearly hairless from a serious illness, self-consciously meets her father's family whom she has never known. Adjusting to a stepfather proves difficult, especially in the extremely rough environment of a logging camp. A fast-paced story with interesting characters and believable adjustment to problems.

JOHNSON, ANNABEL AND EDGAR. *The Grizzly.* Har-Row, 1964, $3.95. David's parents have been separated and David fears his father with an unreasoning fear. David remembers his parents fighting over the possibility of his becoming a sissy and he has a premonition that a weekend fishing trip has been planned to be some sort of test for him. On the trip father and son encounter a bear. They become tentatively close, and David comes to realize how important having a son is to his father.

* JOHNSON, DORIS. *Su An.*

KRUMGOLD, JOSEPH. *And Now Miguel.* il. by Jean Charlot. TY Crowell, 1953, $4.50 (P/Apollo, $1.65). Miguel, who is twelve, hopes to help the men in his family take the sheep to camp in the Sangre de Cristo Mountains. He desperately tries to prove that he is ready. In getting his wish, Miguel grows from boy to man and learns some valuable lessons about growing up and about giving and receiving.

LADD, ELIZABETH. *Meg of Heron's Neck.* il. by Mary Stevens. Morrow, 1961, $3.95. Meg, an orphaned young girl, lives on a barge with her much older, irresponsible half brother. The villain in the story wants the brother to do something illegal and informs an uncle as to Meg's whereabouts. The uncle takes Meg to live with him and she must adjust to going to school, to new rules of behavior, and to living on a farm. She is a lively, believable character who causes herself and others considerable trouble before she adjusts to her new life.

L'ENGLE, MADELEINE. *Meet the Austins.* Vanguard, 1960, $3.95. The children in the Austin family are four individualists: John wants to be a scientist and is very logical; Vicky is writing a book and wishing she were prettier; Suzy is a sweet, but easily-influenced imp; and Rob includes mashed potatoes and dogs in his prayers. When a tragic accident makes her an orphan, Maggy makes five. Not only does the grapefruit not divide evenly into halves with five children, but Maggy is a completely spoiled, inconsiderate child. Mother insists that if one ten-year-old can upset the family solidarity, they aren't as unique a family as they thought they were. After trying (and interesting) episodes, Maggy does become a part of the family.

* LEVITIN, SONIA. *Journey to America.*

LEWIS, ELIZABETH FOREMAN. *Ho-Ming, Girl of China.* il. by Kurt Wiese. HR & W, 1934, $3.59. Raised in an atmosphere of tradition and superstition, Ho-Ming is not encouraged to think for herself. The Sung family finds it difficult to cope with this "girl child" with the curious mind. Ho-Ming, unhappy with unanswered questions, alters her life and her family's by pursuing an education. Strong family loyalty is emphasized as the Sungs meet obstacles together. Mature elementary students studying China will be interested in its customs.

* LEXAU, JOAN M. *Jose's Christmas Secret.*

LIPKIND, WILLIAM. *Boy of the Islands.* HBJ, 1955, $3.50. A boy of ancient Hawaii visits his uncle's island and discovers that someday he will be a chief and unite the two islands. Very briefly, with a minimum of conflict, his adjustment to his future is shown. He realizes the value of the study he has been doing, decides to accept his destiny, but still wants to be a sailor in keeping with a valued tradition of his people. Simple, direct writing style makes the book easy to read.

LITTLE, JEAN. *Home from Far.* il. by Jerry Lazare. Little, 1965, $3.95. Jenny's twin brother is killed in an automobile accident and Jenny has the secret feeling that she alone really misses him, that her parents and two younger brothers don't feel the same way. The family takes in two foster children who have an equally difficult time facing the loss of their mother. The normal cycle of family events brings out each child's individual problems in adjustment to a new family pattern.

————. *Mine for Keeps.* il. by Lewis Parker. Little, 1962, $3.95. Sally Copeland adjusts to living at a special school for children with physical handicaps. When she learns she is going home to live, she is filled with fear and apprehension for she knows being the only cerebral palsied child in a family and a school would cause many difficulties. With the help of an understanding family, she acquires new attitudes about herself, and when she begins to be thoughtful of others her life becomes more satisfying.

MACGIBBON, JEAN. *Liz.* Scribner, 1969, $3.50. Liz and Milly, two London teenagers, become good friends because of one terrible night of terror during which Liz's brother's life is threatened. The chance of a one-week holiday with Aunt Cora at the sea brings the girls face-to-face with many more emotion-laden experiences, from the thrill of sailing and camping in an abandoned farmhouse to the heroic, tragic death of a friend. The sensitive descriptions of Liz's feelings and her reactions to them make this an excellent book for older girls.

MARTIN, PATRICIA MILES. *One Special Dog.* il. by John and Lucy Hawkinson. Rand, 1968, $3.95. Against the background of life on a Navaho reservation, the problems and relationships of two children are portrayed. Charlie befriends a wild dog from a pack which menaces the sheep that the family raise. Molly is fearful of the dog until it helps to rescue her lamb.

MOLLOY, ANNE. *The Girl from Two Miles High.* il. by Polly Jackson. Hastings, 1967, $4.75. Phoebe must adjust to drastic changes in her life—the death of her father and living with her grandmother in

Maine after leaving behind a pampered, isolated life in Peru. She becomes a successful overseer of a large blueberry crop, learns to make friends by overcoming feelings of rejection and alienation, and begins to anticipate attending public school.

NORDSTROM, URSULA. *The Secret Language*. il. by Mary Chalmers. Har-Row, 1960, $2.95. The first ten days of boarding school are the most devastating that ten-year-old Vicky has ever spent. This is before she meets Martha, who shares with Vicky special made-up words and her complete opposition to the regimented situation. When Martha and Vicky become friends, a new housemother shows some affection and helps both girls adjust to their new environment.

NORRIS, GUNILLA B. *The Good Morrow*. Atheneum, 1969, $3.75. Josie, a young black girl from the city, is sent to camp to experience the joys of the country. Nancy, a white city girl, is sent to the same camp to keep her out from underfoot while her mother has a baby. Josie expects to be rejected because of her color, and Nancy finds it easy to act out her hostility on Josie. By the end, each girl has a better understanding of herself as well as the other girl.

ORMONDROYD, EDWARD. *Time at the Top*. il. by Peggie Bach. Parnassus, 1963, $3.75. Mysterious things happen to Susan Shaw when she takes her usual ride up the elevator to her home. As Susan gets off the elevator, she finds herself in the year 1881. The suspense builds throughout the book and comes to a very satisfying ending. Although the book is a fantasy, it does show how Susan develops some realistic attitudes and personal values.

* PARKER, RICHARD. *Second-Hand Family*.

SHOTWELL, LOUISA R. *Adam Bookout*. Viking Pr, 1967, $3.95. Adam has lived all of his life on a cattle ranch in Oklahoma. After his parents are killed in a plane crash, he is sent to live with two great-aunts. He runs away from them to go to his cousins in Brooklyn. Kate and Gideon welcome Adam and make him feel at home. He goes to school and befriends Saul, a Jewish boy, Magdalena, an intellectually gifted child, and Willie Weggfall, a black boy. When his cousins plan to leave for Europe, Adam has to make some very grown-up decisions.

* SMITH, GEORGE HARMON. *Bayou Boy*.

SORENSEN, VIRGINIA. *Plain Girl*. il. by Charles Geer. HBJ, 1955, $3.75. Ten-year-old Esther, an Amish girl, is thoroughly enjoying school after the authorities force her father to send her there. Although she still loves the ways of the Plain People, she begins to understand why her brother Dan has run away from the strict home discipline. Although Esther is confused by marked social differences, she learns to think for herself and stands her ground with gentle firmness.

* STEPTOE, JOHN. *Stevie.*

* STINETORF, LOUISE A. *A Charm for Paco's Mother.*

STOLZ, MARY. *A Wonderful Terrible Time.* il. by Louis S. Glanzman. Har-Row, 1967, $4.50. Mady and Sue Ellen, best of friends, are treated to two weeks at a summer camp. The experience, which is new to both since they have never left New York City, is rewarding to one and a trial for the other. This book shows how change of environment can intensify fears, the usual problems of a child with one parent, racial problems, and children's need to be accepted by their peers.

* THOGER, MARIE. *Shanta.*

WALKER, MILDRED. *A Piece of the World.* il. by Christine Price. M. K. McElderry, 1972, $5.25. A girl adjusts to her parents' divorce during the summer she spends in Vermont with her grandmother, while her mother sets up a new home for them in California.

* WARD, MARTHA EADS. *Ollie, Ollie, Oxen-Free.*

WEIR, ROSEMARY. *No Sleep for Angus.* il. by Elizabeth Grant. Abelard, 1970, $3.95. Twelve-year-old Angus inadvertently witnesses a bank robbery by two men and a boy who then chase him through London until they capture and kidnap him. As Angus adjusts to this change in his life he manages to help the boy, Ray, and his girl, Polly, capture the rest of the gang before they sail for South America. In an all-night adventure he recovers the money, escapes from the robbers, is recaptured, is rescued by the police, falls in the oily Thames in order to save the bank's money, is rescued from the channel buoy, and identifies the robbers for the police. An exciting, fast-moving mystery story.

* WOJCIECHOWSKA, MAIA. *Shadow of a Bull.*

* WYCKOFF, CHARLOTTE CHANDLER. *Kumar.*

YATES, ELIZABETH. *Carolina's Courage.* il. by Nora S. Unwin. Dutton, 1964, $2.92. When Carolina's father decides to leave their stony New Hampshire farm and move the family west to good rich land, much of what they love is left behind. Carolina is allowed to take only the clothes she wears and her beloved doll, Lydia-Lou. The journey is difficult but love within the family is a source of strength.

ZIM, HERBERT S., AND SONIA BLEEKER. *Life and Death.* Morrow, 1970, $3.50. Two distinguished authors have combined their talents to produce this unsentimental scientific explanation of the role of death in the life cycle of all things. There are many charts, diagrams, and sketches to explain the text. The authors show the difference between sleep and death and mention many burial customs past and present.

Junior

ALLAN, MABEL ESTHER. *The Dancing Garlands: The Ballet Family Again.* il. by Whitear. Criterion, 1968, $3.95. The various members of the dancing Garland family, envied for their talent and charm, are immersed in disturbing personal situations. When the family comes to Paris in April with the Thorburg Ballet, everything changes. There are happy solutions and the Garlands are gay once more.

ANDERSON, LONZO. *Zeb.* il. by Peter Burchard. Knopf, 1966, $3.75. When attempting to cross the Delaware River to reach the unsettled land which is to be their new home, an accident claims the lives of Zeb's father and oldest brother. Zeb is left alone to face the fury of the colonial wilderness.

ANNIXTER, JANE AND PAUL. *Wagon Scout.* il. by Charles Greer. Holiday, 1965, $3.95. After the death of his wagon master father and the disappearance of the wagon train's scout, sixteen-year-old Eric accepts the responsibility of guiding the wagon train on its westward trek across the mountains.

* ARTHUR, RUTH M. *Portrait of Margarita.*

* ———. *The Whistling Boy.*

BALL, ZACHARY. *Swamp Chief.* il. by author. Holiday, 1952, $3.95. Joe Panther and his father, the new Seminole Indian chief, have the difficult task of getting the older Indians to give up their old tribal ways and cooperate with the white man.

* BARNWELL, ROBINSON. *Head into the Wind.*

———. *Shadow on the Water.* McKay, 1967, $4.25. A South Carolina farm girl encounters many problems during the summer. Now that she is thirteen everything seems to be changing at once. Camden, the middle child, tries to untangle several family relationships and learns to deal with adult problems.

BELL, MARGARET E. *Ride out the Storm.* Morrow, 1951, $4.75. Lisbeth, reared in an isolated part of Alaska, makes adjustments when sent to a fashionable boarding school in California.

BENARY-ISBERT, MARGOT. *The Ark.* trans. by Richard and Clara Winston. HBJ, 1953, $4.25. The Lechow family, after nine months of moving from refugee camp to refugee camp following World War II, finally settle in West Germany. The happiness of being together means so much to the family that the oldest boy, Matthias, does work which he dislikes until he and Margret, his sister, find satisfactory employment on a farm and are able to make a home for the family in an old streetcar.

BOTHWELL, JEAN. *The Emerald Clue*. HBJ, 1961, $3.75. Seventeen-year-old Tara finds direction for her future life and love in her rebellion against century-old Indian restrictions.

* BROWN, PAMELA. *The Other Side of the Street*.

* BUCK, PEARL. *The Big Wave*.

BUTTERS, DOROTHY GILMAN. *Heartbreak Street*. Macrae, 1958, $3.95. Kitty Boscz gains a new set of values while she works in a plastics factory the summer after her graduation from high school. Though she lives in a depressed neighborhood and comes from an immigrant background, neither factor proves a hindrance to her success.

* CAVANNA, BETTY. *Jenny Kimura*.

* CLEARY, BEVERLY. *Sister of the Bride*.

* CLEWS, DOROTHY. *Guide Dog*.

COLMAN, HILA. *A Girl from Puerto Rico*. Morrow, 1961, $4.25 (P/Dell, $.50). To the outsider, is the United States the end of the rainbow as a place to live? The author treats this question sensitively through the eyes of a widow whose teenage daughter convinces her to move where wealth and contentment are reputed to be beautiful. However, the family quickly feels the constraints of living in New York's ghettos and anguishes in the difficulties of finding employment and psychological acceptance among the larger Anglo community.

* ———. *Mixed-Marriage Daughter*.

* DARINGTON, HELEN FERN. *Adopted Jane*.

DAVID, JANINA. *A Touch of Earth*. Grossman, 1969, $4.95. Miss David escaped from the Warsaw ghetto in January 1943. Fleeing to a convent, she was forced to change her name and adopt the Catholic religion. She did so willingly, with conviction and relief. This is an autobiographical memoir recalling the feelings of a young girl adopting a strange way of life: making friends with a German soldier and weeping for the death of his family as the war, deprivation, and illness surround her.

DENKER, NAN WATSON. *The Bound Girl*. FS & G, 1957, $2.95. Felicity Charreau, a Huguenot refugee, escapes religious persecution in France by coming to America. Here she learns to work and keep her place as a "bound girl" in the home of a severe Puritan family in Boston. At first, her gay and carefree manners make many enemies among the strict Puritans, but in time she succeeds in charming all the members of the Todd family and in winning their respect for her new-found sense of responsibility. When Felicity has an opportunity to return to France and to her former luxurious way of life, her decision to stay in America and work for freedom is proof of her mature judgment and sense of values.

DUNN, MARY LOIS. *The Man in the Box: A Story from Vietnam.* il. by Nicholas Fasciano. McGraw, 1968, $4.50. Chau Li's father had been tortured and killed by the Viet Cong. Then a captured American is brought to his Montagnard village. The American is imprisoned in the tiny box in which Chau Li's father had suffered. The villagers had been too frightened and Chau Li had been too small to help his father. He is bigger now and he is determined to help the strange-looking foreigner. Chau Li overcomes fear and extraordinary difficulties to help a strange American escape, his only reward a feeling of personal satisfaction.

DU SOE, ROBERT C. *Three without Fear.* il. by Ralph Ray. Longmans, 1946, $3.25. When shipwrecked off the southern coast of California, an American boy is aided by two Indian orphans. Sharing hardships and dangers with real courage, they are able to make their way up the coast to civilization.

EVARTS, HAL G. *Smuggler's Road.* Scribner, 1968, $3.95. Sixteen-year-old Kern Dawson is classed as a rogue by the vice principal, following his latest trouble. His counselor, Mr. Garth, gives him a choice—Juvenile Hall or working for a medical clinic in Baja California for the summer. Ex-Marine Sergeant Bull Kalinski grudgingly accepts Kern at the clinic. The change to such primitive conditions gives Kern the opportunity to develop self-reliance and responsibility. His artistic talent enables him to make friends as well as piece together a puzzle which leads to the arrest of a ring of smugglers. The suspense and realism make this an excellent book for intermediate and junior readers.

FRANCIS, HENRY, AND PHILIP SMITH. *Defrosting Antarctic Secrets.* Hale, 1962, $2.43. The authors of this book first went to the Antarctic as part of the United States program for the International Geophysical Year. This is the story of the new explorers, modern scientists, and the ways they use to meet the challenge of the frozen frontier.

* GEORGE, JEAN. *My Side of the Mountain.*

GORDON, ETHEL E. *So Far from Home.* TY Crowell, 1969, $3.95. After the sudden death of her parents, Miranda Curtis is separated from her brother and sent to school in Switzerland. Her travels in Europe with her grandmother and friends from school seem unreal and she longs to be part of a family again. However, her experiences finally lead to a surprising new awareness of herself and others.

———. *Where Does the Summer Go?* TY Crowell, 1967, $3.95. (P/WSP, $.75). Fifteen-year-old Freddy Brewer finds that this summer at the beach is different from other summers because of changes in family relationships, friends, and most of all herself. Freddy's adjustment to changing personal relationships shows her readiness to assume adult responsibility.

* HICKOK, LORENA A. *The Touch of Magic.*

ISSLER, ANNE ROLLER. *Young Red Flicker.* McKay, 1968, $3.75. The conflicting demands of two cultures gets seventeen-year-old Red Flicker into trouble with the authorities, his family, and his friends. He is a young rebel trying to balance his pride in being Indian with the awareness that he must live in a white man's society.

JUDSEN, CLARA INGRAM. *The Green Ginger Jar.* il. by Paul Brown. HM, 1949, $3.50. Chicago-born Chinese-American children protest traditional values of parents and grandparents. Finally the grandmother arranges to help Lu with his medical education.

* KILLILEA, MARIE L. *Karen.*

KLABEN, HELEN. *Hey, I'm Alive!* P/Schol Bk Serv, 1964, $.60. As a result of a plane crash, the author and her pilot, both badly injured, spent forty-nine days in the frozen Yukon. The account of their experiences is a story of courage, hope, and faith. After her rescue, Helen finds that she is now more aware of the power of love as a basis for human action.

LAWRENCE, MILDRED. *The Treasure and the Song.* HBJ, 1966, $3.75. After the divorce of her parents, Binnie Brannon moves from New York City to a small Florida town to live with her aunt and attend a small junior college. A search for Spanish treasure and the problems of a new friend draw Binnie from her self-absorption and isolation into a new life.

* MACGIBBON, JEAN. *Liz.*

MCKOWN, ROBIN. *Girl of Madagascar.* Messner, 1968, $3.50. Set in Madagascar during its period of transition from a French colony to the independent Malagasy Republic, this novel is about Sahondra, a young Malagasy orphan girl who grows up with her country. Sahondra overcomes seemingly insurmountable obstacles until she finally makes decisions and takes on responsibility. This book is valuable as it illustrates the traditions of Malagasy society influenced by another culture.

MARK, POLLY. *The Way of the Wind.* il. by Ursula Koering. McKay, 1965, $3.75. In Borneo girls are meant to work in the fields, not waste their time with books. Mari's desire for an education causes conflict with her family and the traditional values of her people.

MEANS, FLORENCE CRANNELL. *The Moved-Outers.* il. by Helen Blair. HM, 1945, $3.25. The tragedy inherent in the breakup of homes among the Japanese-Americans and the problems of living in relocation camps are shown. The Ohara family, especially its adolescent members, Sue and Kim, try valiantly to adapt themselves to the deprivations and humiliations they cannot escape; they come through still hopeful about finding a place in American life.

* NEWELL, HOPE. *A Cap for Mary Ellis.*

* NOBLE, IRIS. *Megan.*

————. *One Golden Summer.* Messner, 1959, $3.50. This is an account of pretty Lisa Penhold's summer on the McKellway Ranch, where she works as a chambermaid. It is the summer before she enters college and she is seen growing and gaining responsibility as her likable personality quickly earns her friends. During the summer she experiences her first love, she helps a shy girl come out of her shell, and she learns what personality traits are admirable. *One Golden Summer* is a book which shows a young girl growing up.

OGILVIE, ELISABETH. *Blueberry Summer.* McGraw, 1956, $3.95 (P/ Schol Bk Serv, $.60). Cass wants very much to have a job this summer and spend her vacation away from the family. However, her mother must leave home to nurse a sick relative and Cass is left with her younger brother, the house, and the farm to care for. Cass is desperately sad until she meets Adam Ross and Jeff Marshall.

* PEYTON, K. M. *Flambards.*

* POHLMANN, LILLIAN. *Sing Loose.*

QUIMBY, MYRTLE. *The Cougar.* il. by Theresa Brudi. Criterion, 1968, $3.95. Against his mother's wishes, Jerry Foster is sent to a one-room schoolhouse where he is tormented and teased because his father is white and his mother is Indian. He runs away to stay with John Stink, an old Indian who believes in proving one's manhood by killing a cougar. Jerry cannot bring himself to kill the cougar so he goes home. His one friend, Bess, has reported his mistreatment and he realizes that all white people are not bad.

* RICHTER, CONRAD. *A Country of Strangers.*

SAMS, JESSIE. *White Mother.* McGraw, 1957, $4.95. A poignant autobiography of two young black girls who become the sole support of their invalid father. In desperation one girl goes to the homes of various whites in northern Florida until she finds a sympathetic woman who helps the girls by hiring them to do odd jobs around her house. The story traces the slow, patient manner in which the white woman helps the girls grow up and set worthwhile goals for themselves. One, married ill-advisedly at fifteen, sees her mistake and eventually returns to school to become a nurse. The author stubbornly holds to her goal of becoming an elementary-school teacher, eventually teaching in the Los Angeles City Schools.

* SHERBURNE, ZOA. *Stranger in the House.*

SOMMERFELT, AIMEE. *No Easy Way.* il by Theresa Brudi. Criterion, 1967, $3.95. In spite of her Norwegian father's disapproval, Tonia Rosted manages to get enough money for lessons with a leading actor to satisfy her ambition to go on the stage. She works hard and finally gets permission from her father to do so.

* STRACHAN, MARGARET P. *Patience and a Mulberry Leaf.*

* THOGER, MARIE. *Shanta.*

VINSON, KATHRYN. *Run with the Ring.* HBJ, $3.95. Mark Mansfield, a teenager accustomed to success in athletics and science, suffers an accident while participating in a track meet. Left permanently blind, adjustment is slow and bitter, particularly toward his opponent whom he feels is to blame. Personal growth becomes evident as Mark adjusts to new goals.

VROMAN, MARY ELIZABETH. *Harlem Summer.* Putnam, 1967, $3.49 (P/Berkley Pub, $.60). "Young John" Brown, a sixteen-year-old black student from Montgomery, Alabama, sees the complexities of black ghetto life as he works and spends the summer with his aunt and uncle in Harlem. The characterizations are strong and particularly impressive as these characters come to grips with degrading poverty.

* WALKER, MILDRED. *A Piece of the World.*

WEBER, LENORA M. *Come Back, Wherever You Are.* TY Crowell, 1969, $4.50. Beany Malone finds her marriage threatened while she is trying to care for a disturbed child, but she discovers that problems can lead to happiness and contentment.

———. *I Met a Boy I Used to Know.* TY Crowell, 1967, $4.50. The author of the Beany Malone stories adds another title to her series about the Belford family. Katie Rose becomes friend and protector to a new boy in school who has many personal problems. She is finally forced to make a difficult decision about her justifications for his personality and behavior.

WELLS, HELEN. *Doctor Betty.* Messner, 1969, $3.50. Betty Beton wants to be wife and doctor but is forced to choose between the two. She chooses medicine. She completes her medical training and is ready for her internship. Her friends have all married and she begins to realize that something is missing. When she meets Jack Gage, she struggles to meet the challenge of being a wife and doctor.

WIER, ESTER. *The Loner.* McKay, 1963, $3.75. Completely alone and convinced that the only way to get along is to look out for oneself, the boy picks crops in different parts of the country. His very first friend is Raidy, who gives him a name, but who is killed when her hair is caught in a farm machine. Sick with grief, the boy wanders for miles and is found by Boss, who tends a flock of sheep. From

Boss and her friends the boy develops a sense of responsibility for the flock and a sense of belonging, and he earns the name David. When Boy becomes David, his big step toward a new life has been made.

* WILLARD, BARBARA. *Storm from the West.*

* YOUNG, BOB AND JAN. *Where Tomorrow.*

Senior

* ANNIXTER, PAUL. *Swiftwater.*

ARNOTHY, CHRISTINE. *I Am Fifteen—And I Don't Want to Die . . .* P/Schol Bk Serv, 1956, $.50. The author describes her experiences during the siege of Budapest in World War II when she was fifteen. She relates her fear of death and the uncertainties of life during this period.

BAKER, LOUISE M. *Out on a Limb.* McGraw, 1946, $4.95. Louise Baker finds herself out on a limb, as she humorously puts it, when at the age of eight she loses her leg in an automobile accident. How she skates, skis, rides horseback, and, despite her grandmother's grim prediction that "Louise will never get a man," marries twice, is a tale full of fun and courage, a reproof to those inclined to pity themselves.

BARBER, ELSIE O. *The Trembling Years.* Macmillan, 1949, $4.95. A college freshman contracts polio, which cripples her emotionally as well as physically. She learns to face her situation realistically and goes on to complete her college education.

* BOTHWELL, JEAN. *The Silver Mango Tree.*

BRADBURY, BIANCA. *The Blue Year.* Washburn, 1967, $3.75. Joan, a senior in high school, finds it hard to accept her parents' divorce. The year of the separation seems to be her "blue year." She thinks the solution to the problem is uniting her mother and father but finds that they do not agree. This story offers insight into what makes people "tick" as well as a realistic appraisal of divorce.

* ———. *Lots of Love, Lucinda.*

———. *Red Sky at Night.* Washburn, 1968, $3.95. Jo Whittier's father buys a boat with television contest prize money. The boat is a delight for everyone except Jo, who is scared the moment it hits water. How Jo finally learns to accept the boat, the death of her mother, and other aspects of her life make poignant reading for some teenagers.

BUCK, PEARL S. *A Bridge for Passing.* John Day, 1962, $5.95 (P/PB, $.50). A famous writer, faced with the emptiness that comes with the death of her husband, tells of her adjustment to loss, her final acceptance, and the semipeace that comes with it.

BURGESS, PERRY. *Who Walk Alone.* HR & W, 1940, $5.95. Many years after his return from the Philippines, this Spanish-American war veteran contracted leprosy, which resulted in separation from his old life and adjustment to a new and frightening world.

BUTLER, BEVERLY. *Captive Thunder.* Dodd, 1969, $3.75. An unhappy home and school situation in a small town in Wisconsin causes Nancy Essen to run away to Milwaukee. With the help of an understanding relative, Nancy becomes involved as a volunteer in a Project Head Start program and gradually finds a purpose in her life.

CLEARY, BEVERLY. *Sister of the Bride.* Morrow, 1963, $5.50. Sixteen-year-old Barbara feels left out when her older sister plans to be married. Finally she realizes that she has her own life to live and that it can be exciting and interesting too.

CLEWES, DOROTHY. *Guide Dog.* il. by Peter Burchard. Coward, 1965, $3.29. At the age of nineteen, Roley Rolandson has a bomb blow up in his face causing permanent blindness. How can he become a doctor now? Roley would have given up but for his two friends, Susan and Steven, who encourage him to get a guide dog. The adjustment to the loss of sight and to using a guide dog makes this a moving and meaningful story.

COLMAN, HILA. *Mixed-Marriage Daughter.* Morrow, 1968, $3.95. Sophie Barnes, a teenage girl with a background of two different cultures, finds herself forced to accept only one of them as her own. She is the child of a mixed marriage, having lived in a Christian culture for the first seventeen years of her life. Suddenly, she is requested to think, feel, and behave as a girl brought up in an Orthodox Jewish home. Her approach to the dilemma is honest and realistic.

DEAN, NELL M. *Nurse in Vietnam.* Messner, 1969, $3.50. In this exciting novel, Second Lieutenant Lisa Blake, USAF, has volunteered for duty as a flight nurse in the area where her fiance was killed in action. In her work among the wounded men evacuated to the Philippines, Lisa's grief is somewhat lessened. Her friendship and romance with a Green Beret captain add to the adventure and realism of the setting of this timely story of bravery in the face of danger.

DOOLEY, THOMAS A. *The Night They Burned the Mountain.* FS & G, 1960, $4.95 (P/NAL, $.60). The young American doctor, who after the war returned to the remote villages of Laos, tells of the personal battle he fought against the cancer which ultimately claimed him while he was healing the sick in the jungles of Asia.

ESTES, WINSTON M. *Another Part of the House.* Lippincott, 1970, $5.95 (P/Popular Lib, $.75). Larry Morrison is ten years old at the time of the Depression. Through him, we experience a warm happy life in a small Texas Panhandle community, where his father is the local druggist. There are times, however, when adverse events shake Larry's secure world, and his reactions to such problems as death and dishonesty are revealed in this touching novel.

FALK, ANN MARI. *A Place of Her Own.* HBJ, $3.25. After the sudden death of her parents, a fifteen-year-old girl finds a new life in Stockholm and regains her self-confidence. Her family and new friends help her learn to appreciate differences in people.

FIELD, RACHEL. *And Now Tomorrow.* Macmillan, 1942, $5.95. Emily Blair spends her early years as a member of a prominent family of factory owners in a New England mill town. The river is a barrier that protects her social life from contact with the Polish mill hands. When deafness makes Emily reach out for new friends, young Dr. Vance helps her understand the people who work for their daily bread. Personal contacts and interpretation break down the invisible barriers between one section of a community and another.

* GREGORY, SUSAN. *Hey, White Girl!*

* GRIFFIN, JOHN HOWARD. *Black Like Me.*

GUNTHER, JOHN. *Death Be Not Proud.* Har-Row, 1949, $4.95 (P/Har-Row, $.60). John Gunther has written a step-by-step account of his seventeen-year-old son's heroic battle against the inexorable progress of a tragic and fatal illness. Bravery and strength in the face of odds are the keynote of this personal story. Johnny's father and mother were divorced before his illness, but the entire book reveals their great love and devotion to Johnny throughout his gallant fight for life.

HALACY, D. S. JR. *High Challenge.* Macmillan, 1957, $3.00. Steve West does not overcome his difficulty of being physically unable to fly a plane. Instead he learns to accept his disability and to live with it.

* HART, MOSS. *Act One.*

HAUTZIG, ESTHER. *The Endless Steppe: Growing up in Siberia.* TY Crowell, 1968, $4.50. The author's account of the five years spent in Siberia with her family after the Russians occupied Poland is a story of the triumph of trust and affection over hardships and suffering. Mrs. Hautzig's experiences emphasize the human ability to adjust to extreme changes in environment and to withstand emotional stress.

HAYCRAFT, MOLLY COSTAIN. *The Reluctant Queen.* Lippincott, 1962, $6.50. After her brother Henry VIII became King of England, Mary Tudor found her life was not her own. Forced to marry aging Louis XII, King of France, instead of the man she loved, tender, willful, courageous Mary Tudor lived her life as queen with dignity. On the death of the king, she was freed.

* HEAD, ANN. *Mr. and Mrs. Bo Jo Jones.*

* HEYERDAHL, THOR. *Kon-Tiki.*

* ISSLER, ANNE ROLLER. *Young Red Flicker.*

KILLILEA, MARIE L. *Karen.* P-H, 1952, $3.95 (P/several). A gallant mother and a courageous and devoted family help a little girl, born with cerebral palsy, to conquer her disability.

* KLABEN, HELEN. *Hey, I'm Alive!*

LADER, LAWRENCE AND MILTON MELTZER. *Margaret Sanger: Pioneer of Birth Control.* TY Crowell, 1969, $4.50. This is the inspiring life story of a great woman whose ideas were far ahead of her time. Through her nursing experiences at the turn of the century, Margaret Sanger was moved to a then revolutionary and startling concept: the idea of birth control and family planning. A lovely soft-spoken lady, she was ridiculed and jailed for crusading on behalf of birth control. Her work in founding International Planned Parenthood has affected the lives of millions.

* LAWRENCE, MILDRED. *The Treasure and the Song.*

LEWITON, MINA. *The Divided Heart.* McKay, 1947, $3.89 (P/Berkley Pub, $.50). The divided parental loyalties of a fifteen-year-old only child present complex problems at the time of separation and divorce. Julie's ability to cope with this situation is the central theme of this touching story.

LINDBERGH, ANN MORROW. *Listen, the Wind.* HBJ, 1938, $3.95. This true adventure story tells about the experience of a famous pioneer flyer and his wife who seek to study the air routes between America and Europe.

* McKOWN, ROBIN. *Girl of Madagascar.*

MEHTA, RAMA. *The Life of Kesbau.* McGraw, 1969, $5.95. Kesbau's struggle to get educated becomes a family project. Through the simplicity and directness of her narrative, the author gives Western readers a unique, poignant, and absorbing picture of today's India.

MOODY, RALPH. *The Fields of Home.* Norton, 1950, $3.95. When he becomes involved in a misdemeanor, Little Britches is sent to work on his grandfather's farm in Maine. To make the farm pay and to modernize it against his grandfather's wishes require perseverance, tact, and patience.

NAYLOR, PHYLLIS R. *Dark Side of the Moon.* P/Fortress, 1969, $1.95. Fear and shame imprison an alcoholic's family. A bitter girl represses her mother's death. A white boy and Negro girl are slandered. A son faces his father's adultery. A brother's psychosis disrupts a girl's life.

A teenage marriage is on the rocks. An unmarried sister has a baby. A boy questions his own indifference to life. These dramatic short stories do an excellent job of interpreting the feelings and perplexities of young people.

PEDERSEN, ELSA. *Fisherman's Choice.* il. by Alvin Smith. Atheneum, 1964, $3.95. Dave Moffitt, seventeen, has never worked anywhere except on the family farm. He takes a job on a fishing boat to earn money to help clear the family's Alaskan homestead. By the end of the summer, in spite of problems and a mystery about the boat, Dave is sure he is meant for the sea. Dave's parents cannot understand this, and his battle for freedom makes him a man, but almost costs him his family.

PHELAN, MARY KAY. *Probing the Unknown: The Story of Dr. Florence Sabin.* TY Crowell, 1969, $4.50. A modest and humble woman, Florence Sabin was an outstanding medical scientist at Johns Hopkins whose research led to the discovery of the origin of the lymphatic system in 1902. She headed the Rockefeller Institute in New York, where extensive study and work was done on the tubercle bacillus, thus laying the foundation for tuberculosis control. Returning to her native Colorado upon reaching retirement age, she became active in the field of public health, and her tireless crusading resulted in greatly improved health programs.

POHLMANN, LILLIAN. *Sing Loose.* Westminster, 1968, $3.95. "Sing Loose" is Maria's theme song on her guitar. But how can she sing loose when everyone in her new high school is sure to find out that her father is serving time in San Quentin for embezzlement? In spite of her decision not to get involved at school, Maria finds new friends and the solution to her problems.

* RAWLINGS, MARJORIE KINNAN. *The Yearling.*

* RICHTER, CONRAD. *Light in the Forest.*

ROSE, KAREN. *A Single Trail.* Follett, 1969, $3.95. Ricky has just moved to Los Angeles to a racially divided neighborhood and an integrated high school. Morale is low in school and antagonism between blacks and whites is high. Ricky has a number of rough encounters with Earl, a tough black student. After the students endure several poor teachers, a good one finally manages to bring some order and purpose into the classroom. Then a school gang tampers with the teacher's parked car and she has a serious accident. During her hospital stay she tutors the two boys in reading. One night as they walk home from the hospital, a rival gang attacks them. The two unite for the first time after beating the others. The theme of this novel for adolescents is that people who share common interests can overcome their prejudices.

* SAMS, JESSIE. *White Mother.*

* SANSAN, *Eighth Moon.*

SCHULTZ, GLADYS DENNY. *Jenny Lind, the Swedish Nightingale.* Lippincott, 1962, $6.50. Jenny Lind was probably the most famous and beloved singer of the nineteenth century. Noted for her intelligence, her compassion, her kindness, and her magnificent voice, few people knew that she was beset by loneliness and sadness. Few knew of the scheming and greediness of her parents, of her disappointments in love before finally she could marry and have her family.

* STEINBECK, JOHN. *The Pearl.*

STRACHAN, MARGARET P. *What Is to Be.* Washburn, 1966, $3.50. A popular girl looking forward to her senior year in high school finds she and her family must move to an old farm outside the city. Babs and her brothers will have to go to a new school; she will have to cope with housekeeping without electricity or water while her mother works. How Babs faces her responsibility in spite of her dismay makes for an interesting novel.

STRASSOVA, HELENA. *The Path.* trans by Peter Freixa. Grossman, 1969, $5.95. This is the story of a young Jewish girl alone during World War II, living as a fugitive, then a refugee. Nell, the narrator, is deeply attached to her parents and especially to her twin brother with whom she forms a remarkable bond. Her family is separated from her, never to be seen again. But in her flight, she meets people who influence the rest of her life.

* VINSON, KATHRYN. *Run with the Ring.*

WEST, JESSAMYN. *Cress Delahanty.* HBJ, 1954, $4.95 (P/Avon, $.95). Growing up on a ranch in California, thirteen-year-old Cress hopes to gain a place for herself in school by inventing "the Delahanty law."

* WESTHEIMER, DAVID. *My Sweet Charlie.*

WHITNEY, PHYLLIS A. *Linda's Homecoming.* McKay, 1950, $4.95. Linda Hollis helps her mother and stepfather build a happy, affectionate family by learning to get along with Roddy and Babs, her stepbrother and stepsister.

WOLFF, RUTH. *Linsey, Herself.* P/Schol Bk Serv, 1965, $.75. With the death of her father, Linsey is forced to drop out of school to help support her family of five. New friends help her begin a career as a folksinger and she discovers the value of close family ties.

WOODY, REGINA J. *The Young Medics.* Messner, 1968, $3.50. Amanda Davis begins a nursing program but withdraws and enters an M.D. program even though her doctor grandfather had taught her that nursing is for women and medicine is for men. Convinced that there is a place for women she learns how to combine a demanding career with marriage.

Mature

BOOTH, ESMA RIDEOUT. *The Village, the City, and the World.* McKay, 1966, $4.95. An African family leaves the village to make a home in the city. The parents' two different tribes battle for power, and the United Nations sends forces. The family realizes how much understanding is required to remain together in spite of national conflict.

BUCK, PEARL S. *Imperial Woman.* John Day, 1956, $7.95. Tzu Hsi, the last ruling Empress of China, was both loved and hated. A talented woman, contradictory in behavior, she despised the encroachment of the changes seeping through China. She clung to the old ways, believing them better. When she saw that change was inevitable, she accepted it with outer grace but with an unchanged heart.

——. *My Several Worlds.* John Day, 1954, $6.75 (P/PB, $.95). This is the true story of a woman who has lived in many worlds and in many cultures. The first part of her life she spent in China until turmoil and political forces created such danger that many were forced to flee. The last part of her life she has spent in America. Her insights are penetrating, exciting, and rare.

FISHER, AILEEN, AND OLIVE RABE. *We Alcotts.* il. by Ellen Raskin. Atheneum, 1968, $4.95. This carefully researched biography of Louisa May Alcott's mother gives an authentic picture of family life in early nineteenth-century New England.

FURUYA, MIYUKI. *Why, Mother, Why?* Kodansha International, 1966, O.P. Brief, unrhymed, evocative poems by a fifth-grade Japanese girl record her grief over her mother's untimely death and the strangeness of a household left bereaved by the sudden tragedy. The accompanying black and white photographs of Miyuki, her teacher father and young brother sustain the tone of a genuinely moving book that expresses a sorrow free of sentimentality.

MARKANDAYA, KAMALA. *Nectar in a Sieve.* John Day, 1955, $5.95 (P/NAL, $.95). A woman, married as a child to a tenant farmer she had never seen, lives simply and gallantly as a peasant. In spite of poverty and change, she and her husband are happy until the coming of the tannery brings changes almost too great to bear.

NARAYAN, R. K. *The Vendor of Sweets.* Viking Pr, 1967 (P/Avon, $1.45). Jagan, a candy maker in a small town in India, is faced with conflict when his nonconforming son returns home from his studies in America with new ideas. The reader can sympathize with the father's reverence for tradition, as well as with the son's desire for progress and change. This is an amusing picture of contemporary Indian life.

RICH, LOUISE DICKINSON. *Mindy.* Lippincott, 1959, $4.95. Mindy, daughter of a Cape Cod fisherman, faces the choice of marrying when she finishes high school or of going on to college and breaking the pattern of generations.

SERGEANT, ELIZABETH. *Robert Frost: The Trial by Existence.* HR & W, 1960, $6.50. This book about the poet laureate of America, Robert Frost, reveals the emergence of the poet and the man and shows a magnificent human being who dared to live differently from others, to think deeply, to feel keenly. In times of failure and personal tragedy, Frost somehow remained undestroyed by what might have broken lesser men. As teacher, as poet, as man, Frost discovered his own differences early and dedicated himself to finding out what they meant.

SHUTE, NEVIL. *On the Beach.* Morrow, 1957, $5.95 (P/several). As the result of a devastating atomic war, radioactive fallout has completely obliterated human life in the Northern Hemisphere. The winds are slowly carrying the deadly radioactivity into the Southern Hemisphere. This novel recounts the final months in the lives of an American submarine commander stationed in Australia and his Australian acquaintances as they prepare for death.

STEINBECK, JOHN. *The Grapes of Wrath.* Viking Pr, 1939, $7.50 (P/several). A sharecropper family piles a few household goods onto its broken-down car and migrates from the dust bowl to California, where as migratory workers they experience deprivation and rejection.

* STRASSOVA, HELENA. *The Path.*

Coping with Social and Economic Change

Primary

BEHRENS, JUNE. *Soo Ling Finds a Way.* il. by Taro Yashima. Golden Gate, 1965, $3.50. Little Soo Ling watches a laundromat going up right across from her grandfather's Chinese hand laundry. Soo Ling's sadness and worry give way to a solution for all. Illustrations are in Taro Yashima's very unique style with soft and attractively cool colors.

BULLA, CLYDE ROBERT. *White Bird.* il. by Leonard Weisgard. TY Crowell, 1966, $3.75. Like Moses, John Thomas is found floating in his cradle on the swollen spring river. His parents are never found so he grows up with Luke. The poor farm land and the isolation eventually force the other pioneer families further west leaving them alone. Suspicious of the outside world and all people, Luke treats John in a ruthlessly possessive manner. When John's white crow is stolen by some visitors to Half-Moon Valley, he leaves to search for them. His confrontation with the outside world immediately widens his perspectives.

BURTON, VIRGINIA LEE. *Mike Mulligan and His Steam Shovel.* HM, 1939, $3.75. This popular picture book tells the story of an old-fashioned steam shovel finding a useful occupation when more modern engines have replaced it.

DUVOISIN, ROGER. *Lonely Veronica.* Knopf, 1963, $3.00. When Veronica's peaceful river is invaded by men, machines, and a new city, the older hippopotami see the end of the good old days and leave. But young Veronica stays to find the good new days, and ends up in America where she is trapped in a construction site for a time, but finally finds her place on a farm.

EVER, ALF. *Abner's Cabin.* Watts, 1957, O.P. The history of a little country house and how it changes with increasing urbanization up to the present day. Just as the house is about to be torn down to make way for a new highway, someone recalls its earlier tradition and the town decides to make it a part of the town's museum.

JUSTUS, MAY. *New Boy in School.* il. by Joan Balfour Payne. Hastings, 1963, $3.25. When Lennie Lane, a first grader, moves from a country school in the South to the city, he longs for his old school and friends. Lennie must adjust not only to city life but also to being the only Negro in his class.

————. *A New Home for Billy.* il. by Joan Balfour Payne. Hastings, 1966, $3.25. Six-year-old Billy Allen and his parents want to move from their cramped apartment in the city to a little house in the suburbs. While house hunting with his father, Billy hears a man tell his father he will not rent to little Billy. He has been raised in an integrated setting and cannot understand why this man would be silly enough to like or dislike people by their color. Billy's new neighbors prove there are people who judge the person, not the skin color.

KEATS, EZRA JACK. *Apt. 3.* il. by author. Macmillan, 1971, $5.95. "Someone in the building playing a harmonica" starts Sam and Ben off on a search. Before they find the blind man with the secrets in Apt. 3, they discover some secrets of their own. The apartment interiors depicted are more somber than those in *Hi Cat* and *Goggles* but they convey that special feeling for ghetto life unique to Keats.

* KEITH, EROS. *A Small Lot.*

* LONERGAN, JOY. *Brian's Secret Errand.*

MORGAN, GEOFFREY. *A Small Piece of Paradise.* Knopf, 1968, $3.95. The land behind the junkyard in London is a small piece of paradise, brilliant and beautiful. It is also a sanctuary for the owner, Joe, and all the animals. Progress almost destroys this beauty spot, but Joe's devotion and love for it save it for a park area.

PEET, BILL. *Farewell to Shady Glade.* il. by author. HM, 1966, $3.50. Sixteen animals have their own paradise in Shady Glade until they are threatened by urbanization. The wise old raccoon helps the group through their difficulty by leading them on a long journey to other places until they find a suitable home.

————. *The Wump World.* il. by author. HM, 1970, $3.95. The Wump creatures live simply and happily in their small Wump World. There is plenty to eat, they all get along beautifully and life is without problems. Suddenly from Outer Space come the Pollutions from the planet Pollutus. They take over everything everywhere and the Wumps are forced to go underground. The Wump World eventually becomes uninhabitable, the Pollutions take off for greener pastures and the Wumps are left to rebuild their world again. The message is there, subtly told in a simple straightforward manner.

WISE, WILLIAM. *The Story of Mulberry Bend.* il. by Hoot Von Zitzewitz. Dutton, 1963, $3.46. Jacob Riis, a writer for a newspaper in New York City in the year 1888, visits Mulberry Bend, a dark, desolate street of old houses and very poor people, and talks with a small boy who has never seen flowers. After his daughters Kate and Clara send flowers to Mulberry Bend, Jacob, touched by the reactions of the children when they see flowers for the first time, writes a story for his newspaper. After reading Jacob's story, people fill a big wagon with flowers for Jacob to take to Mulberry Bend. Because people become interested, change takes place on Mulberry Bend. Old houses are torn down; new houses and a playground are built. A beautiful, simply told, powerful story based upon a true incident, showing what people can do to bring about change.

Intermediate

BAKER, BETTY. *Shaman's Last Ride.* il. by Leonard Shortall. Har-Row, 1963, $3.95. Eban and his twin sister are excited because their great-grandfather from the Indian reservation is coming to spend the summer with them. They devise a plan to use their grandfather, a shaman who still believes in the old ways, to help them get in a TV movie being filmed at the reservation. Eban becomes absorbed in learning the old Apache ways. The book touches with humor on both the generation gap and the changing ways of a culture.

BARRINGER, D. MOREAU. *And the Waters Prevailed.* il. by P. A. Hutchison. Dutton, 1956, $4.95. While on a reconnaissance trip, young Andor discovers that the Great Sea will eventually break through and inundate his Stone Age village. Andor spends much of his lifetime trying to convince his village of the danger; only a few believe him. When he is an old man the flood comes and he succumbs with most of his village—a dramatic example of failure to cope with changing conditions.

BAUM, BETTY. *A New Home for Theresa.* il. by James Barkley. Knopf, 1968, $3.95. Because Theresa and her mother have been close to each other and no one else, Theresa is terrified when her mother suddenly dies. Placed in a foster home with a more affluent couple, Theresa is caught between Mrs. Chinton's distrust of white people and Mr. Chinton's faith in integration and acceptance of individuals without prejudice about color. Events in a troubled integrated school bring Theresa's problems to a climax.

BAWDEN, NINA. *Squib.* P/Lippincott, 1971, $1.95. Divergent social groups intermingle in a tense, sensitive story of four English children who daringly come to the rescue of a silent, lonely, mistreated little boy.

* BRADBURY, BIANCA. *The Undergrounders.*

* BRADLEY, DUANE. *Meeting with a Stranger.*

BRINK, CAROL RYRIE. *Winter Cottage.* il. by Fermin Rocker. Macmillan, 1968, $4.95. Thirteen-year-old Minty Sparkes is intensely aware of the hardships which the Depression has placed on her dreamer father and younger sister. She becomes the acting leader of the family as first they decide to move into a vacant summer cottage and then include Joe, a runaway, in their plans. The chance of a new home rather than the constantly changing rented room gives Minty a new-found sense of responsibility and pride which the whole family shares. In an effort to win the money to pay rent for their "borrowed" cottage, the children plot together to discover Pop's secret recipe for pancakes in order to enter a contest. The family relationships and adjustments to change make this an enjoyable book.

* BRO, MARGUERITTE H. *Su Mei's Golden Year.*

BUCK, PEARL S. *Matthew, Mark, Luke and John.* il. by Mamoru Funai. John Day, 1967, $3.50. Matthew, no more than a boy himself, finds himself the father figure for three younger boys (Mark, Luke, and John). The bond that ties these homeless boys together is their being half American and half Korean, rejected by Korean society and abandoned by their Korean mothers. Matthew's unselfish devotion to his adopted orphans leads to a satisfying ending. A touching story honestly written with warmth and humor.

BULLA, CLYDE. *Indian Hill.* il. by James J. Spanfeller. TY Crowell, 1963, $3.00. When Kee's family moves from a Navajo hogan to an apartment in the city, Kee is unhappy. When he and his mother return to the reservation to care for a sick friend, they reflect upon the old and the new and how people adjust to new environments.

CLARK, ANN NOLAN. *Summer Is for Growing.* il. by Agnes Tait. FS & G, 1968, $3.50. Set in 1851, this story vividly describes the life on a Spanish hacienda in the Southwest. The tradition of the Maman training her daughter to supervise and manage the staff who produce all the necessary goods and services for the hacienda is outlined in detail. The indirect effect of the incorporation of the hacienda in the new territory of "New Mexico of the United States of America" is mentioned as well as the encounters with the Indians. Spanish terms included in the text add to the authenticity of the story. An excellent book for children studying this region of early America.

CROWELL, ANN. *A Hogan for the Bluebird.* il. by Harrison Begay. Scribner, 1969, $3.50. Singing Willow has just graduated from the reservation mission school and her education there continues to influence her reactions to life around her on her return to the family hogan. The life and customs of the Indians are realistically described in detail as many attempts are made to help Singing Willow readjust to life. Her greatest longing is for the piano which she has mastered and which she longs to play again. The self-sacrifice of her brother Little Eagle and the kind understanding of her parents and the mission school enable her to retain the best of both worlds in which she has lived.

* DE GERING, ETTA. *Wilderness Wife: The Story of Rebecca Bryan Boone.*

EDWARDSON, CORDELIA. *Miriam Lives in a Kibbutz.* il. with photographs by Anna Riwkin-Brick. Lothrop, 1971, $3.75. Five-year-old Miriam and her parents come to Israel from Morocco to settle on a kibbutz. Miriam is unhappy at having to live in the children's house away from her parents and dislikes the kibbutz until an older boy befriends her, takes her on a tour, and helps her adjust to the strange new life. Many photographs, well integrated with the text, give an adequate introduction to life on a kibbutz.

* FITCH, BOB AND LYNNE. *Soy Chicano, I Am Mexican-American.*

FRIEDMAN, FRIEDA. *Carol from the Country.* il. by Mary Barton. Morrow, 1950, $3.95. As a result of an economic change, Carol and her family are forced to give up their home and business in the country and move to an apartment in New York City. At eleven and a half, Carol is forced to make a greater adjustment to the new environment than her neighbor Frank, who has recently emigrated from Italy. At first she is unable to accept the characteristics of her new economic status and rebuffs all attempts to involve her in the new neighborhood. Finally, as a result of a heroic exploit, she is accepted and realizes that friends are found wherever you live.

GEORGE, JEAN CRAIGHEAD. *Coyote in Manhattan.* il. by John Kaufmann. TY Crowell, 1968, $3.95. Those living on 109th Street in New York come from all over the world and prize freedom above all else. In this imaginative and deeply moving story, these people quietly and effectively support the efforts of Tako, a coyote, for survival and freedom against those who wish him captured and killed. Throughout the fast-moving narrative one sees clearly the concerns of the young and their similarity to nature's creatures, as they attempt to find a liveable world in the demanding complexity of city life.

HIRSH, CARL S. *This is Automation.* Anthony Ravielli. Viking Pr, 1964, $3.56. The book explains briefly the industrial revolution, the growth of automation, and the computer and how it works, and it tells of the new skills needed by man and woman because of automation. The benefits and limitations of computers are presented, the future use of computers suggested. The case for the changing role of today's human work force is convincingly stated.

* HOFF, SYD. *Irving & Me.*

HUNT, MABEL LEIGH. *Ladycake Farm.* Lippincott, 1952, $3.79. The Freeds, who are black, move from town to an old farm and must adjust to being the only blacks in a white school, faced with the attitudes of bigoted neighbors. The Freeds do, however, overcome this hardship with honesty, hard work, kindness, and a sense of humor.

JONES, WEYMAN. *The Talking Leaf.* il. by E. Harper Johnson. Dial, 1965, $3.50. Atsee grows up and decides the old ways of his Cherokee father are not the way to lead his people out of the wilderness. Teaching his people to read and write is Atsee's way of blazing new trails. The story is based on a real Cherokee who was one of the first teachers to translate English to Cherokee.

KRUMGOLD, JOSEPH. *Henry Three.* Atheneum, 1968, $4.75. Henry doesn't want it known that he has an I.Q. of 154. He and his family have just moved into a high-toned suburb and they all want more than anything to make good with the right crowd. Henry has discovered that when people know how smart he is, they tend to shy away from him. No one finds out about his brilliance and he is accepted by the "right" crowd until his family has a bomb shelter installed in their backyard. He figures that the only way to solve his problems is to find a way to stop the possibility of war. Scathingly real scenes between Henry and his father, his mother, and his peers make this book a brilliant examination of contemporary social problems.

————. *The Most Terrible Turk: A Story of Turkey.* TY Crowell, 1969, $3.75. The modernization of Turkey creates grave problems for Mustafa, Ali's only surviving relative. Not only is Mustafa unable to read the new alphabet, but he cannot understand the need for the super highways that drive the game from his lands. He is driven to "killing trucks" by blowing out the tires with his long blue rifle. Ali's efforts to disuade his uncle are original and amusing in this easy-to-read adventure.

LAMPMAN, EVELYN SIBLEY. *Half-Breed.* il. by Ann Grifalconi, Doubleday, 1967, $3.95. Pale Eyes, a young Crow and grandson of a chief, leaves his mother and his Crow people to join his white father. Now that he has decided to find his father, Pale Eyes assumes his Christian name—Hardy Hollingshead. Hardy soon learns that the white man's ways are quite different from the life, love, and warmth he has been accustomed to with the Crows. From white eyes he learns the bitter meaning of half-breed. Hardy's patience and perseverance reflect the realities of life faced by numerous youngsters of minority groups. The majestic beauty, excitement, and hardships of early pioneer days are presented in robust style.

* LAST, JEFF, AND U. P. TISNA. *The Bamboo School in Bali.*

McNEILL, JANET. *Goodbye, Dove Square.* il. by Mary Russon. Little, 1969, $4.50. Matt, a young boy once outgoing and concerned, is affected by the transition from his old, established city neighborhood, "Dove Square," to a modern apartment complex. Matt misses the things he once enjoyed and has little interest in the new neighborhood. When making some visits back to Dove Square, Matt and his friends are faced with some unpleasant incidents. A mystery develops and is solved, and Matt gradually accepts his new neighborhood.

MEADOWCROFT, ENID LA MONTE. *By Secret Railway.* TY Crowell, 1948, $4.50. David Morgan, who is twelve, makes friends with Jim, a young exslave, who comes to live at the Morgan home. When Jim is kidnapped and sold back into slavery, David goes on an adventure-filled journey to rescue Jim and bring him back to Chicago. Set in the period of Lincoln's election, this historical novel deals with the social and political problems of that day, as well as the warm and loyal friendship between two boys.

* MONTGOMERY, JEAN. *The Wrath of Coyote.*

MORROW, HONORE W. *On to Oregon.* il. by Edward Shenton. Morrow, 1926, $4.50 (P/NAL, $.60). The nine members of the Sager family are traveling westward with a large wagon train toward Oregon where they are to build their new home. After the death of his parents, thirteen-year-old John Sager is left responsible for his younger brothers and sisters. Facing near starvation and other perils of the wilderness trail, John and his tiny bank of children trek across the Rocky Mountains alone and follow the Snake River into Oregon.

NEVILLE, EMILY CHENEY. *Berries Goodman.* Har-Row, 1965, $3.50. Berries Goodman and his whole family move from New York City to the suburbs. Though feeling uprooted and out of place, Berries makes friends with the girl next door and Sidney Fine, another outsider in his class. Berries is baffled by the snobbish provincialism and anti-Semitism which he encounters. A fine book for the sophisticated middle-grade, or junior-high student.

* O'NEILL, MARY. *Ali.*

POLLAND, MADELEINE. *The Queen's Blessing.* il. by Betty Fraser. HR & W, 1964, $3.50. Merca and Day are left homeless orphans when their eleventh century Scottish village is destroyed by the war. The two children are sold into slavery, escape, and eventually are befriended by the gentle Queen Margaret. Merca vows revenge on the king whose army killed her parents, but her hatred for the king slowly dies as she learns more about him. A mature and beautiful historical novel which shows the timelessness of the necessity to understand others and the need for behavior appropriate to changed understanding.

ROBINSON, JACKIE, AND ALFRED DUCKETT. *Breakthrough to the Big League.* Har-Row, 1965, $3.95. Jackie Robinson describes his impoverished childhood and early racial degradation, a stay at a college in Los Angeles where he began a career in sports, and even greater racial problems when he became the first Negro in the major leagues. The chatty text becomes vivid because it is so clearly drawn from Robinson's own speech. As a plain-speaking, highly personal sharing of experience, the book is a forceful picture of the challenge of crossing barriers.

SACHS, MARILYN. *Bears' House.* il. by Louis Glanzman. Doubleday, 1971, $3.95. Fran Ellen is one of the children you do not hear too much about, but they exist in suburbs and cities, pushed back into the corners of our minds and hearts, left alone to make out as best they can. Faced with a dismal, dreary reality, she escapes into the fantasy world at the bears' house where she finds security and love.

SHECTER, BEN. *Someplace Else.* il. by author. Har-Row, 1971, $3.95. Arnie's family is forced to move into a rundown and depressing neighborhood. Arnie is a frustrated, lonely, sensitive boy who is preparing for his bar mitzvah. His hostility for the Rabbi is so intense that he feels guilt when the Rabbi disappears. The style and format are simple and open; yet sophisticated questions are raised. Despite the humor, a tone of pathos exists. The book ends with the death of Arnie's father.

* SMITH, GEORGE HARMON. *Bayou Belle.*

* SMUCKER, BARBARA C. *Wigwam in the City.*

* SPEEVACK, YETTA. *The Spider Plant.*

STERLING, PHILIP, AND RAYFORD LOGAN. *Four Took Freedom: The Lives of Harriet Tubman, Frederick Douglass, Robert Small, and Blanche K. Bruce.* il. by Charles White. Doubleday, 1967, $2.95 (P/Doubleday, $1.45). Succinct accounts of the lives of four American blacks and their escape from slavery. The drama, pathos, and great excitement of these biographies will cause children to be interested in learning more about Harriet Tubman, Frederick Douglass, Robert Small, and Blanche K. Bruce. Well-selected and well-told incidents from these lives give the reader an understanding of some social issues facing us today.

VALENS, EVANS G. *Wildfire*. il. by Clement Hurd. World, 1963, $3.75. The devastating changes caused by a forest fire are described in poetic prose. How the birds and animals react and how the life cycle resumes after the fire are told with suspense and unusual sensitivity. Mr. Hurd's striking illustrations, making use of leaves and weeds lithographed on weathered wood, produce a remarkable forest before us.

* VAN STOCKUM, HILDA. *The Winged Watchman.*

Junior

ALCOCK, GUDRUN. *Turn the Next Corner*. Lothrop, 1969, $3.95. Ritchie Osborne is hurt and angry when his father is convicted of embezzlement and sent to prison. Ritchie and his mother must move from the comfortable suburbs to the inner city. There they try to conceal their family shame and to adopt a more modest standard of living. Slugger, a Negro boy living in the same building, and Ritchie become friends. An accident made Slugger a cripple but he is fiercely independent. Together, Ritchie and Slugger learn to accept each other and the strengths and weaknesses they discover in themselves.

ALDRICH, BESS STREETER. *Lantern in Her Hand*. G & D, 1928, $2.95 (P/ several). The absorbing story of a woman and her family who settle in Nebraska in the 1870s when every day brings new threats of Indians, accidents, prairie fires, or blizzards. Faith and hard work finally make real their dreams of productive farms and prosperous towns. In the 1920s old Abbie Deal can look back with pride and wonder to her own part in the miracle.

* BONHAM, FRANK. *Durango Street.*

* ———. *The Nitty Gritty.*

BRADBURY, BIANCA. *The Undergrounders*. il. by Jon Nielsen. Washburn, 1966, $3.25. Fourteen-year-old Jess Wright and his family live in the North, but become deeply involved with slaves fleeing from the South and escaping to Canada.

BRO, MARGUERITTE H. *Su Mei's Golden Year*. il. by Kurt Wiese. Doubleday, 1950, $3.50. A Chinese village faces the challenges of the new technology after World War II. Showing faith in her father's new knowledge, Su Mei shows the village how to rid itself of a blight. In addition to the maturing of a twelve-year-old girl in the environment of technological change, the book pictures Chinese customs, festivals, and attitudes, and contains a beautiful segment describing the Chinese theatre.

DE ANGELI, ARTHUR CRAIG. *The Door in the Wall*. il. by Marguerite De Angeli. Doubleday, 1968, $3.95. The notes on props, stage settings, and directions should be helpful in staging this fine adaptation of the Newbery Award winner. The play brings to life again the courage of crippled Robin during plague-ridden thirteenth-century London.

DE GERING, ETTA. *Wilderness Wife: The Story of Rebecca Bryan Boone.* il. by Ursula Koering. McKay, 1966, $3.95. As the wife of the famed frontiersman, Daniel Boone, Rebecca faced many challenges in the untamed wilderness of Kentucky and Missouri. Her loyalty to her husband and her own strength of character helped her adapt to new situations and changing times.

* EMERY, ANNE. *Tradition.*

* FITCH, BOB AND LYNNE. *Soy Chicano, I Am Mexican-American.*

HOFF, SYD. *Irving & Me.* Har-Row, 1967, $3.95. Artie Granick's father wants to get away from the perils of inner-city Brooklyn, so the whole family moves to Florida where Artie meets Irving, a tanned buck-toothed pal who leads him into new scrapes. Artie regrets leaving his friends, and diminishing his chances of getting back that $1.50 Howie Mannheim owes him, but he becomes so busy at the Jewish youth center and with a new love interest that he has little time to think of the past. Written in tongue-in-cheek, breezy style, it nevertheless does deal with the serious problem of being uprooted.

KROEBER, THEODORA. *Ishi, Last of His Tribe.* il. by Ruth Robbins. Parnassus, 1964, $4.50. The dramatic account of the few survivors of the Yahi tribe of Indians. When only Ishi remains, he lives alone, then is discovered and joins the world of the white men. The biography shows the changes the tribe survivors and Ishi are compelled to make, but also presents a compelling picture of the Yahi tribal codes of conduct.

MERRILL, JEAN. *The Pushcart War.* il. by Ronni Solbert. WR Scott, 1964, $3.95 (P/G & D, $.60). The citizens are unhappy about the traffic situation in New York. Looking for a scapegoat, the truckers decide that the solution to the problem would be to abolish the pushcarts. A full-scale war develops between the 500 pushcart peddlers and the big three in the trucking industry. Complete with colorful heroes, nasty villains, and a mayor who plays poker with the truckers, this tongue-in-cheek satire says a great deal about our society.

* NEUFELD, JOHN. *Edgar Allen.*

RAYMOND, CHARLES. *Up from Appalachia.* Follett, 1966, $3.95. When the Cantrells move from Kentucky to Chicago, they are ridiculed and labeled "hillbillies" by their new neighbors. Through Gramma's understanding of human nature, the family finally gets "settled in," and a vacant lot becomes a Street People's Park.

* SACHS, MARILYN. *Bear's House.*

* SHECTER, BEN. *Someplace Else.*

* SMITH, GEORGE HARMON. *Wanderers of the Field.*

TOWNSEND, JOHN ROWE. *Hell's Edge.* Lothrop, 1969, $4.25 (P/Penguin, $.95). Amaryllis Terry, after moving to Hallersage (Hell's Edge), must make adjustments to a strange town, new friends, and growing up. With her cousin, Norman, Amaryllis becomes involved with solving a hundred-year-old mystery, with the fate of the town in the balance.

* WENTWORTH, ELAINE. *Mission to Metlakatla.*

* ZIEGLER, ELSIE REIF. *The Face in the Stone.*

Senior

* BARRIO, RAYMOND. *The Plum Plum Pickers.*

* BONHAM, FRANK. *Durango Street.*

COHEN, FLORENCE CHANOCK. *Portrait of Deborah.* Messner, 1961, $3.50. With the promise of an outstanding piano scholarship, teenaged Deborah Rose had anticipated a bright future. Suddenly her family must move from their inner-city Chicago neighborhood to the suburbs. With shattered hopes, Debbie wants to forget her music. Her new romance with Steve Randall seems to compensate for the void, until his family's anti-Jewish sentiment interferes. Circumstances force Debbie's change of attitude and help her to achieve maturity in her personality and artistry.

* GRAHAM, LORENZ. *South Town.*

HILL, MARGARET. *Time to Quit Running.* Messner, 1970, $3.50. How does an attractive, intelligent teenager from an impoverished home in the most run-down neighborhood in town overcome her environment? Valerie Leslie's valiant efforts to rise above her circumstances cause her to become enmeshed in a series of entangling falsehoods, and an exciting turn of events helps her to suddenly gain an insight into her perplexing problem. The author of this novel, a high school guidance counselor, writes with keen sympathy for this situation.

KISSIN, EVA H. (ed.). *Stories in Black & White.* Lippincott, 1970, $4.95 (P/Lippincott, $1.95). This is a collection of stories by both black and white writers, an outpouring of what they have felt and seen in their experiences with each other. It is particularly appropriate in helping to illustrate the one-to-one relationships often overlooked in describing group attitudes.

MELTZER, MILTON. *Langston Hughes: A Biography.* TY Crowell, 1968, $4.50. Langston Hughes has been called the poet laureate of the Negro people. His poetic and dramatic interpretations of Negro life have revealed an unusual sensitivity for his people. Hughes lived a life of adventure with times of discouragement and success. The author of this book, a personal friend of Hughes, has included many of Hughes' poems in the text.

* RODMAN, BELLA. *Lions in the Way.*

* SILBERMAN, CHARLES. *Crisis in Black and White.*

Mature

LEINWAND, GERALD. *The Negro in the City.* P/WSP, 1969, $.75. Black leadership speaks out about life in the ghetto, the effects of racism, and the so-called new mood of the black people. The focus is on the inner-city problems of black people and their search for a better life. Fifteen candid articles and over fifty photographs document this examination of the black American in urban society.

* LEWIS, OSCAR. *The Children of Sanchez.*

* PATON, ALAN. *Cry, the Beloved Country.*

Coping with Political Change

Intermediate

ALBRECHT, LILLIE V. *The Grist Mill Secret.* il. by Lloyd Coe. Hastings, 1962, $3.50. The Copley family has to leave their comfortable city home and live at a grist mill where they secretly operate a musket-making factory for the Minutemen. The drama of divided loyalties between family members, of keeping their "secret," makes this an exciting story of the way a family has to change its way of life at the time of the Revolutionary War.

ARNOLD, ELLIOTT. *A Kind of Secret Weapon.* Scribner, 1969, $3.95. Lars and Lise Anderson are deeply involved in the Danish underground. Their son, Peter, twelve, takes part as he helps to publish and distribute their underground newspaper. The changes which the Germans bring to their country are partially countered by such activities, and the emphasis on helping one's country in her hour of need is reiterated again and again. The ultimate consequence of such personal involvement is exemplified by Mr. Anderson's arrest, torture, and ultimate death as a martyr. Before they flee to Sweden, Peter, the new head of the family, asserts himself in order to publish and distribute his father's final edition which discredits the local German commander. Excitement and suspense for intermediate-age and junior readers.

BONTEMPS, ARNA. *Frederick Douglass: Slave-Fighter Freeman.* il. by Harper Johnson. Knopf, 1959, $3.64. A dramatic short biography of Frederick Douglass, which is compelling reading. The changes in his character as a result of the trauma of slavery are characterized in the statement attributed to him: "If there is no struggle, there is no progress. Those who profess to favor freedom, and yet deprecate agitation are men who crop without plowing. . . . They want the ocean without the awful roar of its many waters." The struggles of this great American are sensitively presented.

COATSWORTH, ELIZABETH. *The Lucky Ones: Five Journeys toward a Home.* il. by Janet Doyle. Macmillan, 1968, $3.95. These refugee children are called "the lucky ones" only because they survived the danger and hardship of escaping from the enemy and of adapting to a whole new culture and way of life. Even though the stories are brief, the reader is given a real feeling for the culture of the beloved homelands of China, Tibet, Hungary, Rwanda, and Algeria, as well as sympathy for the five distinctly different families as they relocate in alien lands. Together or singly, these stories should motivate good classroom discussion.

HAUGAARD, ERIK CHRISTIAN. *Orphans of the Wind.* il. by Milton Johnson. HM, 1966, $3.50 (P/Dell, $.75). At twelve, Jim is signed on as deckboy for the Civil War blockade runner *Four Winds* by his selfish uncle. Leaving Bristol and sailing to Charleston, his life is changed by the people he meets and the things that happen. Many crewmen are concerned about slavery and question the ship's cargo of guns and powder. When the ship is burned Jim and three of his fellow crewmen row to shore. In order to travel North to join what they feel is the right cause, they travel with the Confederate Army. Their feelings as men in battle as well as their desire to do the right thing are well described.

* HUNT, IRENE. *Across Five Aprils.*

LIFTON, BETTY JEAN. *Return to Hiroshima.* il. by Eikoh Hosoe. Atheneum, 1970, $5.95. When the author went to live in Hiroshima with her husband, Robert J. Lifton, who was studying the psychological effects of the bomb on the survivors, she made a film of the young people. She asked the photographer to help her tell the story of the survivors in book form. The reader becomes a survivor himself and it is hoped he will grasp the nature of the weapons that man has created.

* REBOUL, ANTOINE. *Thou Shalt Not Kill.*

SERRAILLIER, IAN. *The Silver Sword.* il. by C. Walter Hodges. SG Phillips, 1959, $4.95. As a result of World War II, the Balicki family of

Warsaw are separated from one another. Living in bombed-out cellars or the countryside the children are helped by Edek until his arrest for smuggling and from then on by Jan, a sullen orphan. The privations of each member of the family, especially the children, are graphically described as each works toward their rendezvous, Switzerland, and freedom. A suspense-filled, exciting story.

* STEVENSON, WILLIAM. *The Bushbabies.*

TAYLOR, THEODORE. *The Cay.* Doubleday, 1969, $3.50 (P/Avon, $.75). When the freighter which was to take Phillip and his mother from wartime Curacao to the United States is torpedoed, Phillip finds himself afloat on a small raft with a huge, old, very black West Indian man. Phillip becomes blind from injuries and resents his dependence upon old Timothy. Through exciting adventures on a very small cay (coral island), Phillip learns to overcome his prejudice toward Timothy and to see him as a man and a friend. Following the aftermath of a fierce tropical storm, Timothy dies. Phillip survives to live a more complete life because of his friend and because he has grown with the changes that occurred in his life.

UCHIDA, YOSHIKO. *Journey to Topaz.* il. by Donald Carrick. Scribner, 1971, $4.50. The moving story of Yuki, an eleven-year-old Japanese-American girl who, in December of 1941, suddenly finds herself, her mother and her older brother being sent from their comfortable home in Northern California to an internment camp in Utah, while her father is sent elsewhere. The humiliation and suffering inflicted on the Japanese during the war is made very evident in the story. The courage, the dignity, and the patriotism not only of Yuki and her family but of the other people in the camp come through very well.

VAN STOCKUM, HILDA. *The Winged Watchman.* FS & G, 1963, $3.95. During the occupation of Holland in World War II, the Verhagens adjust to the hardships—physical danger, cruelties, and food shortages. They maintain their loyalty to their country and participate in the underground movement. The book presents a dramatic picture of how political events can affect the daily life of individuals.

WATSON, SALLY. *Other Sandals.* HR & W, 1966, $3.50. Debra Meyer, raised on a kibbutz, outspokenly despises all Arabs. Eytan, her cousin, raised in the city of Haifa, indulges in self-pity over a permanent limp resulting from an accident. Their parents decide a "sandal swap" would profit both. Living in each others' shoes is quite an adjustment for both. After some painful events, they gain a wider view of their world and the consequences of living in an era of political and social upheaval.

WILLIAMSON, JOANNE S. *And Forever Free.* il. by Jim McMullan. Knopf, 1966, $3.95. Martin Herter, an eighteen-year-old German immigrant comes to America at the time of the Civil War and the Emancipation Proclamation. He must adjust to the new land, the people, the differing attitudes, and freedom. Martin finds the new environment difficult to understand. Eventually he finds himself, his own set of values, and his own definition of freedom.

ZEI, ALKI. *Wildcat under Glass.* trans. by Edward Fenton. HR & W, 1968, $4.50. In 1936, fascism envelops all of Greece and reaches out to clutch at every facet of Greek daily life. In Melia's own family the threads of fascism are constantly at work changing lives, splitting loyalties, and capturing the minds of the youth.

Junior

* AMES, FRANCIS. *That Callahan Spunk.*

* ARNOLD, ELLIOTT. *A Kind of Secret Weapon.*

BARTHOLOMEW, CAROL. *My Heart Has Seventeen Rooms.* Macmillan, 1959, $4.95. This true story of the author's experiences in India during a two-year period shows the changes involved in moving from one country to another. The author's work in a seventeen-room Indian hospital and her honest involvement with the people result in a positive experience for her entire family.

* DE JONG, MEINDERT. *The House of Sixty Fathers.*

* DE TREVINO, ELIZABETH BARTON. *I, Juan De Pareja.*

* FORMAN, JAMES. *Ring the Judas Bell.*

* ———. *The Traitors.*

* GALT, TOM. *Peter Zenger: Fighter for Freedom.*

GRAHAM, GAIL. *Cross Fire.* il. by author. Pantheon, 1972, $4.95. A young American soldier, the only surviving member of a small scouting mission, and four Vietnamese children are the only survivors in a fire-bombed village. Beyond the barriers of languages and cultures, the soldier and the oldest girl reach out to each other, with gentleness and humor, as they share the responsibility for the younger children. The stark ending reveals far better than newspaper accounts the ugliness and violence of the Vietnamese War.

* HAUTZIG, ESTHER. *The Endless Steppe: Growing up in Siberia.*

* HENRY, MARGUERITE. *Mustang: Wild Spirit of the West.*

* HOLM, ANNE S. *North to Freedom.*

* KENNEDY, JOHN F. *Profiles in Courage.*

KUGELMASS, J. ALVIN. *Ralph J. Bunche: Fighter for Peace.* Messner, 1962, $3.50. Overcoming poverty and prejudice, Ralph J. Bunche becomes a leading statesman.

MEADER, STEPHEN W. *The Sea Snake.* il. by Edward Shenton. HBJ, 1943, $4.25. As a coast watcher, sixteen-year-old Barny is involved in the war effort (World War II). Following his suspicions about Caldee Island, he attempts to spy on the activities there. He is captured by the Germans and placed on board a U-boat. The resourcefulness which he demonstrates as he adjusts to this change and the adventures which follow make an exciting story. His escape with Grauner, one of the crew members, eventually leads to Barney's work with government intelligence and a congratulatory meeting with the president.

PEARE, CATHERINE OWENS. *The F.D.R. Story.* TY Crowell, 1962, $4.50. Franklin Delano Roosevelt grew up in an atmosphere of love and luxury. An adoring mother and father secured for him every privilege. His vibrant personality, great energy, and contagious enthusiasm soon established him as a leader in all schools he attended. Success seemed to attend every experience until he was stricken with polio. Struggling courageously to overcome this tremendous physical handicap, he rose to become one of the greatest leaders of the Western World. He also became a leader in the successful battle against polio.

REBOUL, ANTOINE. *Thou Shalt Not Kill.* SG Phillips, 1969, $4.95. A novel set during the 1967 Arab-Israeli War. Both fourteen years old and separated from their troops, Slimane, an Egyptian boy, and Simmy, an Israeli girl, meet in the Sinai Desert. The first intent of each is to kill the other; instead they join forces and fight their immediate enemy —the desert. Their uneasy alliance quickly turns to respect, acceptance, and friendship. Interesting, fast moving, and simply written.

* SERRAILLER, IAN. *Escape from Warsaw.*

* ———. *The Silver Sword.*

* SOMERFELT, AIMÉE. *Miriam.*

STEELE, MARY Q. *Journey Outside.* il. by Rocco Negri. Viking Pr, 1969, $4.50. Fast-paced, filled with action and excitement, this book is the story of a boy's search for real answers in a bewildering and strange world that is both beautiful and terrifying.

* STERNE, EMMA GOLDERS. *Benito Juarez: Builder of a Nation.*

STILES, MARTHA BENNETT. *Darkness over the Land.* Dial, 1966, $3.95. Mark Elend grew up in Nazi Germany. He was puzzled by an apparent conflict between family loyalty and "patriotism." His confusion gradually gave way to personal convictions. The Elends, and many other Germans, suffered at the hands of the Nazis. Immediately after the war, though, there were no "good" Germans. Mark had the unusual opportunity to leave Germany and to begin life anew elsewhere. Family love and a strong character helped Mark in making his decision.

* TAYLOR, THEODORE, *The Cay.*

* TUNIS, JOHN R. *His Enemy, His Friend.*

* UCHIDA, YOSHIKO. *Journey to Topaz.*

* VAN STOCKUM, HILDA. *The Winged Watchman.*

* WIBBERLEY, LEONARD. *Peter Treegate's War.*

Senior

ABERNETHY, ROBERT G. *Introduction to Tomorrow: The United States and the Wider World, 1945-1965.* HBJ, 1966, $5.25. The author, a well-known NBC news reporter, presents a readable history of the twenty years following World War II. He describes the changing roles of other nations, as well as American participation in the sequence of such events as the end of the war, the development of the bomb, and the missile buildup. The inclusion of brief biographical sketches of influential men of the period helps to make this an interesting overview of the times for young adult readers.

* ADOFF, ARNOLD (ed.). *Black on Black: Commentaries by Black Americans.*

ALLEN, MERRITT P. *The White Feather.* McKay, 1944, $4.50. Conflicts between loyalty to the North and to the South arise between an illiterate, tyrannical Kentucky mountaineer grandfather and his sensitive, well-educated seventeen-year-old grandson. The white feather, given as a symbol of cowardice and betrayal, becomes a badge of courage when the boy joins Morgan's Raiders. No reconciliation of conviction is possible but respect for honesty and idealism bridges the gap between generations.

BLATTER, DOROTHY. *Cap and Candle.* Westminster, 1961, $3.95. This story of Filiz of Istanbul, her training to become a nurse, and her later experiences in outlying villages reads more like a firsthand account of actual experience than a novel.

BOYLE, SARAH PATTON. *The Desegregated Heart: A Virginian's Stand in Time of Transition.* P/Apollo, 1966, $2.95. Integration in the South in the 1950s is presented through the author's personal struggle with racial problems in her state and community. These experiences force her to reexamine her traditional Southern values and her relationships with all people. Her crusade for civil rights results in new perceptions about the brotherhood of man.

BRADDON, RUSSELL. *When the Enemy Is Tired.* Viking Pr, 1969, $7.95 (P/Popular Lib, $.75). Chinese Communist Major Lim forces Australian Colonel Anthony Russell to write detailed memoirs of his boyhood. The writings are used as a basis for brainwashing. Despite psychological terrorism and physical abuse Russell maintains his sanity and his integrity. When returned to his own people, they, because of fear, proceed to destroy what the Communists could not.

DOOLEY, THOMAS A. *Deliver Us from Evil.* FS & G, 1956, $5.95 (P/NAL, $.75). A young American, Dr. Tom Dooley, after his experience as a navy doctor, returned to a land that desperately needed help. There, he devoted the remainder of his life to helping one-half million Vietnamese refugees.

* ———. *The Edge of Tomorrow.*

EMERY, ANNE. *Carey's Fortune.* Westminster, 1969, $3.95. Nancy Carey, a popular seventeen-year-old belle in nineteenth-century Annapolis, has a comfortable future in prospect as the fiancee of a well-to-do family friend. Suddenly, when her brother Tom arrives home from college with new Republican ideas, there is an abrupt change in Nancy's complacent life. She meets Nick, and their exciting secret romance is affected by political intrigue, with the ultimate decision resting upon the presidential election results.

FOSTER, G. ALLEN. *Votes for Women.* il. with photographs. Criterion, 1966, $4.95. With ratification of the Nineteenth Amendment in 1920, the eighty-year battle for women's right to vote was won. Events of the period are recreated in this interesting account of the struggle and its relation to such other historical happenings as the abolitionist movement, the Civil War, and World War I. The author tells about many outstanding suffragettes: Lucretia Mott, Elizabeth Cady Stanton, Lucy Stone, Susan B. Anthony, Julia Ward Howe, Victoria Woodhull, and Carrie Chapman Catt.

GOFF, GERALD M. *Voices of Man: Homecoming.* P/A-W, 1969, $2.96. The poems, short stories, and art prints in this anthology explore the theme of personal experience and expectation as forces for motivating one's reactions to various situations. Emphasis is placed on success as a result of a positive self-image and the will to overcome obstacles.

* GOLDING, WILLIAM. *Lord of the Flies.*

* GRAHAM, GAIL. *Cross Fire.*

GUARESCHI, GIOVANNI. *The Little World of Don Camillo.* trans. by Una V. Troubridge. FS & G, 1951, $4.95 (P/several). A realistic, vigorous, warm-hearted Italian priest manages again and again to confound the Communist captors of his native village. This funny but moving story gives heart in troubled times.

HANNUM, ALBERTA. *Spin a Silver Dollar.* Viking Pr, 1945, $6.50. A young couple, recently graduated from the University of Chicago, go to Arizona and buy an old trading post. Through dealing with the Indians they learn to understand Navaho customs and superstitions.

* HENTOFF, NAT. *I'm Really Dragged, but Nothing Gets Me Down.*

HERSEY, JOHN. *A Bell for Adano.* Knopf, 1944, $4.95 (P/Bantam, $.75). A young Italian-American major shows a starved and demoralized Italian village how the people can get back to work and once more believe in themselves.

* HOWELL, BETH PRIM. *Lady on a Donkey.*

JONES, LEROI. *Home: Social Essays.* P/Apollo, 1967, $1.95. The two dozen essays that constitute this book were written during a five year span. It was a turbulent and critical period for Negroes and whites. The progressive changes LeRoi Jones noted looking at America are recorded with honesty, anger, and passion. These social essays are appropriate to illustrate black viewpoints and feelings during the Cuban Revolution, the Birmingham bombings, the Harlem riots, etc.

* KENNEDY, JOHN F. *Profiles in Courage.*

KINNICK, B. J., AND JESSE PERRY. *I Have a Dream: Voices of Man.* P/ A-W, 1969, $2.40. The selection of writings, poems, and illustrations provokes thought regarding man's present state and future course, emphasizing the theme that each man does have a choice in determining the direction of humanity through his own behavior.

* KOSTERINA, NINA. *The Diary of Nina Kosterina.*

LEDERER, WILLIAM J. *A Nation of Sheep.* Norton, 1961, $4.95 (P/ Fawcett World, $.60). Mr. Lederer's book is a battle plan for the ordinary citizen rather than for his often remote leaders. Factually, the book chronicles a number of American blunders and scandals in foreign affairs and sketches certain mechanisms of deceit in government itself. These general studies are followed by specific recommendations for reform at the national and personal level.

MACGREGOR-HASTIE, ROY. *Africa: Background for Today.* Criterion, 1967, $4.50. An easy-to-read survey of this history of major political, social and economic change in Africa. It contains some history, some reporting, and some social commentary. A chronological table is provided in the index.

McLEOD, RUTH. *Buenos Dias, Teacher.* Messner, 1970, $3.50. Set in a large city in California, this touching novel tells of the trials Jennifer Meade encounters in her first year of teaching. Her inner-city third graders from many backgrounds present her with challenges and frustrations.

MEDEIROS, V. *The Eyes of Love.* A-W, 1969, $2.48. The poems, short stories, and art prints in this anthology explore the themes of love and hate as motivating forces for human action. Included are selections from the works of Anton Chekov, Somerset Maugham, Langston Hughes, Jesse Stuart, and other well-known writers, both classic and modern.

MERRIAM, EVE. *Growing up Female in America: Ten Lives.* il. by author. Doubleday, 1971, $7.95. Ten fascinating American women are introduced through excerpts from diaries, letters, journals, and autobiographies. This book supplies some of the missing history of women.

SEVERN, BILL. *Toward One World: The Life of Wendell Wilkie.* Washburn, 1967, $4.50. This book shows how a man can suffer defeat in school, in the courtroom, in love, in finances, and in politics (1940 presidential candidate against Franklin D. Roosevelt) and still make the last years of his life the most fruitful—as a writer, lecturer, and political liaison between the Republican and Democratic parties.

SNEIDER, VERN. *Teahouse of the August Moon.* Putnam, 1951, $5.95 (P/NAL, $.75). It is hard to decide who is the conquered and who is the conqueror in this hilarious World War II story of the American armed services' attempts to change the way of life of the Okinawan peasants.

STEINBECK, JOHN. *Travels with Charley: In Search of America.* Viking Pr, 1962, $4.95 (P/several). Deciding it is time for him to rediscover the America he has been writing about for so long, John Steinbeck departs with his large poodle and a camper truck to tour parts of America. His report touches on such experiences as eating lobster in Maine, meeting a transient actor, refusing to shoot two coyotes in the Mojave, viewing with sinking heart the atrocities against small Negro school children, getting lost in New York, and finally returning home to reflect on his America.

STERNE, EMMA GELDERS. *They Took Their Stand.* Macmillan, 1968, $4.50. In these biographical sketches, eleven men and women are described, who at various times in American history have worked selflessly for equal rights for Negroes: a Southern colonial patriot who saw the need to emancipate the Negro during the American Revolution; a native Virginian and West Point graduate who was called a traitor when he chose to fight for the Union cause; several Southern clergymen who bravely spoke out against injustices as they saw them; and contemporary leaders in the struggle for open housing and equal education for all men.

STILLER, RICHARD. *Queen of the Populists: The Story of Mary Elizabeth Lease.* TY Crowell, 1970, $4.50. Mary Elizabeth Lease, born in 1853, was the first important female politician in American history. Her early life on the Kansas prairie, first as a teacher, then as a housewife, mother, and lawyer, gave her an insight into the need for speaking out on behalf of the farmers, who were exploited by big business, especially the banks and railroads. Though she never ran for political office, her campaigns on behalf of the Populist party advocated ideas that were far ahead of the times and since have become a reality.

SUHL, YURI. *Eloquent Crusader—Ernestine Rose.* Messner, 1970, $3.50. This is the life story of one of the early crusaders for the emancipation of women. Born in a Polish ghetto in 1810, this daughter of a rabbi emigrated to the United States in 1836 and joined the early suffragist and abolitionist movements here. An eloquent but controversial crusader for social reform, she spoke widely of the evils of the time and helped change the thinking of an entire nation.

SUMMERS, JAMES L. *You Can't Make It By Bus.* Westminster, 1969, $3.95. Paul Guevara is a leader in his high school in East Los Angeles. He has good grades, is a track star, and has a beautiful girl friend, Lura Golden. But because of his Mexican-American background, Paul is pushed into a perplexing problem: his association with the leader of the Brown Berets, who demands that he lead a strike of his Chicano group. Paul's trip to Mexico creates an additional dilemma, and his painful inner conflict reflects the actual problems confronting this minority segment of our society.

VAN WYCK MASON, F. *American Men at Arms.* Little, 1964, $6.95 (P/PB, $.95). These stories are sometimes humorous, sometimes bitter, sometimes sad, but always entertaining and informative. The selection of writings about American men in the armed forces reflects the traditional American suspicion of professional soldiers and the folk hero anachronism of the civilian soldier with a plow in one hand and a rifle in the other. The stories are fiction but all have a dramatic force that shows how men who happen to be soldiers face danger, fear, death, and the military way of doing things.

VISCARDI, HENRY, JR. *A Laughter in the Lonely Night.* il. by Charles Rowe. Eriksson, 1961, $5.00. This book tells the stories of fifteen people whom the world has rejected as hopeless cripples, all so severely disabled they cannot become more than burdens on the state. The author, a man without legs, decides to do something about these people and establishes an electronic company fittingly called Abilities, Inc., in which men and women, despite unbelievable handicaps, display their ability to work and live fully and with dignity.

* WALLACE, IRVING. *The Man*

WERSTEIN, IRVING. *Pie in the Sky.* Delacorte, 1969, $4.50. The Industrial Workers of the World, or the IWW, played an important role in the development of industrial unions for the working class in America. From 1905 to 1924, this group, also known as "The Wobblies," helped organize workers. They also fought for improved conditions for Negro and migrant laborers. This book tells the history of the movement up to its final stages when the CIO rose to inherit its legacy.

YOUNGER, SUSIE. *Never Ending Flower.* il. with a map. John Day, 1969, $5.50. In 1959, at the age of twenty-three, Susie Younger went to South Korea after a year's social work in England. She adopted the country as her own. She paints vivid pictures of this country and of its gay, patient, hard working, and desperately poor people, whose life she shares. The appendix consists of her account of accepting Catholicism which led her to the religious life of a lay-person in Korea.

Mature

ARON, RAYMOND. *The Industrial Society.* Praeger, 1967, $4.95 (P/ S & S, $1.95). A prominent French sociologist examines aspects of current industrial societies and analyzes writings of other well-known scholars in this field. He explores the nature of Marxist and Western industrial development, with their conflicts and problems. Both societies share the same history and must learn to live with their differences, tolerating the rights and opinions of others. These three essays study in depth such problems as social order, national growth, and technological development.

* BALDWIN, JAMES. *Nobody Knows My Name.*

BOUMAN, PIETER M. *Can the World Share the Wealth?* P/Friend Pr, 1969, $.75. Vital world concerns such as overpopulation, famine, widening gap between rich and poor, and a plea for economic justice are presented. Examples of these problems are cited, along with concrete suggestions for individual and group involvement. The author has had experience working with the World Council of Churches and the United Nations.

CAROTHERS, J. EDWARD. *Can Machines Replace Men?* P/Friend Pr, 1966, $.75. With the advent of computers, the relationship between men and machines has become more complex and is constantly changing. The author of this small pamphlet raises many provocative questions and shows how men's lives have been altered by machines in the past. He feels that a lag between religion and moral perception is causing society to be more the victim than the master of machines, and this trend must be reversed if humanity is to benefit.

CARSON, RACHEL. *Silent Spring.* HM, 1962, $5.95 (P/Fawcett World, $.95). A sensitive, distinguished scientist cites many examples of the dreadful effect chemicals have wrought upon our changing environment and the serious consequences which have developed. She examines and describes the pollution which has resulted from man's careless attempts to control unwanted plant and animal life and shows how disastrous this may be in upsetting the balance of nature both now and in the future.

DRURY, ALLEN. *Advise and Consent.* Doubleday, 1959, $7.95 (P/PB, $1.25). In this realistic story of life and politics in Washington, the reader sees the men and women who conduct the business of the United States as people with the same courage, love, wisdom, and frailities as the rest of the population. In addition, the complex, sometimes confusing, processes of government are presented in believable, understandable form.

ELDREDGE, H. WENTWORTH. *The Second American Revolution.* P/WSP, $.90. According to the author, the present American form of government is an anachronism: it is dead but it refuses to lie down. This idea is sure to raise comment. The author hopes to stimulate creative thinking as well. The ability of the present form of government to meet modern demands is inadquate. Yet America seems unwilling to adopt any other form of rule. Many forms of government are examined briefly and more critical examination is urged. The choice presented by the author is change or die.

HALL, EDWARD T. *The Silent Language.* Doubleday, 1959, $5.50 (P/ Fawcett World, $.75). This is an anthropologist's interesting observation of the complex nature of culture and its effect on human behavior. Examples of various stages and levels of communication are given. Organized differently in each culture, time and space are powerful means of conveying ideas. Hall believes that we Americans tend to misunderstand other peoples and would benefit from a study of this nonverbal aspect of human relations.

HERNDON, JAMES. *The Way It Spozed to Be.* S & S, 1968, $4.95 (P/ Bantam, $.95). An account of James Herndon's year of teaching in an inner-city junior high school. Herndon cites inconsistencies and elaborate efforts by administration and teachers to maintain order to survive. Rarely does real teaching or learning take place. Complicated rules are established for games of "the way it spozed to be," with no one actually being deceived. There are no solutions. It is an account which provokes the desire to change the system.

* LUTHULI, ALBERT. *Let My People Go.*

ORWELL, GEORGE. *Animal Farm.* HBJ, 1946, $4.50 (P/several). This frightening fable tells of the successful rebellion of the farm animals against their human masters. Although the animals set up a "classless" society, the pigs become the rulers, and the other animals find themselves in varying degrees of slavery. "Some are more equal than others," explain the pigs.

PERRY, JOHN. *Our Polluted World: Can Man Survive.* Watts, 1967, $4.95. The author believes that a crucial point in human development has been reached and that the overwhelming problem of wastes in the air and water must be solved. Our very survival depends upon this. With the naturalist's eye, he cites examples of changes in our environment which have resulted from misuse of natural resources and industrialization. While this is undoubtedly a complex concern with varying degrees of pessimism, Perry feels it is not too late to preserve ourselves from extinction.

* TOLSTOY, LEO. *Anna Karenina.*

TURNBULL, COLIN M. *The Lonely African.* S & S, 1962, $5.50 (P/S & S, $2.95). Today's Africa is made up of nations of young people who are finding their voices, beliefs, and commitments. Though much of what is taking place there may seem strange, the world must learn to listen to and understand the changing problems and pressures of Africa and its lonely, seeking men.

URIS, LEON. *Exodus.* Doubleday, 1958, $5.95 (P/Bantam, $1.25). The establishment of a Jewish homeland is told dramatically through the personal experience of Jews and gentiles. The author controls the vast range of this novel and maintains reader interest in the characters as well as in the task of building a new nation. *Exodus* will be condemned by some critics for its partisan attitude toward Judaism. Despite this charge, it ranks as one of the fine novels in this century.

* YOUNGER, SUSIE. *Never Ending Flower.*

Directory of Publishers

ABELARD Abelard-Schuman Limited, 257 Park Ave. S., New York, N.Y. 10010

ABINGDON Abingdon Press, 201 Eighth Ave. S., Nashville, Tenn. 37203

ACE American Council on Education, One Dupont Circle, N.W., Washington, D.C. 20036

ACE BKS Ace Books, Inc., 1120 Ave. of the Americas, New York, N.Y. 10036

AFT American Federation of Teachers, 1012 14th St. N.W., Washington, D.C. 20005

ALA American Library Association, 50 E. Huron St., Chicago, Ill. 60611

APPLETON Appleton-Century-Crofts, 440 Park Ave. S., New York, N.Y. 10016

APOLLO Apollo Editions, Inc., 666 Fifth Ave., New York, N.Y. 10019

ARIEL See FS & G

ASCD Association for Supervision and Curriculum Development, 1201 16th St. N.W., Washington, D.C. 20036

ATHENEUM Atheneum Publishers, 122 E. 42nd St., New York, N.Y. 10017

ASTOR-HONOR Astor-Honor, Inc., 67 Southfield Ave., Stamford, Conn. 06904

AVON Avon Books, 959 Eighth Ave., New York, N.Y. 10019

A-W Addison-Wesley Publishing Co., Inc., Reading, Mass. 01867

A WHITMAN Albert Whitman & Co., 560 W. Lake St., Chicago, Ill. 60606

BALLANTINE Ballantine Books, Inc., 101 Fifth Ave., New York, N.Y. 10003

BANTAM Bantam Books, Inc., 666 Fifth Ave., New York, N.Y. 10019

BERKLEY PUB Berkley Publishing Corp. See PUTNAM

BOBBS Bobbs-Merrill Co., 4300 W. 62nd St., Indianapolis, Ind. 46268

BORDEN Borden Publishing Co., 1855 W. Main St., Alhambra, Calif. 91801

BOWKER R. R. Bowker Co., 1180 Ave. of the Americas, New York, N.Y. 10036

BOWMAR Bowmar Publishing Corp., 662 Rodier Dr., Glendale, Calif. 91201

BRADBURY Bradbury Press, Inc., 2 Overhill Rd., Scarsdale, N.Y. 10583

BROWN See WM C. BROWN

C E TUTTLE Charles E. Tuttle Co., Inc., 28 S. Main St., Rutland, Vt. 05701

CHANDLER PUB Chandler Publishing Co., 124 Spear St., San Francisco, Calif. 94105

CHILDRENS   Childrens Press, Inc., 1224 W. Van Buren St., Chicago, Ill. 60607

CHILTON   Chilton Book Company, 401 Walnut St., Philadelphia, Pa. 19106

CIBC   Council on Interracial Books for Children, 29 W. 15th St., New York, N.Y. 10011

COLLINS   See W COLLINS

COWARD   Coward, McCann and Geoghegan, Inc., 200 Madison Ave., New York, N.Y. 10016

CREATIVE ED   Creative Educational Society, Inc., 515 N. Front St., Mankato, Minn. 56001

CRITERION   Criterion Books, 257 Park Ave. S., New York, N.Y. 10010

CROWELL   See TY CROWELL

CROWN   Crown Publishers, Inc., 419 Park Ave. S., New York, N.Y. 10016

CURTIS   Curtis Books, Inc., Chestnut East Bldg., Philadelphia, Pa. 19107

DAY   See JOHN DAY

DELACORTE   See DELL

DELL   Dell Publishing Co., Inc., 750 Third Ave., New York, N.Y. 10017

DIAL   See DELL

DODD   Dodd, Mead & Co., 79 Madison Ave., New York, N.Y. 10016

DOUBLEDAY   Doubleday & Co., Inc., Garden City, N.Y. 11530

DUTTON   E. P. Dutton & Co., Inc., 201 Park Ave. S., New York, N.Y. 10003

D WHITE   David White Co., 60 E. 55th St., New York, N.Y. 10022

ENCYCLOPAEDIA BRITANNICA   Encyclopaedia Britannica, Educational Corporation, 425 N. Michigan Ave., Chicago, Ill. 60611

ERICKSSON   Paul S. Ericksson, Inc., 119 W. 57th St., New York, N.Y. 10019

EVANS   See M EVANS

FAWCETT WORLD   Fawcett World Library: Crest, Gold Medal & Premier Books, 1 Astor Plaza, New York, N.Y. 10036

FEARON   Fearon Publishers, 6 Davis Dr., Belmont, Calif. 94002

FOLLETT   Follett Publishing Co., 1010 W. Washington Blvd., Chicago, Ill. 60607

FORTRESS   Fortress Press, 2900 Queen Lane, Philadelphia, Pa. 19129

FOUR WINDS   See SCHOLASTIC MAGAZINES

FRIEND PR   Friendship Press, 475 Riverside Dr., New York, N.Y. 10027

FS & G   Farrar, Straus & Giroux, Inc., 19 Union Square W., New York, N.Y. 10003

FUNK & W   Funk & Wagnalls Co., Inc., 53 E. 77th St., New York, N.Y. 10021

GARRARD   Garrard Publishing Co., 1607 N. Market St., Champaign, Ill. 61820

G & D   Grosset & Dunlap, Inc., 51 Madison Ave., New York, N.Y. 10010

GIBSON   C. R. Gibson Co., Knight St., Norwalk, Conn. 06856

GOLDEN GATE   Golden Gate Junior Books, Box 398, 343 Old Country Rd., San Carlos, Calif. 94070

GROSSMAN Grossman Publishers, 625 Madison Ave., New York, N.Y. 10022

GROVE Grove Press, 53 E. 11th St., New York, N.Y. 10003

HALE E. M. Hale & Co., 1201 S. Hasting Way, Eau Claire, Wis. 54701

HAR-ROW Harper & Row, Publishers, 10 E. 53rd St., New York, N.Y. 10022

HASTINGS Hastings House Publishers, Inc., 10 E. 40th St., New York, N.Y. 10016

HAWTHORN Hawthorn Books, Inc., 70 Fifth Ave., New York, N.Y. 10011

HBJ Harcourt Brace Jovanovich, Inc., 757 Third Ave., New York, N.Y. 10017

HILL & WANG Hill and Wang, Inc., 19 Union Sq. W., New York, N.Y. 10003

HM Houghton Mifflin Co., 2 Park St., Boston, Mass. 02107

HOLIDAY Holiday House, Inc., 18 E. 56th St., New York, N.Y. 10022

HORN BOOK Horn Book, 585 Boylston St., Boston, Mass. 02116

HR & W Holt, Rinehart & Winston, Inc., 383 Madison Ave., New York, N.Y. 10017

JOHN DAY John Day Co., Inc., 257 Park Ave. S., New York, N.Y. 10016

KNOPF Alfred A. Knopf, Inc. See RANDOM

KODANSHA INTERNATIONAL Kodansha International/USA, 599 College Ave., Palo Alto, Calif. 94306

KTAV Ktav Publishing House, Inc., 120 E. Broadway, New York, N.Y. 10002

LANCER Lancer Books, Inc., 1560 Broadway, New York, N.Y. 10036

LANTERN Lantern Press, Inc., 354 Hussey Rd., Mt. Vernon, N.Y. 10552

LIBRARY OF CONGRESS Library of Congress, Washington, D.C. 20540

LINCOLN FILENE/TUFTS Lincoln Filene Center for Citizenship and Public Affairs, Tufts University, Medford, Mass. 02155

LIPPINCOTT J. B. Lippincott Co., E. Washington Square, Philadelphia, Pa. 19105

LITTLE Little, Brown & Co., 34 Beacon St., Boston, Mass. 02106

LONGMANS See McKAY

LOTHROP Lothrop, Lee & Shepard. See MORROW

McGRAW McGraw-Hill Book Co., 330 W. 42nd St., New York, N.Y. 10036

McKAY David McKay Co., Inc., 750 Third Ave., New York, N.Y. 10017

MACMILLAN Macmillan Co., 866 Third Ave., New York, N.Y. 10022

MACRAE Macrae Smith Co., 225 S. 15th St., Philadelphia, Pa. 19102

MERRILL Charles E. Merrill Publishing Co., 1300 Alum Creek Dr., Columbus, Ohio 43216

MESSNER Julian Messner, Inc., 1 W. 39th St., New York, N.Y. 10018

M EVANS M. Evans & Co., Inc., 216 E. 49th St., New York, N.Y. 10017

M K McELDERRY Margaret K. McElderry Books. See ATHENEUM

MODERN LIB Modern Library, Inc. See RANDOM

MORROW William Morrow & Co., Inc., 105 Madison Ave., New York, N.Y. 10016

NAL   New American Library, Inc., 1301 Ave. of the Americas, New York, N.Y. 10019

NCCJ   National Conference of Christians and Jews, 43 W. 57th St., New York, N.Y. 10019

NCSS   National Council for the Social Studies, 1201 16th St. N.W., Washington, D.C. 20036

NCTE   National Council of Teachers of English, 1111 Kenyon Rd., Urbana, Ill. 61801

NELSON   Thomas Nelson Inc., Copewood & Davis Sts., Camden, N.J. 08103

NEW DIRECTIONS   New Directions Publishing Corp., 333 Ave. of the Americas, New York, N.Y. 10014

NEW YORK TIMES   New York Times, Book Div., 330 Madison Ave., New York, N.Y. 10017

NOBLE   Noble & Noble, Publishers, Inc. See DELL

NORTHLAND   Northland Press, Box N, Flagstaff, Ariz. 86001

NORTON   W. W. Norton & Co., Inc., 55 Fifth Ave., New York, N.Y. 10003

N.Y. PUBLIC LIBRARY   New York Public Library, Fifth Ave. and 42nd St., New York, N.Y. 10018

OREG ST U PR   Oregon State University Press, 101 Waldo Hall, Corvallis, Oreg. 97331

PALO VERDE   Palo Verde Publishing Company, P.O. Box 5783, Tucson, Ariz. 85700

PANTHEON   Pantheon Books, Inc. See RANDOM

PAPERBACK LIB   Paperback Library, 315 Park Ave. S., New York, N.Y. 10010

PARENTS'   Parents' Magazine Press, 52 Vanderbilt Ave., New York, N.Y. 10017

PARNASSUS   Parnassus Press, 2721 Parker St., Berkeley, Calif. 94705

PB   Pocket Books, Inc. See S & S

PENGUIN   Penguin Books, Inc., 7110 Ambassador Rd., Baltimore, Md. 21207

P-H   Prentice-Hall, Inc., Englewood Cliffs, N.J. 07632

PHILLIPS   See S G PHILLIPS

POPULAR LIB   Popular Library, Inc., 355 Lexington Ave., New York, N.Y. 10017

PRAEGER   Praeger Publishers, Inc., 111 Fourth Ave., New York, N.Y. 10003

PUTNAM   G. P. Putnam's Sons, 200 Madison Ave., New York, N.Y. 10016

PYRAMID PUBNS   Pyramid Publications, 444 Madison Ave., New York, N.Y. 10022

QUADRANGLE   Quadrangle Books, Inc., 330 Madison Ave., New York, N.Y. 10017

RAND   Rand McNally & Co., 8255 Central Park Ave., Skokie, Ill. 60076

RANDOM   Random House, Inc., 201 E. 50th St., New York, N.Y. 10022

REILLY   Reilly & Lee, Henry Regnery Co., 114 W. Illinois St., Chicago, Ill. 60610

RITCHIE   Ward Ritchie Press, 3044 Riverside Dr., Los Angeles, Calif. 90039

SATURDAY REVIEW   Saturday Review, Inc., 380 Madison Ave., New York, N.Y. 10017

SCHOLASTIC MAGAZINES   Scholastic Magazines, Inc., 50 W. 44th St., New York, N.Y. 10036

SCHOL BK SERV   Scholastic Book Services, 50 W. 44th St., New York, N.Y. 10036

SCOTT   See W R SCOTT

SCOTT F   Scott, Foresman & Co., 1900 E. Lake Ave., Glenview, Ill. 60025

SCRIBNER   Charles Scribner's Sons, 597 Fifth Ave., New York, N.Y. 10017

SEABURY   Seabury Press, Inc., 815 Second Ave., New York, N.Y. 10017

S G PHILLIPS   S. G. Phillips, Inc., 305 W. 86th St., New York, N.Y. 10024

SIERRA   Sierra Club Books, 1050 Mills Tower, San Francisco, Calif. 94104

S & S   Simon & Schuster, Inc., 630 Fifth Ave., New York, N.Y. 10020

ST. MARTIN   St. Martin's Press, Inc., 175 Fifth Ave., New York, N.Y. 10010

STECK   Steck-Vaughn Company, Box 2028, Austin, Texas 78767

TRI-OCEAN   Tri-Ocean Books, 62 Townsend St., San Francisco, Calif. 94107

TUTTLE   See C E TUTTLE

TY CROWELL   Thomas Y. Crowell Co., 201 Park Ave. S., New York, N.Y. 10003

U CHI PR   University of Chicago Press, 5801 Ellis Ave., Chicago, Ill. 60637

U CONN ENGLISH DEPT   English Department, University of Connecticut. Order from the University of Connecticut Bookstore, Storrs, Conn. 06268

U PITT PR   University of Pittsburgh Press, 127 N. Bellefield Ave., Pittsburgh, Pa. 15213

U.S. DEPT. OF H.E.W.   United States Department of Health, Education & Welfare, 300 Independence Ave. S.W., Washington, D.C. 20201

VANGUARD   Vanguard Press, 424 Madison Ave., New York, N.Y. 10017

VIKING PR   Viking Press, Inc., 625 Madison Ave., New York, N.Y. 10022

WALCK   Henry Z. Walck, Inc., 19 Union Sq. W., New York, N.Y. 10003

WALKER   Walker & Company, Div. of Walker Publishing Co., Inc., 720 Fifth Ave., New York, N.Y. 10019

WARNE   Frederick Warne & Co., Inc., 101 Fifth Ave., New York, N.Y. 10003

WASHBURN   Ives Washburn, Inc. See McKAY

WATTS   Franklin Watts, Inc., 845 Third Ave., New York, N.Y. 10022

W COLLINS   William Collins Sons & Co., Ltd., 215 Park Ave., New York, N.Y. 10003

WEATHERHILL   John Weatherhill, Inc., 149 Madison Ave., New York, N.Y. 10016

WESTERN PUB   Western Publishing Co., Inc., 1220 Mound Ave., Racine, Wis. 53404

WESTMINSTER   Westminster Press, Witherspoon Bldg., Philadelphia, Pa. 19107

WHITE   See D WHITE

A WHITMAN   Albert Whitman & Co., 560 W. Lake St., Chicago, Ill. 60606

WHITMAN   See WESTERN PUB

WILSON   H. W. Wilson Co., 950 University Ave., Bronx, N.Y. 10452

WINDMILL   Windmill Books, Inc., 201 Park Ave. S., New York, N.Y. 10010

WM C BROWN   William C. Brown & Co., 135 S. Locust, Dubuque, Iowa 52003

WORLD PUB   World Publishing Co., 110 E. 59th St., New York, N.Y. 10022

W R SCOTT   William R. Scott, Inc., 333 6th Ave., New York, N.Y. 10003

WSP   Washington Square Press, Div. of Pocket Books, Inc. See S & S

XEROX   Xerox College Publishing, 191 Spring St., Lexington, Mass. 02173

YALE U PR   Yale University Press, 92a Yale Station, New Haven, Conn. 06520

Author Index

Title Index

AMERICAN COUNCIL ON EDUCATION

ROGER W. HEYNS, *President*

The American Council on Education, founded in 1918, is a *council* of educational organizations and institutions. Its purpose is to advance education and educational methods through comprehensive voluntary and cooperative action on the part of American educational associations, organizations, and institutions.